tfm Publishing Limited, Castle Hill Barns, Harley, Shrewsbury, SY5 6LX, UK
Tel: +44 (0)1952 510061; Fax: +44 (0)1952 510192

E-mail: info@tfmpublishing.com; Web site: www.tfmpublishing.com

Cover photos: © Ben Lawrence and Paul Lawrence

Other photographs: Jim Holmes, Malcolm Almond, John Moon and Lawrence Clift

First edition: © 2023
Hardback   ISBN: 978-1-913755-48-5

The entire contents of *Roger Albert Clark Rally: the first 20 years — The story of Britain's most challenging rally* is copyright tfm publishing Ltd. Apart from any fair dealing for the purposes of research or private study, or criticism or review, as permitted under the Copyright, Designs and Patents Act 1988, this publication may not be reproduced, stored in a retrieval system or transmitted in any form or by any means, electronic, digital, mechanical, photocopying, recording or otherwise, without the prior written permission of the publisher.

The author and publisher gratefully acknowledge the permission granted to reproduce the copyright material where applicable in this book. Every effort has been made to trace copyright holders and to obtain their permission for the use of copyright material. The publisher apologises for any errors or omissions and would be grateful if notified of any corrections that should be incorporated in future reprints or editions of this book.

Printed by L&C PRINTING GROUP, Tadeusza Romanowicza 11, 30-702 Kraków, Poland
Tel: +48 690 565 600; E-mail: office@lcprinting.eu; Web site: www.lcprinting.eu

Kielder 2008: (L-R) Steve Herbert, Colin Heppenstall, Paul Lawrence and the late David Winstanley

Welcome to the story of the first 20 years of the Roger Albert Clark Rally.

This fantastic book charts the development of the rally that has been so close to our hearts for the last two decades. It tells the story of each of the 15 rallies that have taken place with detailed reports and many previously unseen photographs. We have statistics, results and commentary to make it a complete record of this amazing event.

Way back in 2004 we ran the first edition and many people really didn't know what to expect. Since then, there have been ups and downs and some incredible weather challenges. There have been many, many highs and I believe that we have delivered a true rallying challenge for hundreds and hundreds of competitors. I pay particularly tribute to our loyal competitors who have returned time and again to support the event.

This book will serve as an enduring record of what we have all achieved so far and it is only with the support of so many people that it has been possible. So I pay tribute to all of our officials and marshals as well as our competitors for believing in what we were doing and being part of the first 20 years of the Roger Albert Clark Rally story.

Colin Heppenstall
December 2023

Introduction: Colin Heppenstall

Bring on the cars! The 2021 event in Pundershaw

Martin McCormack, Escort Mk2, Ae forest and sunshine. How good is that?

In November 2004 I ventured north for the inaugural Roger Albert Clark Rally, not really knowing what to expect.

The first running of this new multi-day rally aimed at historic crews had caught my interest but it was a journey into the unknown as I headed for the Don Valley Stadium in Sheffield.

Three days later, I got home tired, wet and weary, but utterly elated having experienced an event of the like that I thought I would never again see in British rallying.

Back through the late 1960s, '70s and '80s, I never missed the original RAC Rally. Now 20 years on here was an event that recaptured that sense of adventure in the UK forests.

Of course, in the ensuing 20 years the rally has grown beyond all recognition and is now a must-do event on the calendar for hundreds of competitors and thousands of spectators.

Across the 15 rallies that have run in 20 years, I don't think I've missed a day and I've loved every minute of it. This rally has given me so many special moments

and for all of that I have to thank the Heppenstall family, headed by Colin, for producing a rally that has captured our hearts and entertained us magnificently across two decades.

Of course, it has not always been plain sailing and in 2015 the future of the event seemed very shaky. That year's rally was sadly cancelled shortly before the event as insufficient entries were received to make it anywhere near viable.

Colin and Nicola could easily have pulled the plug and given up but they are made of tougher stuff than that. After a break, the rally regrouped and came back bigger and better than ever before.

We've survived the snow of 2010 and Storm Arwen in 2021. There have even been days when the sun has shone.

The snow of 2010 at Oliver's Mount

Many moments and situations stand out in my Roger Albert Clark memory bank. Being on the finish line of the Kershope stage in 2012, when the battle between Martin McCormack and Steve Bannister was finally resolved by just 17 seconds. The atmosphere was electric as a small group of us waited on the stop line for the final result to unfold.

Simply experiencing the 2010 event and the way that the organising team pulled a rabbit out of the hat to run a rally, when the odds were so heavily stacked against them, was another highlight. Battling out of Kielder on Friday evening of the 2021 rally as Storm Arwen started to hit was memorable, albeit for different reasons. Had I waited another half an hour, I would probably have been one of those to spend a night in the forest.

We've had shooting stars over Shepherdshield, crisp, frosty mornings in Ae, thick fog in Radnor, snow and ice at Oliver's Mount and just about every other imaginable weather condition.

I remember a beautiful sunset late one afternoon in Kershope with an incredible colour to the sky as the sun went down and Saab 96s and the Lancia Stratos provided the soundtrack. Listening to the Stratos blasting along the river in Ae forest was another highlight as has been the sound of so many BDA and BDG engines revving hard in any number of forests. It's a sound, you can never have enough of!

I've been lucky enough to be involved, in a modest way, in the organisation of the event on the media side of the rally and it has been an absolute honour to work on this rally.

Many of my days out in the forest have been spent with great friends, which has simply made it even more special: notably Ian Burnell, Russ Otway, Paul Otway and Penny and Andy Smith have usually been there to enjoy a shared experience that is hard to explain to those who don't love this sport.

Most recently, my son Ben has joined me and has quickly come to love the event as much as I do. Here's to the first 20 years and here's to the future editions that, God willing, we will all continue to enjoy as much as we have done the 15 rallies that have gone before.

Paul Lawrence
November 2023

Page		Title
8		Roger Clark – the inspiration
10	Chapter 1	The build-up to the first event
14	Chapter 2	2004: the original Stig delivers in the first edition
26	Chapter 3	2005: Higgins beats the weather
42	Chapter 4	2006: Easson's heartbreak
58	Chapter 5	2007: Bannister's overall victory
74	Chapter 6	2008: Wilson wins his hero's rally
90	Chapter 7	2009: Evans above
106	Chapter 8	2010: The year of the snow
122	Chapter 9	2010: Colin Heppenstall's story of 2010: Pulling off a miracle
138	Chapter 10	2011: Evans at the double
154	Chapter 11	2012: McCormack the first
172	Chapter 12	2013: Bannister's second win
188	Chapter 13	2014: Robinson takes over
204	Chapter 14	2017: McCormack wins on the rally's return
224	Chapter 15	2019: McCormack does it again
244	Chapter 16	2021: Champion the wonder Porsche
264	Chapter 17	2021 Storm Arwen: Rallying and the storm
270	Chapter 18	2023: McCormack makes it four
294	Chapter 19	The unsung heroes
296	Chapter 20	What the rally means to me
302	Chapter 21	The event statistics

In his earlier years with the works Rover on the RAC Rally

Roger Clark:
a rallying inspiration

Roger Albert Clark MBE was a legend of British rallying. More than just about anyone, he brought British rallying to the forefront of public attention through the 1960s and 1970s and inspired a generation of competitors and fans with his sublime handling of a whole range of cars and, most notably, Ford Escorts.

Perhaps his biggest claim to fame was winning our very own RAC Rally, first in 1972 with Tony Mason, and then again in 1976 with Stuart Pegg. He was the first British driver to take on and beat the Scandinavians in the forests of England, Scotland and Wales after a decade of domination by Finnish and Swedish drivers. That huge achievement earned Roger fame and popularity far beyond the rallying fraternity.

This rally celebrates the life, character, achievements and driving style of Roger Clark

As many people remember him: Roger on the limit in OOO 96M

and there is no more fitting tribute than a tough five-day rally in the forests where he delivered so much excitement and drama.

Born in August 1939, Clark grew up in the motor trade and worked for the family business, along with his younger brother Stan. Roger joined the garage as an apprentice and helped grow the franchise.

He passed his driving test at the age of 17 in 1956 and joined the local Leicester Car Club where he

On the Scottish Rally in a TR7 V8

met Jim Porter, who would become a longtime co-driver. Roger's first rally was that same year in a pre-war Ford Prefect and he then progressed via a Ford 100E van to a Mini Cooper, in which Clark and Porter won the East Midlands championship in 1961 and 1962.

They soon moved up the rallying ladder and competed on bigger events like the Circuit of Ireland, the Welsh Rally and the Scottish Rally. Roger's pace and natural ability brought him to the notice of the works teams and in 1963 he drove a Triumph TR4 on the incredibly tough Spa-Sofia-Liege Rally. He also drove for Reliant in the Sabre and then agreed a two year deal with Rover to compete internationally.

Alongside the Rover 2000, he drove a private Ford Cortina and won the 1964 Scottish Rally before scoring the first of four British Rally Championship victories in 1965.

His career stepped up a further gear in 1966 when Roger signed to drive for Ford in a partnership that lasted 15 years. He started in a Ford Cortina, but quickly switched to the Ford Escort for a 12-year career in the Mk1 and then the Mk2. The Ford deal brought him three more British titles through the 1970s but it was success on the RAC Rally that really made him a household name. Britian finally had a rally driver who could take on, and beat, the Scandinavians.

With sponsorship first from Esso Uniflo and then Cossack hairspray, he thrilled the fans with sensational performances or both gravel and tarmac and chalked up around 40 national and international victories. With Jim Porter he won the 1968 Acropolis Rally and led the 1973 East African Safari Rally by over an hour before the car gave up the challenge.

Roger famously competed in the Tour of Britain, trading times and paintwork with racer Gerry Marshall in a pair of Escort RS2000s and also competed in rallycross. In 1975, along with Porter, they received the Segrave Trophy for the most outstanding performance in motor sport and Roger was awarded an MBE in 1979.

Though into the 1980s his rallying schedule eased back, he never really retired and still drove whenever the opportunity came up, with some great performances in Porsches. In the mid-1990s, despite ill health, he created Roger Clark Motor Sport with his sons, Matt and Olly.

Sadly, at the age of just 58, he died in January 1998 But his memory lives on and shines bright through his sons and his wife Judith and in the memory of so many rally fans.

Roger's son Olly said: "Rallying gave him so much global exposure and he gave back to the sport. His family endorse the Roger Albert Clark Rally and its contribution to British rallying."

The Roger Albert Clark Rally is a fitting tribute to a man who did so much to make rallying popular in the UK. Roger Clark was truly a legend of British rallying.

Photos: fotoracing.co.uk

The build up

It was the late Paul Adams from South Wales, a rally enthusiast through and through, who first came up with the idea of running a 'proper rally'. Fortunately, he contacted Brian Avery from De Lacy Motor Club who brought Colin Heppenstall to the project. The rest, of course, is history.

The idea came at a time when Britain's round of the World Rally Championship had been shortened and condensed to fit the new format of WRC events and some UK competitors were looking for a bigger challenge.

Adams sought Avery out at Autosport International, probably at the 2003 edition, and floated his idea. Avery said: "I don't think you're the only person in the world thinking that because we've been sat in the local pub at De Lacy Motor Club. This is an idea we've come up with as well and I think it's a brilliant idea."

Avery continues: "Paul Adams said: 'I'm going to try and get some interested parties together. Are you on board and would you come along to a meeting? Because you've already been running an international rally.' That was the Mintex International Rally.

"So that was arranged and as the meeting went on, it became clear that a lot of people were interested. There were a lot of ideas and people were saying well, we need to have this and we'll need to do that. And we'll need to run 180 cars, and at night. Someone said you can't do that. You will need to have a Schedule 4 and everybody looked blank.

"I knew that De Lacy had got a Schedule 4 permission to run an event with 180 cars at night. I waited until the coffee break, went outside and phoned Geoff Round from De Lacy. And he said: 'Yes, I think we can help.' So we left it at that. I went back into the meeting and announced that the Schedule 4 would not be a problem. Well, the room was dumbstruck. De Lacy Motor Club has the use of a Schedule 4 and I've spoken to them and they're interested. And from there, that's where it started.

"Brian Heppenstall, Colin's father, was heavily involved in the club and that's when Colin got involved. Graham James, Nicola Heppenstall's

The late Paul Adams

dad, was also involved from the beginning.

"The first event lost a significant amount of money. Hindsight being the perfect science, we probably shouldn't have carried on. But Colin bit the bullet and we went from that. The way I explain it is that it's an event run by a dictator. We ran the first two or three years with virtually no money and then it started to work and more money came in. It's only Colin's stubbornness that kept it running."

In the early stages of planning, the operation known as 'Stuttgart and Oval' had taken the lead for raising sponsorship. Unfortunately, this did not materialise and the 2004 event lost money. It was probably a case of being over ambitious in terms of what they thought they could deliver. However, if they had not been ambitious the event may never have run, because common sense would have kicked in sooner.

The rally was launched in Sheffield

The Roger Albert Clark Rally: The build up

The Croft service area in 2005

Colin Heppenstall takes up the story. "Brian Avery came to us, probably during 2003, and asked if we would get involved with it? So after getting an understanding of what it was all about and realising that it was the type of thing that I thought would work, I said I was more than happy to get involved. But it would only work if I had total control over it. With too many people getting involved, it doesn't work. So we decided to split it into two with me doing the event and Stuttgart and Oval doing the promotion and everything else. And that's how it was set up for the first year.

"Here we are now, 20 years later, still organising it. For the first event, entries were a challenge and

Hannu Mikkola and Malcolm Wilson in 2004

David Winstanley interviews Mark Higgins in 2005

2004: Chris and Hilary Green go over the start ramp at the Don Valley Stadium

we got 52. But we actually only started with 37.

"The biggest challenge was actually knowing who to speak to because regional associations didn't want this outside event coming into their association area. Motorsport UK, the MSA as it was then, called Brian and I down to their offices because they'd heard that we'd got no permissions.

"I had a lever arch file full of all the necessary paperwork, because in the good old days, you had it all in writing. I had to get the folder out and show that I'd got permission for everything. The Chief Executive apologised for dragging us all the way down for a file because people had told him we hadn't got permissions. That was really the start of my relationship with Motorsport UK which is still on-going.

"So for the first year it was a miracle that it ever ran and it only ran because my wife Nicola had to have an operation. I had to stop at home to look after her for two months and that's the time I had to run the event and finish it all off."

The Roger Albert Clark Rally: The build up

Roger Albert Clark Rally 2004:
the first edition

Overall winners: Stig Blomqvist and Ana Goni

The original Stig delivers in the first edition

The 2004 rally
Saturday 20 to Tuesday 23 November
179 stage miles
25 special stages
Start: Don Valley Stadium, Sheffield
Overnight 1: Don Valley Stadium, Sheffield
Overnight 2 & 3: Carlisle Airport
Finish: Don Valley Stadium, Sheffield
39 starters
23 finishers

Open Rally winners: Steve Bannister and Kevin Rae

Roger Albert Rally 2004: the first edition

Steve Perez and Neil Dashfield

The inaugural Roger Albert Clark Rally took a lot of people by surprise. Many in the sport doubted that it would ever run, even in the days leading up to the start. Some thought that hardly any of the 39 starters would survive to the finish. Some simply thought that no one would turn out to watch it. They were all very wrong.

The event grew out of an idea from Paul Adams to run a 'proper rally'. The RAC Rallies of the 1960s and 1970s were remembered with great affection, but times had changed and the demands of the current WRC mean that, like it or loathe it, the format of Wales Rally GB was very different.

Instead, De Lacy Motor Club took hold of the project and resolved to run an event that would, as far as possible, recreate the RAC Rallies of old. The route offered four days of competition, centred on the Scottish borders and finished with an assault on Kielder on the morning of the final day.

But the build up to the event did not bring the level of entry needed to make it work financially. In truth, the stretched organisers did not communicate very well with potential competitors and, with an entry fee of £2500 for around 180 stage miles, many crews kept their hands in their pockets.

The final tally was 39 starters, 29 in the three historic classes and ten in the Open event for any two-wheel drive car. In money terms, it was little short of a disaster, but De Lacy dug deep and pushed ahead to run a very slick event.

The Don Valley Stadium in Sheffield provided a

Alexander Hack

Hannu Mikkola was a star in 2004

Bob Bean in his battered Lotus Cortina

Bryan Gill

good event base, but it was when the crews arrived at Rother Valley for the opening stage on Saturday afternoon that the first signs emerged that the rally had captured the imagination of the fans. The stage was lined with people, many there to see Hannu Mikkola, Stig Blomqvist and Malcolm Wilson in Ford Escort Mk2s.

That level of enthusiasm continued into Sunday. "I last did the RAC in 1996 and going into Gisburn forest was like a World Championship rally," said Bryan Gill, back in an Opel Kadett for the event. "The spectators could have joined hands and lined the stage from the start to the finish!" Tarmac ace Eian Pritchard, out for a very rare gravel rally, was equally overwhelmed. "I haven't seen spectators like this on an event for a long, long time," he said at Carlisle.

At the head of the rally, a fine battle developed between Wilson and Blomqvist as electrical dramas on Monday evening cost Mikkola around seven minutes. Richard Tuthill/John Bennie could have topped the Escorts in their Porsche 911 but dropped five minutes when the throttle cable broke in Ae as dawn broke on Monday morning.

Roger Albert Rally 2004: the first edition

David Stokes and Guy Weaver

Willi Polesznig

David McErlain in his Porsche 911

Wilson's spectacular charge finally came to an end far up a Kielder firebreak on Tuesday morning. Now, Blomqvist had a big lead but you'd never have thought it as he threw the car around the final stage on the race circuit at Croft. That last stage, in front of a couple of thousand spectators, was a case of who can get an Escort sideways for longest, and the fans loved it!

Blomqvist, like his fellow legends, signed autographs every time he stepped out of the car. "It is no different to 1983. This is the way the rally is supposed to be," he said, part way through the Kielder leg on Tuesday. In fact, the Kielder stagers drew widespread praise. "They are fantastic stages!" raved fourth-placed Ray Bellm. "I've never seen any of them before," he added, rightly claiming to be the best of the rallying novices after finishing behind Blomqvist, Jeremy Easson and Mikkola.

"Unbelievable crowds; absolutely fantastic," said Grant Shand on his way to sixth place, a minute down on Phil and Mick Squires in their famous Mk2 Escort. "This event has been the highlight of my rallying career," said Phil. "To all those who didn't enter, you really missed a challenge. You must come and do it next year, don't stay away."

Hannu Mikkola and Ieuan Thomas

The sentiments of Squires echoed those of thousands of fans as well as the organisers. "This event has brought back all the enthusiasm that we lost in the last five years of Rally GB," said a spectating Jock Simpson.

OK, the entry was small. But it was crammed with quality and the friendly atmosphere on the stages amongst the fans and marshals was straight out of 1979. Over 1200 marshals were on duty and more than adequate safety, radio and medical cover proved that it wasn't just the fans who got behind the event. Modern day issues of greatly increased safety needs and risk assessment matters had been well covered.

As the 28 proud survivors filtered back into the finish at Sheffield, Olly, Stan and Judy Clark were there to represent the man whose name graced the rally. "It's wonderful," said Judy. "It's just so sad that Roger's not here to see it, because it's just overwhelming. I hope this is the first of many to come."

Stig Blomqvist

Mikkola finished third

Roger Albert Rally 2004: the first edition

Ray Bellm

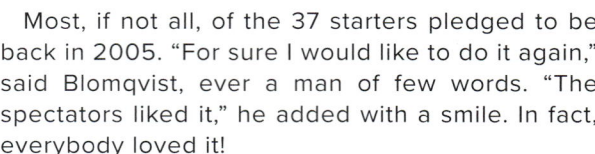
Phil and Mick Squires

Easson and Cook finished second

Most, if not all, of the 37 starters pledged to be back in 2005. "For sure I would like to do it again," said Blomqvist, ever a man of few words. "The spectators liked it," he added with a smile. In fact, everybody loved it!

Out in the Open
The Roger Albert Clark Rally cannot survive on period cars alone, and so an Open event ran in tandem with the historics to cater for any two-wheel drive cars. Steve Bannister and Kevin Rae duly dominated, with a typically blistering performance in Banner's faithful Mk2 Escort. His total time for the rally, albeit in a non-period specification car, was 1m40s up on Blomqvist.

"It has been a marvellous event! Those who didn't do it have missed out," said the Yorkshire legend. "The stages have been brilliant and I just hope it runs again next year with a full entry."

Rob Dick and Baz Green led the chase of Bannister in their Mk2, while Rodger Fowler/Chris Dewsnap (Astra) and Julius Deane/Charlie Chatburn (Peugeot 205 GTi) completed the finishers. "All I've ever wanted to do is Kielder on

Alexander Hack

Craig Salter and Preston Ayres

Malcolm Wilson

Polesznig in his Porsche 911

the RAC," said Deane, who had earlier managed to trash the front of his car on the first proper corner of the rally!

The entry in the Open category is going to be hugely significant to the future viability of the rally, though the cost of competing is an obvious barrier for many clubmen. But Dave Hemingway and Jim Plevey, who got their Escort home in the Trophy rally for early retirees from the main event, reckoned on a spend of around £2000 on top of the entry fee. A slap up meal for eight at a Little Chef was one of Hemingway's major costs!

Stephen Hall's TR7 V8

The Squires brothers

2004 ROGER ALBERT CLARK RALLY: ENTRY LIST

No	Driver	Co-driver	Car	Class
1	Steve Perez	Neil Dashfield	Porsche 911	C5
2	Chris Green	Hilary Green	Ford Lotus Cortina Mk1	B4
3	David McErlain	Andrew Merifield	Porsche 911	B5
4	Rob Pilcher	Roger Burkill	Ford Lotus Cortina Mk1	B4
11	Richard Tuthill	John Bennie	Porsche 911	C4
12	Ray Bellm	Dorian Evans	Ford Escort RS1600	C5
15	David Stokes	Ian Oakey	Ford Escort Mk1 RS1600	C5
16	Richard Gower	Carl Williamson	Ford Escort RS1600	C5
18	Jeremy Easson	Alun Cook	Ford Escort RS2000	C5
19	Willi Polesznig	Peter Stark	Porsche 911	C4
21	Anthony Ward	Mark Crisp	Ford Escort RS1600	C5
22	Craig Salter	Preston Ayres	Ford Escort Mk1	C5
23	Terry Nowlan	Nick Barrington	Ford Escort Mk1 RS1600	C5
24	Keith Scarr	Paul Hudson	Ford Escort Mk1 RS1600	C5
25	Garry Preston	Mike Sones	Mini Clubman GT	C2
26	Peter Hall	John Billett	Ford Escort	C3
27	Alexander Hack	Rob Richardson	Ford Escort RS1600	C5
28	Mark Butler	Richard Forster	Ford Escort Mk1 RS1600	C5
41	Stig Blomqvist	Ana Goni	Ford Escort Mk2 RS	D5
42	Hannu Mikkola	Ieuan Thomas	Ford Escort RS1800	D5
43	Richard Lepley	Ian Bevan	Ford Escort RS1600	D5
44	Robert Dick	Barry Green	Ford Escort Mk2	F4
45	Grant Shand	Frank Richer	Ford Escort Mk2	D5
46	Stephen Hall	Aggie Foster	Triumph TR7 V8	D4
47	Malcolm Wilson	Peter Martin	Ford Escort Mk2	D5
48	Bryan Gill	Nigel Hutchinson	Opel Kadett GTE	D3
49	Philip Squires	Michael Squires	Ford Escort RS1800	D5
50	Robin Morgan	Mike Robinson	Opel Kadett GTE	D3
51	Ralph Abel	Mark Swallow	Ford Escort RS1800	D5
52	Eian Pritchard	Martin Jones	Ford Escort Mk2 RS	D5
61	Steve Bannister	Kevin Rae	Ford Escort Mk2	E3
62	Dave Hemingway	Jim Plevey	Ford Escort Mk2	E3
63	Mark Fowler	Chris Dewsnap	Opel Manta 400	E4
64	Tony Jardine	Maurice Hamilton	MG ZR 160	F3
65	Steve Blunt	Gawaine Clark	Peugeot 306 GTi	F3
66	Martin Kilburn	Tim Buckley	Ford Escort Mk2	E3
67	Redmond Barry	Robert Hay	Proton Satria Kit Car	F2
68	Julius Deane	Charlie Chatburn	Peugeot 205 GTi	F2
69	Steve Graham	Tony Graham	Peugeot 205	F2

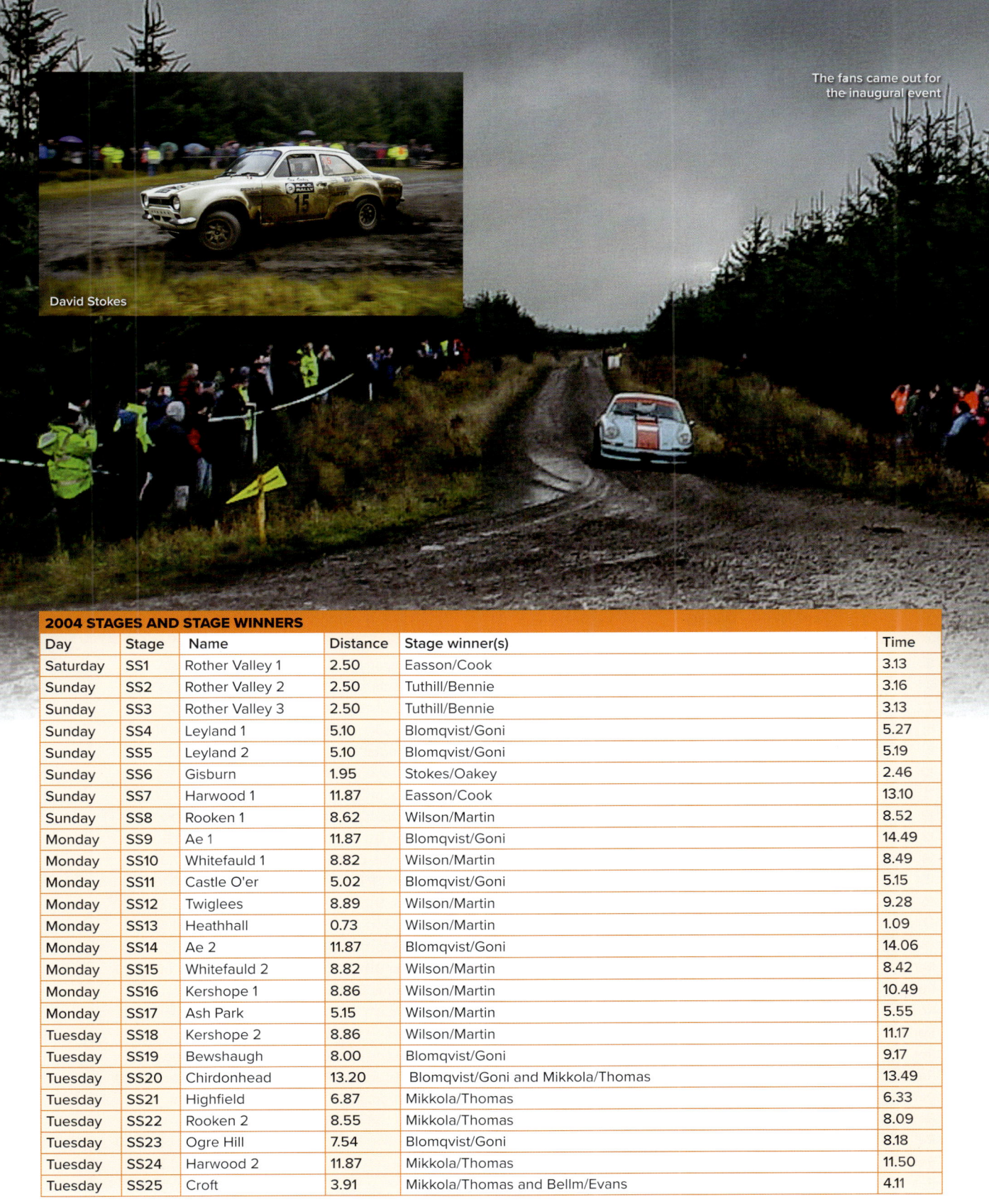

The fans came out for the inaugural event

David Stokes

2004 STAGES AND STAGE WINNERS

Day	Stage	Name	Distance	Stage winner(s)	Time
Saturday	SS1	Rother Valley 1	2.50	Easson/Cook	3.13
Sunday	SS2	Rother Valley 2	2.50	Tuthill/Bennie	3.16
Sunday	SS3	Rother Valley 3	2.50	Tuthill/Bennie	3.13
Sunday	SS4	Leyland 1	5.10	Blomqvist/Goni	5.27
Sunday	SS5	Leyland 2	5.10	Blomqvist/Goni	5.19
Sunday	SS6	Gisburn	1.95	Stokes/Oakey	2.46
Sunday	SS7	Harwood 1	11.87	Easson/Cook	13.10
Sunday	SS8	Rooken 1	8.62	Wilson/Martin	8.52
Monday	SS9	Ae 1	11.87	Blomqvist/Goni	14.49
Monday	SS10	Whitefauld 1	8.82	Wilson/Martin	8.49
Monday	SS11	Castle O'er	5.02	Blomqvist/Goni	5.15
Monday	SS12	Twiglees	8.89	Wilson/Martin	9.28
Monday	SS13	Heathhall	0.73	Wilson/Martin	1.09
Monday	SS14	Ae 2	11.87	Blomqvist/Goni	14.06
Monday	SS15	Whitefauld 2	8.82	Wilson/Martin	8.42
Monday	SS16	Kershope 1	8.86	Wilson/Martin	10.49
Monday	SS17	Ash Park	5.15	Wilson/Martin	5.55
Tuesday	SS18	Kershope 2	8.86	Wilson/Martin	11.17
Tuesday	SS19	Bewshaugh	8.00	Blomqvist/Goni	9.17
Tuesday	SS20	Chirdonhead	13.20	Blomqvist/Goni and Mikkola/Thomas	13.49
Tuesday	SS21	Highfield	6.87	Mikkola/Thomas	6.33
Tuesday	SS22	Rooken 2	8.55	Mikkola/Thomas	8.09
Tuesday	SS23	Ogre Hill	7.54	Blomqvist/Goni	8.18
Tuesday	SS24	Harwood 2	11.87	Mikkola/Thomas	11.50
Tuesday	SS25	Croft	3.91	Mikkola/Thomas and Bellm/Evans	4.11

Roger Albert Rally 2004: the first edition

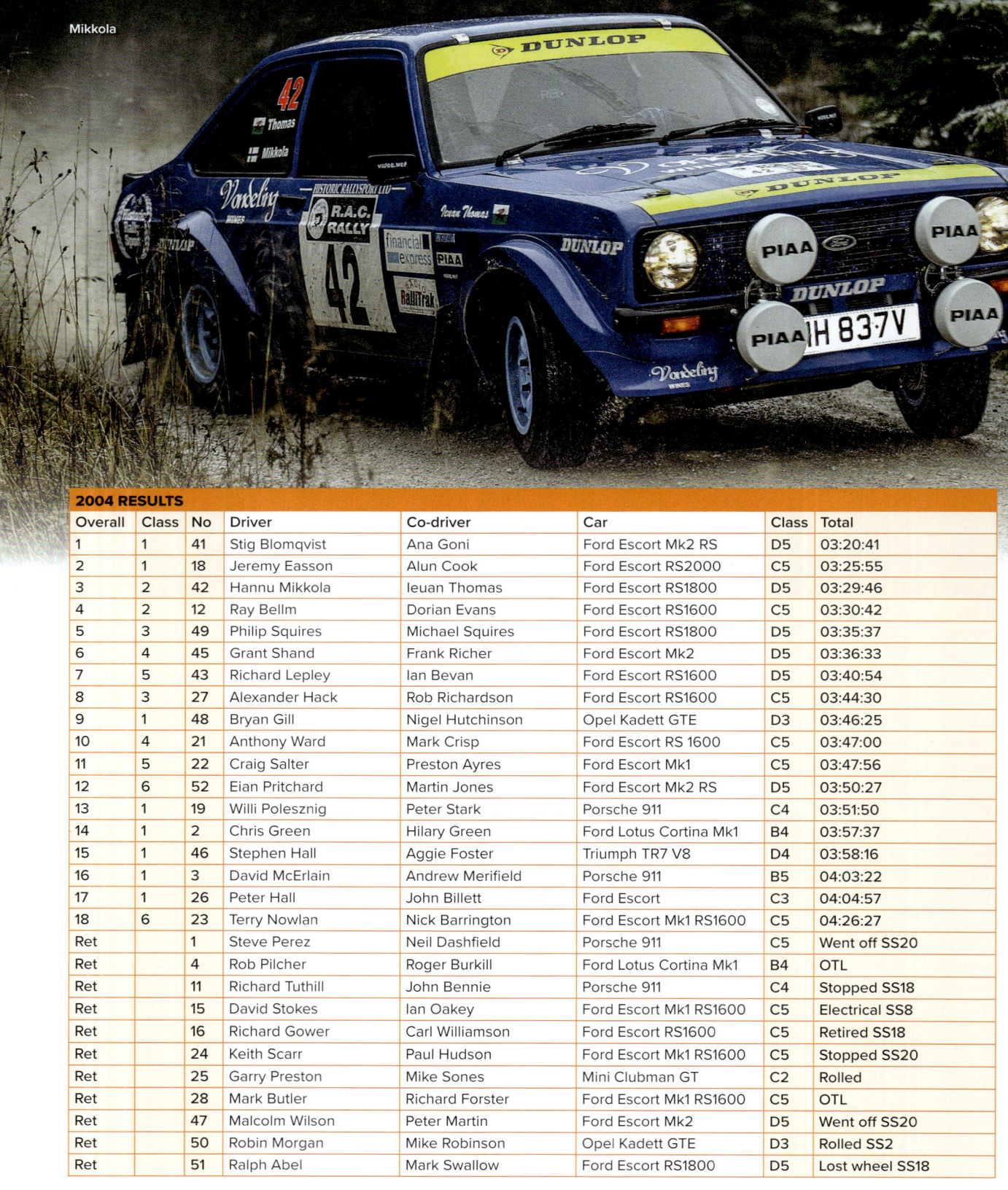

Mikkola

2004 RESULTS

Overall	Class	No	Driver	Co-driver	Car	Class	Total
1	1	41	Stig Blomqvist	Ana Goni	Ford Escort Mk2 RS	D5	03:20:41
2	1	18	Jeremy Easson	Alun Cook	Ford Escort RS2000	C5	03:25:55
3	2	42	Hannu Mikkola	Ieuan Thomas	Ford Escort RS1800	D5	03:29:46
4	2	12	Ray Bellm	Dorian Evans	Ford Escort RS1600	C5	03:30:42
5	3	49	Philip Squires	Michael Squires	Ford Escort RS1800	D5	03:35:37
6	4	45	Grant Shand	Frank Richer	Ford Escort Mk2	D5	03:36:33
7	5	43	Richard Lepley	Ian Bevan	Ford Escort RS1600	D5	03:40:54
8	3	27	Alexander Hack	Rob Richardson	Ford Escort RS1600	C5	03:44:30
9	1	48	Bryan Gill	Nigel Hutchinson	Opel Kadett GTE	D3	03:46:25
10	4	21	Anthony Ward	Mark Crisp	Ford Escort RS 1600	C5	03:47:00
11	5	22	Craig Salter	Preston Ayres	Ford Escort Mk1	C5	03:47:56
12	6	52	Eian Pritchard	Martin Jones	Ford Escort Mk2 RS	D5	03:50:27
13	1	19	Willi Polesznig	Peter Stark	Porsche 911	C4	03:51:50
14	1	2	Chris Green	Hilary Green	Ford Lotus Cortina Mk1	B4	03:57:37
15	1	46	Stephen Hall	Aggie Foster	Triumph TR7 V8	D4	03:58:16
16	1	3	David McErlain	Andrew Merifield	Porsche 911	B5	04:03:22
17	1	26	Peter Hall	John Billett	Ford Escort	C3	04:04:57
18	6	23	Terry Nowlan	Nick Barrington	Ford Escort Mk1 RS1600	C5	04:26:27
Ret		1	Steve Perez	Neil Dashfield	Porsche 911	C5	Went off SS20
Ret		4	Rob Pilcher	Roger Burkill	Ford Lotus Cortina Mk1	B4	OTL
Ret		11	Richard Tuthill	John Bennie	Porsche 911	C4	Stopped SS18
Ret		15	David Stokes	Ian Oakey	Ford Escort Mk1 RS1600	C5	Electrical SS8
Ret		16	Richard Gower	Carl Williamson	Ford Escort RS1600	C5	Retired SS18
Ret		24	Keith Scarr	Paul Hudson	Ford Escort Mk1 RS1600	C5	Stopped SS20
Ret		25	Garry Preston	Mike Sones	Mini Clubman GT	C2	Rolled
Ret		28	Mark Butler	Richard Forster	Ford Escort Mk1 RS1600	C5	OTL
Ret		47	Malcolm Wilson	Peter Martin	Ford Escort Mk2	D5	Went off SS20
Ret		50	Robin Morgan	Mike Robinson	Opel Kadett GTE	D3	Rolled SS2
Ret		51	Ralph Abel	Mark Swallow	Ford Escort RS1800	D5	Lost wheel SS18

Eian Pritchard and Martin Jones

Blomqvist

2004 RESULTS: OPEN RALLY

Overall	Class	No	Driver	Co-driver	Car	Class	Total
1	1	61	Steve Bannister	Kevin Rae	Ford Escort Mk2	E3	03:19:03
2	1	44	Robert Dick	Barry Green	Ford Escort Mk2	F4	03:28:39
3	1	63	Mark Fowler	Chris Dewsnap	Opel Manta 400	E4	04:07:29
4	1	68	Julius Deane	Charlie Chatburn	Peugeot 205 GTi	F2	04:14:37
Ret		62	Dave Hemingway	Jim Plevey	Ford Escort Mk2	E3	
Ret		64	Tony Jardine	Maurice Hamilton	MG ZR 160	F3	
Ret		65	Steve Blunt	Gawaine Clark	Peugeot 306 GTi	F3	
Ret		66	Martin Kilburn	Tim Buckley	Ford Escort Mk2	E3	
Ret		67	Redmond Barry	Robert Hay	Proton Satria Kit Car	F2	

2004 RESULTS: TROPHY RALLY TWO

Overall	Class	No	Driver	Co-driver	Car	Total
1	1	15	David Stokes	Ian Oakey	Ford Escort Mk1 RS1600	02:39:15
2	1	62	Dave Hemingway	Jim Plevey	Ford Escort Mk2	02:58:48
Ret	2	4	Rob Pilcher	Roger Burkill	Ford Lotus Cortina Mk1	Stopped in service

2004 RESULTS: TROPHY RALLY THREE

Overall	Class	No	Driver	Co-driver	Car	Total
1	1	28	Mark Butler	Richard Forster	Ford Escort Mk1 RS1600	01:27:39
2	1	69	Steve Graham	Tony Graham	Peugeot 205	01:45:46
3	1	25	Garry Preston	Mike Sones	Mini Clubman GT	01:50:30

Anthony Ward

David McErlain

Roger Albert Rally 2004: the first edition

Roger Albert Clark Rally 2005:
the second edition

Overall winners: Mark Higgins and Peter Martin

Higgins beats the weather

The 2005 rally

Saturday 19 to Tuesday 22 November
179 stage miles
29 special stages
Start: Don Valley Stadium, Sheffield
Overnight 1: Don Valley Stadium, Sheffield
Overnight 2 & 3: Carlisle Airport
Finish: Don Valley Stadium, Sheffield
50 starters
23 finishers

Open Rally winners: Steve Bannister and Kevin Rae

Roger Albert Rally 2005: the second edition

Blomqvist and Goñi finished second

The second Roger Albert Clark Rally was a real toughie, as fog and ice covered 29 difficult stages in some of Britain's most challenging forests.

"It's just like a proper RAC Rally," said Mark Higgins after dominating the event.

Partnered by Peter Martin and driving a Mk1 Escort from Historic Rallysport, the reigning British Rally champion won the four-day classic rally by over four minutes. It was a crushing performance.

Michael and David Pedley

For the second running of the rally, De Lacy MC stuck with the format that had worked well a year earlier. Spectator stages over the weekend preceded the real competition, which started with two Scottish stages on Sunday night. More Scottish stages followed through Monday before a 5am start on Tuesday for over 70 stage miles in Kielder and then two blasts around Croft on the way back to Sheffield.

Historic cars again took pride of place, but an Open Rally catered for non-period two-wheel drives and two trophy rallies mopped up early retirements who were able to get running again. The field of 50 cars was up on 2004 but was still some way adrift of where the event really needs to be. Nevertheless, a projected financial break even for the 2005 rally was a big step in the right direction.

What the event did once more was capture the hearts of the spectators. Freezing fog and pre-dawn starts failed to dampen the enthusiasm of the thousands of fans who turned out to see the type of rallying many of them remembered from the 1970s.

Right from the opening two stages at the Don

Charlie Taylor and Steve Bielby

John Taylor

Higgins at Bramham Park

Valley Stadium in Sheffield, Higgins was on it. By the time he arrived at Carlisle on Sunday evening, he had a 15s lead over the Mk2 Escort of Stig Blomqvist/Ana Goni, and that margin would steadily increase over the next two days. Chasing was the Porsche 911 of Jimmy McRae and Campbell Roy, but they dropped a lot of time with an off in Ae on Monday morning and eventually retired with engine problems on Tuesday morning.

Before that, the very icy stages on Monday morning caught out many crews as well as McRae. Steve Bannister/Kevin Rae, leaders of the Open Rally in their Escort Mk2, spent three minutes on the roof in Whitefauld Hill, but later regained the lead when Mick Jones/Andy Morgan lost four minutes changing a puncture on their Escort on the second run through Ae.

By Monday afternoon, with the ice clearing, Higgins extended his lead and arrived at service in Dumfries with a 1m45s lead. "We've got more of a gap now. She's an old girl and we've got to look after her," he joked of the car. Blomqvist continued to be troubled by a misfire but held second as a typically neat and tidy run from Jeremy Easson and Alun Cook put their Escort Mk1 into third.

Mark Fowler on the opening stage at the Don Valley Stadium

Perez in the Stratos

Martin Freestone

Though the ice had gone, the fog was back for the final two stages of Monday afternoon in the dark of Kershope and Ash Park. In more trouble were David Stokes and Ian Oakey when their Escort Mk1 slid wide and hit something in the undergrowth. They limped out of Ash Park on a shattered rim and with a bent axle. However, that was changed back at Carlisle, thanks to the generosity of Martin Freestone who loaned his spare axle. Stokes/Oakey would go on to finish fourth, beating the Mk2 Escort of Freestone/Joanne Lockwood in the process!

The final day was a real sting in the tail as seven stages in Kielder, with only one brief service, kept up the pressure. Before dawn, with the temperature well below freezing and patches of fog lying in wait, the leaders were into Kershope and then Bewshaugh. Along with McRae, out went Will Onions/Tim Hobbs (Escort Mk2) from fourth in the Open Rally, while Phil and Mick Squires effectively ended their rally when they went off backwards in Kershope. Jones/Morgan, meanwhile, finally put their Escort off terminally in Chirdonhead but immediately vowed to return in 2006.

Through it all, Higgins set a punishing pace. But it so nearly went wrong for the rally leaders on the

Jimmy McRae and Campbell Roy

second run through Bewshaugh when the Escort slithered up a firebreak. "Fortunately, there were plenty of spectators there and without them we wouldn't have got back on," admitted Higgins, who lost only a minute in the incident.

Just to prove a point, Higgins then stormed the 16-miler in Pundershaw, beating the bogey by 56s and catching Blomqvist on the finish line. Having escaped the clutches of Kielder, just two stages at Croft remained for a final chance to wow the fans as a misty darkness started to fall over the race circuit. The sight of the Mk1 in a glorious power slide, with Higgins waving out of the window to his watching parents brought the curtain down in style for the 2005 Roger Albert Clark Rally. "It's been an absolutely amazing event and made me realise again why I started rallying," said the winner.

Blomqvist/Goni took a clear second from Easson/Cook, who enjoyed a mighty run to third. "Perfect! A brilliant rally," said Easson after scarcely putting a wheel wrong. Stokes/Oakey and Freestone/Lockwood wrapped up the top five in the historic event as a fabulous sixth went to the 1600cc Escort of Vincent Bristow/Dean Mitchell.

In the Open Rally, Bannister/Rae finished a remarkable 13m51s ahead of Jason Lepley/Simon Sparey, who overcame a catalogue of dramas to get their Escort home ahead of the similar Mk2s of Rob Archer/Peter Field and Dave Hemingway/Jim Plevey. "The conditions were as bad as you'd expect. It's been a great event," said Bannister.

Easson took third overall

Roger Albert Rally 2005: the second edition 31

Steve and Tony Graham used an MG before their Lancia Fulvia was ready

Of course, on such a tough rally, simply finishing was a mighty achievement and many were elated just to return to Sheffield on Tuesday evening. Dave Watkins and Neil Duncan took ninth historic and second in class in their ex-Roger Clark Escort, having changed 14 tyres and just one fog light bulb in four days!

Further down, Garry Preston/Mike Sones got their Mini Clubman to the finish and typified the spirit of the rally. On the first lap of Croft on Sunday, they spotted the other Mini of Keith Bird/Ken Bills stopped on the stage. Preston stopped and told Bird to get the tow rope ready and then stopped again on the second lap to tow his rival out of the stage. It was that sort of rally!

The classes and the trophy rallies
While Higgins and Blomqvist grabbed the limelight, all the way down the event were heroic tales from club competitors tackling the biggest rally of their lives.

Higgins at Don Valley

Easson at Bramham Park

Nigel Talton in the Clubmans Rally

Will Onions

Jason Lepley

"This is a real challenge for the crew, the car and the service crew," reckoned Chris Green. Partnered by his wife Hilary, Green ran a newly prepared Escort Mk1 to 11th in the historics, despite a bush repair to failed engine mounts using a lump of wood.

In the main historic event, Bristow/Mitchell were awesome on their way to Class C2 victory. "I've never seen so many different conditions," reckoned Mitchell, after his team changed a failing head gasket on Sunday evening. The next three places in C2 fell to twin-cam Escorts as Watkins/Duncan headed home John Dixon/Gavin Heseltine and the Greens.

Eilir Morris/Phil Clarke won class C3 from eighth overall in the historics in their Escort RS2000, while Chris Worrall/Howard Pridmore (Talbot Sunbeam) and Robin Morgan/Mike Robinson (Opel Kadett GTE) also won their classes. "We've had a wonderful rally, it's been a great event," said Morgan.

To no-one's great surprise Bannister dominated the Open Rally, but one of the star turns came from Matt Barker and Dave Lucas in Barker's Peugeot 205 GTi. They spent four minutes off the road in Kershope on Tuesday morning but got back on when Andy Madge/Pat Cooper stopped their Toyota Corolla and towed the 205 out of the ditch!

Roger Albert Rally 2005: the second edition

Chris Worrall and Howard Pridmore

Rob Pilcher

Andy Madge

Tony Jardine/Maurice Hamilton claimed the final Open class in their Skoda Fabia, finishing well clear of the delayed MG ZR of brothers Steve and Tony Graham.

Despite putting their Escort Mk2 on its side in Greystoke, Peter Beer and John Pickavance returned to win the Monday/Tuesday Trophy Rally, while the Tuesday only Trophy event fell to the Opel Kadett of Bryan Gill/Nigel Hutchinson.

Finally, a Clubmans Rally added another 20 crews to the event for a run through most of Monday's stages in the Scottish borders. Once again, Escorts dominated, with Mk2s taking the top four places as Keith Robathan/Martin Forrest won by nearly a minute from Geoff Wilson/Simon Martin. Tim Jones and Don James trekked up from Wales with their Mk2 to claim third on a rare foray into the region.

Insight: Steve Perez (Lancia Stratos)
What put you out of the rally?
"We first had some problems on Sunday night. Then, halfway through the first stage on Monday morning in Ae Forest, we started to lose oil pressure and it looks like we've done a piston. It was always a chance when we brought the car out because we hadn't had time to rebuild the engine."

What has the reaction been to the Stratos?
"What's been great is that there has just been

Keith Bird and Ken Bills at Bramham Park

so much interest in the car. I'm sorry for all the spectators that we retired early. It's great to have something different to all the Escorts!"

What's it like to drive?
"I really needed another day to get to know the car better, but the time I had in the car was fantastic. I never really got the chance to drive the car before the start of the rally. But it is a very tricky and quite temperamental car to drive. It's very twitchy! But the times were coming along and it's been a fantastic experience. We had a good go in the car but it wasn't to be in the end."

What next?
"I'll do a couple of BHRC events next year and we'll certainly be out for the Roger Albert Clark again next year. I've had two goes at it and not finished yet, and I hope to be back next year to see the finish ramp and be in with a shout of victory!"

Stig Blomqvist

Grant Shand

2005 ROGER ALBERT CLARK RALLY: ENTRY LIST

No	Driver	Co-driver	Car	Class
1	Stig Blomqvist	Ana Goni	Ford Escort Mk2 RS	D5
2	Mark Higgins	Peter Martin	Ford Escort Mk1 RS1600	C5
3	Steve Perez	Steve Harris	Lancia Stratos	D4
4	Jeremy Easson	Alun Cook	Ford Escort RS2000	C5
5	Jimmy McRae	Campbell Roy	Porsche 911RS	C5
7	David Stokes	Ian Oakey	Ford Escort Mk1 RS1600	C5
8	Ray Bellm	Patrick Walsh	Ford Escort RS1600	C5
9	Rikki Proffitt	Phill Harrison	Ford Escort Mk1 RS1600	C5
11	Phil Squires	Michael Squires	Ford Escort RS1800	D5
12	Graham Samuel	Tony Phillips	Ford Escort RS2000	C5
14	Grant Shand	Chris Parsons	Ford Escort RS	D5
15	Martin Freestone	Joanne Lockwood	Ford Escort Mk2	D5
16	Eilir Morris	Phil Clarke	Ford Escort RS2000	C3
18	Chris Green	Hilary Green	Ford Escort Mk1	C2
19	Charlie Taylor	Steve Bielby	Ford Escort Mk2	D5
21	Craig Salter	Preston Ayres	Ford Escort RS1600	C5
22	Vincent Bristow	Dean Mitchell	Ford Escort Mk1	C2
23	David Cobb	Allen Craven	Toyota Corolla 1600 GT	D2
24	David Watkins	Neil Duncan	Ford Escort Twin Cam	C2
25	Robin Morgan	Mike Robinson	Opel Kadett GTE	D3
26	Chris Worrall	Howard Pridmore	Talbot Sunbeam Ti	D2
28	Russell Morgan	Rob Fairhurst	Ford Escort Mexico	C2
29	Sean Lockyear	Christopher Wood	Porsche 911	C5
30	Keith Cornell	Tony Hunter	Ford Escort Mk2	D5
31	John Dixon	Gavin Heseltine	Ford Escort Mk1	C2
32	Keith Bird	Ken Bills	Mini Cooper S	C1
33	Garry Preston	Mike Sones	Mini Clubman GT	C2
34	Michael Pedley	David Pedley	Triumph TR7 V8	D4
35	David Winstanley	Terri Metcalfe	Ford Escort Mk2 RS2000	D3
36	Bryan Gill	Nigel Hutchinson	Opel Kadett GTE	D3
41	Rob Pilcher	Roger Burkill	Porsche 911S	B5
42	Bob Bean	Bill Stevenson	Ford Lotus Cortina Mk1	B4
51	Steve Bannister	Kevin Rae	Ford Escort Mk2	E4
52	'Mad' Mick Jones	Andy Morgan	Ford Escort Mk2	E3
53	Jason Lepley	Simon Sparey	Ford Escort Mk2 RS1800	E4
54	Peter Beer	John Pickavance	Ford Escort Mk2	E3
55	Dave Hemingway	Jim Plevey	Ford Escort Mk2	E3
57	Robert Archer	Peter Field	Ford Escort Mk2	E3
58	Mark Fowler	Christopher Dewsnap	Opel Manta	E4
59	Colin Barber	Martin Barber	Vauxhall Astra Sport	E3
60	John Taylor	Mark Ingram	Ford Escort Mexico	E2
62	William Onions	Tim Hobbs	Ford Escort Mk2	E4
63	Andy Madge	Pat Cooper	Toyota Corolla GT Coupe	E2
64	Austin Mckinlay	Dominic Brown	Peugeot 205 1.9 GTi	E3
65	Matt Barker	Dave Lucas	Peugeot 205 GTi	E3
66	Ralph Abel	Samuel Armida	Ford Escort RS	E4
67	Tony Jardine	Maurice Hamilton	Skoda Fabia	E2
69	Trevor Silcock	Pam Silcock	Vauxhall Astra GTE	E3
70	Julius Deane	Charles Chatburn	Peugeot 205 GTi	E2
71	Steve Graham	Tony Graham	MG ZR	E2

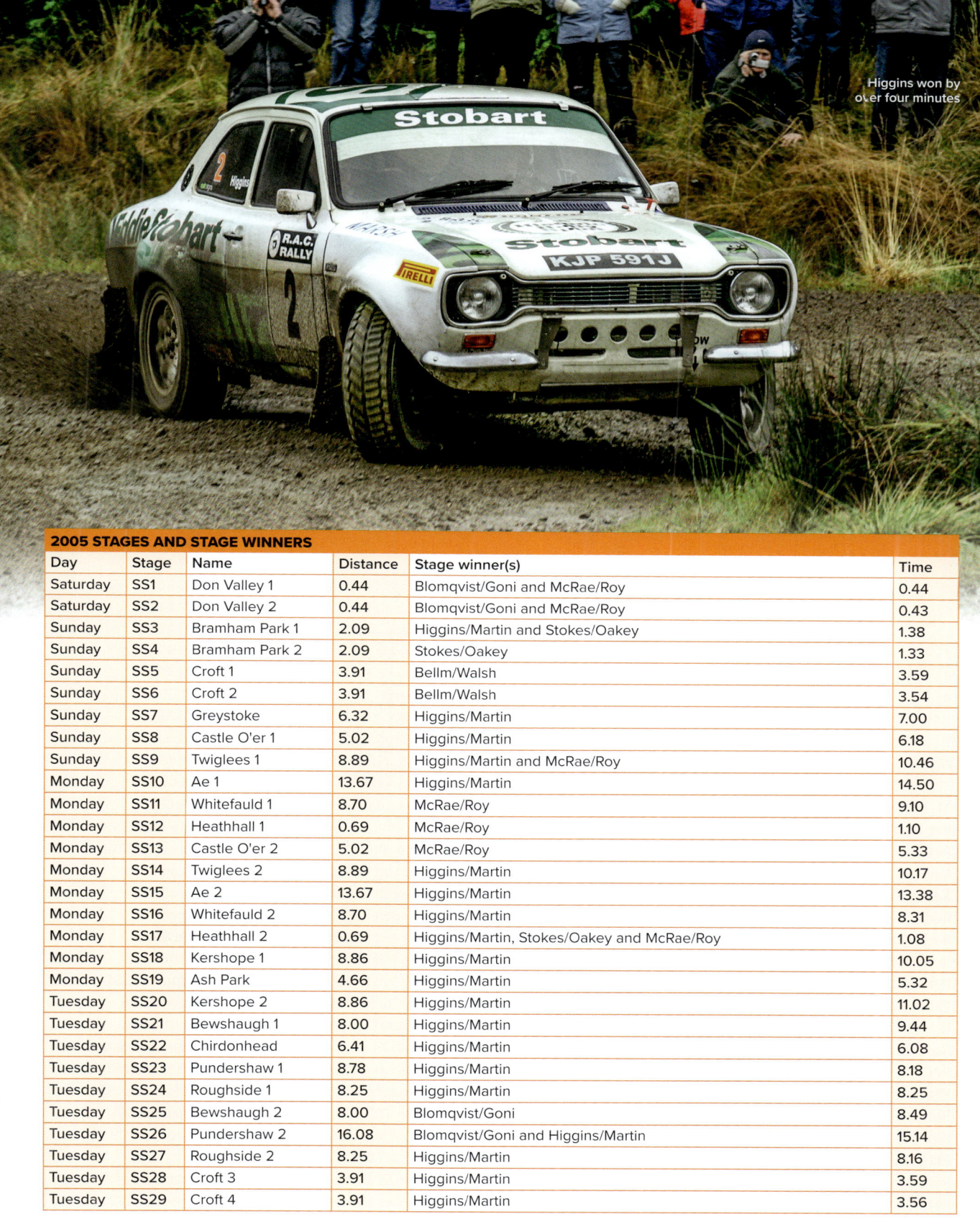

Higgins won by over four minutes

2005 STAGES AND STAGE WINNERS

Day	Stage	Name	Distance	Stage winner(s)	Time
Saturday	SS1	Don Valley 1	0.44	Blomqvist/Goni and McRae/Roy	0.44
Saturday	SS2	Don Valley 2	0.44	Blomqvist/Goni and McRae/Roy	0.43
Sunday	SS3	Bramham Park 1	2.09	Higgins/Martin and Stokes/Oakey	1.38
Sunday	SS4	Bramham Park 2	2.09	Stokes/Oakey	1.33
Sunday	SS5	Croft 1	3.91	Bellm/Walsh	3.59
Sunday	SS6	Croft 2	3.91	Bellm/Walsh	3.54
Sunday	SS7	Greystoke	6.32	Higgins/Martin	7.00
Sunday	SS8	Castle O'er 1	5.02	Higgins/Martin	6.18
Sunday	SS9	Twiglees 1	8.89	Higgins/Martin and McRae/Roy	10.46
Monday	SS10	Ae 1	13.67	Higgins/Martin	14.50
Monday	SS11	Whitefauld 1	8.70	McRae/Roy	9.10
Monday	SS12	Heathhall 1	0.69	McRae/Roy	1.10
Monday	SS13	Castle O'er 2	5.02	McRae/Roy	5.33
Monday	SS14	Twiglees 2	8.89	Higgins/Martin	10.17
Monday	SS15	Ae 2	13.67	Higgins/Martin	13.38
Monday	SS16	Whitefauld 2	8.70	Higgins/Martin	8.31
Monday	SS17	Heathhall 2	0.69	Higgins/Martin, Stokes/Oakey and McRae/Roy	1.08
Monday	SS18	Kershope 1	8.86	Higgins/Martin	10.05
Monday	SS19	Ash Park	4.66	Higgins/Martin	5.32
Tuesday	SS20	Kershope 2	8.86	Higgins/Martin	11.02
Tuesday	SS21	Bewshaugh 1	8.00	Higgins/Martin	9.44
Tuesday	SS22	Chirdonhead	6.41	Higgins/Martin	6.08
Tuesday	SS23	Pundershaw 1	8.78	Higgins/Martin	8.18
Tuesday	SS24	Roughside 1	8.25	Higgins/Martin	8.25
Tuesday	SS25	Bewshaugh 2	8.00	Blomqvist/Goni	8.49
Tuesday	SS26	Pundershaw 2	16.08	Blomqvist/Goni and Higgins/Martin	15.14
Tuesday	SS27	Roughside 2	8.25	Higgins/Martin	8.16
Tuesday	SS28	Croft 3	3.91	Higgins/Martin	3.59
Tuesday	SS29	Croft 4	3.91	Higgins/Martin	3.56

Roger Albert Rally 2005: the second edition

The Stratos on the opening stage

2005 RESULTS

Overall	Class	No	Driver	Co-driver	Car	Class	Total
1	1	2	Mark Higgins	Peter Martin	Ford Escort MK1 RS1600	C5	03:21:21
2	1	1	Stig Blomqvist	Ana Goni	Ford Escort Mk2 RS	D5	03:25:50
3	2	4	Jeremy Easson	Alun Cook	Ford Escort RS2000	C5	03:29:22
4	3	7	David Stokes	Ian Oakey	Ford Escort Mk1 RS1600	C5	03:35:50
5	2	15	Martin Freestone	Joanne Lockwood	Ford Escort Mk2	D5	03:37:34
6	1	22	Vincent Bristow	Dean Mitchell	Ford Escort Mk1	C2	03:46:00
7	3	19	Charlie Taylor	Steve Bielby	Ford Escort Mk2	D5	03:48:22
8	1	16	Eilir Morris	Phill Clarke	Ford Escort RS2000	C3	03:49:46
9	2	24	David Watkins	Neil Duncan	Ford Escort Twin Cam	C2	04:01:05
10	3	31	John Dixon	Gavin Heseltine	Ford Escort Mk1	C2	04:05:36
11	4	18	Chris Green	Hilary Green	Ford Escort Mk1	C2	04:05:52
12	1	26	Chris Worrall	Howard Pridmore	Talbot Sunbeam Ti	D2	04:08:16
13	1	25	Robin Morgan	Mike Robinson	Opel Kadett GTE	D3	04:18:07
14	5	33	Garry Preston	Mike Sones	Mini Clubman GT	C2	04:35:05
Ret		3	Steve Perez	Steve Harris	Lancia Stratos	D4	Engine after SS10
Ret		5	Jimmy McRae	Campbell Roy	Porsche 911RS	C5	Engine after SS23
Ret		8	Ray Bellm	Patrick Walsh	Ford Escort RS1600	C5	Went off SS21
Ret		9	Rikki Proffitt	Phill Harrison	Ford Escort Mk1 RS1600	C5	Went off SS9
Ret		11	Phil Squires	Michael Squires	Ford Escort RS1800	D5	Stopped SS20
Ret		12	Graham Samuel	Tony Phillips	Ford Escort RS2000	C5	Rolled S16
Ret		14	Grant Shand	Chris Parsons	Ford Escort RS	D5	Rolled SS9
Ret		21	Craig Salter	Preston Ayres	Ford Escort RS1600	C5	Headgasket SS7
Ret		23	David Cobb	Allen Craven	Toyota Corolla 1600 GT	D2	Accident SS16
Ret		28	Russell Morgan	Rob Fairhurst	Ford Escort Mexico	C2	Went off SS19
Ret		29	Sean Lockyear	Christopher Wood	Porsche 911	C5	Stopped on road section
Ret		30	Keith Cornell	Tony Hunter	Ford Escort Mk2	D5	Stopped after SS7
Ret		32	Keith Bird	Ken Bills	Mini Cooper S	C1	Electrical after SS6
Ret		34	Michael Pedley	David Pedley	Triumph TR7 V8	D4	Mechanical SS11
Ret		35	David Winstanley	Terri Metcalfe	Ford Escort Mk2 RS2000	D3	Stopped at PC9
Ret		36	Bryan Gill	Nigel Hutchinson	Opek Kadett GTE	D3	OTL
Ret		41	Rob Pilcher	Roger Burkill	Porsche 911S	B5	Accident in service
Ret		42	Bob Bean	Bill Stevenson	Ford Lotus Cortina Mk1	B4	Mechanical SS9

Mark Higgins and Peter Martin

2005 RESULTS: OPEN RALLY

Overall	Class	No	Driver	Co-driver	Car	Class	Total
1	1	51	Steve Bannister	Kevin Rae	Ford Escort Mk2	E4	03:31:42
2	2	53	Jason Lepley	Simon Sparey	Ford Escort Mk2 RS1800	E4	03:45:33
3	1	57	Robert Archer	Peter Field	Ford Escort Mk2	E3	03 46:46
4	2	55	Dave Hemingway	Jim Plevey	Ford Escort Mk2	E3	03:50:03
5	3	65	Matt Barker	Dave Lucas	Peugeot 205 GTi	E3	03:54:38
6	4	64	Austin Mckinlay	Dominic Brown	Peugeot 205 1.9 GTi	E3	04:01:06
7	5	69	Trevor Silcock	Pam Silcock	Vauxhall Astra GTE	E3	04:04:10
8	1	67	Tony Jardine	Maurice Hamilton	Skoda Fabia	E2	04:07:53
9	2	71	Steve Graham	Tony Graham	MG ZR	E2	04:22:10
Ret		52	'Mad' Mick Jones	Andy Morgan	Ford Escort Mk2	E3	Rolled SS22
Ret		54	Peter Beer	John Pickavance	Ford Escort Mk2	E3	Rolled SS7
Ret		58	Mark Fowler	Christopher Dewsnap	Opel Manta	E4	Did not start Leg 2
Ret		59	Colin Barber	Martin Barber	Vauxhall Astra Sport	E3	Went off SS9
Ret		60	John Taylor	Mark Ingram	Ford Escort Mexico	E2	Lost wheel SS11
Ret		62	William Onions	Tim Hobbs	Ford Escort Mk2	E4	Mechanical after SS24
Ret		63	Andy Madge	Pat Cooper	Toyota Corolla GT Coupe	E2	Stopped SS8
Ret		66	Ralph Abel	Samuel Armida	Ford Escort RS	E4	Did not start
Ret		70	Julius Deane	Charles Chatburn	Peugeot 205 GTi	E2	Rolled SS24

Roger Albert Rally 2005: the second edition

Blomqvist tackles the opening stage

2005 RESULTS: CLUBMANS RALLY

Overall	Class	No	Driver	Co-driver	Car	Class	Total
1	1	109	Keith Robathan	Martin Forrest	Ford Escort Mk2	F3	00:58:03
2	1	120	Geoff Wilson	Simon Martin	Ford Escort Mk2	F4	00:58:58
3	2	102	Tim Jones	Don James	Ford Escort Mk2	F3	00:59:24
4	3	107	Marcus Noble	Richard Todd	Ford Escort Mk2	F3	01:00:46
5	2	112	Jim McDowall	Eric McClurg	Talbot Lotus Avenger	F4	01:00:55
6	3	104	Paul Drinkall	Ken Bowman	Porsche 911RS	F4	01:01:05
7	4	105	Nigel Talton	Guy Scarbrough	Triumph Dolomite Sprint	F3	01:02:22
8	5	110	Paul Dolby	Cyril Jones	Ford Escort	F3	01:03:41
9	6	115	Darren Grimston	Larry Carter	Ford Escort Mk2	F3	01:04:13
10	1	111	Brian Middlemas	Steve Grigor	Hillman Avenger	F2	01:05:01
11	7	106	Robert Adamson	Jim Howie	Talbot Sunbeam	F3	01:05:08
12	2	121	Richard Perry	Clive Townend	Talbot Sunbeam Ti	F2	01:06:08
13	4	113	Richard Naylor	Kevin Watts	Ford Escort RS1800	F4	01:08:09
14	5	103	Andrew Borthwick	Fiona Gourlay	Ford Escort Mk1	F4	01:08:34
15	8	114	Peter Roughan	Peter Norris	Ford Escort Mk2	F3	01:11:56
16	1	118	Clive Baty	Stephen Prince	Toyota Yaris	F1	01:14:41
Ret		101	David Hughes	Bruce Harper	Vauxhall Chevette HSR	F4	Stopped SS17
Ret		108	Neil Rudd	Brian Hodgson	Ford Escort Twin Cam	F3	Mechanical SS16
Ret		116	Richard Simpson	Craig Wallace	Saab 96 V4	F3	Went off in SS16
Ret		117	Martin Shaw	Ian Prout	Ford Escort RS1400	F1	Clutch SS17
Ret		119	Tony Racey	Gawaine Clark	Peugeot 205 GTi	F2	Stopped SS15
Ret		122	Derek Lord	Adam Lord	Talbot Sunbeam	F4	Stopped SS13
Ret		123	Clive Alcock	Mal Capstick	Saab 96 V4	F3	Hit bridge SS19

Jason Lepley was second in the Open Rally

2005 RESULTS: TROPHY RALLY TWO

Overall	Class	No	Driver	Co-driver	Car	Class	Total
1	1	54	Peter Beer	John Pickavance	Ford Escort Mk2	T2	03:04:11
2	2	63	Andy Madge	Pat Cooper	Toyota Corolla GT Coupe	T2	03:10:54

2005 RESULTS: TROPHY RALLY THREE

Overall	Class	No	Driver	Co-driver	Car	Class	Total
1	1	36	Bryan Gill	Nigel Hutchinson	Opel Kadett GTE	T2	01:36:47
2	2	60	John Taylor	Mark Ingram	Ford Escort Mexico	T2	01:48:17

Perez prepares to launch

Shand at Bramham Park

Roger Albert Rally 2005: the second edition

Roger Albert Clark Rally 2006:
the third edition

Overall winners: Jimmy McRae and Andy Richardson

Easson's heartbreak
The 2006 rally

Saturday 18 to Monday 20 November
189 stage miles
27 special stages
Start: Yorkshire Event Centre, Harrogate
Overnight 1 & 2: Rosehill Car Park, Carlisle
Finish: Yorkshire Event Centre, Harrogate
70 starters
36 finishers

Open Rally winners: Steve Bannister and Kevin Rae

Roger Albert Rally 2006: the third edition

Perez on a charge in the Stratos

Jimmy McRae, former multiple British Rally Champion, returned to the forest special stages of Ae, Castle O'er and Twiglees en route to winning the third Roger Albert Clark Rally.

Lanark-based McRae and co-driver Andy Richardson were driving a Ford Escort Mk2 on the rally that recreates the Lombard RAC Rallies of the 1970s. A field of 70 cars lined up for the event.

The three-day rally started and finished in Harrogate and took in special stages in Yorkshire, the Scottish borders and Kielder forest. The stages in Ae forest on Sunday morning proved some of the toughest of the rally as overnight snow and patches of ice caught out several leading crews.

It was Jeremy Easson and Alun Cook who were central to the dramatic conclusion to the 2006 event, when they seemed set for victory as they headed into the final stage of the rally.

Jeremy Easson

Mark Fowler

44   The Roger Albert Clark Rally: The first 20 years

McRae in the snow in Ae

Paul Kirtley

Gareth Lloyd

Easson had driven a fine rally and took a small lead into the final stage at Croft circuit as McRae and Richardson continued to chase. Easson looked to have done enough as he had a 15s lead with only a mile to go until disaster struck.

Unbelievably, the rally was decided in that final mile when Easson's throttle linkage came apart and he lost two minutes repairing the problem and certain victory as McRae swept ahead to score a dramatic win.

Up into second place, by just eight seconds went Welsh crew Gareth Lloyd anc Ryland James, while Carlie Taylor and Steve Bielby claimed fourth. Further down, Steve Perez and Peter Martin got the crowd-pleasing Lancia Stratos to the finish in 18th place.

In the Open Rally, Steve Bannister and Kevin Rae were dominant once more in their Ford Escort Mk2, finishing a whopping 15 minutes clear of John Reid and Frank Richer.

Steve Magson's Opel Ascona 400

Jimmy McRae

Charlie Taylor

Insight: Jimmy McRae (Ford Escort Mk2)
What are your thoughts on the event?
"It was a cracking event, I thoroughly enjoyed it and the car ran faultlessly. It was just a typical RAC Rally. But thankfully we didn't have the fog this year and I didn't miss that! But we had snow and we had rain and gales."

How did the first two days go?
"The first day in Yorkshire was alright, but we had a problem in the first two Dalby stages when the engine went onto three cylinders. We probably dropped 40 or 50 seconds, but it was OK after service. On Sunday, Ae was a bit rough in places, but OK. Then in Kershope we had a front puncture and drove about five miles out of the stage. That probably lost us nearly a minute."

What about Monday, the final day?
"We were trying a bit harder in Kielder on Monday and had no problems at all. We caught Jeremy Easson a wee bit asleep on the first stage; it must have been the Scots porridge oats for breakfast! We had a good run and decided to chase Jeremy all the way to Croft. We just kept up our pace to see what happened. But we couldn't have gone much

Andrew Bowen in the Open Rally

faster without bringing the car back in a skip. We pushed really hard and got a fair bit of time back from Jeremy. I do feel a bit gutted for Jeremy. But that's rallying and it's happened to us all and no doubt he'll come back and fight next year again."

What about the event format?
"We were talking in the car on the way back to the finish on Monday afternoon. We started on Monday morning at half past seven in Carlisle and by half past one, we had done about 60 stage miles. That puts some of the World Championship rallies to shame!"

And next year?
"I'd love to come back and do it again next year. The bug has bitten again. I never managed to win it when it was the original RAC Rally, but this is a pretty good substitute."

Andrew Haddon

Jim Valentine

Dave Watkins in his ex-works Escort Mk1

Rikki Proffitt

David Luton

Personal view: Paul Lawrence

When was the last time your journey home from a rally was badly delayed by a consignment of lobsters?

No, me neither. That little story made my four days on the Roger Albert Clark Rally seem almost tame. Nevertheless, 9 to 12 November 2007 is already in the diary for edition four of the event that has rapidly become a highlight of the rally season.

The lobster affair was a peculiar drama that befell one dedicated spectator on his way home from the Roger Albert. But Jarrod Tuck is no ordinary spectator. Although originally from Somerset, he fell in love with the Isle of Harris in the Outer Hebrides and so decided to live there.

The only problem with living in such a remote place is the distance he has to travel to watch a rally. While I hopped in the car for a three-hour trip to Harrogate on Friday morning, he was already on the road, having taken an early ferry from Harris to Skye. Then came a simple 11-hour drive into the heart of the Yorkshire forests and a night in 'hotel Clio' ready for Saturday's stages.

The Bewshaugh roller-coaster

Richard Lepley

Dave Hemingway

Roger Albert Rally 2006: the third edition

Jeremy Easson in Punondershaw

Ray Bellm

David Stokes

Then it was up to Ae forest, another night in the car and another day of rallying on Sunday before a final night tucked up in the depths of Kielder and the last leg of stages on Monday morning. While the rain and wind lashed against my hotel room window in Carlisle on Sunday night I did spare a thought for this most dedicated of fans.

But there he was on Monday morning at the end of that incredible roller-coaster straight in Bewshaugh in typically good spirits, genuinely disappointed that this was his last stage and that he would soon be heading home. But only when the course-closing car finally confirmed that there were no more cars to come would he accept that his rally was over.

While I headed for the finish at Harrogate and a very tight copy deadline for the Motorsport News report, Jarrod was on the road north. He would get to Skye too late for the last ferry of Monday so, after another night away from home, the final two-hour ferry leg of his journey was finished on Tuesday morning.

But it was on this last leg that the lobsters intervened and delayed the ferry, so he was even later getting back than expected. But that was a minor inconvenience compared to his return from the 2005 Roger Albert, when winter storms left the ferries in the harbour and

Ronnie Roughead and Ian Canavan

Grant Shand

Stuart Rolt

Mick Jones

Jarrod stranded on Skye for two days.

Even before the RAC finished, Jarrod was eagerly planning a trip to the Robin Hood Stages in March to catch the opening round of the British Historic Championship. Then in November, he'll repeat his trek to the Roger Albert. He's got hooked on historics and that's easy to understand, for the appeal of the event is building year on year, both with competitors and fans.

I'll be back as well. But I'll never again bemoan traffic jams on the M62 around Manchester on the way home. Compared to ferries delayed by lobsters, three lanes of stationery traffic is no big deal!

Roger Albert Rally 2006: the third edition

2006 ROGER ALBERT CLARK RALLY: ENTRY LIST

No	Driver	Co-driver	Car	Class
1	Steve Perez	Peter Martin	Lancia Stratos	D5
2	Ray Bellm	Mark Solloway	Ford Escort RS1600	C5
3	David Stokes	Ian Oakey	Ford Escort RS1600	C5
4	Jeremy Easson	Alun Cook	Ford Escort RS2000	C5
5	Gareth Lloyd	Ryland James	Ford Escort Mk2	D5
6	Richard Lepley	Ian Bevan	Porsche 911RS	C4
7	Jimmy McRae	Andy Richardson	Ford Escort RS1800	D5
8	Andrew Haddon	Mark Crisp	Porsche 911RS	C4
9	Craig Salter	Preston Ayres	Ford Escort RS1600	C5
10	Steve Smith	Paul Morris	Ford Escort Mk2 RS1800	D5
11	Graham Samuel	Tony Phillips	Ford Escort RS2000	C5
12	Ken Forster	John Stanger-Leathes	Ford Escort Mexico	C2
14	Rikki Proffitt	Phill Harrison	Ford Escort Mk1 RS1600	C5
15	Martin Freestone	Joanne Oakey	Ford Escort Mk2	D5
16	Sean Lockyer	Chris Wood	Porsche 911RS	C4
17	Ian Rix	Daniel Stone	Ford Escort Mk1	C5
18	Geoffrey Crabtree	Liz Jordan	Ford Escort RS1800	D5
19	Philip Squires	Michael Squires	Ford Escort Mk2 RS1800	D5
20	Stephen Magson	Geoff Atkinson	Opel Ascona 400	D5
21	Peter Egerton	Russ Langthorne	Ford Escort RS2000	C3
22	Charlie Taylor	Steve Bielby	Ford Escort RS1800	D5
23	Paul Kirtley	Jim Kitson	Ford Escort Mk1 RS2000	C3
24	Tim Mason	'Captain' Thompson	Porche 911	C4
25	Derek Belbin	Michael Davison	Ford Escort Mexico	C2
26	Russell Morgan	Martin Kenyon	Ford Escort Mexico	C2
27	Grant Shand	Chris Dewsnap	Ford Escort RS	D5
28	Reg Britton	Gerry Buckley	Ford Escort RS1800	D5
29	Robin Shuttleworth	Mark Midgley	Ford Escort Mexico	C2
30	Martin Kenny	Dave Stocking	Ford Escort Mk1	C3
31	Terry Nowlan	Nick Barrington	Ford Escort RS1600	C5
32	Neil Parsons	Chris Parsons	Ford Escort RS1600	C5
33	David Watkins	Neil Duncan	Ford Escort Twin Cam	C3
34	Dave Cobb	Tony Cobb	Toyota Corolla	D2
35	Keith Cornell	Brynmor Pierce	Ford Escort Mk2 RS1800	D5
36	Steve Graham	Tony Graham	Lancia Fulvia	C1
37	John Dixon	Gavin Heseltine	Ford Escort Twin Cam	C2
38	David Pedley	Steven Warrington	Triumph TR7 V8	D4
39	Scott Armstrong	Andrew Johnstone	Datsun Stanza PA10	D3
40	Tony Ginns	Mark Ellis	Ford Escort Mexico	C2
41	Keith Bird	Ken Bills	Austin Mini Cooper S	C1
42	Adrian Young	Dylan Jenkins	Ford Escort Mk2 RS	D3
43	Peter Hall	Jim Hurman	Ford Escort RS2000	C3
45	Bob Bean	Malcolm Smithson	Ford Lotus Cortina Mk1	B4
46	Stuart Rolt	Richard Pomfret	Porsche 911	B5
47	Ronnie Roughead	Ian Canavan	Ford Cortina Mk1 GT	B3
48	David Luton	Norman Quayle	Ford Lotus Cortina Mk1	B4
49	Jim Valentine	Julian Stocks	Saab 96 Two Stroke	B1
50	Nick Pinkett	Caroline Lodge	Saab 96 Sport	B3
51	Steve Bannister	Kevin Rae	Ford Escort Mk2	E3
52	Glen Workman	Kevin Hare	Talbot Sunbeam	E3

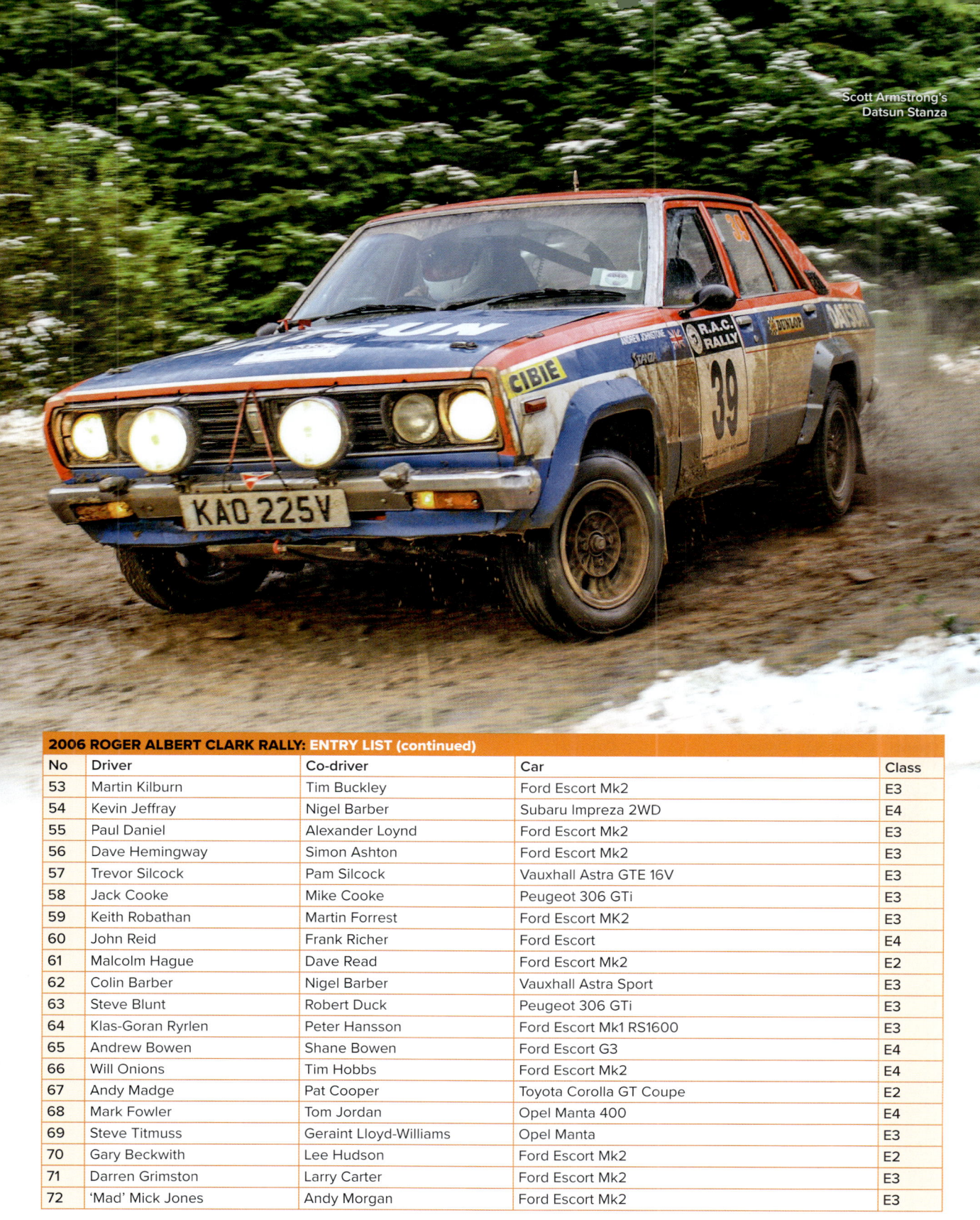

Scott Armstrong's Datsun Stanza

2006 ROGER ALBERT CLARK RALLY: ENTRY LIST (continued)

No	Driver	Co-driver	Car	Class
53	Martin Kilburn	Tim Buckley	Ford Escort Mk2	E3
54	Kevin Jeffray	Nigel Barber	Subaru Impreza 2WD	E4
55	Paul Daniel	Alexander Loynd	Ford Escort Mk2	E3
56	Dave Hemingway	Simon Ashton	Ford Escort Mk2	E3
57	Trevor Silcock	Pam Silcock	Vauxhall Astra GTE 16V	E3
58	Jack Cooke	Mike Cooke	Peugeot 306 GTi	E3
59	Keith Robathan	Martin Forrest	Ford Escort MK2	E3
60	John Reid	Frank Richer	Ford Escort	E4
61	Malcolm Hague	Dave Read	Ford Escort Mk2	E2
62	Colin Barber	Nigel Barber	Vauxhall Astra Sport	E3
63	Steve Blunt	Robert Duck	Peugeot 306 GTi	E3
64	Klas-Goran Ryrlen	Peter Hansson	Ford Escort Mk1 RS1600	E3
65	Andrew Bowen	Shane Bowen	Ford Escort G3	E4
66	Will Onions	Tim Hobbs	Ford Escort Mk2	E4
67	Andy Madge	Pat Cooper	Toyota Corolla GT Coupe	E2
68	Mark Fowler	Tom Jordan	Opel Manta 400	E4
69	Steve Titmuss	Geraint Lloyd-Williams	Opel Manta	E3
70	Gary Beckwith	Lee Hudson	Ford Escort Mk2	E2
71	Darren Grimston	Larry Carter	Ford Escort Mk2	E3
72	'Mad' Mick Jones	Andy Morgan	Ford Escort Mk2	E3

Roger Albert Rally 2006: the third edition

2006 STAGES AND STAGE WINNERS

Day	Stage	Name	Distance	Stage winner(s)	Time
Saturday	SS1	Harrogate Showground 1	0.50	McRae/Richardson	0.50
Saturday	SS2	Harrogate Showground 2	0.50	Smith/Morris	0.49
Saturday	SS3	Dalby 1	9.00	Lloyd/James	10.31
Saturday	SS4	Staindale 1	4.65	Haddon/Crisp	5.19
Saturday	SS5	Langdale 1	8.41	McRae/Richardson	8.30
Saturday	SS6	Dalby 2	9.00	Lloyd/James	10.17
Saturday	SS7	Staindale 2	4.65	Easson/Cook and Lloyd/James	5.18
Saturday	SS8	Langdale 2	8.41	Easson/Cook	8.27
Saturday	SS9	Croft 1	3.91	Haddon/Crisp	4.30
Saturday	SS10	Croft 2	3.91	Bellm/Solloway and Shand/Dewsnap	4.20
Saturday	SS11	Greystoke	6.32	Smith/Morris	7.34
Sunday	SS12	Ae 1	16.01	Britton/Buckley	18.36
Sunday	SS13	Heathhall 1	0.68	Easson/Cook	1.07
Sunday	SS14	Ae 2	16.01	Easson/Cook	17.17
Sunday	SS15	Heathhall 2	0.68	Lloyd/James	1.06
Sunday	SS16	Castle O'er	5.02	McRae/Richardson	5.27
Sunday	SS17	Twiglees	8.89	McRae/Richardson	9.26
Sunday	SS18	Kershope 1	8.86	Easson/Cook and Lloyd/James	10.01
Sunday	SS19	Ash Park	4.66	Lloyd/James	5.21
Monday	SS20	Kershope 2	8.86	McRae/Richardson	9.39
Monday	SS21	Bewshaugh 1	8.00	McRae/Richardson	8.50
Monday	SS22	Roughside	8.76	McRae/Richardson	9.10
Monday	SS23	Pundershaw 1	8.78	Easson/Cook	8.06
Monday	SS24	Bewshaugh 2	8.00	McRae/Richardson	8.53
Monday	SS25	Pundershaw 2	18.85	McRae/Richardson	18.27
Monday	SS26	Croft 3	3.91	McRae/Richardson	4.24
Monday	SS27	Croft 4	3.91	McRae/Richardson	4.16

2006 RESULTS

Overall	Class	No	Driver	Co-driver	Car	Class	Total
1	1	7	Jimmy McRae	Andy Richardson	Ford Escort RS1800	D5	03:29:06
2	2	5	Gareth Lloyd	Ryland James	Ford Escort Mk2	D5	03:30:56
3	1	4	Jeremy Easson	Alun Cook	Ford Escort RS2000	C5	03:31:04
4	3	22	Charlie Taylor	Steve Bielby	Ford Escort RS1800	D5	03:33:24
5	4	19	Philip Squires	Michael Squires	Ford Escort Mk2 RS1800	D5	03:34:26
6	5	15	Martin Freestone	Joanne Oakey	Ford Escort Mk2	D5	03:43:39
7	6	18	Geoffrey Crabtree	Liz Jordan	Ford Escort RS1800	D5	03:44:26
8	1	12	Ken Forster	John Stanger-Leathes	Ford Escort Mexico	C2	03:47:19
9	2	14	Rikki Proffitt	Phill Harrison	Ford Escort Mk1 RS1600	C5	03:49:03
10	2	29	Robin Shuttleworth	Mark Midgley	Ford Escort Mexico	C2	03:50:18
11	1	23	Paul Kirtley	Jim Kitson	Ford Escort Mk1 RS2000	C3	03:50:59
12	3	17	Ian Rix	Daniel Stone	Ford Escort Mk1	C5	03:51:39
13	4	11	Graham Samuel	Tony Phillips	Ford Escort RS2000	C5	03:52:16
14	1	46	Stuart Rolt	Richard Pomfret	Porsche 911	B5	03:52:23
15	1	24	Tim Mason	'Captain' Thompson	Porsche 911	C4	03:53:53
16	3	25	Derek Belbin	Michael Davison	Ford Escort Mexico	C2	03:55:26
17	2	30	Martin Kenny	Dave Stocking	Ford Escort Mk1	C3	03:55:34
18	7	1	Steve Perez	Peter Martin	Lancia Stratos	D5	03:56:48
19	8	28	Reg Britton	Gerry Buckley	Ford Escort RS1800	D5	03:56:51
20	3	21	Peter Egerton	Russ Langthorne	Ford Escort RS2000	C3	03:57:49
21	4	33	David Watkins	Neil Duncan	Ford Escort Twin Cam	C3	04:01:26
22	1	47	Ronnie Roughead	Ian Canavan	Ford Cortina Mk1 GT	B3	04:05:35
23	1	42	Adrian Young	Dylan Jenkins	Ford Escort MK2 RS	D3	04:08:05

Steven Smith in the VK-backed Escort

2006 RESULTS (continued)

Overall	Class	No	Driver	Co-driver	Car	Class	Total
24	1	38	David Pedley	Steven Warrington	Triumph TR7 V8	D4	04:21:41
25	2	39	Scott Armstrong	Andrew Johnstone	Datsun Stanza PA10	D3	04:31:22
Ret		2	Ray Bellm	Mark Solloway	Ford Escort RS1600	C5	Mechanical after SS16
Ret		3	David Stokes	Ian Oakey	Ford Escort RS1600	C5	Fire end SS8
Ret		6	Richard Lepley	Ian Bevan	Porsche 911RS	C4	Mechanical SS24
Ret		8	Andrew Haddon	Mark Crisp	Porsche 911RS	C4	Mechanical after leg 1
Ret		9	Craig Salter	Preston Ayres	Ford Escort RS1600	C5	Oil leak SS6
Ret		10	Steve Smith	Paul Morris	Ford Escort Mk2 RS1800	D5	Slid off SS12
Ret		16	Sean Lockyer	Chris Wood	Porsche 911RS	C4	Mechanical SS16
Ret		20	Stephen Magson	Geoff Atkinson	Opel Ascona 400	D5	Retired
Ret		26	Russell Morgan	Martin Kenyon	Ford Escort Mexico	C2	Stopped SS23
Ret		27	Grant Shand	Chris Dewsnap	Ford Escort RS	D5	Stopped SS25
Ret		31	Terry Nowlan	Nick Barrington	Ford Escort RS1600	C5	OTL
Ret		32	Neil Parsons	Chris Parsons	Ford Escort RS1600	C5	Mechanical SS7
Ret		34	Dave Cobb	Tony Cobb	Toyota Corolla	D2	Overheating at PC27
Ret		35	Keith Cornell	Brynmor Pierce	Ford Escort Mk2 RS1800	D5	Rolled SS12
Ret		36	Steve Graham	Tony Graham	Lancia Fulvia	C1	Mechanical after SS23
Ret		37	John Dixon	Gavin Heseltine	Ford Escort Twin Cam	C2	Blown engine SS21
Ret		40	Tony Ginns	Mark Ellis	Ford Escort Mexico	C2	Mechanical SS6
Ret		41	Keith Bird	Ken Bills	Austin Mini Cooper S	C1	Accident SS6
Ret		43	Peter Hall	Jim Hurman	Ford Escort RS2000	C3	Blown engine SS3
Ret		45	Bob Bean	Malcolm Smithson	Ford Lotus Cortina Mk1	B4	Retired
Ret		48	David Luton	Norman Quayle	Ford Lotus Cortina Mk1	B4	OTL
Ret		49	Jim Valentine	Julian Stocks	Saab 96 Two Stroke	B1	Rolled SS3
Ret		50	Nick Pinkett	Caroline Lodge	Saab 96 Sport	B3	Engine after SS2

Roger Albert Rally 2006: the third edition

Sean Lockyear

Paul Daniel

2006 RESULTS: OPEN RALLY

Overall	Class	No	Driver	Co-driver	Car	Class	Total
1	1	51	Steve Bannister	Kevin Rae	Ford Escort Mk2	E3	03:25:25
2	1	60	John Reid	Frank Richer	Ford Escort	E4	03:40:31
3	2	56	Dave Hemingway	Simon Ashton	Ford Escort Mk2	E3	03:50:54
4	1	67	Andy Madge	Pat Cooper	Toyota Corolla GT Coupe	E2	03:51:33
5	3	62	Colin Barber	Nigel Barber	Vauxhall Astra Sport	E3	03:52:32
6	4	57	Trevor Silcock	Pam Silcock	Vauxhall Astra GTE 16V	E3	04:01:15
7	2	68	Mark Fowler	Tom Jordan	Opel Manta 400	E4	04:04:00
8	5	63	Steve Blunt	Robert Duck	Peugeot 306 GTi	E3	04:11:38
9	2	70	Gary Beckwith	Lee Hudson	Ford Escort Mk2	E2	04:12:45
10	6	69	Steve Titmuss	Geraint Lloyd-Williams	Opel Manta	E3	04:16:20
11	7	58	Jack Cooke	Mike Cooke	Peugeot 306 GTi	E3	04:23:23
Ret		52	Glen Workman	Kevin Hare	Talbot Sunbeam	E3	Suspension SS25
Ret		53	Martin Kilburn	Tim Buckley	Ford Escort Mk2	E3	OTL at MC1
Ret		54	Kevin Jeffray	Joe Parsons	Subaru Impreza 2WD	E4	Driveshaft
Ret		55	Paul Daniel	Alexander Loynd	Ford Escort Mk2	E3	Engine after SS24
Ret		59	Keith Robathan	Martin Forrest	Ford Escort Mk2	E3	Oil pressure SS14
Ret		61	Malcolm Hague	Dave Read	Ford Escort Mk2	E2	Mechanical SS4
Ret		64	Klas-Goran Ryrlen	Peter Hansson	Ford Escort Mk1 RS1600	E3	Mechanical SS6
Ret		65	Andrew Bowen	Shane Bowen	Ford Escort G3	E4	Rolled SS12
Ret		66	Will Onions	Tim Hobbs	Ford Escort Mk2	E4	In ditch SS12
Ret		71	Darren Grimston	Larry Carter	Ford Escort Mk2	E3	Blown engine SS12
Ret		72	'Mad' Mick Jones	Andy Morgan	Ford Escort Mk2	E3	Engine SS23

2006 RESULTS: KALL KWIK RALLY

Overall	Class	No	Driver	Co-driver	Car	Class	Total
1	1	104	Darren Moon	John McNichol	Ford Escort Mk2	F3	00:48:47
2	1	120	Chris Peart	Gordon Blyth	Proton Satria Kit Car	F2	00:50:35
3	1	103	Richard Welford	Richard Ross	Ford Escort Mk2	F4	00:51:14
4	2	102	Ian Jemison	Owen Wallbank	Porsche Boxster	F4	00:51:30
5	2	106	Philip Welch	Mark Ellerker	VW Golf GTi Kit Car	F3	00:52:34
6	3	113	Tony Jardine	Jonathan McEnvoy	Ford Fiesta ST	F3	00:52:34
7	2	105	Robert Close	Mike Reynolds	Toyota Corolla	F2	00:52:37
8	4	109	Robert Carr	Gavin Fielding	Ford Escort Mk2	F3	00:52:41
9	5	107	Steven Finch	Stanley Graham	Ford Escort Mk2	F3	00:52:49
10	6	118	Stuart Adamson	John Adamson	Ford Escort RS	F3	00:55:12
11	7	110	Richard Poulter	Peter Scott	Ford Escort	F3	00:55:31
12	8	116	Cliff Richards	Reg Day	Ford Escort Mk2	F3	00:56:12
13	9	111	Robert Cholmondeley	Dave Evans	Ford Escort Mk2	F3	00:56:58
14	10	124	James Everard	David Everard	Ford Fiesta ST	F3	00:57:03
15	11	114	Kev Wilson	Alastair Roe	Talbot Sunbeam	F3	01:02:33
16	3	122	Jon Finch	Paul Vasey	BMW 318i	F4	01:03:56
Ret		101	Neil Weaver	Nick Thornton	Ginetta GT4	F2	Stopped
Ret		117	Ton Hewick	Sam Collins	Ford Escort	F3	Gearbox SS3
Ret		119	Robert Archer	Timothy Rodgers	Ford Fiesta	F3	Overheating SS3
Ret		121	Mark Mitchell	Mike Scrimgour	Vauxhall Astra	F3	Mechanical

Glen Workman and Kevin Hare

2006 RESULTS: CLUBMANS RALLY

Overall	Class	No	Driver	Co-driver	Car	Class	Total
1	1	138	Marcus Noble	Simon Martin	Ford Escort Mk2	G3	00:53:41
2	1	126	Geoff Wilson	Alex Benn	Ford Escort Mk2	G4	00:54:17
3	2	132	Sandy Arbuthnott	Christopher Hunter	Ford Escort Mk2	G3	00:55:59
4	2	125	Paul Drinkall	Ken Bowman	Porsche 911	G4	00:56:54
5	3	127	Neil Rudd	Brian Hodgson	Ford Escort Twin Cam	G3	00:58:56
6	1	130	Richard Perry	Clive Townend	Talbot Sunbeam	G2	00:58:59
7	4	131	Magic McCombie	Fiona Gourlay	Saab 900	G3	00:59:17
8	3	139	Mark Holmes	Anthony Ross	Ford Escort Mk2	G4	01:01:12
9	5	133	Peter Roughan	Peter John Norris	Ford Escort	G3	01:02:09
10	6	136	Simon Rigby	Nigel Gilbride	Ford Escort Mk2	G3	01:03:14
Ret		129	James McDowell	Eric McClurg	Talbot Lotus Avenger	G4	Retired after SS17
Ret		134	Roger Ray	Paul Ray	Ford Escort Mexico Mk1	G2	Retired after SS15
Ret		135	David Killin	Clive Black	Opel Kadette Coupe	G2	Retired after SS16
Ret		137	Fraser Gellan	Melvin Gellan	Ford Escort Mk2	G2	Stopped SS14

2006 RESULTS: TROPHY RALLY 1

Overall	Class	No	Driver	Co-driver	Car	Class	Total
1	1	48	David Luton	Norman Quayle	Ford Lotus Cortina Mk1	B4	02:46:57
2	1	41	Keith Bird	Ken Bills	Austin Mini Cooper S	C1	02:56:13
Ret		3	David Stokes	Ian Oakey	Ford Escort RS1600	C5	Stopped after SS23
Ret		20	Stephen Magson	Geoff Atkinson	Opel Ascona 400	D5	Mechanical SS14
Ret		32	Neil Parsons	Chris Parsons	Ford Escort RS1600	C5	Stopped SS22
Ret		45	Bob Bean	Malcolm Smithson	Ford Lotus Cortina Mk1	B4	Mechanical SS14
Ret		53	Martin Kilburn	Tim Buckley	Ford Escort Mk2	E3	Retired
Ret		61	Malcolm Hague	Dave Read	Ford Escort Mk2	E2	Engine after SS20

2006 RESULTS: TROPHY RALLY 2

Overall	Class	No	Driver	Co-driver	Car	Class	Total
1	1	10	Steve Smith	Paul Morris	Ford Escort Mk2 RS1800	D5	01:20:54
2	1	65	Andrew Bowen	Shane Bowen	Ford Escort G3	E4	01:24:06
3	1	31	Terry Nowlan	Nick Barrington	Ford Escort RS1600	C5	01:24:45
4	2	54	Kevin Jeffray	Joe Parsons	Subaru Impreza 2WD	E4	01:29:06
Ret		16	Sean Lockyer	Chris Wood	Porsche 911RS	C4	Stopped after SS23
Ret		45	Bob Bean	Malcolm Smithson	Ford Lotus Cortina Mk1	B4	Head gasket SS23
Ret		53	Martin Kilburn	Tim Buckley	Ford Escort Mk2 RS1800	E3	Stopped SS20

Roger Albert Rally 2006: the third edition

Roger Albert Clark Rally 2007:
the fourth edition

Overall winners: Steve Bannister and Kevin Rae

Bannister's overall victory

The 2007 rally

Saturday 17 to Monday 19 November
178 stage miles
28 special stages
Start: Temple Newsam Park, Leeds
Overnight 1 & 2: Carlisle Airport
Finish: City Centre, Carlisle
48 starters
36 finishers

Open Rally winners: Richard Hill and Patrick Cooper

Roger Albert Rally 2007: the fourth edition

Simon Tysoe and Rob Dyson

"We're both getting on but we can still drive a bit," said Steve Bannister after winning an epic Roger Albert Clark Rally. For three days, Bannister and Kevin Rae fought a mighty battle with Jimmy McRae and Andy Richardson and only when McRae punctured on the final day was the result anything like settled.

The two legends of British rallying thrilled the fans throughout another brilliant Roger Albert Clark and went into the final day in Kielder split by just four seconds. But it was a puncture in Roughside and then another on the second run through the same stage that cost McRae his chance of taking back-to-back victories.

"It wasn't to be, but we've really enjoyed it," said Richardson after a typically attacking performance from McRae. Jeremy Easson/Alun Cook claimed another fine result in third, while Martin McCormack/Phil Clarke were an amazing fourth. The young charger would have won the event but for sliding into a ditch in Greystoke and taking a stage maximum.

Also in superb form were Richard Hill and Phil Cooper as they won the Open Rally, while veteran Bob Bean and Malcolm Smithson were the best of the Category 1 field.

Day one: Saturday
"This is 'Banner' country," said McRae before the start of the opening forest stage in Dalby on Saturday morning. He knew that the opening six

Marty McCormack

Andy Madge

Richard Hill's four-door Escort

Derek Belbin

stages through the Yorkshire forests was a time for damage limitation; keeping Bannister's lead as small as possible as the Yorkshireman rallied in his own back yard.

Despite a catalogue of electrical dramas, Bannister was as quick as expected and emerged from the second Langdale stage with a 40s lead over McCormack and McRae.

However, the pair of stages in a wet and slippery Greystoke that wrapped up the first leg would turn things around. Bannister admitted to a poor run by his own standards and his lead over McRae dropped to 24s. But the big loser was McCormack, who slithered into a ditch on the first Greystoke stage and picked up a stage maximum, a massive six-minute penalty. Once out of the ditch, he flew the second Greystoke to be considerably quicker than everyone.

The Hillman Avenger of Steve French

Steve Bannister

Steve Perez

Keeping the leaders firmly in sight as crews arrived in Carlisle for the overnight halt was Easson (Escort Mk1), only 14s down on McRae. With McCormack dumped down to 14th place, battling for fourth at the end of day one was the Porsche 911 of Andrew Haddon/Mark Crisp and the Escorts of Paul Griffiths/John Madoc-Jones and David Stokes/Guy Weaver. "In all the years I've been rallying, I'd never driven a Mk2 Escort," said Griffiths as he started a hugely impressive run.

The most notable day one retirement was the Lancia Stratos of Steve Perez/Stewart Merry with engine failure in Yorkshire, while engine dramas also side-lined the Escort Mk1 of Tim Jones/Don James.

In the Open Rally, Hill and Cooper swept into an immediate lead in Hill's freshly prepared four-door Escort Mk2, complete with a 16-valve Vauxhall power unit. "Not bad for a standard engine," said Hill as he

Jimmy McRae in Dalby on Saturday morning

finished the leg with a two and a half minute lead over Irish crew Brian Lawlor/Peter Kavanagh (Escort Mk2).

Day two: Sunday
With mist hanging over Ae forest, Sunday started as Saturday had finished, with Bannister and McRae trading times and setting a ferocious pace. While Yorkshire had been Bannister country, now the action was in Scotland and McRae was on his home stages.

Initially, Bannister extended his lead again but, bit-by-bit as the day progressed, McRae nibbled away at the leader and went one second ahead after the first Kershope stage. Bannister had caught the Porsche 911 of Geoff Stewart in Twiglees and, though Stewart pulled over as quickly as he could, Bannister lost more than 15s.

Second time through Twiglees, Bannister reclaimed 11s and by the time they concluded the toughest day of the rally, Bannister led by just four seconds. Both drivers had driven superbly and their contest thrilled the thousands of fans who lined the Scottish border stages.

However, some of the fastest stage times of all came from McCormack who was nothing short of sensational as he took fastest time of seven of the day's 12 stages. Incredibly, by the end of Sunday he was back up to fifth overall behind Easson and Griffiths. "Unbelievable," said the Irish charger. "This is the best rally I've ever done," he said.

Darren Yarney

Roger Albert Rally 2007: the fourth edition

"We can't go with those guys," said Easson after a largely trouble-free day, while Griffiths kept up his impressive pace to end the day fourth from McCormack, Stokes and Haddon.

Hill's domination of the Open Rally continued unabated and took his lead over Lawlor out to over seven minutes. "Touch wood, it's going quite well," he said. Things were much closer in the battle for third as Alan Gardiner/Robin Nicholson battled ahead of fellow Escort crew Dave Hemingway/Simon Ashton. Just 16s split them as they prepared for the third and final day and six stages in Kielder.

Day three: Monday

Six tough stages in a wet and slippery Kielder would decide the destiny of a battle that had gripped the fans. In the spirit and atmosphere that are hallmarks

Another podium finish for Jeremy Easson

of this tough rally, it had been a marvellous contest, but only one crew could win. It was nip and tuck through the opening two stages, but not far into Roughside the crucial moment came.

"We punctured and had to drive five miles out," explained Richardson. Suddenly, Bannister led by 55s, but McRae pulled 13 back on the first stage of the final leg, Hopehouse. Bannister responded to match McRae in Broomyllin and surely had enough in hand for the final six miles. "More or less at the same location we got another puncture," said Richardson.

"That's one of my best ever results," said Bannister. Having won the Open Rally three times running, he had now taken the big prize in the Escort Mk2 borrowed from Steve Perez.

Easson bagged third, but the McCormack sensation continued as he got to within 18s of the podium after a truly epic performance. Into fifth after a final day battle with Stokes went Haddon's Porsche while a cracking drive from Griffiths ended in ninth having lost a lot of time after sliding off in Roughside.

The classes

With only three cars starting the event in Category 1, all of them were destined to be class winners if they could survive three tough days. In a tremendous performance, Bob Bean and Malcolm Smithson headed the category in their Lotus Cortina and took B4 spoils in the process. The experience gained from contesting 27 RAC Rallies guided Bean around any major problems.

McRae in Hopehouse

Roger Albert Rally 2007: the fourth edition

Roger Kilty and Lynette Banks

Despite struggling with the loss of second gear from the opening day, Geoff Stewart and Bill Stevenson got their Porsche 911 to the finish to win class B5, while B1 fell to the two-stroke Saab 96 of Jim Valentine/Julian Stocks. Having stopped on Sunday afternoon with electrical failure, they got going again to claim a deserved finish.

Steve and Tony Graham were the only starters in C1 in their Lancia Fulvia, but sadly rolled on the final leg of stages. In category 2, the 1600cc C2 class was set to be another battle between the Escort Mexicos of Ken Forster/John Stanger-Leathes and John Worthing/Bill Robertson. However, Worthing was in big trouble in Yorkshire when a significant engine fire came close to ending their rally. They continued under the super rally regulations, but then had a suspension failure on Sunday. Meanwhile, Forster/Stanger-Leathes pressed on in style to take the class and an overall place just outside the top 10.

With Richard and Pat Egger out very early with engine problems, Andrew Siddall and 'Captain' Thompson worked hard to win C3 in their Escort Mk1. They claimed a gate post in Temple Newsam and later did more damage in Kershope but battled on to win the class.

On his first visit to the Scottish border stages, Haddon proved to be the only non-Escort in the overall top 10 when, partnered by Mark Crisp, he took his Porsche 911 to victory in Class C4. Easson/Cook won C5.

Craig Salter

Geoff Stewart's Porsche 911 in Dalby

Seamus O'Connell

Phil Squires

While the battle for overall victory also resolved class D5, the D3 class for 2-litre category 3 cars was blitzed by Will Onions/Tim Hobbs in their Escort RS2000. "It goes well downhill," said Onions after stepping back from his more powerful Escort Mk2 for the event.

In the 1600cc class in the Open Rally, the Rover K Series-engined Mk2 Escort of Phil Jobson and Caroline Lodge led by a big margin, only to go off in the penultimate stage. Instead, the hard-driven Toyota Corolla of Andy Madge/Pat Cooper took the class. Hill/Cooper won the 2-litre class and the over 2-litre class was won by the Irish crew of Lawlor and Kavanagh.

Roger Albert Rally 2007: the fourth edition

2007 ROGER ALBERT CLARK RALLY: ENTRY LIST

No	Driver	Co-driver	Car	Class
1	Jimmy McRae	Andy Richardson	Ford Escort RS1800	D5
2	Jeremy Easson	Alun Cook	Ford Escort RS2000	C5
3	David Stokes	Guy Weaver	Ford Escort RS1600	C5
4	Steve Perez	Stewart Merry	Lancia Stratos	C5
5	Steve Bannister	Kevin Rae	Ford Escort Mk2	D5
6	Andrew Haddon	Mark Crisp	Porsche 911	C4
7	Martin McCormack	Phil Clarke	Ford Escort RS1800	D5
8	John Worthing	Bill Robertson	Ford Escort Mk1 Mexico	C2
9	Paul Griffiths	Jon Madoc-Jones	Ford Escort Mk2	D5
10	Craig Salter	Preston Ayres	Ford Escort RS1600	C5
11	Tim Mason	Graham Wild	Porsche 911	C4
12	Martin Healer	Peter Thomas	Ford Escort Mk2	D5
14	Phil Squires	Mick Squires	Ford Escort RS1800	D5
15	Charlie Taylor	Steve Bielby	Ford Escort RS1800	D5
16	Geoff Crabtree	Ian Oakey	Ford Escort RS1800	D5
17	Graham Samuel	Tony Phillips	Ford Escort RS2000	C5
20	Ken Forster	John Stanger-Leathes	Ford Escort Mexico	C2
21	Derek Belbin	Michael Davison	Ford Escort Mexico Mk1	C2
22	Ian Rix	Daniel Stone	Ford Escort RS1600	C5
23	Will Onions	Tim Hobbs	Ford Escort RS2000	D3
24	Tim Jones	Don James	Ford Escort Mk1 RS1600	C3
25	Keith Cornell	Graham Wride	Ford Escort Mk1	C5
26	Adrian Young	Den Golding	Ford Escort RS2000	D3
27	Neil Rudd	Brian Hodgson	Ford Escort Twin Cam	C3
28	Simon Tysoe	Rob Dyson	Ford Escort RS1800	D5
30	Roger Kilty	Lynette Banks	Vauxhall Chevette HSR	D5
31	Steve Graham	Tony Graham	Lancia Fulvia	C1
32	Andrew Siddal	Colin Thompson	Ford Escort Mk1	C3
33	Richard Egger	Pat Egger	Ford Escort Mk1	C3
34	Roger Platt	Peter Gilbert	Renault Alpine A110	C2
35	Darren Yarney	Stephen Richards	Hillman Avenger	C2
41	Geoff Stewart	Bill Stevenson	Porsche 911	B5
42	Bob Bean	Malcolm Smithson	Ford Lotus Cortina Mk1	B4
43	Jim Valentine	Julian Stocks	Saab 96 Two Stroke	B1
51	Richard Hill	Patrick Cooper	Ford Escort Mk2	E3
52	Dave Hemingway	Simon Ashton	Ford Escort Mk2	E3
53	Brian Lawlor	Peter Kavanagh	Ford Escort Mk2	E4
54	Andy Madge	Pat Cooper	Toyota Corolla GT	E2
55	Kevin Jeffray	Joe Parsons	Subaru Impreza RWD	E4
56	Steve Blunt	Robert Duck	Ford Fiesta ST	E3
57	Stephen French	Colin Booth	Hillman Avenger	E3
58	Phil Jobson	Caroline Lodge	Ford Escort Mk2	E2
60	Malc Hague	Dave Read	Ford Escort MK2	E2
61	Mark Fowler	Chris Dewsnap	Opel Manta 400	E4
62	Alan Gardiner	Robin Nicholson	Ford Escort Mk2	E3
63	John Taylor	Lindsey Watson	Ford Escort RS1600	E2
64	Garry Preston	Mike Sones	Ford Escort RS2000	E3

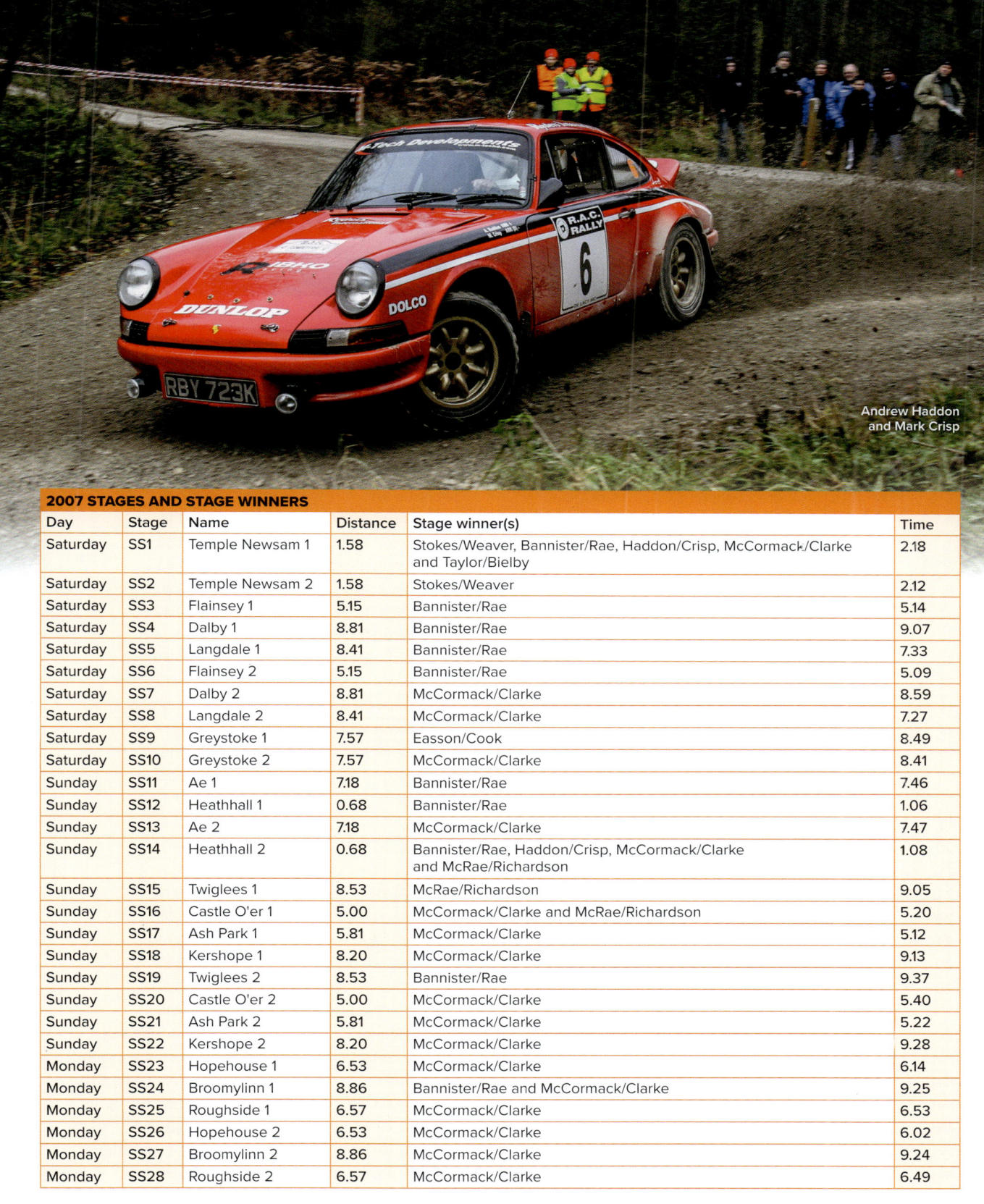

Andrew Haddon and Mark Crisp

2007 STAGES AND STAGE WINNERS

Day	Stage	Name	Distance	Stage winner(s)	Time
Saturday	SS1	Temple Newsam 1	1.58	Stokes/Weaver, Bannister/Rae, Haddon/Crisp, McCormack/Clarke and Taylor/Bielby	2.18
Saturday	SS2	Temple Newsam 2	1.58	Stokes/Weaver	2.12
Saturday	SS3	Flainsey 1	5.15	Bannister/Rae	5.14
Saturday	SS4	Dalby 1	8.81	Bannister/Rae	9.07
Saturday	SS5	Langdale 1	8.41	Bannister/Rae	7.33
Saturday	SS6	Flainsey 2	5.15	Bannister/Rae	5.09
Saturday	SS7	Dalby 2	8.81	McCormack/Clarke	8.59
Saturday	SS8	Langdale 2	8.41	McCormack/Clarke	7.27
Saturday	SS9	Greystoke 1	7.57	Easson/Cook	8.49
Saturday	SS10	Greystoke 2	7.57	McCormack/Clarke	8.41
Sunday	SS11	Ae 1	7.18	Bannister/Rae	7.46
Sunday	SS12	Heathhall 1	0.68	Bannister/Rae	1.06
Sunday	SS13	Ae 2	7.18	McCormack/Clarke	7.47
Sunday	SS14	Heathhall 2	0.68	Bannister/Rae, Haddon/Crisp, McCormack/Clarke and McRae/Richardson	1.08
Sunday	SS15	Twiglees 1	8.53	McRae/Richardson	9.05
Sunday	SS16	Castle O'er 1	5.00	McCormack/Clarke and McRae/Richardson	5.20
Sunday	SS17	Ash Park 1	5.81	McCormack/Clarke	5.12
Sunday	SS18	Kershope 1	8.20	McCormack/Clarke	9.13
Sunday	SS19	Twiglees 2	8.53	Bannister/Rae	9.37
Sunday	SS20	Castle O'er 2	5.00	McCormack/Clarke	5.40
Sunday	SS21	Ash Park 2	5.81	McCormack/Clarke	5.22
Sunday	SS22	Kershope 2	8.20	McCormack/Clarke	9.28
Monday	SS23	Hopehouse 1	6.53	McCormack/Clarke	6.14
Monday	SS24	Broomylinn 1	8.86	Bannister/Rae and McCormack/Clarke	9.25
Monday	SS25	Roughside 1	6.57	McCormack/Clarke	6.53
Monday	SS26	Hopehouse 2	6.53	McCormack/Clarke	6.02
Monday	SS27	Broomylinn 2	8.86	McCormack/Clarke	9.24
Monday	SS28	Roughside 2	6.57	McCormack/Clarke	6.49

Roger Albert Rally 2007: the fourth edition

Neil Rudd

Kevin Jeffray

2007 RESULTS

Overall	Class	No	Driver	Co-driver	Car	Class	Total
1	1	5	Steve Bannister	Kevin Rae	Ford Escort Mk2	D5	03:10:13
2	2	1	Jimmy McRae	Andy Richardson	Ford Escort RS1800	D5	03:12:15
3	1	2	Jeremy Easson	Alun Cook	Ford Escort RS2000	C5	03:14:29
4	3	7	Martin McCormack	Phil Clarke	Ford Escort RS1800	D5	03:14:47
5	1	6	Andrew Haddon	Mark Crisp	Porsche 911	C4	03:17:36
6	2	3	David Stokes	Guy Weaver	Ford Escort RS1600	C5	03:18:14
7	4	15	Charlie Taylor	Steve Bielby	Ford Escort RS1800	D5	03:21:30
8	5	14	Phil Squires	Mick Squires	Ford Escort RS1800	D5	03:21:43
9	6	9	Paul Griffiths	Jon Madoc-Jones	Ford Escort Mk2	D5	03:22:10
10	7	16	Geoff Crabtree	Ian Oakey	Ford Escort RS1800	D5	03:24:43
11	1	23	Will Onions	Tim Hobbs	Ford Escort RS2000	D3	03:28:34
12	1	20	Ken Forster	John Stanger-Leathes	Ford Escort Mexico	C2	03:30:30
13	3	17	Graham Samuel	Tony Phillips	Ford Escort RS2000	C5	03:35:10
14	1	42	Bob Bean	Malcolm Smithson	Ford Lotus Cortina Mk1	B4	03:35:56
15	4	22	Ian Rix	Daniel Stone	Ford Escort RS1600	C5	03:38:19
16	5	25	Keith Cornell	Graham Wride	Ford Escort Mk1	C5	03:41:15
17	1	32	Andrew Siddal	Colin Thompson	Ford Escort Mk1	C3	03:42:32
18	2	21	Derek Belbin	Michael Davison	Ford Escort Mexico Mk1	C2	03:49:30
19	3	35	Darren Yarney	Stephen Richards	Hillman Avenger	C2	03:52:12
20	2	27	Neil Rudd	Brian Hodgson	Ford Escort Twin Cam	C3	03:56:09
21	2	26	Adrian Young	Den Golding	Ford Escort RS2000	D3	03:57:32
22	1	41	Geoff Stewart	Bill Stevenson	Porsche 911	B5	03:58:04
23	8	28	Simon Tysoe	Rob Dyson	Ford Escort RS1800	D5	04:15:03
24	1	31	Steve Graham	Tony Graham	Lancia Fulvia	C1	04:43:09
25	1	43	Jim Valentine	Julian Stocks	Saab 96 Two Stroke	B1	04:43:53
26	4	8	John Worthing	Bill Robertson	Ford Escort Mk1 Mexico	C2	04:50:20
27	9	30	Roger Kilty	Lynette Banks	Vauxhall Chevette HSR	D5	05:27:16
Ret		4	Steve Perez	Stewart Merry	Lancia Stratos	C5	Engine after SS4
Ret		10	Craig Salter	Preston Ayres	Ford Escort RS1600	C5	Went off SS24 finish
Ret		11	Tim Mason	Graham Wild	Porsche 911	C4	Alternator after SS9
Ret		12	Martin Healer	Peter Thomas	Ford Escort Mk2	D5	Gearbox after SS26
Ret		24	Tim Jones	Don James	Ford Escort Mk1 RS1600	C3	Retired
Ret		33	Richard Egger	Pat Egger	Ford Escort Mk1	C3	Ignition problems
Ret		34	Roger Platt	Peter Gilbert	Renault Alpine A110	C2	Drive shaft SS1

Dave Hemingway and Simon Ashton

2007 RESULTS: OPEN RALLY

Overall	Class	No	Driver	Co-driver	Car	Class	Total
1	1	51	Richard Hill	Patrick Cooper	Ford Escort Mk2	E3	03:13:10
2	1	53	Brian Lawlor	Peter Kavanagh	Ford Escort Mk2	E4	03:23:48
3	2	62	Alan Gardiner	Robin Nicholson	Ford Escort MK2	E3	03:30:52
4	3	52	Dave Hemingway	Simon Ashton	Ford Escort Mk2	E3	03:31:23
5	4	56	Steve Blunt	Robert Duck	Ford Fiesta ST	E3	03:50:12
6	1	54	Andy Madge	Pat Cooper	Toyota Corolla GT	E2	04 00:07
7	5	64	Garry Preston	Mike Sones	Ford Escort RS2000	E3	04:03:17
8	2	63	John Taylor	Lindsey Watson	Ford Escort RS1600	E2	04:04:14
9	3	60	Malc Hague	Dave Read	Ford Escort Mk2	E2	05:33:54
Ret		55	Kevin Jeffray	Joe Parsons	Subaru Impreza RWD	E4	Went off SS27
Ret		57	Stephen French	Colin Booth	Hillman Avenger	E3	Mechanical SS23
Ret		58	Phil Jobson	Caroline Lodge	Ford Escort Mk2	E2	Went off SS27
Ret		61	Mark Fowler	Chris Dewsnap	Opel Manta 400	E4	Gearbox after SS7

Roger Albert Rally 2007: the fourth edition

Malc Hague and Dave Read

2007 RESULTS: KALL KWIK RALLY

Overall	Class	No	Driver	Co-driver	Car	Class	Total
1	1	116	Darren Moon	John McNichol	Ford Escort Mk2	F3	00:48:18
2	1	119	Seamus O'Connell	Sean Magee	Ford Escort Mk2	F4	00:48:59
3	1	105	Robert Close	Mike Reynolds	Toyota Corolla	F2	00:49:44
4	2	104	Ian Jemison	Mick Quinn	Porsche Boxster	F4	00:50:05
5	2	106	Philip Welch	Plug Pulleyn	Volkswagen Golf Kit Car	F3	00:51:07
6	3	103	Steve Magson	Geoff Atkinson	Opel Ascona 400	F4	00:51:11
7	3	114	Gareth Hooper	Michael Calvert	Opel Manta	F3	00:51:50
8	4	117	Yuk Hodgson	Jemma Hodgson	Ford Escort Mk1	F3	00:52:02
9	4	112	Scott Smith	Andrew Richards	Ford Escort Mk2	F4	00:52:22
10	5	110	Daniel Hart	Rob Hardy	Opel Manta	F4	00:52:56
11	5	108	Robin Shuttleworth	Mark Midgley	Ford Escort Mk1	F3	00:55:37
12	2	109	Raymond Barnes	Geoffrey Watson	Leyland Mini	F2	00:56:26
13	6	102	David Marshall	Chris Hudson	Ford Escort RS1600	F3	00:56:36
14	3	115	Rob Pilcher	Roger Burkill	Ford Lotus Cortina Mk1	F2	00:56:43
15	7	107	Mike Collins	Mike Robinson	Ford Escort Mk2	F3	00:59:13
Ret		101	Richard Welford	Richard Ross	Ford Escort Mk2	F4	Alternator
Ret		111	Anthony Cox	Martyn Clark	Ford Ka	F2	Missed SS5

David Stokes and Guy Weaver

2007 RESULTS: CLUBMANS RALLY

Overall	Class	No	Driver	Co-driver	Car	Class	Total
1	1	138	Marcus Noble	Malcolm Capstick	Ford Escort Mk2	G3	00:52:46
2	1	136	James McDowell	Colin Johnstone	Talbot Lotus Sunbeam	G4	00:54:44
3	1	131	Gordon Boyd	Fred Bell	Ford Lotus Cortina	G2	00:55:53
4	2	133	Brian Middlemas	Steve Grigor	Hillman Avenger	G2	00:59:15
5	2	135	Simon Rigby	Eddie Myatt	Ford Escort	G3	01:00:13
Ret		132	Pete Roughaw	Barry Sharpe	Ford Escort	G3	Clutch SS11
Ret		134	Mike Axford	Dave Thomason	Ford Fiesta RS	G2	Stopped SS15
Ret		137	Gordon McCrombie	Eric Bridgewater	Saab 900	G3	Did not start SS11

Graham Samuel

Steve Perez

Roger Albert Rally 2007: the fourth edition

Roger Albert Clark Rally 2008:
the fifth edition

Overall winners: Malcolm Wilson and John Millington

Wilson wins his hero's rally

The 2008 rally
Friday 14 to Monday 17 November
204 stage miles
31 special stages
Start: Elland Road Car Park, Leeds
Overnight 1: Elland Road Car Park, Leeds
Overnight 2 & 3: Carlisle Airport
Finish: City Centre, Carlisle
50 starters
36 finishers

Open Rally winners: Dave Hemingway and Simon Ashton

Roger Albert Rally 2008: the fifth edition

Wilson on his way to victory: Millington head down as usual over the maps

Malcolm Wilson and John Millington ran out convincing winners of the fifth Roger Albert Clark after three long and challenging days of rallying in the forests of Yorkshire and the Scottish borders.

"It's a very tough event," said Wilson after an impeccable drive. "It's so sweet to win my hero's rally. It is good to come back and do it in a Mk2 Escort; the car he made famous."

The big threat to Wilson came from the similar Ford Escort Mk2 of Martin McCormack and Phil Clarke and the scene was set for a grandstand finish as McCormack tigered back into contention through Sunday after several time consuming moments on Saturday.

But a deceptive corner in Craik on Sunday afternoon pitched McCormack into a ditch and out of the rally after he'd taken 50s back from Wilson during Sunday's early stages. "We were getting there and making some progress," said McCormack after a stirring performance.

With McCormack out, it was the Escort Mk1 of David Stokes and Guy Weaver that took second overall after one of the best drives of the rally. "That's my best result so far on this event; I guess we can't be expected to beat Malcolm," said Stokes. Meanwhile, Irishman Seamus O'Connell and Paul Wakely were elated to bag a hard-earned third after a raft of dramas.

Dave Hemingway and Simon Ashton won the Open Rally after a fine performance, aided by the demise of Mick Jones/Andy Morgan with diff failure in Castle O'er on Sunday evening.

McCormack and Clarke led the challenge

The Roger Albert Clark Rally: The first 20 years

Phil Collins and David Stokes battled at Oliver's Mount

The mighty Lancia Stratos of Steve Perez

Seamus O'Connell in Castle O'er

Day one and two: Friday and Saturday

After two runs through Temple Newsam on Friday evening, Saturday started with another pair of stages at the Leeds country park before the field headed for the meat of the day's action in the Yorkshire forests.

Wilson quickly asserted his authority on the rally to take a 29s lead after the first forest stage in Langdale. By the time the first pair of asphalt stages at Oliver's Mount were done, the Ford WRC team boss was 47s clear as Stokes/Weaver slotted very happily into second place.

After a dramatic start, including sliding off on the second corner of the rally and demolishing a chicane at Oliver's Mount, McCormack/Clarke got more into their stride to take second by the time the rally left Yorkshire, but they were already over a minute down on Wilson.

The day finished late in the evening with two runs through Wilson's own stage in Greystoke and McCormack was conscious that he'd gone off there a year earlier. "He's going to blow us away in here," said McCormack as he waited to start the first Greystoke stage. Sure enough, by the time crews reached the overnight halt at Carlisle, Wilson's lead was 1m42s.

Roger Albert Rally 2008: the fifth edition 77

Richard Lepley and Ian Bevan in Temple Newsam

The crowds were out at Oliver's Mount

Marcus Noble and Brian Hodgson in the Open Rally

"It's been a good day; just getting the hang of the car," said Wilson. "The only problems have been driver inflicted mistakes," he added.

Stokes was sitting quietly in third while Jeremy Easson/Alun Cook were fourth, having not enjoyed Oliver's Mount. Worse was to come, however, when an electrical problem cost them more time in Greystoke.

Wrapping up the top six historic crews were Richard Lepley/Ian Bevan (Porsche 911RS) and O'Connell/Wakely (Escort Mk2), but out in Langdale with a blown engine went the Porsche 911 of Andrew Haddon/Mark Crisp.

In the small Category 1 field, Bob Bean and Malcolm Smithson were setting a roaring pace in their Ford Lotus Cortina and, having gone way clear of their category rivals they set about getting the 45-year old car as far up the overall leader board as possible.

Over in the Open Rally, Jones and Morgan were quickly in control and ended the day nearly three minutes up on the similar Escorts of Hemingway/Ashton and Marcus Noble/Brian Hodgson. However, in trouble was the Mk2 Escort of Phil Burton/Mal Capstick, which snapped a camshaft at Oliver's Mount. Undeterred, they set about planning an engine change in order to rejoin on Sunday.

Tim Mason's Porsche 911 in Falstone

Day three: Sunday

Any thoughts that Wilson would now run away and hide were quickly dispelled in the first stage on Sunday morning, Ae. "I love that stage; we were on the door handles," reported McCormack. By the time they completed the second run through Ae, McCormack had pulled back 28s from Wilson. With more time taken from the leader in Twiglees and Castle O'er, McCormack got the margin back to under a minute with still 50 stage miles to go, running into the dark of Sunday evening.

Unfortunately, it was all to go wrong for McCormack in Craik. "We were making some progress, but I just got caught out on a deceptive right-hander and hit a tree lying in the ditch." With a bent axle, his rally was over and spectators were denied what was shaping up to be a dramatic conclusion to the rally.

"The boys did a great job fixing the car; we had problems with the alternator and a steering arm," said Wilson. "He was driving very, very quickly; probably just a little too quickly," he said of his young adversary. "I'm more than twice his age and I know how I used to drive then!"

With McCormack gone, Wilson suddenly had a much bigger lead and could concentrate on dealing with the car problems that were troubling him. Some quick work at management service kept the Stobart-liveried Escort running well, but they used up most of their penalty-free lateness in the process. However, as they arrived back in Carlisle at the end of the day, Wilson now led by nearly five minutes over Stokes who was, in turn, three minutes up on O'Connell.

George and Jacqueline Bryson

Roger Albert Rally 2008: the fifth edition

Richard and Pat Egger

Phil Collins and Nicky Grist in Ae forest

Phil Welch in the Kall Kwik Rally in his VW Golf kit car

"It's been a good day and I'm glad we're back here tonight," said Stokes on a day when other leading runners fell by the wayside. A failed oil seal ended the rally for Easson and Lepley's excellent run stopped with gearbox failure. Tim Mason/Graham Wild (Porsche 911) dropped a lot of time in Newcastleton, so through to third came O'Connell after a remarkable day that included a roll in Ae, a gearbox out and an axle change at the side of the road. Through it all he drove superbly to take third from the flying Charlie Taylor/Steve Bielby (Escort Mk2) and Phil and Mick Squires in their Escort.

Bean/Smithson moved well inside the overall top 10 with another mighty day, while Jones went out of the Open Rally lead when his diff clattered into oblivion in the second Castle O'er stage. That left Hemingway at the head of the Open Rally from Noble, who spent much of the day changing gearboxes and looking for brakes.

Day four: Monday
With the key positions looking settled, Monday morning's five stages in Kielder still offered around 50 stage miles and a real sting in the tail with the concluding 18-miler in Broomylinn.

"I'm glad I'm not in a battle," admitted Wilson at

McCormack on the attack in Ae forest

service at Kielder water, having found the first leg of three stages very slippery. "Just very gentle," he said of his approach to the last two stages.

Stokes was on a similar mission. "I'm not pushing; just going fast and holding station," said Stokes. After his traumatic day on Sunday, O'Connell was relieved to have less drama in Kielder on his way to a brilliant third, while Taylor wrapped up his excellent performance with fourth, taking a cushion when Squires punctured in Falstone and lost some time driving out on a flat tyre.

Wilson emerged from the final 18-miler in Broomylinn to celebrate an emotional victory in honour of Roger Clark. Like every competitor, he had tackled a tough rally and the sense of achievement in reaching the finish ran all the way through the field. Sadly, out on the final stage with oil pressure woes went the Lancia Stratos of Steve Perez/Kevin Rae when heading for seventh place. They were still classified tenth, however.

The Eggers finished 19th overall

Phil Burton and Mal Capstick in the Open Rally

Roger Albert Rally 2008: the fifth edition

David Stokes and Guy Weaver finished second overall

Perez took the Stratos to 10th overall

The Class D2 winning Sunbeam of Richard Perry

There was also a late scare for Bean/Smithson, who did most of Broomylinn in second gear, but they were still all smiles at the finish. So too, were Hemingway/Ashton after a great win in the Open Rally.

The classes
With Bob Bean winning Category 1 for the historic cars, the only other category finisher was the two-stroke Saab 96 of Jim Valentine/Andy Harris, which had a great run on such a tough event. They duly won Class B1 and the hearts of many fans for a truly spirited performance.

The same can be said for the Lancia Fulvia of Steve and Tony Graham, the only starter in Class C1 for the smaller post-historic cars. They had to miss stages on Saturday while sorting out a major misfire but rejoined to claim class victory.

The Super Rally regulations worked well for a number of cars, including the Class C2 winning Ford Escort Mk1 of George and Jacqueline Bryson. Built up for the event and to mark 40 years of both the Ford Escort and the driver, they hit problems on Saturday when a dry sump pipe came off, but they got going again later for a deserved finish.

A dominant Class C3 victory went to the Escort Mk1 of Andrew Siddall/Captain Thompson, who also

Stuart Newby finished third in the Open Rally

Reg Britton and Gerry Buckley

Guy Woodcock and Iwan Jones

Bob Bean and Malcolm Smithson were a remarkable ninth overall

got well into the top 10 overall. They had a relatively trouble free run and like many, eased their pace back in Kielder to avoid any late dramas.

Despite time spent in ditches in Craik and Falstone, Mason/Wild got their Porsche 911 around to take C4 spoils, having set some very rapid stage times until caught out in the dark of Sunday late afternoon.

Victory in Class D2 was just reward for Richard Perry/Clive Townend and their efforts to get their Talbot Sunbeam around the daunting event. They stopped in Oliver's Mount with electrical problems, but later got going again.

Another praiseworthy performance earned D3 victory for Adrian Young/Den Golding in their Escort Mk2. They kept out of trouble and were knocking on the door of an overall top 10 finish by the end of the rally.

Despite an engine change late on Saturday, Burton/Capstick won Class E4 in the Open Rally in their Escort Mk2. The engine they started the rally with suffered a broken cam at Oliver's Mount, but in the true spirit of the rally, they rejoined on Sunday morning with a spare fitted.

Phil Jobson/Caroline Lodge earned E2 victory after changing a gearbox on Saturday. That made life much easier in the Escort Mk2 and they even moved up to second overall in the Open Rally.

On Sunday, the Clubmans Rally ran through a loop of the Scottish border stages and it was a repeat victory for Paul Drinkall/Roy Brown in their Porsche 911. They finished over two minutes ahead of the Escort of Mark Jackson/Philip Ellison.

Finally, on Monday morning was the Kielder Challenge over three stages and from three starters, only the Proton Satria of Peter Mayland/Paul Hughes emerged from the last stage to take victory.

Roger Albert Rally 2008: the fifth edition

2008 ROGER ALBERT CLARK RALLY: ENTRY LIST

No	Driver	Co-driver	Car	Class
41	Bob Bean	Malcolm Smithson	Ford Lotus Cortina Mk1	B4
42	Pete 'Pop' Gunson	Pete G Gunson	Ford Lotus Cortina MK1	B4
43	Jim Valentine	Andy Harris	Saab 96 Sport	B1
2	Jeremy Easson	Alun Cook	Ford Escort RS2000	C5
3	Malcolm Wilson	John Millington	Ford Escort Mk2 RS1800	D5
4	Steve Perez	Kevin Rae	Lancia Stratos	C5
5	David Stokes	Guy Weaver	Ford Escort RS1600	C5
6	Martin McCormack	Phil Clarke	Ford Escort Mk2	D5
7	Andrew Haddon	Mark Crisp	Porsche 911	C5
9	Phil Collins	Nicky Grist	Opel Ascona 400	D5
10	Richard Lepley	Ian Bevan	Porsche 911	D5
11	Tim Mason	Graham Wild	Porsche 911	C4
12	Charlie Taylor	Steve Bielby	Ford Escort Mk2	D5
14	Phil Squires	Mick Squires	Ford Escort RS1800	D5
15	Paul Griffiths	Sam Collis	Ford Escort RS1800	D5
16	Rikki Proffitt	John H Roberts	Ford Escort RS1600	C5
17	William Onions	Tim Hobbs	Ford Escort RS1800	D5
18	Seamus O'Connell	Paul Wakely	Ford Escort Mk2	D5
19	Stefaan Stouf	Joris Erard	Ford Escort RS1600	C5
20	Bo Axelsson	Eugen Damstedt	Ford Escort Mk1	C5
21	Ian Drummond	Yvonne Coppin	Ford Escort RS2000	C3
22	Andrew Siddall	'Captain' Thompson	Ford Escort RS2000	C3
23	Terry Nowlan	Nick Barrington	Ford Escort Mk1 RS1600	C5
25	Geoff Bell	Wayne Kieswetter	Ford Escort RS1800	D5
26	Reg Britton	Gerry Buckley	Ford Escort Mk2 RS1800	D5
27	Matt Fowle	Andy Ballantyne	Ford Escort Mexico Mk1	C2
28	Guy Woodcock	Iwan Jones	Ford Escort RS2000	D3
29	Richard Egger	Pat Egger	Ford Escort Mk1	C3
30	Adrian Young	Den Golding	Ford Escort Mk2 RS2000	D3
31	Steve Graham	Tony Graham	Lancia Fulvia	C1
32	George Bryson	Jacqueline Bryson	Ford Escort Twin Cam	C2
33	Christopher Langthorne	Michael Hollis	Ford Escort Mk2	D3
34	Rob Smith	Shaun O'Gorman	Ford Escort RS1600 Mk1	C5
35	Richard Perry	Clive Townend	Talbot Sunbeam Ti	D2
36	Tony Ginns	Mark Ellis	Ford Escort Mexico	C2
37	Garry Preston	Mike Sones	Ford Escort RS2000	D3
45	Dave Hemingway	Simon Ashton	Ford Escort Mk2	E3
46	Andy Madge	Pat Cooper	Toyota Corolla	E2
47	Robert Collins	Cliff Simmons	Ford Escort Mk2 RS1800	E3
48	Brian Lawlor	Peter Kavanagh	Ford Escort Mk2	E4
49	Ray Barnes	Geoffrey Watson	Austin Mini	E2
50	Phil Jobson	Caroline Lodge	Ford Escort Mk2	E2
51	Brian Maguire	Anthony Helliwell	Peugeot 205GTi	E3
52	Phil Burton	Mal Capstick	Ford Escort Mk2	E4
53	Martin Shaw	Dave Evans	Ford Escort Mk2	E2
54	Colin Hope	Nick Patrick	Proton Satria	E2
55	Clive Baty	Joe Parsons	Toyota Yaris	E1
56	'Mad' Mick Jones	Andy Morgan	Ford Escort Mk2	E3
57	Marcus Noble	Brian Hodgson	Ford Escort Mk2	E3
58	Stuart Newby	Giles Brooksbank	Ford Escort Mk2	E3

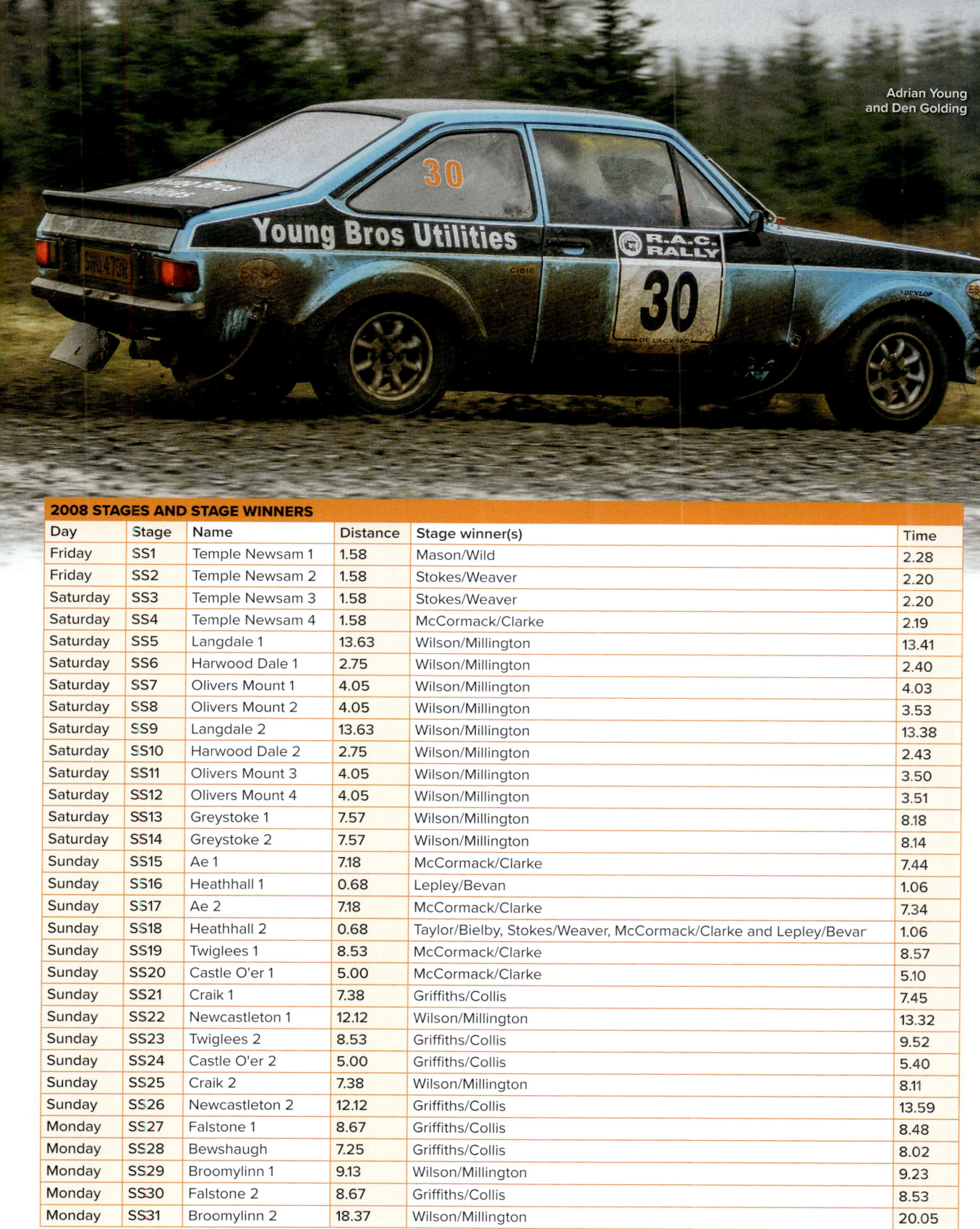

Adrian Young and Den Golding

2008 STAGES AND STAGE WINNERS

Day	Stage	Name	Distance	Stage winner(s)	Time
Friday	SS1	Temple Newsam 1	1.58	Mason/Wild	2.28
Friday	SS2	Temple Newsam 2	1.58	Stokes/Weaver	2.20
Saturday	SS3	Temple Newsam 3	1.58	Stokes/Weaver	2.20
Saturday	SS4	Temple Newsam 4	1.58	McCormack/Clarke	2.19
Saturday	SS5	Langdale 1	13.63	Wilson/Millington	13.41
Saturday	SS6	Harwood Dale 1	2.75	Wilson/Millington	2.40
Saturday	SS7	Olivers Mount 1	4.05	Wilson/Millington	4.03
Saturday	SS8	Olivers Mount 2	4.05	Wilson/Millington	3.53
Saturday	SS9	Langdale 2	13.63	Wilson/Millington	13.38
Saturday	SS10	Harwood Dale 2	2.75	Wilson/Millington	2.43
Saturday	SS11	Olivers Mount 3	4.05	Wilson/Millington	3.50
Saturday	SS12	Olivers Mount 4	4.05	Wilson/Millington	3.51
Saturday	SS13	Greystoke 1	7.57	Wilson/Millington	8.18
Saturday	SS14	Greystoke 2	7.57	Wilson/Millington	8.14
Sunday	SS15	Ae 1	7.18	McCormack/Clarke	7.44
Sunday	SS16	Heathhall 1	0.68	Lepley/Bevan	1.06
Sunday	SS17	Ae 2	7.18	McCormack/Clarke	7.34
Sunday	SS18	Heathhall 2	0.68	Taylor/Bielby, Stokes/Weaver, McCormack/Clarke and Lepley/Bevan	1.06
Sunday	SS19	Twiglees 1	8.53	McCormack/Clarke	8.57
Sunday	SS20	Castle O'er 1	5.00	McCormack/Clarke	5.10
Sunday	SS21	Craik 1	7.38	Griffiths/Collis	7.45
Sunday	SS22	Newcastleton 1	12.12	Wilson/Millington	13.32
Sunday	SS23	Twiglees 2	8.53	Griffiths/Collis	9.52
Sunday	SS24	Castle O'er 2	5.00	Griffiths/Collis	5.40
Sunday	SS25	Craik 2	7.38	Wilson/Millington	8.11
Sunday	SS26	Newcastleton 2	12.12	Griffiths/Collis	13.59
Monday	SS27	Falstone 1	8.67	Griffiths/Collis	8.48
Monday	SS28	Bewshaugh	7.25	Griffiths/Collis	8.02
Monday	SS29	Broomylinn 1	9.13	Wilson/Millington	9.23
Monday	SS30	Falstone 2	8.67	Griffiths/Collis	8.53
Monday	SS31	Broomylinn 2	18.37	Wilson/Millington	20.05

Roger Albert Rally 2008: the fifth edition

Charlie Taylor and Steve Bielby took fourth overall

Ian Jemison was second in the Kall Kwik Rally

2008 RESULTS

Overall	Class	No	Driver	Co-driver	Car	Class	Total
1	1	3	Malcolm Wilson	John Millington	Ford Escort Mk2 RS1800	D5	03:42:01
2	1	5	David Stokes	Guy Weaver	Ford Escort RS1600	C5	03:48:25
3	2	18	Seamus O'Connell	Paul Wakely	Ford Escort Mk2	D5	03:51:57
4	3	12	Charlie Taylor	Steve Bielby	Ford Escort Mk2	D5	03:52:20
5	4	14	Phil Squires	Mick Squires	Ford Escort RS1800	D5	03:53:35
6	5	17	William Onions	Tim Hobbs	Ford Escort RS1800	D5	03:58:12
7	6	26	Reg Britton	Gerry Buckley	Ford Escort Mk2 RS1800	D5	04:03:10
8	1	22	Andrew Siddall	'Captain' Thompson	Ford Escort RS2000	C3	04:03:29
9	1	41	Bob Bean	Malcolm Smithson	Ford Lotus Cortina Mk1	B4	04:03:32
10	2	4	Steve Perez	Kevin Rae	Lancia Stratos	C5	04:10:45
11	3	16	Rikki Proffitt	John H Roberts	Ford Escort RS1600	C5	04:12:17
12	1	30	Adrian Young	Den Golding	Ford Escort Mk2 RS2000	D3	04:15:35
13	4	19	Stefaan Stouf	Joris Erard	Ford Escort RS1600	C5	04:17:41
14	7	15	Paul Griffiths	Sam Collis	Ford Escort RS1800	D5	04:20:35
15	8	25	Geoff Bell	Wayne Kieswetter	Ford Escort RS1800	D5	04:24:16
16	2	21	Ian Drummond	Yvonne Coppin	Ford Escort RS2000	C3	04:43:18
17	5	20	Bo Axelsson	Eugen Damstedt	Ford Escort Mk1	C5	04:57:49
18	1	35	Richard Perry	Clive Townend	Talbot Sunbeam Ti	D2	04:58:20
19	3	29	Richard Egger	Pat Egger	Ford Escort Mk1	C3	05:00:07
20	1	43	Jim Valentine	Andy Harris	Saab 96 Sport	B1	05:12:15
21	1	11	Tim Mason	Graham Wild	Porsche 911	C4	05:30:11
22	1	32	George Bryson	Jacqueline Bryson	Ford Escort Twin Cam	C2	05:55:27
23	1	31	Steve Graham	Tony Graham	Lancia Fulvia	C1	06:04:14
24	2	37	Garry Preston	Mike Sones	Ford Escort RS2000	D3	07:42:47
25	2	36	Tony Ginns	Mark Ellis	Ford Escort Mexico	C2	07:57:05
Ret		42	Pete 'Pop' Gunson	Pete G Gunson	Ford Lotus Cortina Mk1	B4	Headgasket SS20
Ret		2	Jeremy Easson	Alun Cook	Ford Escort RS2000	C5	Engine SS16
Ret		6	Martin McCormack	Phil Clarke	Ford Escort Mk2	D5	Went off SS21
Ret		7	Andrew Haddon	Mark Crisp	Porsche 911	C5	Engine SS5
Ret		9	Phil Collins	Nicky Grist	Opel Ascona 400	D5	Rolled SS19
Ret		10	Richard Lepley	Ian Bevan	Porsche 911	D5	Gearbox after SS22
Ret		23	Terry Nowlan	Nick Barrington	Ford Escort Mk1 RS1600	C5	Cam belt SS5
Ret		27	Matt Fowle	Andy Ballantyne	Ford Escort Mexico Mk1	C2	Holed piston SS7
Ret		28	Guy Woodcock	Iwan Jones	Ford Escort RS2000	D3	Second blown engine SS22
Ret		33	Christopher Langthorne	Michael Hollis	Ford Escort Mk2	D3	Navigator ill
Ret		34	Rob Smith	Shaun O'Gorman	Ford Escort RS1600 Mk1	C5	Rolled SS13

Ray Barnes and Geoff Watson were 10th in the Open Rally in their Mini

Charlie Taylor entertained the crowds at Oliver's Mount

2008 RESULTS: OPEN RALLY

Overall	Class	No	Driver	Co-driver	Car	Class	Total
1	1	45	Dave Hemingway	Simon Ashton	Ford Escort Mk2	E3	04:00:29
2	1	50	Phil Jobson	Caroline Lodge	Ford Escort Mk2	E2	04:09:38
3	2	58	Stuart Newby	Giles Brooksbank	Ford Escort Mk2	E3	04:10:21
4	3	57	Marcus Noble	Brian Hodgson	Ford Escort Mk2	E3	04:11:59
5	2	53	Martin Shaw	Dave Evans	Ford Escort Mk2	E2	04:14:23
6	3	46	Andy Madge	Pat Cooper	Toyota Corolla	E2	04:29:30
7	1	52	Phil Burton	Mal Capstick	Ford Escort Mk2	E4	04:35:36
8	4	54	Colin Hope	Nick Patrick	Proton Satria	E2	04:36:32
9	4	51	Brian Maguire	Anthony Helliwell	Peugeot 205GTi	E3	04:43:46
10	5	49	Ray Barnes	Geoffrey Watson	Austin Mini	E2	05:39:21
Ret		47	Robert Collins	Cliff Simmons	Ford Escort Mk2 RS1800	E3	Electrical problems
Ret		48	Brian Lawlor	Peter Kavanagh	Ford Escort Mk2	E4	Accident SS14
Ret		55	Clive Baty	Joe Parsons	Toyota Yaris	E1	Oil leak SS7
Ret		56	'Mad' Mick Jones	Andy Morgan	Ford Escort Mk2	E3	Differential SS24

Roger Albert Rally 2008: the fifth edition

2008 RESULTS: KALL KWIK RALLY

Overall	Class	No	Driver	Co-driver	Car	Class	Total
1	1	103	Andy Davison	Mike Curry	BMW 325i	F4	00:49:33
2	2	101	Ian Jemison	Graham Wride	Porsche Boxster	F4	00:49:36
3	1	115	Matthew Smith	Darren Smith	Peugeot 205 GTi	F2	00:50:06
4	2	143	Dan Corner	Will Rutherford	Peugeot 205	F2	00:50:09
5	1	111	Mark Bentley	Ed Bentley	Ford Escort Mk2	F3	00:50:23
6	3	113	Russ Thompson	Andy Murphy	Peugeot 205 GTi	F2	00:51:03
7	3	106	Andrew Fox	Jamie-Lee Fox	BMW 325i	F4	00:51:16
8	4	118	Jamie Anderson	Jon Scott	Peugeot 205 GTi	F2	00:51:18
9	2	104	Philip Welch	Plug Pulleyn	Volkswagen Golf Kit Car	F3	00:51:24
10	5	122	Chris Woodward	Richard Pover	Peugeot 205 GTi	F2	00:51:37
11	4	112	Richard Felgate	Mark Mason	BMW 325i	F4	00:52:14
12	5	108	Simon Cole	Ian Jackson	BMW 325i	F4	00:52:59
13	6	117	Gawaine Clark	Bob Duck	Peugeot 206 GTi	F2	00:53:07
14	3	145	Yuk Hodgson	Jemma Hodgson	Ford Escort Mk1	F3	00:53:21
15	7	132	Andrew Smith	Darren MacDonald	Peugeot 205	F2	00:54:10
16	4	109	David Marshall	Mark Midgley	Ford Escort RS1600	F3	00:54:23
17	6	116	Barney Johnson	Neil Merriman	BMW 325 E30	F4	00:54:27
18	7	139	John Clayton	Marc Clayton	BMW 325	F4	00:55:29
19	8	140	Andrew Chalmers	Timothy Young	Peugeot 206XS	F2	00:55:50
20	5	123	Matthew Walker	Bryan Merrison	Vauxhall Astra GTE 16v	F3	00:55:54
21	9	128	Lee Burgess	Joe Pattison	Peugeot 205 GTi	F2	00:57:03
22	10	144	Richard Evans	Jonathan Evans	Peugeot 106 GTi	F2	00:57:33
23	6	134	David May	David McLachlan	BMW 318Ti Compact	F3	00:58:13
24	1	136	Mick Smith	Paul Osmond	Nissan Micra	F1	00:58:31
25	11	133	Paul Metcalfe	Graham Shults	Peugeot 205 GTi	F2	01:00:15
26	12	124	Andrew Frost	Miles Cartwright	Ford Escort Mk1 Mexico	F2	01:00:55
27	13	130	Graham Webb	Andy May	Peugeot 205	F2	01:01:39
28	14	138	Sam Jones	Graham Fraser	Peugeot 205XT	F2	01:02:07
29	15	142	Phil Hall	Aggie Foster	Peugeot 205	F2	01:06:23
Ret		102	Toni Carannante	Ella Flynn	BMW 316i	F4	Accident SS5
Ret		105	Gareth Hooper	Michael Calvert	Opel Manta	F3	Stopped SS9
Ret		110	Richard Poulter	Peter Scott	Ford Escort	F3	OTL
Ret		114	Martin Auskerin	Jon Ross	Peugeot 205 GTi	F2	Accident SS2
Ret		119	Dave Bennett	Alastair McNeil	Vauxhall Corsa	F2	Gearbox fell out after S8
Ret		120	Damien Smith	Frazer Hutchinson	Peugeot 205 GTi	F2	Mechanical SS5
Ret		121	John Sutton	Michael Downborough	Porsche 914/6	F4	Stopped after SS4
Ret		125	Gary Beckwith	Kirsty Beckwith	Ford Escort Mk2	F2	Retired
Ret		126	Clive Wilson	Peter Meyers	Ford Escort Mk2	F3	Missed SS8
Ret		127	Chris Boffin	James Waller	Peugeot 205 GTi	F2	Accident SS2
Ret		129	Chris Hellings	Nick Farmer	Peugeot 205XS	F1	Rolled SS9
Ret		131	Jonathan Williams	Simon Atkinson	Peugeot 205	F2	Mechanical SS6
Ret		137	Rob Richards	Wendy Gibson	Peugeot 106 GTi	F2	Gearbox SS5
Ret		141	Andrew Hebron	Simon Illsley	Peugeot 205 GTi	F2	Accident SS5
Ret		146	Dave Brick	Rob Woodhouse	Ford Escort RS	F4	Stopped after SS4

Brian Lawlor and Peter Kavanagh retired from the Open Rally

2008 RESULTS: CLUBMANS RALLY

Overall	Class	No	Driver	Co-driver	Car	Class	Total
1	1	60	Paul Drinkall	Roy Brown	Porsche 911	G4	00:52:17
2	1	70	Mark Jackson	Philip Ellison	Ford Escort Mk2	G3	00:54:35
3	2	61	Pete Roughan	Barry Sharpe	Ford Escort	G3	00:57:29
4	1	66	Helen Hall	Mike Dunning	Talbot Sunbeam	G2	01:14:46
Ret		62	Alexander Curran	Stephen Marshall	Talbot Sunbeam Ti	G2	OTL
Ret		63	Dominic Foister	Sharron Dean	Ford Escort Mk1 Mexico	G3	Retired
Ret		64	Baz Wheeler	John Pickavance	Ford Escort RS	G3	OTL
Ret		65	Allan McDowell	Gavin Heseltine	Opel Kadett	G3	Stopped SS21

2008: RESULTS: KIELDER CHALLENGE

Overall	Class	No	Driver	Co-driver	Car	Class	Total
1	1	69	Peter Mayland	Paul Hughes	Proton Persona Compact	K2	00:30:39
Ret		68	Bill Lymburn	Stuart Hastings	Ford Escort Mk2	K4	Stopped SS28
Ret		70	Mark Jackson	Philip Ellison	Ford Escort Mk2	K3	OTL after being in ditch

Roger Albert Rally 2008: the fifth edition

Roger Albert Clark Rally 2009:
the sixth edition

Overall winners: Gwyndaf Evans and John Millington

Evans above

The 2009 rally
Friday 13 to Monday 16 November
145 stage miles
27 special stages
Start: Pickering Showground
Overnight 1: Pickering Showground
Overnight 2 & 3: Carlisle Airport
Finish: City Centre, Carlisle
66 starters
44 finishers

Open Rally winners: Marcus Noble and Brian Hodgson

Roger Albert Rally 2009: the sixth edition

Jim Valentine's Saab in Ae Forest

With a stunning performance, Gwyndaf Evans and John Millington won the sixth Roger Albert Clark after four tough days of rallying. Eventually, they won by over three minutes, but this was no cruise to victory for the Welshman as he tackled the event for the first time.

"It's a tough rally, but I'm really, really pleased," said Evans as he stopped at the end of the final stage in a wet Kielder at lunchtime on Monday. "I'll treasure this result," he said before paying tribute to his co-driver Millington, who made it two wins in a row.

Taking the fight to Evans in the early stages were Steve Bannister/Kevin Rae and Martin McCormack/Phil Clarke, but over the second half of the rally it was Jeremy Easson/Alun Cook who moved through to a fine second with a mighty performance. Paul Griffiths/Sam Collis also played a starring role as they fended off Bannister for third while another drive of the rally came from Steven Smith and Patrick Walsh who forged their Pinto-powered Escort into fifth overall after a giant killing campaign.

In the Open Rally, Marcus Noble and Brian Hodgson took control early on and never faltered en route to a well-deserved victory.

Once again, the Roger Albert Clark Rally had been a resounding success, both with the competitors and the thousands of fans who followed the event. Steve Perez summed up the feelings of every crew that finished the rally. "We've made it; what an event," he said after getting his Lancia Stratos through the entire rally at the fifth attempt.

Steve Bannister at Oliver's Mount

Frank Cunningham and Ryland James in Kielder

Stig Blomqvist didn't finish

Andy Madge in Scotland

Day one: Friday

"That was horrendous in there," said Evans as he reflected on the crucial stage of Friday evening. In the dark and in heavy rain, seven miles in Langdale delivered tough conditions and most crews were simply glad to survive and get back to service in Pickering, where the first and third stages were short blasts around the Showground.

While Evans jumped straight into a slender lead over Bannister, things did not go so well in Langdale for others and the seven miles claimed some notable scalps. Rolling out at the first corner went David Stokes/Guy Weaver (Escort Mk1), while later in the stage Phil Collins and Nicky Grist put their Opel Ascona into the undergrowth.

Having been anxious about going back to maps after two decades on notes, Evans was surprised to lead at the end of the evening but the gaps were small as McCormack slotted into third. "You just had to drive to the conditions," said McCormack after a measured start.

Seamus O'Connell/Ian Oakey and Easson/Cook packed out the top five, while Stig Blomqvist and Ana Goni eased themselves into the rally with sixth place. "It's very wet and very slippery," said Blomqvist, echoing the comments of just about every crew.

Steve Perez got the Stratos to the finish

Steve Magson and Geoff Atkinson

Jeremy Easson and Alun Cook

Another maximum went to Richard Lepley/Ian Bevan who parked their Porsche 911 on its side and were finally rescued by spectators, while Tim Mason/Graham Wild (Porsche 911) nearly joined Stokes when they spun at the same corner.

Right in the thick of the massed ranks of more powerful cars came the Pinto-engined Escort Mk1 of Smith/Walsh. They took a superb ninth overall as Smith drove the car for the first time. "It was a learning curve," he said of a giant-killing performance.

In the Open rally, Noble and Hodgson put their Escort Mk2 straight into the lead from the similar cars of Stuart Newby/Andy Morgan and Dave Hemingway/Simon Ashton.

Day two: Saturday
After the warm-up of Friday evening, the meat of the rally started on Saturday with four asphalt stages at Oliver's Mount, three Yorkshire gravel stages and then a real sting with four stages in the dark of Kielder before a late finish in Carlisle.

First to hit trouble was Blomqvist, who collected a pheasant on the run out and had to spend the morning with a badly broken screen before the crew could change it at service. To compound his problems, a low sun made life even more difficult. Evans was immediately on it and added 20s to his lead during two stages at Oliver's Mount. But it all changed on the short forest stage of Harwood Dale. "The gear lever

Darren Moon in the Showground on Friday evening

came off in my hand," said Evans as he lost 40s. A half-spin followed in the Langdale test and by the time they reached service at Pickering, Evans was 38s down on Bannister, who now led from McCormack.

Unfortunately, one of the next two stages at Oliver's Mount was cancelled after Darren Moon/Chris Parsons went off, so next was the long haul north for double runs through Shepherdshield and Chirdonhead. Many felt that these four stages would be a true pointer to the final result and Evans decided to attack. "It felt right to push," said Evans, who was quickest on all four stages. But there was disaster for Bannister when he slid off on the first Chirdonhead, losing three minutes. "It was going fine," said Bannister. "One very loose corner caught me out. That's how it goes sometimes."

The problem for Bannister should have been good news for McCormack, but his rally was already over. At Oliver's Mount, a conrod had ventilated the block and he was going no further. Instead, Easson/Cook slotted into second as Bannister quickly recovered to third. "Absolutely spot-on; couldn't be better," said Easson after a fine day's work.

Griffiths/Collis moved up to hold a cracking fourth place ahead of another crew turning in a great run; Rob Smith and Shaun O'Gorman in their Vauxhall Chevette. In the Open Rally, Noble/Hodgson had a very strong day to take their lead out to more than two minutes.

Aside from McCormack, the day also claimed the Collins Opel Ascona with a broken oil pump pulley and the Escort of O'Connell with a roll in Langdale.

Stouf and Erard at Oliver's Mount

The winners in Kielder on Monday morning

Stuart Rolt

Mick Plowman

Day three: Sunday

Evans didn't put a wheel wrong through Sunday, taking fastest time on all six forest stages as he built his lead to more than three minutes over Easson. It was a case of a measured attack for Evans. "We've been going reasonably," he said of the four stages in Ae, before dominating two runs through Greystoke at the end of day. In 14 miles, he was 44s faster than anyone else to end the day with a crushing performance.

Evans took time out of everyone, notably Bannister who had run him so close over the early stages. A broken brake calliper in Hope House and a puncture in Ae ended the possibility of a Bannister fight back and he ended the leg down in fourth.

Holding a fine second was Easson after another straightforward day in the office. "We're not chasing Gwyndaf," he said. "We're just trying to hold the gap to the rest," said Easson.

The pace of Griffiths just got better and better and he jumped ahead of Bannister to take third. "We've had a good day," he said with a measure of understatement, having led the chase of Evans on several of the days longer forest stages.

Another great performance was coming from

Dave Watkins in 'LAR 801P' in the Kielder gloom

Smith in a Pinto-powered Escort Mk1. When it was foggy in Ae and dark in Greystoke, he was a match for anyone bar Evans and his pace in the Peter Egerton car took him ahead of Rob Smith later in the day for fifth overall.

Smith was still having a fine rally in his Chevette, despite a brief off into a ditch. He ended the day only 8s down on Steven Smith and poised to rechallenge during Monday's five stages in Kielder.

Out with an accident in Greystoke went Blomqvist, so it was Mason, Charlie Taylor/Steve Bielby and Simon Tysoe/Cliff Simmons packing out the top 10, all of them enjoying excellent runs.

Still going like a train to lead the Open Rally by nearly five minutes was Noble. His pace was too strong for the rest, though a good run from the Vauxhall Astra of Nigel Barber/Stuart Popplewell took it up to second as Newby dropped two minutes driving out of Ae with a puncture.

Phil Collins

Charlie Taylor

Roger Albert Clark Rally 2009: the sixth edition

Paul Griffiths and Sam Collis in Ae

McCormack challenged for victory

Steve Bannister and Kevin Rae

Day four: Monday

Five stages in Kielder was the real sting in the tail on Monday morning and fog lay over the forest as crews started the opening Hope House stage. That was soon replaced by heavy rain to complete the Kielder experience. However, there was no change at the head of the leader board as Evans completed his faultless performance to score a resounding win.

Easson was justifiably delighted with second overall and an extension of his remarkable record on this tough event. "Very slippery, very fast," he said of Kielder. "An excellent rally."

Monday's big battle was over third as Griffiths drove his socks off to fend off the attacking Bannister. But it was close and Griffiths thought he'd thrown it away with a big moment on the last stage. "I thought he was going to catch us," said Griffiths. Bannister, having lost time Sunday afternoon with a steady run through Greystoke was still pleased with fourth. "Same as always; a very good event," he said.

Steven Smith headed Rob Smith for fifth, but Rob was elated to get his Chevette home among the front-running Escorts. "There's a big row of Escorts with the Chevette in the middle: spot on," he said.

Noble wrapped up the Open Rally with a good final day, while Barber ran well on his first taste of Kielder to bring the Astra home in second.

Seamus O'Connell bounced back after rolling

Personal view: Paul Lawrence

There's no question that the Roger Albert Clark is the toughest rally of the UK season. It is meant to be tough, for it relives the era when the RAC Rally was a five-day marathon slog.

Rally manager Colin Heppenstall designs the event to be a challenge, with plenty of stage mileage in the dark, some early starts and late finishes. But he also creates an event where the competitors' enjoyment and their opportunity to stay in the rally are uppermost. "It is a tough rally, but we want people to stay in, even if they miss stages and rejoin under super rally rules," said Heppenstall. "We want to get as many finishers as we possibly can."

That outlook runs through the competitors and their service crews, and tales of heroic efforts to keep cars running are part of this remarkable event. Take flying Irishman Seamus O'Connell, who rolled his Escort in Langdale on Saturday morning. Undeterred, his crew found a willing body shop in Penrith and, five hours later, after a session on a jig the car was ready to rejoin on Sunday.

Dave Hemingway, winner of the 2008 Open Rally, hit a cam pulley problem on Saturday. An internet plea sourced replacements in Dumfries and he was back out rallying during Sunday.

The service crew of Mick Plowman/Nigel Boston worked through Saturday night to solve clutch problems in their Escort Mk2, while the team behind the Vauxhall Chevette of Rob Smith/Shaun O'Gorman started taking the gearbox out well after midnight at the end of the long Saturday leg. It's that sort of rally.

Russell Morgan

2009 ROGER ALBERT CLARK RALLY: ENTRY LIST

No	Driver	Co-driver	Car	Class
1	Gwyndaf Evans	John Millington	Ford Escort RS1800	D5
2	Steve Bannister	Kevin Rae	Ford Escort Mk2	D5
3	Stig Blomqvist	Ana Goni	Ford Escort RS1800	D5
4	Martin McCormack	Phil Clarke	Ford Escort Mk2	D5
5	Darren Moon	Chris Parsons	Ford Escort Mk2	D5
6	Seamus O'Connell	Ian Oakey	Ford Escort Mk2	D5
7	David Stokes	Guy Weaver	Ford Escort RS1600	C5
8	Jeremy Easson	Alun Cook	Ford Escort RS1600	C5
9	Steve Perez	Carl Williamson	Lancia Stratos	C5
10	Stefaan Stouf	Joris Erard	Ford Escort RS1600	C5
11	Rob Smith	Shaun O'Gorman	Vauxhall Chevette	D5
12	Richard Lepley	Ian Bevan	Porsche 911	C4
14	Tim Mason	Graham Wild	Porsche 911RS	C4
15	Andrew Haddon	Mark Crisp	Porsche 911	C4
16	Phil Collins	Nicky Grist	Opel Ascona 400	D5
17	Steve Magson	Geoff Atkinson	Opel Ascona 400	D5
18	Phil Squires	Mick Squires	Ford Escort RS1800	D5
19	Alex Sabater	Iain Tullie	Ford Escort Mk2	D5
20	Charlie Taylor	Steve Bielby	Ford Escort Mk2	D5
21	Simon Tysoe	Cliffy Simmons	Ford Escort Mk2	D5
22	Russell Morgan	Martin Kenyon	Ford Escort RS2000	C3
23	Bob Bean	Malcolm Smithson	Ford Escort RS2000	C5
24	Frank Cunningham	Ryland James	Ford Escort RS1800	D5
25	Graham Samuel	Tony Phillips	Ford Escort Mk1	C5
26	Andrew Siddall	Colin Thompson	Ford Escort RS2000	D5
27	David Watkins	Paul Train	Ford Escort Mk2	D5
28	William Onions	Tim Hobbs	Ford Escort RS1800	D5
29	Ken Forster	John Stanger-Leathes	Ford Escort Mk1	C3
30	Peter Smith	Russ Langthorne	Porsche 911RS	C4
31	Steve Graham	Tony Graham	Lancia Fulvia	C1
32	Steve Smith	Patrick Walsh	Ford Escort Mk1	C3
33	Chris Blake	Tony Walker	Ford Escort Mk1	C2
34	Adrian Young	Gwynfor Jones	Ford Escort RS2000	D3
35	Geoff Bell	Paul Wakely	Ford Escort Mk2	D5
36	Paul Griffiths	Sam Collis	Ford Escort RS1800	D5
37	Tony Thompson	Peter Grant	Vauxhall Chevette HSR	D5
38	Mark Bentley	Edward Bentley	Ford Escort Mk2	D5
39	Leigh Armstrong	Chris Armstrong	Ford Escort Mk2	D5
40	Guy Woodcock	Iwan Jones	Ford Escort Mk2	D3
43	Ian Drummond	Yvonne Coppin	Ford Escort RS2000	C3
44	Tony Ginns	Mark Ellis	Ford Escort Mexico	C2
46	John McIlwraith	Andrew Irving	Ford Escort Mk2	D3
47	Mick Plowman	Nigel Boston	Ford Escort RS1800	D5
48	David Pedley	Steve Warrington	Triumph TR7 V8	D4
49	Matt Fowle	Andy Ballantyne	Ford Escort Mk2	C2
50	Terry Nowlan	Ben Giles	Ford Escort RS1600	C5
51	Guy Smith	Howard Pridmore	Ford Escort Mk1 RS2000	C3
52	Stuart Rolt	Richard Pomfret	Porsche 911	B5
53	Peter 'Pop' Gunson	Peter Graham Gunson	Ford Lotus Cortina Mk1	B4
54	Jim Valentine	Andy Harris	Saab 96 Sport Two Stroke	B1
55	Dave Hemingway	Simon Ashton	Ford Escort Mk2	E3
56	Phil Jobson	Caroline Lodge	Ford Escort Mk2	E2
57	Alan Gardiner	Robin Nicolson	Ford Escort Mk2	E4
58	Stuart Newby	Andy Morgan	Ford Escort Mk2	E3
59	Colin Hope	Nick Patrick	Proton Satria	E2
60	Marcus Noble	Brian Hodgson	Ford Escort Mk2	E3
61	Martin Shaw	Ian Prout	Ford Escort RS1400	E2
62	Malcolm Mawdsley	Kevin Bardon	Subaru Impreza	E4
63	Kevin Jeffray	Joe Parsons	Subaru Impreza	E4
64	Andy Madge	Pat Cooper	Toyota Corolla	E2
65	Nigel Barber	Stuart Popplewell	Vauxhall Astra Sport	E3
66	John Taylor	Claire Abrey	Ford Escort Mk2	E3
67	John Dixon	Gavin Heseltine	Ford Escort Mk2	E4
68	Thomas Hewick	Mick Johnson	Ford Escort Mk2	D5

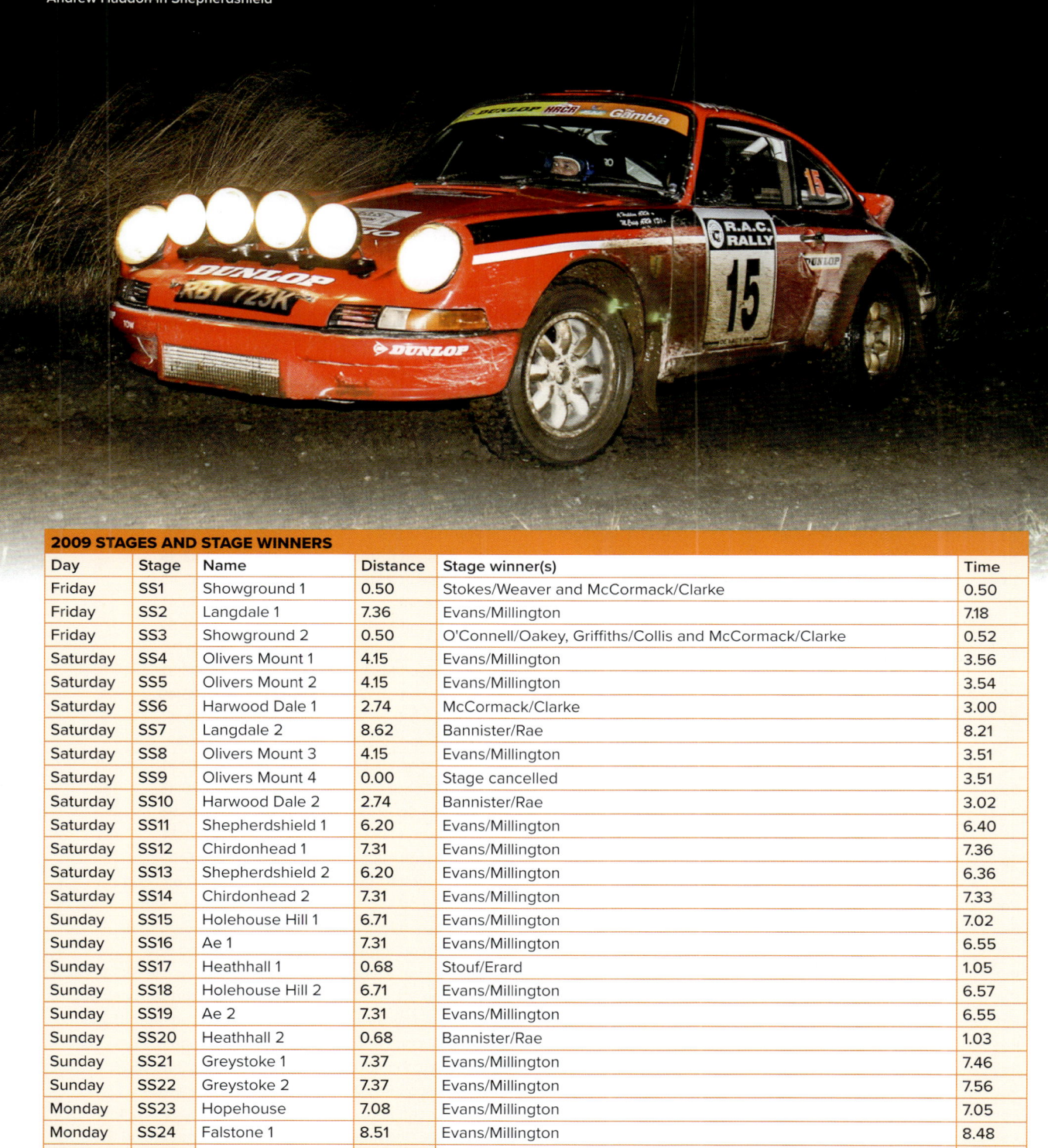

2009 STAGES AND STAGE WINNERS

Day	Stage	Name	Distance	Stage winner(s)	Time
Friday	SS1	Showground 1	0.50	Stokes/Weaver and McCormack/Clarke	0.50
Friday	SS2	Langdale 1	7.36	Evans/Millington	7.18
Friday	SS3	Showground 2	0.50	O'Connell/Oakey, Griffiths/Collis and McCormack/Clarke	0.52
Saturday	SS4	Olivers Mount 1	4.15	Evans/Millington	3.56
Saturday	SS5	Olivers Mount 2	4.15	Evans/Millington	3.54
Saturday	SS6	Harwood Dale 1	2.74	McCormack/Clarke	3.00
Saturday	SS7	Langdale 2	8.62	Bannister/Rae	8.21
Saturday	SS8	Olivers Mount 3	4.15	Evans/Millington	3.51
Saturday	SS9	Olivers Mount 4	0.00	Stage cancelled	3.51
Saturday	SS10	Harwood Dale 2	2.74	Bannister/Rae	3.02
Saturday	SS11	Shepherdshield 1	6.20	Evans/Millington	6.40
Saturday	SS12	Chirdonhead 1	7.31	Evans/Millington	7.36
Saturday	SS13	Shepherdshield 2	6.20	Evans/Millington	6.36
Saturday	SS14	Chirdonhead 2	7.31	Evans/Millington	7.33
Sunday	SS15	Holehouse Hill 1	6.71	Evans/Millington	7.02
Sunday	SS16	Ae 1	7.31	Evans/Millington	6.55
Sunday	SS17	Heathhall 1	0.68	Stouf/Erard	1.05
Sunday	SS18	Holehouse Hill 2	6.71	Evans/Millington	6.57
Sunday	SS19	Ae 2	7.31	Evans/Millington	6.55
Sunday	SS20	Heathhall 2	0.68	Bannister/Rae	1.03
Sunday	SS21	Greystoke 1	7.37	Evans/Millington	7.46
Sunday	SS22	Greystoke 2	7.37	Evans/Millington	7.56
Monday	SS23	Hopehouse	7.08	Evans/Millington	7.05
Monday	SS24	Falstone 1	8.51	Evans/Millington	8.48
Monday	SS25	Archys Rigg	7.20	Easson/Cook, Bannister/Rae and Evans/Millington	6.39
Monday	SS26	Falstone 2	8.51	Bannister/Rae	8.34
Monday	SS27	Samuel Crag	7.62	Bannister/Rae	7.23

2009 RESULTS

Overall	Class	No	Driver	Co-driver	Car	Class	Total
1	1	1	Gwyndaf Evans	John Millington	Ford Escort RS1800	D5	02:29:04
2	1	8	Jeremy Easson	Alun Cook	Ford Escort RS1600	C5	02:33:06
3	2	36	Paul Griffiths	Sam Collis	Ford Escort RS1800	D5	02:33:50
4	3	2	Steve Bannister	Kevin Rae	Ford Escort Mk2	D5	02:33:53
5	4	11	Rob Smith	Shaun O'Gorman	Vauxhall Chevette	D5	02:36:54
6	1	32	Steve Smith	Patrick Walsh	Ford Escort Mk1	C3	02:37:39
7	5	20	Charlie Taylor	Steve Bielby	Ford Escort Mk2	D5	02:40:38
8	6	21	Simon Tysoe	Cliffy Simmons	Ford Escort Mk2	D5	02:41:32
9	7	18	Phil Squires	Mick Squires	Ford Escort RS1800	D5	02:41:41
10	8	24	Frank Cunningham	Ryland James	Ford Escort RS1800	D5	02:42:53
11	9	26	Andrew Siddall	Colin Thompson	Ford Escort RS2000	D5	02:45:58
12	1	34	Adrian Young	Gwynfor Jones	Ford Escort RS2000	D3	02:46:19
13	2	40	Guy Woodcock	Iwan Jones	Ford Escort Mk2	D3	02:46:19
14	2	22	Russell Morgan	Martin Kenyon	Ford Escort RS2000	C3	02:46:23
15	3	29	Ken Forster	John Stanger-Leathes	Ford Escort Mk1	C3	02:47:05
16	10	38	Mark Bentley	Edward Bentley	Ford Escort Mk2	D5	02:47:16
17	11	39	Leigh Armstrong	Chris Armstrong	Ford Escort Mk2	D5	02:47:59
18	12	35	Geoff Bell	Paul Wakely	Ford Escort Mk2	D5	02:48:42
19	13	19	Alex Sabater	Iain Tullie	Ford Escort Mk2	D5	02:50:04
20	2	9	Steve Perez	Carl Williamson	Lancia Stratos	C5	02:50:43
21	1	49	Matt Fowle	Andy Ballantyne	Ford Escort Mk1	C2	02:51:44
22	1	30	Peter Smith	Russ Langthorne	Porsche 911RS	C4	02:52:01
23	14	47	Mick Plowman	Nigel Boston	Ford Escort RS1800	D5	02:53:38
24	15	28	William Onions	Tim Hobbs	Ford Escort RS1800	D5	02:53:45
25	1	52	Stuart Rolt	Richard Pomfret	Porsche 911	B5	02:56:41
26	3	25	Graham Samuel	Tony Phillips	Ford Escort Mk1	C5	02:59:52
27	4	50	Terry Nowlan	Ben Giles	Ford Escort RS1600	C5	03:01:23
28	16	68	Thomas Hewick	Mick Johnson	Ford Escort Mk2	D5	03:05:31
29	4	51	Guy Smith	Howard Pridmore	Ford Escort Mk1 RS2000	C3	03:06:49
30	2	15	Andrew Haddon	Mark Crisp	Porsche 911	C4	03:10:15
31	5	43	Ian Drummond	Yvonne Coppin	Ford Escort RS2000	C3	03:18:19
32	17	27	David Watkins	Paul Train	Ford Escort Mk2	D5	03:20:31
33	1	31	Steve Graham	Tony Graham	Lancia Fulvia	C1	03:28:48
34	1	54	Jim Valentine	Andy Harris	Saab 96 Sport Two Stroke	B1	03:38:55
35	18	6	Seamus O'Connell	Ian Oakey	Ford Escort Mk2	D5	03:51:24
36	3	46	John McIlwraith	Andrew Irving	Ford Escort Mk2	D3	04:07:52
Ret		3	Stig Blomqvist	Ana Goni	Ford Escort RS1800	D5	Went off SS21
Ret		4	Martin McCormack	Phil Clarke	Ford Escort Mk2	D5	Engine SS8
Ret		5	Darren Moon	Chris Parsons	Ford Escort Mk2	D5	Accident SS8
Ret		7	David Stokes	Guy Weaver	Ford Escort RS1600	C5	Rolled SS2
Ret		10	Stefaan Stouf	Joris Erard	Ford Escort RS1600	C5	Hit log pile SS24
Ret		12	Richard Lepley	Ian Bevan	Porsche 911	C4	Retired start day 3
Ret		14	Tim Mason	Graham Wild	Porsche 911RS	C4	Retired after SS24
Ret		16	Phil Collins	Nicky Grist	Opel Ascona 400	D5	Oil pump SS14
Ret		17	Steve Magson	Geoff Atkinson	Opel Ascona 400	D5	Propshaft SS26
Ret		23	Bob Bean	Malcolm Smithson	Ford Escort RS2000	C5	Engine SS7
Ret		33	Chris Blake	Tony Walker	Ford Escort Mk1	C2	Stopped SS24
Ret		37	Tony Thompson	Peter Grant	Vauxhall Chevette HSR	D5	Cylinder head SS21
Ret		44	Tony Ginns	Mark Ellis	Ford Escort Mexico	C2	Stopped SS24
Ret		48	David Pedley	Steve Warrington	Triumph TR7 V8	D4	Engine SS6
Ret		53	Peter 'Pop' Gunson	Peter Gunson	Ford Lotus Cortina Mk1	B4	Did not restart MTC5

Steve and Tony Graham in their Lancia Fulvia

2009 RESULTS: OPEN RALLY

Overall	Class	No	Driver	Co-driver	Car	Class	Total
1	1	60	Marcus Noble	Brian Hodgson	Ford Escort Mk2	E3	02:46:04
2	2	65	Nigel Barber	Stuart Popplewell	Vauxhall Astra Sport	E3	02:50:07
3	3	58	Stuart Newby	Andy Morgan	Ford Escort Mk2	E3	02:51:45
4	1	64	Andy Madge	Pat Cooper	Toyota Corolla	E2	02:52:44
5	2	61	Martin Shaw	Ian Prout	Ford Escort RS1400	E2	03:00:09
6	1	63	Kevin Jeffray	Joe Parsons	Subaru Impreza	E4	03:12:39
7	2	57	Alan Gardiner	Robin Nicolson	Ford Escort Mk2	E4	03:31:42
8	4	55	Dave Hemingway	Simon Ashton	Ford Escort Mk2	E3	03:46:42
Ret		56	Phil Jobson	Caroline Lodge	Ford Escort Mk2	E2	Stopped SS23
Ret		59	Colin Hope	Nick Patrick	Proton Satria	E2	Engine after SS5
Ret		62	Malcolm Mawdsley	Kevin Bardon	Subaru Impreza	E4	Went off SS26
Ret		66	John Taylor	Claire Abrey	Ford Escort Mk2	E3	Stopped SS24
Ret		67	John Dixon	Gavin Heseltine	Ford Escort Mk2	E4	Electrical SS26

Roger Albert Clark Rally 2009: the sixth edition

Hope and Patrick

Smith and Langthorne

2009 RESULTS: KALL KWIK RALLY

Overall	Class	No	Driver	Co-driver	Car	Class	Total
1	1	135	Dave Brick	Rob Woodhouse	Ford Escort RS1600	F4	00:41:47
2	1	106	Nick Cook	Neil Colls	Ford Escort Mk1 Mexico	F3	00:41:55
3	1	107	Carl Tuer	Rob Tuer	MG ZR S1600	F2	00:43:17
4	2	104	Mathew Smith	Darren Smith	Peugeot 205 GTi	F2	00:43:19
5	2	102	Ian Jemison	Graham Wride	Porsche Boxster	F4	00:43:24
6	3	131	Ciro Carannante	Mike Scrimgour	BMW 328i	F4	00:43:28
7	4	109	Toni Carannante	Nicola Fearnley	BMW 316i	F4	00:44:18
8	2	127	Gareth Hooper	Michael Calvert	Opel Manta	F3	00:44:40
9	5	112	John Clayton	Plug Pulleyn	BMW 325i	F4	00:46:38
10	6	111	Simon Cole	Steve Waggett	BMW 325i	F4	00:46:51
11	3	123	Marcus Feeley	James Jolly	Peugeot 205 GTi	F2	00:46:53
12	3	130	David Marshall	John McNichol	Ford Escort RS1600	F3	00:47:26
13	4	121	Martin Eades	Chris Welch	Peugeot 205 GTi	F2	00:48:29
14	5	125	Andrew Thorpe	Gavin Lupton	Vauxhall Corsa	F2	00:48:38
15	4	115	David May	Dave Mclachlan	BMW 325i	F3	00:48:40
16	6	129	Richard Evans	Jonathan Evans	Peugeot 106 GTi	F2	00:48:59
17	7	134	Adam Lawrence	Laura Taylor	Peugeot 205 Rallye	F2	00:49:32
18	8	118	Benjamin Cressey	Andrew Murphey	Peugeot 205 Rallye	F2	00:49:33
19	5	132	John Tillett	Guy Kirby	Ford Escort Mk2	F3	00:50:00
20	9	128	Ant Morthover	Dave Northover	Peugeot 205XS	F2	00:50:21
21	7	114	John Sutton	Paul Osmond	Porsche 914/6	F4	00:50:50
22	10	113	Andrew Frost	Miles Cartwright	Ford Escort Mexico	F2	00:50:55
23	11	122	Andrew Hebron	Simon Illsley	Peugeot 205 GTi	F2	00:51:20
24	6	124	Richard Boyes	Jon Robinson	Opel Kadett GTE	F3	00:54:20
25	12	119	Martin Auskerin	Darren Macdonald	Peugeot 205 GTi	F2	00:56:02
26	13	126	Glyn Casey	Mark Casey	Vauxhall Nova	F2	01:06:42
Ret		101	Andy Davison	Mike Curry	BMW 325i	F4	Stopped SS4
Ret		103	Chris Peart	Jamie Forrest	Vauxhall Astra Sport	F3	Driveshaft after SS10
Ret		105	Chris Birkbeck	Joyce Champion	Opel Kadett	F3	Retired SS8
Ret		108	Ian Winstanley	Neil Bye	BMW 325i	F4	Went off SS11
Ret		116	Thomas Stephenson	Marc Crack	BMW 325i	F4	Stopped SS11
Ret		117	Ed Pead	John Pead	Peugeot 205 GTi	F3	Stopped SS11
Ret		120	Gary Beckwith	Kirsty Beckwith	Ford Escort Mk2	F2	Retired

Rob Smith's Vauxhall Chevette was the leading non-Ford Escort

2009 RESULTS: CLUBMANS RALLY

Overall	Class	No	Driver	Co-driver	Car	Class	Total
1	1	121	Mark Shaw	Ken Willan	Talbot Sunbeam Ti	G2	00:37:41
2	2	120	Helen Hall	Alison Crozier	Talbot Sunbeam	G2	00:44:10
3	3	118	Darren Martin	Martin Steele	Peugeot 205XS	G2	00:45:31
4	1	117	Julian Doroszczuk	Paul Doroszczuk	Rover Mini	G1	00:48:34

Easson was second

Haddon at Oliver's Mount

Roger Albert Clark Rally 2009: the sixth edition

Roger Albert Clark Rally 2010:
the seventh edition

Overall winners: Stefaan Stouf and Joris Erard

The year of the snow

The 2010 rally
Friday 26 to Monday 29 November
104 stage miles
23 special stages
Start: Pickering Showground
Overnight 1: Pickering Showground
Overnight 2 & 3: Carlisle Racecourse
Finish: City Centre, Carlisle
78 starters
53 finishers

Open Rally winners: Dave Hemingway and Simon Ashton

Roger Albert Rally 2010: the seventh edition

Andrew Haddon battles the ice at Oliver's Mount

Anyone who was involved with the 2010 Roger Albert Clark Rally will never forget one of the most challenging rallies ever run in the UK.

The 2010 edition, run in late November, was the seventh running of the event designed to recreate the spirit of the RAC Rallies of the 1970s. Rally manager Colin Heppenstall planned a route covering 170 stage miles in 24 stages: starting in Yorkshire on Friday evening and finishing in Carlisle on Monday afternoon.

Rob Smith at Pickering

A field of 78 cars, predominantly historic, duly gathered at Pickering showground on Friday for the start. However, the forecast was for snow in the east of the country and no one could have predicted just how much that would impact the rally. There were several inches on the ground in Pickering, but up on the Yorkshire moors in the stages like Dalby and Langdale there was much, much more.

While the usual documentation and scrutineering was going on, Heppenstall was in Dalby which was the setting for two runs through a nine-mile stage as Friday evening's opener. Heppenstall said: "There had been snow in the forecast but I was shocked at the snow in Dalby. I just took a blinkered view and it never entered my head to cancel. If I could get the first car into the first stage, I could make the rest up from there." He had been a young organiser when snow hit the 1986 National Breakdown Rally and the show was going to go on.

That first evening was hugely difficult. Heppenstall persuaded a local farmer to plough the route, and duly took the wrath of the Forestry Commission.

The Roger Albert Clark Rally: The first 20 years

Mark and Tim Tugwell in Kershope

Steve Perez

Russell Morgan

Trees had come down under the weight of snow and had to be shifted and at one point Heppenstall towed a huge branch behind his 4x4 as an impromptu snowplough. The stage route had to be shortened and so started a weekend of Heppenstall and members of his organising team meeting competitors at controls and giving them updates on stage routes and where to go next.

It turned into a late night as cars had to be pushed at various points but the rally was running and Rob Smith took the early lead in his Vauxhall Chevette from Belgians Stefaan Stouf and Joris Erard in their Escort Mk1. Given the forecast, Heppenstall had approved the use of snow tyres and Stouf was well set-up with some highly effective Dunlops.

Stuart and Linda Cariss were running near the head of the rally in their 1600cc Escort Mk1. "Heading back to Pickering for service the planned route was impassable, so it was two-way rally traffic on a single width road covered in ice! Along with four other crews, we spent 10 minutes getting Bob Bean and his Cortina back onto the road after he tried to pass an oncoming crew by taking to the snow-covered verge and ended up stuck in a fence."

Roger Albert Clark Rally 2010: the seventh edition

Nick Pinkett's Saab 96 two-stroke in the snow of Kershope

The winners have a quick spin at Oliver's Mount

Mark Higgins

While trying to get the event running on Friday, Heppenstall had also been trying to work out a plan for Saturday which was due to centre on Oliver's Mount and Langdale before heading north and west for stages in Hamsterley and Shepherdshield before the overnight halt in Carlisle.

The asphalt Oliver's Mount stage was covered in snow and ice, but Heppenstall blagged a ton of grit from the venue owners, the local authority, to get it passable. Some inspired thinking by safety officer Brian Avery came up with a shortened Langdale route that was workable and so, once again, it was time to brief crews at the stage starts. While the uphill parts of Oliver's Mount had been gritted, the level sections had not and this prompted a master class of ice driving by Geoff Jones.

While crews were sliding around in Yorkshire, Heppenstall was now tackling the next challenge of how to get the rally out of Yorkshire. The planned route was north over the moors but that was reportedly impassable. Eventually, Heppenstall re-routed the entire rally, including all the service crews, down the A64 past York and then up the A1 heading for Hamsterley.

Pickering-based Steve Magson was competing in his Opel Ascona, complete with a very poor heater. "After Langdale we were re-routed up the A1 and my co-driver

Gwyndaf Evans in Ae with less snow

Geoff Atkinson said there was no rush so we stopped for coffee. The service crew gave us extra socks and coats to cover our legs. Going up the A1, the windscreen froze. We managed to arrive at Hamsterley and found that we were nearly the last car on the road. We had to be pushed off the start line, but we passed two cars."

Having lost some stage mileage in Yorkshire, Heppenstall, who'd managed just three hours in bed on Friday night, pulled another rabbit out of the hat by quickly arranging a double run through Hamsterley.

Dave Price, co-driver for leading contender Nick Elliott, takes up the story. "It was the first time we met the Heppenstalls and their wonderful 'keep the event going' approach. Writing the times for the bonus second Hamsterley run on the back of the time card is a classic moment. Ironically, had there not been this second run, we would have led the rally at the end of the day."

Shepherdshield was another massive challenge for crews and even the management vehicles struggled to get through but, eventually, the survivors reached Carlisle. Stouf now had an 11s lead over Elliott and a minute in hand over Rob Smith and Andrew Haddon.

Co-driver Phil Clarke, who won the rally in 2012 with Marty McCormack, was alongside Welsh ace Geoff Jones. "We went off in Hamsterley and broke a track control arm but Matt Edwards was there spectating and helped us get back on."

Stouf's Dunlops were proving hugely effective but he would have struggled had David Stokes not given him some spare covers. "During the whole event we had only one small moment when we slipped off the road on a square junction," said co-driver Erard. "There was no ditch and no spectators, but in reverse we were able to get out of the field with only a loss of about 10-15s. One good feature of the massive snow was that the darkness in the UK was not so dark anymore!"

"I have very little recollection of the three-hour journey up to Hamsterley," says Heppenstall. "I didn't fall asleep but was on the phone a lot and just thinking about what we had done during the event so far and hoping that the snow didn't fall in Scotland as I knew there was only a very light dusting of snow and all was okay as planned for Sunday."

Evans battles the ice at Oliver's Mount

Higgins in Kershope on Monday

The further west the rally went, the better the conditions and Sunday's stages in Ae and Twiglees had little snow but were still frozen hard. The fact that most of Sunday could run as planned gave Heppenstall a little breathing space as he worked out what to do on Monday when the planned 'sting in the tail' was due to run in the central block of Kielder forest.

Cariss took up the story of the Scottish stages. "Ae was the longest stage at over 14 miles. The surface was frozen but mainly clear of snow. It was our best stage of the event and we really enjoyed it: great fun! Then it was on to Twiglees 1 and back to snow and ice. While waiting for the stage to open, across the valley we saw the Land Rover Freelander opening car go off."

However, Sunday marked Elliott's departure from the lead battle, as Price recalled. "We should have let the event come to us and not pushed hard in Ae on snow tyres, where we punctured twice. Then we over-reacted and fitted gravel tyres for Twiglees to save the snows. Ice and a ditch awaited."

The first Ae stage was as far as Magson got. "We went off and damaged the front end of the car and my wrist. We got to service and the guys strapped my wrist with duct tape. But as we were leaving

Peter Smith's Opel Kadett

service the guys notice a leak from the oil cooler. They were about to bypass the oil cooler, when I said: 'don't worry, I can't drive the car'. I was taken home to Pickering, which was a six-hour journey, and the next day went to the hospital with what turned out to be a fractured wrist."

While all this was going on, Gwyndaf Evans was on a charge in his Viking Motorsport Escort Mk2 after a disastrous start to the rally when Pirelli was caught with no suitable tyres. Evans struggled in Yorkshire before more relevant rubber was flown in from Italy and by the second Twiglees stage he was up to fourth, having ended Friday evening down in 25th place. By the time the crews arrived back in Carlisle, Evans was up to third behind Stouf and Haddon.

Sunday evening's trip into Newcastleton was cut to only one stage instead of two when rescue units got stuck in the snow, which was lying thick. However, it was even worse in the central block of Kielder. "On Sunday evening in Newcastleton we lost nine cars in half a mile of sheet ice," said Heppenstall, who had spent much of Sunday working out a route for Monday. The planned stages were out of the question: the snow was just too deep and though the Forestry Commission was prepared to plough them, the strong winds due for Sunday night would have negated that work as the snow drifted back.

Instead, Heppenstall moved the entire leg into a different forest and plotted a stage in Kershope to be run twice. At one point on Sunday morning, he privately accepted that Monday would have to be cancelled, but an hour later he had a new plan. "There was too much snow in main Kielder, so we arranged two runs at Kershope on Monday. In Kershope it was a foot deep rather than two feet!" Incredible support from the local forestry team made this seemingly impossible plan work and when crews left Carlisle on Monday morning, they were sent straight to Kershope where a team of officials had been working hard to grit the public road up from the bridge and make it passable.

The reduced mileage on Monday probably cost Evans the rally as he pulled back half a minute from Stouf in the pair of five-mile stages.

Steve Perez leads Pascal Regnier

The scene on Monday morning

The planned leg had been 36 stage miles but it was Stouf and Erard who led the field back to the ceremonial finish in the centre of Carlisle. Evans was second from Haddon while Dave Hemingway and Simon Ashton dominated the concurrent Open Rally.

Clarke summed up the event. "It was different for everyone and is the one we'll always remember. I thought the effort from the organisers was amazing. Colin just kept appearing everywhere with new instructions and a 'just get there and forget about the road timing' comment!"

Stouf and Erard took the overall spoils back to Belgium after a fantastic performance, boosted by some very good Dunlops. "The 2010 event was very special for Stefaan and I, because we won the event," says Erard. "Maybe the biggest point for us was to get home to Belgium! We had to go round the M25 with our van, motor home and chase car, but at one point the whole motorway was closed for all traffic. So, we had to sleep in the middle of the M25 in our motor home!"

It had been the adventure of a lifetime for competitors, service crews, marshals, spectators and organisers. A lesser man at the top would have pulled the plug on Friday and sent everyone home. But Colin Heppenstall is a seriously determined character and he had a strong team around him. At the awards' ceremony on Monday afternoon he got a standing ovation and the competitors presented him with the 'spirit of the rally' award.

"If we'd not run it, the rally was never going to run again," said Heppenstall, a decade later. "Fortunately, the crews went with it and at each stage start and stage finish they were getting fresh instructions. I didn't break one rule! We bent some Forestry Commission rules but they were happy to work with me. Every single person worked to make the rally work. It was a complete team effort and

Geoff Jones was stunning on the ice

Alexandre Leens

Andrew Haddon

Mark Higgins

without the whole team it would never have worked. Now, I really still can't believe that we achieved it."

Personal view: Paul Lawrence
Rallying on snow is an awesome spectacle and I've been lucky enough to witness two very snowy rallies in 2010. Back in February, the Boucles de Spa was an amazing experience and the sight of Tim van Parijs on full opposite lock in the Mercedes 500SLC will long live with me. In the spirit of a true showman, he held the slide perfectly with one hand so that he could wave to the crowd with the other hand.

But even that was surpassed on the Roger Albert Clark Rally. The Oliver's Mount stage at Scarborough was covered in snow and ice and the approach to the Mount Hairpin included a fast left-hander over crest on sheet ice. The first few cars were spectacular, but then came Geoff Jones in his Escort Mk2 to completely redefine just what was possible.

At a pace that seemed certain to end in a big accident, he crested the brow and calmly gathered a monster slide with a deft flick of opposite lock, seemingly never even considering backing off. The onlookers collectively held their breath and then burst into chatter and applause as he rocketed out the hairpin and away up the hill.

It was one of the finest pieces of car control I've seen for a long time and I mentioned that to Geoff at the Carlisle service late that night. He smiled modestly and admitted that it had been good fun. I think terrifyingly spectacular would have been a better description.

Roger Albert Clark Rally 2010: the seventh edition

2010 ROGER ALBERT CLARK RALLY: ENTRY LIST

No	Driver	Co-driver	Car	Class
65	Bob Bean	Don Griffiths	Ford Lotus Cortina Mk1	B4
66	Richard Simpson	Debby Myers	Saab 96 V4	B4
67	Stuart Cariss	Linda Cariss	Ford Escort Sport	C1
68	Jim Valentine	Andy Harris	Saab 96 Sport	B1
69	Nick Pinkett	Mark Casey	Saab 96 2 Stroke	B1
1	Gwyndaf Evans	John Millington	Ford Escort Mk2	D5
2	Mark Higgins	Dale Furniss	Ford Escort RS1800	D5
3	Nick Elliott	Dave Price	Ford Escort Mk2	D5
4	Geoff Jones	Phil Clarke	Ford Escort Mk2	D5
5	Will Onions	Paul Wakely	Ford Escort Mk2 RS	D5
6	David Stokes	Guy Weaver	Ford Escort RS1600	C5
7	Paul Griffiths	Sam Collis	Ford Escort RS1800	D5
8	Rob Smith	Shaun O'Gorman	Vauxhall Chevette	D4
9	Darren Moon	Malcolm Smithson	Ford Escort RS1800	D5
10	Phil Collins	Nicky Grist	Opel Ascona 400	D5
11	Steve Smith	Andrew Edwards	Ford Escort RS1800	C5
12	Stefaan Stouf	Joris Erard	Ford Escort RS1600	C5
14	Steve Perez	Paul Spooner	Lancia Stratos	C5
15	Tim Mason	Graham Wild	Porsche 911RS	C4
16	Warren Philliskirk	Eurig Evans	Ford Escort Mk2	D5
17	Andrew Haddon	Mark Crisp	Ford Escort RS1800	D5
18	Steve Magson	Geoff Atkinson	Opel Ascona 400	D5
19	Arnaud Clause	Jonathan Lemaire	Ford Escort Mk2	D5
20	Herve Guignard	Didier Meffre	Porsche 911SC	D4
21	Pascal Regnier	Maryline Furnemont	Ford Escort RS1800	D5
22	Eric Guignard	Serge Le Gars	Porsche 911SC	D4
23	Sebastien Cuvelier	Jean-Noel Gregoire	Ford Escort RS2000	D3
24	Charlie Taylor	Steve Bielby	Ford Escort Mk2	D5
25	Phil Squires	Mick Squires	Ford Escort RS1800	D5
26	David Greer	Brian Crawford	Opel Ascona 400	D5
27	Neville Jones	Ian Capewell	Ford Escort Mk2	D5
28	David Watkins	Paul Train	Ford Escort RS1800	D5
29	Andrew Siddall	'Captain' Thompson	Ford Escort Mk1	C3
30	Russell Morgan	Martin Kenyon	Ford Escort RS2000	C3
31	Steve Graham	Tony Graham	Lancia Fulvia	C1
32	Leigh Armstrong	Chris Armstrong	Ford Escort Mk2	D5
33	Guy Woodcock	Iwan Jones	Ford Escort Mk2	D3
34	Ricky Evans	Ian Butcher	Ford Escort Mk2	D3
35	Adrian Young	Gwynfor Jones	Ford Escort RS2000	D3
37	Peter Smith	Russ Langthorne	Opel Kadett GTE	D3
38	Christophe Jacob	Isabelle Regnier	Ford Escort Mk2	D5
39	Alex Sabater	Iain Tullie	Ford Escort RS2000	C3
40	Francis Tuthill	Franca Davenport	Porsche 911	D4
41	Pierre Bonnardel	Bruno Ceccarelli	Porsche 911	D4
42	Stephane Modini	Robert Jaudel	Porsche 911SC	D4
43	Paul Chieusse	James Bocognano	Renault R5 Turbo	D3
44	Julien Elleboudt	Lul Joassin	Ford Escort Mk2	D3
45	Jean-Pierre Ansiaux	Laurent Joassin	Talbot Sunbeam Lotus	D5
46	James Slaughter	Phil Peak	Ford Escort Mk1	C3
48	Robin Eyre-Maunsell	Peter Scott	Talbot Sunbeam Lotus	D5

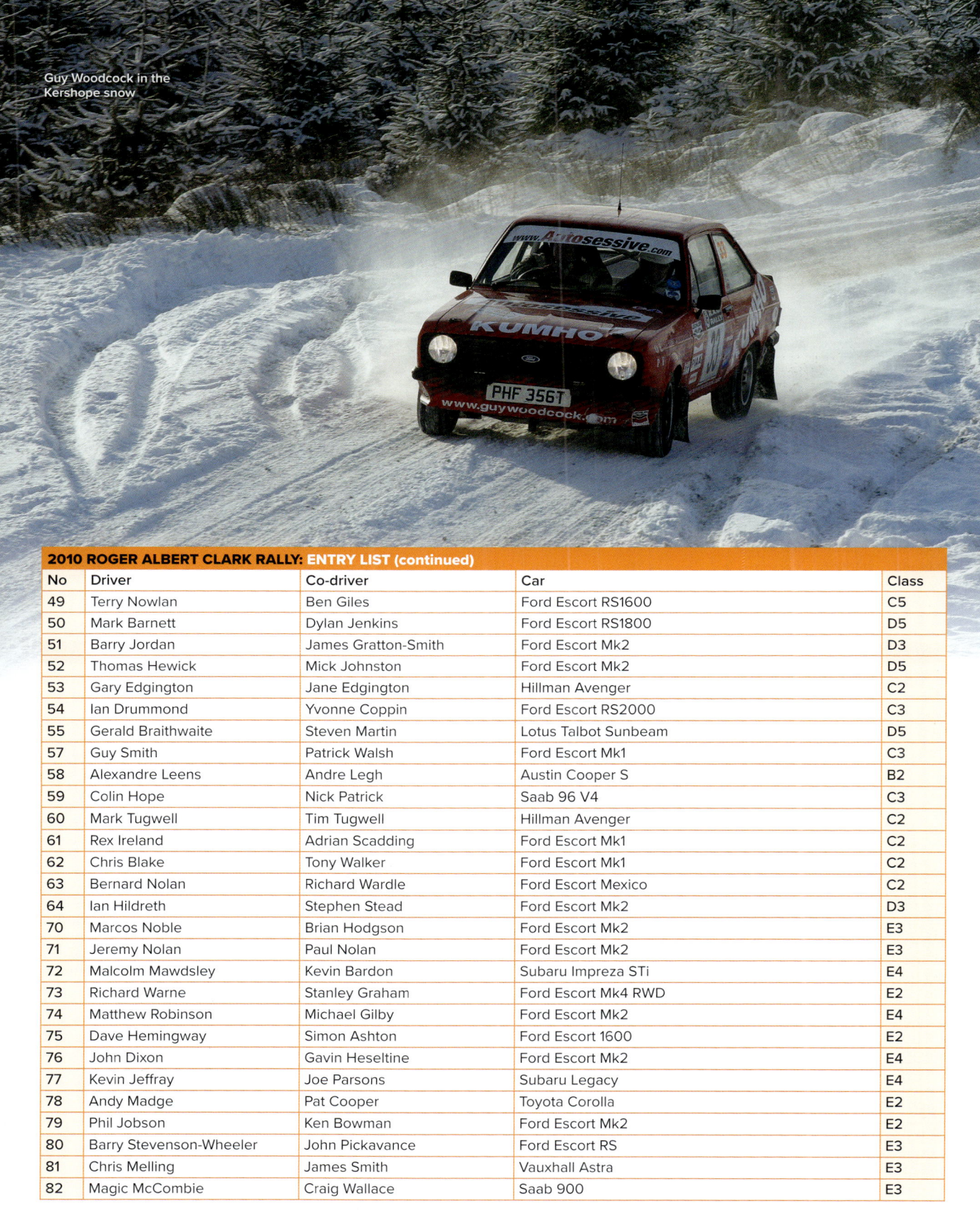

Guy Woodcock in the Kershope snow

2010 ROGER ALBERT CLARK RALLY: ENTRY LIST (continued)

No	Driver	Co-driver	Car	Class
49	Terry Nowlan	Ben Giles	Ford Escort RS1600	C5
50	Mark Barnett	Dylan Jenkins	Ford Escort RS1800	D5
51	Barry Jordan	James Gratton-Smith	Ford Escort Mk2	D3
52	Thomas Hewick	Mick Johnston	Ford Escort Mk2	D5
53	Gary Edgington	Jane Edgington	Hillman Avenger	C2
54	Ian Drummond	Yvonne Coppin	Ford Escort RS2000	C3
55	Gerald Braithwaite	Steven Martin	Lotus Talbot Sunbeam	D5
57	Guy Smith	Patrick Walsh	Ford Escort Mk1	C3
58	Alexandre Leens	Andre Legh	Austin Cooper S	B2
59	Colin Hope	Nick Patrick	Saab 96 V4	C3
60	Mark Tugwell	Tim Tugwell	Hillman Avenger	C2
61	Rex Ireland	Adrian Scadding	Ford Escort Mk1	C2
62	Chris Blake	Tony Walker	Ford Escort Mk1	C2
63	Bernard Nolan	Richard Wardle	Ford Escort Mexico	C2
64	Ian Hildreth	Stephen Stead	Ford Escort Mk2	D3
70	Marcos Noble	Brian Hodgson	Ford Escort Mk2	E3
71	Jeremy Nolan	Paul Nolan	Ford Escort Mk2	E3
72	Malcolm Mawdsley	Kevin Bardon	Subaru Impreza STi	E4
73	Richard Warne	Stanley Graham	Ford Escort Mk4 RWD	E2
74	Matthew Robinson	Michael Gilby	Ford Escort Mk2	E4
75	Dave Hemingway	Simon Ashton	Ford Escort 1600	E2
76	John Dixon	Gavin Heseltine	Ford Escort Mk2	E4
77	Kevin Jeffray	Joe Parsons	Subaru Legacy	E4
78	Andy Madge	Pat Cooper	Toyota Corolla	E2
79	Phil Jobson	Ken Bowman	Ford Escort Mk2	E2
80	Barry Stevenson-Wheeler	John Pickavance	Ford Escort RS	E3
81	Chris Melling	James Smith	Vauxhall Astra	E3
82	Magic McCombie	Craig Wallace	Saab 900	E3

2010 STAGES AND STAGE WINNERS

Day	Stage	Name	Distance	Stage winner(s)	Time
Friday	SS1	Showground 1	0.78	Armstrong/Armstrong	1.32
Friday	SS2	Dalby 1	4.12	Moon/Smithson	6.11
Friday	SS3	Showground 2	0.78	Stokes/Weaver	1.32
Friday	SS4	Dalby 2	4.12	Stouf/Erard	6.07
Saturday	SS5	Olivers Mount 1	1.55	Philliskirk/Evans	1.29
Saturday	SS6	Olivers Mount 2	1.55	Onions/Wakely and Stouf/Erard	1.52
Saturday	SS7	Langdale 1	4.22	Bennett/Jenkins and Haddon/Crisp	5.50
Saturday	SS8	Olivers Mount 3	1.55	Stouf/Erard	1.42
Saturday	SS9	Olivers Mount 4	1.55	Stouf/Erard	1.42
Saturday	SS10	Langdale 2	4.22	Stouf/Erard	5.08
Saturday	SS11	Hamsterley 1	5.80	Elliott/Price	7.58
Saturday	SS11A	Hamsterley 2	5.80	Stouf/Erard	7.55
Saturday	SS12	Shepherdshield	6.28	Elliott/Price	8.29
Sunday	SS13	Ae 1	14.34	Griffiths/Collis	16.16
Sunday	SS14	Twiglees 1	8.47	Evans/Millington	10.20
Sunday	SS15	Heathhall 1	0.68	Griffiths/Collis	1.13
Sunday	SS16	Ae 2	14.34	Griffiths/Collis	15.27
Sunday	SS17	Heathhall 2	0.68	Smith/O'Gorman, Moon/Smithson, Stouf/Erard and Taylor/Bielby	1.12
Sunday	SS18	Twiglees 2	8.47	Smith/O'Gorman and Higgins/Furniss	10.04
Sunday	SS19	Newcastleton 1	0.00	Cancelled	0.00
Sunday	SS20	Newcastleton 2	4.69	Evans/Millington	7.00
Monday	SS21	Kershope 1	4.78	Evans/Millington	6.38
Monday	SS22	Kershope 2	4.78	Griffiths/Collis	6.35
		Total Miles	103.55		

2010 RESULTS

Overall	Class	No	Driver	Co-driver	Car	Class	Total
1	1	12	Stefaan Stouf	Joris Erard	Ford Escort RS1600	C5	02:17:19
2	1	1	Gwyndaf Evans	John Millington	Ford Escort Mk2	D5	02:18:37
3	2	17	Andrew Haddon	Mark Crisp	Ford Escort RS1800	D5	02:19:02
4	3	7	Paul Griffiths	Sam Collis	Ford Escort RS1800	D5	02:20:05
5	4	10	Phil Collins	Nicky Grist	Opel Ascona 400	D5	02:20:18
6	5	9	Darren Moon	Malcolm Smithson	Ford Escort RS1800	D5	02:22:46
7	6	2	Mark Higgins	Dale Furniss	Ford Escort RS1800	D5	02:22:48
8	1	30	Russell Morgan	Martin Kenyon	Ford Escort RS2000	C3	02:25:34
9	7	50	Mark Barnett	Dylan Jenkins	Ford Escort RS1800	D5	02:27:11
10	8	24	Charlie Taylor	Steve Bielby	Ford Escort Mk2	D5	02:27:55
11	2	11	Steve Smith	Andrew Edwards	Ford Escort RS1800	C5	02:28:08
12	2	29	Andrew Siddall	'Captain' Thompson	Ford Escort Mk1	C3	02:29:45
13	9	26	David Greer	Brian Crawford	Opel Ascona 400	D5	02:30:57
14	10	38	Christophe Jacob	Isabelle Regnier	Ford Escort Mk2	D5	02:31:38
15	11	16	Warren Philliskirk	Eurig Evans	Ford Escort Mk2	D5	02:33:05
16	1	33	Guy Woodcock	Iwan Jones	Ford Escort Mk2	D3	02:33:21
17	3	14	Steve Perez	Paul Spooner	Lancia Stratos	C5	02:33:35
18	2	37	Peter Smith	Russ Langthorne	Opel Kadett GTE	D3	02:38:03
19	12	48	Robin Eyre-Maunsell	Peter Scott	Talbot Sunbeam Lotus	D5	02:39:16
20	1	53	Gary Edgington	Jane Edgington	Hillman Avenger	C2	02:39:43
21	2	62	Chris Blake	Tony Walker	Ford Escort Mk1	C2	02:40:31
22	3	34	Ricky Evans	Ian Butcher	Ford Escort Mk2	D3	02:41:20
23	13	19	Arnaud Clause	Jonathan Lemaire	Ford Escort Mk2	D5	02:41:27
24	4	6	David Stokes	Guy Weaver	Ford Escort RS1600	C5	02:41:38
25	14	52	Thomas Hewick	Mick Johnston	Ford Escort Mk2	D5	02:41:49
26	15	25	Phil Squires	Mick Squires	Ford Escort RS1800	D5	02:42:30

2010 RESULTS (continued)

Overall	Class	No	Driver	Co-driver	Car	Class	Total
27	3	39	Alex Sabater	Iain Tullie	Ford Escort RS2000	C3	02:48:16
28	1	40	Francis Tuthill	Franka Davenport	Porsche 911	D4	02:54:00
29	16	45	Jean-Pierre Ansiaux	Laurent Joassin	Talbot Sunbeam Lotus	D5	02:54:37
30	17	21	Pascal Regnier	Maryline Furnemont	Ford Escort RS1800	D5	02:56:04
31	4	59	Colin Hope	Nick Patrick	Saab 96 V4	C3	02:57:06
32	2	22	Eric Guignard	Serge Le Gars	Porsche 911SC	D4	02:58:34
33	18	28	David Watkins	Paul Train	Ford Escort RS1800	D5	02:58:58
34	4	44	Julien Elleboudt	Lul Joassin	Ford Escort Mk2	D3	02:59:11
35	3	60	Mark Tugwell	Tim Tugwell	Hillman Avenger	C2	03:06:35
36	5	49	Terry Nowlan	Ben Giles	Ford Escort RS1600	C5	03:09:32
37	1	58	Alexandre Leens	Andre Legh	Austin Cooper S	B2	03:11:42
38	4	63	Bernard Nolan	Richard Wardle	Ford Escort Mexico	C2	03:15:31
39	1	67	Stuart Cariss	Linda Cariss	Ford Escort Sport	C1	03:19:49
40	5	64	Ian Hildreth	Stephen Stead	Ford Escort Mk2	D3	03:20:52
41	1	69	Nick Pinkett	Mark Casey	Saab 96 2 Stroke	B1	03:34:06
42	2	68	Jim Valentine	Andy Harris	Saab 96 Sport	B1	03:36:31
43	2	31	Steve Graham	Tony Graham	Lancia Fulvia	C1	04:07:11
		65	Bob Bean	Don Griffiths	Ford Lotus Cortina Mk1	B4	Various problems TC16A
		66	Richard Simpson	Debby Myers	Saab 96 V4	B4	Stopped SS21
		3	Nick Elliott	Dave Price	Ford Escort Mk2	D5	Stuck in ditch SS14
		4	Geoff Jones	Phil Clarke	Ford Escort Mk2	D5	Broken coil SS13
		5	Will Onions	Paul Wakely	Ford Escort Mk2 RS	D5	Broken fuel union SS13
		8	Rob Smith	Shaun O'Gorman	Vauxhall Chevette	D4	Went off SS20
		15	Tim Mason	Graham Wild	Porsche 911RS	C4	Broken steering column
		18	Steve Magson	Geoff Atkinson	Opel Ascona 400	D5	Oil cooler
		20	Herve Guignard	Didier Meffre	Porsche 911SC	D4	Went off SS20
		23	Sebastien Cuvelier	Jean-Noel Gregoire	Ford Escort RS2000	D3	Retired SS18
		27	Neville Jones	Ian Capewell	Ford Escort Mk2	D5	Retired SS20
		32	Leigh Armstrong	Chris Armstrong	Ford Escort Mk2	D5	OTL
		35	Adrian Young	Gwynfor Jones	Ford Escort RS2000	D3	Retired SS20
		41	Pierre Bonnardel	Bruno Ceccarelli	Porsche 911	D4	Retired SS13
		42	Stephane Modini	Robert Jaudel	Porsche 911SC	D4	Retired SS11
		43	Paul Chieusse	James Bocognano	Renault R5 Turbo	D3	Engine TC14A
		46	James Slaughter	Phil Peak	Ford Escort Mk1	C3	Loss of steering SS16
		51	Barry Jordan	James Gratton-Smith	Ford Escort Mk2	D3	Engine TC14A
		54	Ian Drummond	Yvonne Coppin	Ford Escort RS2000	C3	Blown engine SS2
		55	Gerald Braithwaite	Steven Martin	Lotus Talbot Sunbeam	D5	Retired SS15
		57	Guy Smith	Patrick Walsh	Ford Escort Mk1	C3	Stopped SS21
		61	Rex Ireland	Adrian Scadding	Ford Escort Mk1	C2	Broken diff SS15

Nick Elliott in Ae with a puncture

Herve Guignard

Roger Albert Clark Rally 2010: the seventh edition

Bob Bean at Oliver's Mount

2010 RESULTS: OPEN RALLY

Overall	Class	No	Driver	Co-driver	Car	Class	Total
1	1	75	Dave Hemingway	Simon Ashton	Ford Escort 1600	E2	02:33:46
2	1	70	Marcos Noble	Brian Hodgson	Ford Escort Mk2	E3	02:36:50
3	2	78	Andy Madge	Pat Cooper	Toyota Corolla	E2	02:40:43
4	3	79	Phil Jobson	Ken Bowman	Ford Escort Mk2	E2	02:44:09
5	2	71	Jeremy Nolan	Paul Nolan	Ford Escort Mk2	E3	02:53:23
6	1	77	Kevin Jeffray	Joe Parsons	Subaru Legacy	E4	02:56:30
7	3	81	Chris Melling	James Smith	Vauxhall Astra	E3	03:09:39
8	2	74	Matthew Robinson	Michael Gilby	Ford Escort Mk2	E4	03:12:07
9	4	80	Barry Stevenson-Wheeler	John Pickavance	Ford Escort RS	E3	03:18:29
10	3	76	John Dixon	Gavin Heseltine	Ford Escort Mk2	E4	03:20:27
Ret		72	Malcolm Mawdsley	Kevin Bardon	Subaru Impreza STi	E4	Retired SS20
Ret		73	Richard Warne	Stanley Graham	Ford Escort Mk4 RWD	E2	Co-driver ill MTC5
Ret		82	Magic McCombie	Craig Wallace	Saab 900	E3	Gearbox casing SS17

Rob Smith

Robin Eyre-Maunsell

The Roger Albert Clark Rally: The first 20 years

Paul Chieusse

Steve Graham

2010 RESULTS: KALL KWIK RALLY

Overall	Class	No	Driver	Co-driver	Car	Class	Total
1	1	106	Stuart Wood	Errol Bairstow	Opel Astra	F3	00:28:51
2	2	107	Conor Flynn	Mark Mason	Peugeot 306 GTi	F3	00:30:20
3	3	108	Tony Jardine	Byron Young	Ford Fiesta ST150	F3	00:32:53
4	4	104	Terrence Cree	Richard Shores	BMW 2002Ti	F3	00:35:16
5	1	117	Nigel Barrett	Simon Law	Nissan Micra	F1	00:36:39
6	1	115	Ian Cartwright	Ian Jackson	Peugeot 205 GTi	F2	00:36:55
7	5	105	Philip Welch	Fred Roberts	VW Golf Kit Car	F3	00:37:24
8	6	103	Chris Langthorne	Nigel Wetton	Ford Escort	F3	00:37:48
9	2	109	Martin Auskerin	Darren MacDonald	Peugeot 205 GTi	F2	00:40:00
10	3	112	Mike Kent	Miles Cartwright	Talbot Sunbeam Ti	F2	00:44:38
11	7	119	Mike Dowson	Nigel Boston	Ford Escort Mk2	F3	00:45:24
12	4	120	Stuart Ingham	Mat Tinker	Peugeot 205 GTi	F2	00:51:11
13	5	111	Richard Evans	David Evans	Peugeot 106 GTi	F2	00:51:22
Ret		101	Dave Brick	Rob Woodhouse	Ford Escort RS	F4	Gearbox MTC3
Ret		102	Ian Jemison	Graham Wride	Porsche Boxster	F4	Engine SS6
Ret		110	David May	Dave Mclachlan	BMW E36 Compact	F4	No drive
Ret		113	Gary Beckwith	Kirsty Beckwith	Ford Escort Mk2	F3	Retired after SS7
Ret		114	John O'Gorman	John Rutter	BMW E30	F4	Went off SS8
Ret		116	Wayne Bale	Daren Bale	Peugeot 205 GTi	F2	In ditch SS7
Ret		118	Brian Maguire	Ant Hellewell	Peugeot 205 GTi Ml16	F3	Retired

2010 RESULTS: DALBY NIGHT RALLY

Overall	Class	No	Driver	Co-driver	Car	Class	Total
1	1	87	Amanda Cornforth	Derek Cornforth	Ford KA	G2	00:28:16
2	1	84	Clive Baty	Simon Bentley	Ford Escort RS2000	G3	00:28:51
3	2	86	Micheal Raw	Dave Raw	Ford Fiesta	G2	00:32:14
Ret		85	Bill Douglas	Dave Tearl	Volvo 244	G4	Retired after SS3

2010 RESULTS: CLUBMANS RALLY

Overall	Class	No	Driver	Co-driver	Car	Class	Total
1	1	92	James Robertson	Claire Robertson	Citroen C2	J2	00:59:11
2	2	89	Mike Axford	Dave Thomason	Ford Fiesta RS	J2	01:01:30
3	1	95	Nigel Talton	Dominic Foister	Rover SDI	J4	01:06:58
4	1	94	Darren Martin	Martin Steele	Skoda Felicia	J1	01:12:25
5	3	88	Mark Shaw	Ken Willan	Talbot Sunbeam	J2	01:12:37
Ret		90	David Perkins	Paul Morgan	Talbot Sunbeam	J3	Half shafts TC14A
Ret		91	Roy Eide Johansen	Amanda Burney	Ford Escort Mk1	J3	Went off SS13
Ret		93	Tam Brown	Michael Curry	Peugeot 205 GTi	J2	In ditch SS18

The 2010 event was snow-bound

Pulling off a miracle
2010: The Colin Heppenstall view

The 2010 Roger Albert Clark Rally ran in the face of almost insurmountable odds as heavy snow fell in the north east of England. After the event, Rally Manager Colin Heppenstall recorded his honest and open experience of running an event that came close to never happening.

Being a 19-year-old on the organising team of the 1986 National Breakdown Rally when snow hit the event, I knew that the principles of the De Lacy Motor Club were to make the event work at whatever cost, and give the competitors, marshals and spectators something to do and watch. In 2010, this had to be achieved for the future of the Roger Albert Clark Rally.

During the week leading up to the event, the weather forecast said snow was coming and probably a lot of it on the east coast but they didn't know how far inland it would come.

Wednesday evening came and the senior management team travelled to Pickering. However, even this didn't go to plan. We dropped off the equipment van at one of the team's homes for the morning and pulling out of the housing estate we realised we had a flat tyre, with the van crammed to the roof with boxes and paper. I wasn't going to empty it so the jack had to struggle, but after about 40 minutes we had it changed to the space saver.

As I passed the showground the roads were clear and nothing looked like coming from the sky but how the situation changes in less than a mile. As I entered the 30mph limit for Pickering, it started to snow and snow and snow and by the time we came out of the Chinese restaurant at 11pm there was two to three inches of snow on the ground and then I realised this year's event was going to be a great challenge.

Thursday 25 November

On Thursday morning the team arrived at the showground at 9am to start preparing and were handed the keys to the buildings with one to two inches covering the venue, not too bad and really workable.

As the first equipment van arrived by 10am we got started on building and preparing. Unbeknown to us all, as we were in the building, the snow had started at about 10.30am and did not stop until about 4pm.

At around 2pm I dispatched the Event Safety Officer Brian Avery up into Dalby to take the refreshment wagon into the Woodyard and to have a look at the amount of snow, then on to Oliver's

It started in Pickering Showground

Mount. On reporting back Brian Avery said we had no problems getting into the woodyard, about four to five inches of snow, and we should be able to make this work OK. This gave me the confidence that the Safety Officer was being economical with the depth of the snow, or the amount of ice there actually was, but knowing Brian if he said the stages would run then I had confidence in him.

The whole team went down to the Black Bull pub just outside the showground, which does exceptional pub food, and as we were the only ones daft enough to venture out in the snow, we had a good feed. About 9pm four yellow welly clad men arrived: the Dunlop team had come in for a pint. So after an exchange of views about the snow and what might happen during the event, we all headed off to bed for 11pm.

Friday 26 November

The team was back in the Showground by 7.45am. As more and more officials started to arrive, I got a phone call at 8.20am from the portable toilet people who were telling me they had contacted the Forestry Commission and the road up from Thornton le Dale was blocked with snow and they could not get up into Dalby. Scarborough Council were saying that they would not get up to Oliver's Mount to deliver there either. At 8.30am they phoned again and said they would not set off until they had it confirmed that they could get their vehicle into Dalby.

So the best way of seeing what the actual situation was to go and have a look myself. Off I went into Thornton le Dale and there was only about two inches of snow past the houses going up to Forest Drive. Then at the hill it had been ploughed and scraped and the road had also been gritted, so I continued up the hill with no problems. On the plateau at the top the snow had been ploughed and the banks were one to two feet high, but quite passable with care.

I turned onto the Forest Drive and had to break very hard as the Forestry Commission snow plough was just coming out, so I waited for him to turn around and go back in. As I followed the plough he was now gritting and I followed him all the way into Low Dalby village. As I turned down the road to the Woodyard the snow was six to eight inches deep and this had been clear the previous night so I knew we had some issues in getting Dalby working.

While travelling back to the Showground, I contacted the portable toilet people and told them they could get into Low Dalby village, so they said they would set off. I also contacted Brian Avery and asked him to be ready at the Showground for when I got back to go back up into Dalby.

Back at the Showground for 9.20am, a lot of people had arrived so Nicola had got them all working on various things around the Showground and Brian and myself set off back up into Dalby to look at the stage via rally route. We went via a quick trip into the FC officers in Pickering to introduce myself to Cath the FC liaison officer who I had never met as she was new to the job, and to ask for the combination code for the high security locks in Dalby so we could get through.

Marshals and media at Oliver's Mount

As we turned up the Ebberstone Road, the road had been ploughed and gritted all the way up to Givendale Head Farm. Wow, what a good council we thought but how wrong could we have been? The farmer, who was also doing our bales, had been up since 5am ploughing the road as he was due a delivery of 200 pigs at 9am and he wanted to receive them.

Beyond the farm the road was covered in snow about eight to 10 inches deep with no tracks. Now we knew we had a huge battle on our hands. We struggled to the Fire Tower, opened the gate and the Forest Drive back down towards Low Dalby had been ploughed, so I knew the event could at least get to the start line of the stage.

As we turned off into the forest to head towards the quarry, where the start line was, we came across branches of trees blocking the road. As Brian and I got out to move the first 10 or so, we heard an almighty crack down the road and watched the top of one of the trees break due to the weight of the snow and come crashing down onto the road.

After about 45 minutes we got to the end of the copse of trees around the quarry and had it clear. Brian then found one of the branches that was quite large and like a V, and suggested that we attach it to the back of the vehicle and use it as a plough. There was eight to 10 inches of snow on the road so any reduction would have been welcome. This we did and set off all the way down to Junction 2 and what a difference it made as we managed to get down to Junction 3. On the slight uphill we stopped and weren't going any further, mainly due to the amount of snow we were pulling behind us on our plough, so shovels came out to dig the snow away and we uncoupled the tree so I could make some tracks up to J4, then off we went again.

We eventually managed to get past J5 and came to a full tree across the road: this wasn't going to be easily moved. The time was now 10.30am and we had agreed with the farmer that he would be in the Woodyard with the bales at about 11.15am, so Brian walked off down the track to the Woodyard. As we waited and waited nothing could be heard, so I started to walk towards the Woodyard to be confronted by another 30 or 40 large branches on the road full of snow. Well at least I had something to do while we waited for the farmer.

At 11.30am the farmer appeared and I was soaked to the skin from moving these branches which had fallen snow on them. I was wet and needed

There was little snow in Ae

some good news as all I could see was the event disappearing before me, as we were only about two miles into a nine mile stage and time was against us.

As the farmer arrived in only his tractor with no bales, he said he had cleared four downed trees coming down the rigg we were using to go up, and he had left them at the top of the rigg. As his machine was huge he came up and moved the one blocking us as well. While riding on the footplate I tried to persuade the farmer that looking after his new pigs could wait and could he go back to the farm after he had delivered the bales and put the bucket on and drive the stage, which would be a lot more fun and would at least allow the event to start at 6.30pm.

As the farmer put all the bales out I did not know if he was going to do it. The Forestry Commission do not allow their tracks to be ploughed or if they do consent to it, only people and machinery which has been cleared with the relevant passes and insurance can do it. I had another chat with the farmer and said I would sort the FC out, and on the fact that I said it was my head on the block and not his for coming onto FC land I think we had a deal, well apart from what the cost would be, but like a true Yorkshireman the deal was 'you do this for me and I will see you right'. So the deal was done. My first break of the day so I thought. By now it was 1.30pm and we now had five other 4x4 official vehicles driving the stage to make it run.

I made the decision with the Stage Commander that no two-wheel drive cars would be allowed into the stage, only 4x4s, and the stage would be shortened so we had the necessary cover.

At 2.15pm I took a phone call from the Head Forester at Pickering. To say he was not a happy man was an understatement and I agreed to be summoned directly to Pickering to have a meeting with him. As Brian and I got to the Woodyard two foresters were also looking for us as they had been sent to find us for this meeting. We knew we had some explaining to do as we had ploughed the FC land without permission and made access for the spectators.

We arrived back in Pickering at 2.45pm to be ushered into their conference room. I knew I had upset the top man. After a very good discussion and one which covered sensible topics and included my telling off for breaking the rules, the FC required some new Risk Assessments for the snow. Then they were content that they would do the final stage check at 5.30pm with Brian to allow the stage to run, as long as all we had promised was in place.

Knowing that we had had to offer to cancel Langdale on the Saturday to get Friday, I asked if we could run Dalby again on Saturday as we had managed to get it open. I got a very clear one word answer 'NO'. At this point we shook hands and left at 3.45pm knowing we had an event: well on Friday, anyway.

We headed back to the Showground and arrived at 4pm to finalise what needed to be done prior to the start at 6.30pm. I then met up with my normal driver Bob Lodge who, during the event, is my right hand man and sounding board for decisions. Bob's experience goes back many years with De Lacy in organising the old international rallies and I would not be able to make the many decisions I had to, as quickly as I did, without his input and suggestions.

The public road alongside Kershope

I decided that the best place for the Clerk of the Course to position himself was at Givendale Head Farm on the entrance to the woods. As we were getting up to the farm I had a call to say the exit route down to Allerston was impassable with the trees we had down on the route out of the forest. A quick discussion with my best mate the farmer, who had just had his tea, would not allow us through the farm yard. But he had ploughed the back link road around the farm so we had an exit route, even though not ideal with rally traffic going in and out on the same road, but at least we had a plan.

So as the crews entered the forest on their way to Dalby I stopped each one and issued them their first amendment at the side of the road and drew the new exit route on each crew's maps. Before the event people were asking: would the event be doing pace note checks and map checks? This had been planned, but now I had to see and write on every crew's maps and this would not be the first time during the event. So these checks did take place. What I would like to report back is that only three crews at the back of the field had written on their maps and were warned accordingly. But due to the conditions not a lot of advantage would have occurred.

As the first cars came out of the stage they were reporting it was OK but very slippy and we had an event. I had timed the event so that for the second pass of the stage the crews were coming back before the first had completed their first pass so for the first time in the day at about 8pm I had a sit down in the car and a rest.

This did not last long, as the historic cars were coming out for their second run. Past the farm the road goes narrow with fences on both sides and Bob Bean in the Cortina had stopped and nothing was moving. Bob and I agreed that we would have to run a traffic light system on this stretch of road to keep the cars flowing once we got the Cortina clear. With over 10 cars blocked I had the manpower to move the Cortina, which we achieved, and started to stop cars at both ends of the narrow track to keep them moving. This was working well for all the RAC cars but then a gap came. After about 20 minutes with no cars I phoned my deputy Graham James, who was stopping all non-rally vehicles from coming up Ebberstone, and asked if any of the Kall Kwik crews had started to come up. He said yes, all of them.

So I set off walking back down the track towards Ebberstone and eventually saw loads of headlights in the distance. When I eventually got to the cars they could not get up a very long slight incline. The RAC crews all had snow tyres on so had grip, and as the road had had over 300 cars over it the ice had got very polished and the Kall Kwik crews could not get up on normal tyres.

The Kall Kwik crews were pushing each other up the hill. So I got each crew back into their car and pushed each car up the hill. It didn't need much pushing but it was a long hill for the 15 or so that needed it. As I knew they were all up, I stopped the closing car from coming up the road and decided that I would close the stage, as I wanted to thank the marshals on the car's PA system for coming out.

As we headed into the stage to close we came to the square left after J2 to find six cars all parked up as one of the cars was off and the other crews had got out of their cars to push him back on. It was a very long closing job! About 100 meters before the flying finish line we came across car 86 in a snow bank and it took us 15 minutes of struggling to get him out of the snow and on his way so we could get the marshals out.

Back into the Showground at midnight I was getting reports from Brian Avery who had spoken to the Stage Commanders of Oliver's Mount and Langdale. They both had a lot of snow and the stages were set up but didn't know if the stages were safe to run.

Earlier in the day I had been in discussion with the Scarborough Council about the Mount. The Council refused to plough or grit the Mount due to a landlord issue with residents who live on the Mount, but finally at 4.30pm agreed to allow us to grit the Mount and even provide some grit. I got the Stage Commander to go to the council depot with a trailer and they gave us one ton of grit. This does not do much on the Mount, and most of it was put onto the Mere to try and give us a chance in the morning.

At the Showground on the Friday we used the services of a local farmer's wife who provided sandwiches and warm evening food for the officials. As I sat down to eat the first food since breakfast at 7am at 00.30am in the morning I was hungry to say the least! I managed to get back to the B&B and into bed at 2.30am.

Saturday 27 November
The alarm went off at 5.30am and Nicola got up and got ready. She'd managed to get to bed at about 2am and as she made me get out of bed I crawled into the shower and sat in the basin with the water running on my head, trying desperately to wake up. I was absolutely knackered from everything that had gone on during Friday and knew that Saturday could be another hell of a day. At 5.40am I had no plans of what we were going to do, as I knew we only had about three inches of snow in Hamsterley on the Friday but I needed to find an event on the Saturday in Yorkshire.

As I walked into breakfast at 6am the whole room stopped and looked at me and said 'oh my god, it does live'. I looked shocking and was not up yet. I could not eat anything and had a glass of orange juice and some coffee and was back out in the car with Bob Lodge by 6.30am, heading to the Showground to open up.

To try and make life a little easier, knowing that getting Oliver's up and running was going to be a challenge I delayed the start for the first car by 30 minutes to 9.30am, which meant that first car at Oliver's was now 10.15am As we were about to leave for the Mount I got a phone call from Richard Harrison, the local co-ordinator, to say the bale man had refused to take the bales up to the Mount this morning, due to the ice on the hills, so if we were going to use it then we would have no bales.

I arrived at Oliver's at 7.45am and went straight onto the Mount to look at the conditions. We drove the stage and the monument was very slippy and drifted towards the café doing 20mph. We decided that this part of the stage could not be used or an insurance claim would have been going in for a new cafe. We then got to the top of the Mere Hill; as we went down very carefully you could see the ton of grit that was put on last night had worked and the road would have cleaned up quite quickly. It would have been passable if there had been bales at the bottom, but as we had no bales, the hill had to be pulled as well.

A scene from Monday morning

Roger Albert Clark Rally 2010: the year of the snow

The spectacular scene in Kershope

So what was left was a single straight lap which was 1.55 miles. I went back to the paddock to speak to the Stage Commander and other officials who were now waiting for my decision. It is fair to say everybody was up for the shortened stage as they had something to do. The Commander sent out a set-up crew and Pete Baker was dispatched to find grit so we could put some more down. The council wasn't very helpful so a local builders merchant had 45 bags available which we bought and then started to grit the start, then the hairpin, then the hill, then the new final hairpin and finish line. We tried to put any that was left down on the straights.

After the stage was ready I did a final pass with the Safety Officer and we stopped at the final hairpin, as it was sheet ice, to get some more grit. At this point it was 8.45am and as I stood talking to Brian and Bob I had a brain wave. Without telling them what it was, I said listen to this phone call. I called Jonathan Ferries the forestry liaison officer for Kielder which included Hamsterley and Shepherdshield.

"Jonathan, do you know of the snow conditions in Hamsterley and Shepherdshield this morning?" This was a silly question really as he was sat in the kitchen on his morning off. No, was the reply but I will find out and come back to you. I said I had a thought that, as we have lost so much mileage in Dalby and I don't know about Langdale yet, can we run Hamsterley twice.

Good question was the reply. These things are not easily agreed, and Jonathan said he would have to pass it up the chain but would come back to me. I said I needed an answer by 12 noon so I could plan for it, I left it at this point with fingers crossed. It would at least give crews some mileage back if the FC agreed.

As we were now happy with Oliver's we headed back to the start to write the stage changes. The easiest way to explain to the crews was to draw the new stage onto their maps and this I did prior to the arrival control. The first car entered the stage bang on their revised time so I was very happy.

After about four cars had gone in I got a call from the first 4x4 crew I sent to Langdale at 7.30am to say they had reached the end of the stage and it should work if we ban any two-wheeled drive marshals cars

Bob Bean was first car on the road

as last night, and could they go onto the MOD land now. So I rang the MOD to confirm that we were still planning on coming through.

After a few fraught calls we were allowed to proceed onto their land to see if we could get through the snow. The first 4x4 eventually made it through, but when the second 4x4 arrived we realised that the wrong road inside the MOD property had been opened and this was about to cause an almighty problem.

On MOD property the Police have the final say about any and all security. As the road we had just opened was too close to the very high security outer fence then the answer was no, you cannot come across our land and have a nice day. Great I thought, we have a stage but no way of getting out of it.

As we were already telling crews that Langdale was open and to go there after Oliver's we could not stop them. I put a message over the radio network that we would have to cancel the stage as we couldn't get out of the end of the stage. Brian Avery came back over the management frequency to say we could stop the stage at J8 and come out there

and what did I think? I said you have 40 minutes and the cars were already on their way.

I rang my deputy again, who was now at the junction with the Broxa road stopping all spectators from going up to the stage as it was not fit for two-wheel drive cars, to ask if any crews had passed yet? Yes three was the reply. Stop all other crews on the road until we have decided what to do as the arrival control at Langdale is not the best place to queue the entire event if you are going to have to cancel the stage.

After Bob had briefed somebody else to write on the competitors' maps for the new Oliver's stage, we headed off to Langdale to prepare another bulletin and route amendments and while Bob was driving I was working out times and exit routes to get the crews back to the Showground. When I arrived at the Broxa junction the scene was hectic, not least because the local large snow plough could not get down the road due to parking rally cars and he was not a happy chappy.

After I had been there for about 10 minutes I heard on the radio that Brian was happy with the stage and Lloyd Walker the Chief Timekeeper was entering the stage to do the final check. I then started to issue the crews with their latest amendment to the stage and the route back to the Showground.

Brian was surprised to hear that it was still my intention to let the crews have two more attempts at Oliver's and another Langdale in Yorkshire before we moved away as we were now running 45 minutes late on the revised timetable. As the last cars were entering Langdale 1 I followed the crews back to the Showground via Dalby Forest Drive where by now it was snowing in blizzard conditions and you could not see the road. As we only had 10 to 15 cars left to come across I decided that for the second run of the stage the crews could not come back via this route as it was too dangerous.

The ice of Oliver's Mount

It was now 11.45am and as I got to Givendale Head Farm my phone rang: it was Jonathan from the FC. The snow in Hamsterley is four to six inches and Shepherdshield is six to eight inches. That all should work then I thought, and he said that the big boss says yes you can do the stage twice. Great: we had another plan to work and at least we had an event to Carlisle.

As I was travelling back to the Showground around 1pm the snow that was on the tops in Dalby was now coming down again in Pickering. I then received a phone call from Chrys Worboys who was the Operations Car and runs about an hour in front of the first car to say that he was at a complete standstill in Middlesborough and it was snowing like the clappers. I had heard on the radio that cars were struggling down the Hole of Horcum where the service crews would be going, so I phoned Richard Hinton, who was the Clerk of the Course for the Kall Kwik Rally and was based in the Showground, to stop all service crews from leaving until I had found a route they could go on.

So I rang the Police Traffic Sergeant who came to see me on Friday to ask which roads were open now and would be from 2pm to 6pm. Listening on his radio via the phone, the A169 north, the way we were planning on going, had just been closed. Sutton Bank was likely to be open until about 3pm but was likely to close for large vehicles and currently the A64 was closed at Barton Hill due to a jack-knifed lorry, so there was no way out of Yorkshire. As we were talking he got a message to say the lorry was just being towed away and the road would be reopened in 30 minutes maximum and therefore we had a route out which had the least amount of snow.

It was not the most direct route for the service crews to Carlisle or the competitors to Hamsterley. The route amendments given to the service crews was head south onto the A64, continue past York to the A1M, then north. The rest of the route was unknown but they all had maps and knew where Carlisle was so they too could have their own adventure.

Back in the Showground watching the service crews head south was a fulfilling sight, knowing that they knew we were up against it and were just doing as they were told: a very satisfying situation.

The next plan was what can we give all the crews to get them to Hamsterley. The first crews were already about to start Langdale 2. I spoke to Lloyd and asked him to issue a bulletin at the stop line to send the crews back to the Showground and the passage control would be in the layby outside the venue where more instructions would be issued.

Instructions were very similar to the service crews but we googled the mileages from Malton to the A1M and then up to J58 where we came off onto the A68 for the time control at Swann House. Time for section allowed? We had not got a clue; just get there: these were extreme conditions but you could not speed due to the road conditions and the Competition Trials Regulations were not broken. The time from the Langdale stop to the TC Swann House was a lot longer than expected and by the time the first crews arrived at Hamsterley the rally was three hours late, but at least the crews were doing the stage twice.

Bob and I manned the Passage Control at the Showground as the planned crew had to go home and we managed to speak to all the crews who thought Yorkshire had been one hell of a challenge. How I wished this was going to be the last!

As we had official cars all over the place and the two big 4X4s we had for closing vehicles were tied up doing other jobs, Bob and I decided to close from the Showground up to Carlisle. After the last car had gone we went back into the Showground to say goodbye, as the Kall Kwik competitors were having their presentation, and to thank everybody for a good day's work. Just as I was about to leave at 7pm I had a phone call from two crews who I asked to drive the revised route and it had taken them three hours but all was clear. The whole event was now on a road route from the Showground via Leeds to Hamsterley with us being tail end Charlie.

Coming onto the York bypass we saw Nick Pinkett in the Saab 96 parked up in the lay by. They had called the RAC for recovery up to Carlisle as the engine had blown up. "Not to worry," said Nick. 'I brought a spare engine and we will put it in tonight when we get to Carlisle." Commitment or what we thought! This was the spirit of the Roger Albert Clark Rally coming through, no matter what happens we will continue to run.

I have very little recollection of the journey up to Hamsterley. I didn't fall asleep but was on the phone a lot and just thinking about what we had done during the event so far and hoping that the snow didn't fall in Scotland as I knew we only had a very light dusting of snow and all was planned OK for Sunday.

On coming into Hamsterley down the grove the area was hectic to say the least with competitors and management crews everywhere, a true hive of activity. After we got through them and onto the link road towards the start the road was very icy and we came across the Saab 900, the last car on the road going nowhere up the hill. We got in front and towed him the rest of the way to the start line.

Grit and salt broke up some of the ice

Winner Stefaan Stouf

With the Stage Commander we tried to work out who had done their first lap, who was off in stage and who was doing their second lap. Two more cars arrived to do their second attempt, the Saab who we had just towed said they were only doing it once so we had all crews in. As we came out of the other end we were now four hours behind time, but all the marshals we spoke to were happy that they'd had the chance to see the crews twice, which was a nice bonus.

As we exited Hamsterley towards the PC which was about five miles after the stage at the first place with mobile phone coverage, we were passed by two of the cars which the recovery unit had got out of the ditches and were heading up to Shepherdshield. The A68 at 1am. with the wind blowing the snow across the road. was not a welcoming sight. Bob said to me: "Can you see the road?" "No," was my reply. "Good," said Bob. "I thought I had gone to sleep!" Just then we hit a cat's eye so we found the middle of the road and for the next five or six miles we ran on the cat's eyes but were not sure which side of the road we were on: the conditions were awful.

We arrived at Shepherdshield to be greeted by John Clayton, the Stage Commander, who said: "I thought you could have done our stage twice too". I laughed and he said that at 8.30pm it seemed a good idea but at 2am he was glad they were only running once. The stage, due to the lateness, was as icy as anything. John said all the marshals were coming out reverse direction as the public road out was horrendous and not really passable.

As we were closing the stage we passed the Mini car 58 straddled across a small dyke, not going anywhere. Then we came across the last car on the road not going anywhere up the hill to J10. After trying to push it up the hill for 10 minutes we all reversed back to the bottom of the hill and attached our invisible tow rope to pull him up the hill and to J10 where he managed to pull past us and onto the stop line. The marshals at the PC at the end of the stage were very happy to see us as they had arrived early at the location due to the weather and now, nine hours later, were just standing down but happy they had done a great job for the event.

It was now 2.30am and I managed to contact Nicola in Carlisle to persuade her to go to bed, and not wait up as this was going to be a hell of a drive in. For the first time in seven years she very reluctantly left the Racecourse to go to bed before I arrived back in for the night. How glad I was that she did that. After the stage the road went back into the woods and we came across three cars with management cars stopped in the middle of the road. We didn't know why until we stopped and the road was like glass. Each of the rally cars was just moving behind the management cars to get a tow up the small hills. At least they looked like small hills when I did the road book. But on sheet ice they were mountains and the rally cars were really struggling. After the three crews got to the top and past the radio masts we heard on the radio that the three crews who were off in the stage had been recovered and were on their way via road route to Carlisle. Bob said, they wouldn't get up that hill so we will reverse back and pull them up.

Reversing a Pathfinder in total darkness on sheet ice for about a mile and half was a great piece of driving. When we got to the top of the hill all three cars were happily driving up it. "Why did we bother?" I said to Bob. "Well at least they saw that we cared for them to go back," said Bob and I had to agree.

As we got out onto the Greenhead road there was now a convoy of 18 cars and management crews all travelling together, the conditions were that bad. When we pulled into the Racecourse at 3.30am the Service Area Commander John Linsdey was still taking times off the crews and time cards and greeted me with: "A little later than you said we would be finishing!" What an understatement and what a hell of a day's motor sport.

I said to Bob: "Friday and Saturday were planned as the easy days. The big day starts tomorrow with 71 stage miles planned." By the time we got all the times into the results system and agreed the restart times and order for the morning it was 4am so up to the hotel and hit the bed at 4.30am. First car away in the morning was 8.30am so up out of bed for 7.30am.

Sunday 28 November
My phone rang at 7.20am and t was Franca Davenport from car 40 asking what her restart time was. Yes, I was sound asleep.

Nicola quickly got showered and off to Dumfries to scrutineer the Clubmans crews and Bob and I got into the car to head north. As we pulled onto the M74 I rang Nicola to ask what this black thing was I was driving on. She informed me that it was tarmac: we hadn't seem it for such a long time and it was novel and dry, so Scotland should work.

Not knowing what the weather conditions were going to do, I issued yet another bulletin from the Racecourse for the road section from Ae to Twiglees, as this road was very rural and any snow would have made the road impassable. I knew about this before the event and we had planned a full re-route and had it already drawn and copied so we could issue it to the crews, which we did at the time control prior to Ae.

Bob and I headed to Beattock to see the crews out of Ae. As the course cars came out they said the stage was great and the rally could really start in earnest, which was a great feeling after two very hard days. I then had my morning phone call from the kitchen of Jonathan Ferries' house on the update for the Kielder stages for Monday and Newcastleton later that day. Rooken and Highfield had over 20 inches of snow, and he was still waiting for the plough man to come back to him. Newcastleton had eight to 10 inches of snow, but the stage commander was due there very soon.

As I sat in the car at Beattock for about 30 minutes on the phone to various people, Jonathan phoned back. The plough man had been put on 24-hour call-out and had just moved four inches of snow from the A68 from Carter Bar to Otterburn, which we were using. But the main problem, he said, was the wind that was due on Sunday night and even if he did plough the stages then all the snow would be back in the morning and it would all need doing again. Coupled with this, I needed a service area in Kielder which also needed ploughing, and another landowner to get permission from and additional risk assessments to get approved.

Sunday ran largely to plan in Scotland

I made the decision there and then to cancel the Monday stages, so here we were 10.30am on Sunday morning with the first cars going through Ae with a full day ahead of them, knowing I had cancelled the last day of the rally. However...

"Jonathan," I said, "what do you think would happen if I asked if we could use Kershope on Monday, on the understanding we find a stage and let you know what we use." I knew that the main problem would be closing the wood officially for a CROW order, which are only given for the day of the event and not the day before or after. This would be the stumbling block. Jonathan's reply was that he would have to talk to the big boss. Let's remember that this is now Sunday and we are trying to do something that is not allowed, and by the way can I have an answer by 12 noon please so I can start planning.

Unbeknown to me, after the problems we had had on Friday and Saturday, and surprisingly, the Forestry Commission people do speak to their colleagues in different areas. Jonathan had already made the suggestion to his boss that if I asked this question, what would the answer be.

The main man had already done his homework on the CROW legislation and was wanting to help the event, which I am really grateful for. There is a clause in the legislation which allows him to make the order under extreme circumstances and with the snow that had fallen it was agreed that this was covered by the legislation. By 11.45am I had my answer: we had permission to run Kershope on Monday on the 'find a stage and tell me what you have done' basis. What a top man!

So after a few phone calls as we were heading down to Heathhall I called an officials briefing in the service area at 1pm to discuss what was happening on Monday to formulate a plan. All the course cars that ran at the front of the field were there, my deputy John Trevethick and Competitor Liaison Officer Mike Sones: everybody who needed to be there was.

The phone then rang from Nicola. The two rescue units from Edinburgh were stuck in snow and would not get to the Newcastleton stage. So our only option was to cancel the first running of the stage and send the competitors from Twiglees 2 back to Carlisle to service while the rescue units from Ae moved to Newcastleton for the second run and we could bring this forward by one hour, which we did.

As I was driving to Heathhall, I then got a phone call from Jon Binns, the Stage Commander for Newcastleton, which used the Scottish section of Kershope and the English side. He said that the stage was fully set up on the Scottish side to junction 12, but it was very difficult to get up the hill from 14 to 16 and this was very icy and on the English side the snow was a good 8 to 10 inches.

The adventure of Monday morning

Don't worry I said; I will be there before 2pm to make an assessment as to what we were doing but plan to run the stage full length and don't allow two-wheel drive vehicles into the stage.

So as I headed into Heathhall I knew I had a plan for Monday in the forests but had now been told that these same woods were too deep to rally tonight. What a problem! After rallying the troops and explaining what my thoughts were for Monday, I picked three more of the team to come to Kershope to help. Steve Herbert and Jim Holmes in the Link Car and Bryan Marshal and Paul Arch, both in Land Rover Defenders; what great vehicles for the conditions, plus Nicola who had the trip meter installed in her vehicle, which I would need to do the new mileages and re-routes.

As we arrived at about 3pm we had about an hour of daylight to drive the forest to find the route for Monday and assess the stage for that night. I drew the plan for Monday on the maps of the team who set off and made roads. On the first pass round their answer was wow, what a ride! Well do it again, and wait back here so I followed, with Nicola driving now. Wow was definitely not the word Nicola used. After about three miles, I got: "Oh my god, you are driving this?"

When we got to the top of the hill at J16 I sent the Defenders down and up for an assessment. They reported OK, but we were losing grip from 15 to 16. Remembering Shepherdshield from last night in the ice I decided it was safer for the crews and the stage to cut it short at J12 and bring the crews out at the bottom of the valley onto the tarmac road.

Attention then passed back onto Monday. It was now 4.15pm and the dark was coming in. Looking at the proposed stage again I decided there was a little too much uphill in it and we changed the layout to try and keep as much flat road in the stage or downhill and the new stage was born at 4.78 miles: not bad after no great plan. The Monday stage commanders had come across to set the Kershope stage up.

As we finished the revised stage and got onto the public highway the team split. Nicola went back to Carlisle to receive the crews and draw the new re-route and Bob and I went to Newcastleton. As the crews had already left Carlisle by the time we had shortened the stage I needed to issue yet another amendment for the stage. I also needed to tell them about what was happening on Monday, and that they would get a bulletin back in Carlisle to confirm this.

So I waited on the access road up to the stage to issue the amendment. When Brian Avery arrived I asked him to come back after his run through the stage to help here as it was likely to get busy later on with crews queuing for their amendment and management crews trying to find out what was happening.

We issued all the crews the new stages and told them what we were hoping to do on Monday. I must say what a great reaction I got from each and every crew: it was very much appreciated.

As the stage finished we heard on the radio that nine cars were off in the stage so with the closing car we decided to help and pull some of the cars out. All the offs were cars in ditches not coming back onto the road as it was again sheet ice. When we got back to Carlisle around 10pm, Nicola had re-written the route for Monday and had printed off enough copies for the whole event to be issued at the out control the following morning. Another plan sorted.

Back at the hotel at 11pm I was not sleepy and started to watch the cricket in the bar, having a very nice glass of coke. At 2am the day's adrenalin had worked its way through my body and I went to bed and straight to sleep.

Monday 26 November
Due to the new stages I had put back the start time for the first car from Carlisle to 9am, with the first car into stage at 10.14am. The alarm was on for 6am as we had to be out for 6.30am. Before everyone went to bed I requested that all officials who did not need to be in Carlisle made their way to Kershope as it was going to be busy. We had to stop all management crews and spectator vehicles from going up the hill from Kershope bridge or the road would have got gridlocked and the stage would not have run.

As we arrived at Newcastleton it was obvious that overnight about another two to three inches of snow had fallen. As we got to Kershope Bridge, Chrys Worboys had got the marshals who had arrived early gritting the hill. If we didn't get it clear and wide for two cars to pass we would not get the stage. By 9am we had 20 people moving snow and gritting the

The Sunbeam Lotus of Jen-Pierre Ansiaux

hill and you could see the ice breaking and tarmac coming through: this was going to work.

As we got all the marshals into the stage and the final course cars came through, Brian Avery said he would wait at the exit road to stop vehicles coming the other way so we could keep the route back to the start clear and open for the second pass of the stage.

The only way we could make the stage work and get the leading crews back to Carlisle for the ceremonial finish at 1.30pm was to let the historic cars and the first 15 main event cars into the stage first. Then we held the remainder of the field so we could send the historic cars back in for their second run and the first six main field as these would be required for the procession into Carlisle. After this we then ran the cars in turn into the stage.

As Bob and I moved from the start to the finish of the stage to welcome the crews out of the last stage, all the planning had worked and we followed Steffan Stouf back to the Premier Inn for the last official control. We had done such a good job of getting the cars around the Kershope loop that we were back at 12.15pm and didn't need to leave until 1pm so I told the crews they had 45 minutes to wait before the finish. They didn't seem to mind as they were all out of their cars talking about what they had just done.

Chris Melling

Now was the time to take advantage of the spare 45 minutes and go into the hotel for a quick shower and the first shave of the weekend to look smart for the finish and prize giving. I don't think anybody noticed the car was there but I wasn't. I came back out at 12.50pm just in time to start getting the cars in order for the final procession into the city centre for the ceremonial finish.

As we arrived in the centre of Carlisle the mayor was waiting to receive the crews with Border TV and BBC Radio all covering the finish. Well it was all over. I listened to the comments that the crews were giving to Bob Milloy, the commentator, and it sounded that not only the organisers had had a hard time but every crew had also had their own challenges during the weekend.

As the last car went over the line at 2.45pm, results were due to go provisional at 3pm at the Racecourse so we got up there so that I could sign them off. As 3.30pm came, we went final and 10 minutes later Bob Milloy started the prizegiving and invited me to the stage.

What can I say about the standing ovation that followed as I walked to the stage? It was very emotional for me as four days of total stress had just come to an end and I was getting this wonderful reception from the crews. I could not look out at the crowd as I could feel a tear starting to run down my face but promised myself that I could not do that just quite yet. I wanted to speak and thank everyone for what I believe will be the event remembered for years and years to come.

I don't write a script, and I don't write any notes; I prefer to speak from the heart and say it how it is. I hope that my passion and admiration for the crews, especially the marshals and the spectators, who all made the 2010 Roger Albert Clark Rally a huge success was clear to be seen.

So we got into the presentation and Dave Hemingway, one of the six crews who has done each event and won the Open Rally for the second time wanted to say a few words and embarrass me for a second time. Being given the Spirit of the Rally award by the crews on the event on behalf of the whole organising team was a great feeling, and the whole team appreciated the standing ovation that the team got.

Roger Albert Clark Rally 2010: the year of the snow

Roger Albert Clark Rally 2011:
the eighth edition

Overall winners: Gwyndaf Evans and John Millington

Evans at the double
The 2011 rally
Friday 2 to Monday 5 December
169 stage miles
24 special stages
Start: Duncombe Park, Helmsley
Overnight 1: Duncombe Park, Helmsley
Overnight 2 & 3: Carlisle Racecourse
Finish: Carlisle Racecourse
60 starters
34 finishers

Open Rally winners: Martyn Hawkswell and Nick Welch

Roger Albert Rally 2011: the eighth edition

Steve Perez in the Heathhall stage

Gwyndaf Evans and John Millington dominated the eighth Roger Albert Clark Rally as Evans became the first driver to win the epic event twice and Millington won it for the third time.

Evans, on his first competitive outing since the snowbound 2010 event, was majestic as he powered through the forests in the Ford Escort Mk2 from Viking Motorsport. "It's a proper event and the team has been magnificent again," said the event winner.

This was one of the toughest Roger Albert's yet with many leading runners side-lined before the finish at Carlisle on Monday afternoon including Paul Griffiths and Sam Collis, who took the fight to Evans for the first two days. But the real sting in the tail was 18 miles in the snowbound Kershope stage on Monday morning. That stage cost David Stokes and Guy Weaver second place as Tim Pearcey and Neil Shanks swept ahead thanks to a smart tyre choice.

Day one: Friday

Friday's opening salvo of four stages, two in Duncombe Park and two in Dalby, should have been a modest lead into the real meat of the rally to follow. But Duncombe was very slippery and Dalby was both slippery and rough in places. By the end of the night, the hopes of four leading crews had been dashed.

First to go were 2010 winners Stefaan Stouf and Joris Erard who slid their Escort Mk2 off in the first Dalby and rolled gently. Once recovered, the car restarted and they rejoined on Saturday, but head-gasket woes soon put them out for good. Next, Phil Collins and Nicky Grist slid off on the second run through Dalby and beached the Opel Ascona on a bank. They lost three and a half minutes before getting going again. "I am stupid," said Collins of the incident. A bigger off 24 hours later in Hamsterley ended their rally, while engine and gearbox woes put the Porsche 911 of Tim Mason/Graham Wild out in Dalby.

The other casualty was Marcus Dodd, a late substitution for Peter Egerton in the Escort Mk2 that Dodd's team prepares. "We hit the big hole in Dalby," said Dodd. "It went sideways and I thought it was going to spin but it fell over." Damage was limited, but Dodd and Andrew Bargery elected to retire.

Robin Shuttleworth and
Ron Roughead in Langdale

Andy Madge

David Stokes

Up front, there were no such problems for Evans/Millington and they ended the leg 1m14s ahead of Griffiths and Collis (Escort Mk2). "We've had a good evening, but a big hole in Dalby launched the car in the air and I was worried that we'd damaged something," said Evans. "Gwyndaf is on another planet," acknowledged Griffiths, who took up the early chase of the flying Welshman.

Stokes/Weaver were nicely in contention 19s behind Griffiths but it nearly went wrong on the opening stage when Stokes slid wide in Duncombe Park and whacked a tree with a rear corner of the Escort. Fortunately, damage was cosmetic and it was tidied up at service.

Pearcey/Shanks slotted into fourth, with Pearcey happier once he'd sorted out the brake balance as they ended the opening leg 5s up on Yorkshiremen Charlie Taylor and Steve Bielby at the start of an epic run for their Escort Mk2.

Day two: Saturday
While Friday evening proved to be unexpectedly tough, everyone knew that Saturday would be a real challenge. It started under a blue sky in Yorkshire and ended in rain and sleet in Shepherdshield.

Roger Albert Clark Rally 2011: the eighth edition

Peter Smith and Paul Wakely in Langdale

Tim Pearcey

Stephen Higgins

The bare facts are that Evans extended his lead by 70s, but that doesn't do justice to a long, hard day. "It's been a tough evening," said Evans as he arrived at Carlisle. "I had to do Hamsterley and Shepherdshield with no wipers and that was hard work." Evans also struggled to find his way around Croft on his first visit to the race circuit. Aside from the wiper issue, the Viking Motorsport Escort had run like clockwork through a 13-hour day that comprised over 50 stage miles and nearly 290 road miles.

But the Welshman had been kept on his toes all day by a dogged challenge from Griffiths, who drove a fine day to regularly run within a few seconds of Evans. "We've had a very good day and I've just had to keep it going. But Hamsterley was very slippery," added Griffiths who consolidated second place by extending the margin over Stokes to 1m21s.

To complete a pretty trouble-free day for the top three, Stokes/Weaver also had a clear run with just a puncture towards the end of Shepherdshield to report and that only cost them around 10s as they drove to the finish of the Kielder stage.

But while Evans, Griffiths and Stokes had clean runs, life was much more stressful for Pearcey who ran the second loop of his native Yorkshire stages with only second and fourth gear. He was also on the cusp of maximum lateness for the afternoon after a borrowed gearbox was fitted, but he got to Carlisle

still in fourth, 1m15s down on Stokes.

"I don't think we woke up quickly enough this morning," said Taylor. But once into his stride he had another strong run to keep the pressure on Pearcey to be the best Yorkshireman. "We were steady in the last two," added Taylor of the slippery Hamsterley and Shepherdshield. It was a view shared by many and most of those who were slowed at the scene of Collins' accident in Hamsterley admitted to easing back the pace.

"Phil Collins was off in front of me and I just backed it off after that," said sixth-placed Leigh Armstrong, partnered by his brother Chris in their Escort Mk2. Once again they were running strongly and were embroiled in a battle with Guy Woodcock/Graham Dance (Escort Mk2) and Peter Smith/Paul Wakely (Escort Mk1). Woodcock, in the first non-BDG powered car was driving a blinder with Pinto power and flew the Hamsterley and Shepherdshield stages to make up some of the time he was losing on the power stages. "That was a cracking evening," said Woodcock, one of the only drivers to enjoy the pair of stages.

Day three: Sunday

Ice, snow and sleet were all part of the mix for Sunday, with 60 stage miles in the Scottish borders to keep the survivors working hard on this tough event. First up was 14 miles in Ae, with snow and ice on the later higher sections of the forest and it duly claimed the Armstrong brothers. Griffiths rates Ae as one of his favourite stages and he started the day knowing that this was his best chance to attack Evans. But Evans wasn't about to be caught napping and was 6s faster. Then, with snow falling in Twiglees, Griffiths punctured three miles from the finish and drove out, losing any chance of grabbing time back.

"That was our chance to push and we were trying," said Griffiths. However, on the second run through Ae it all went wrong and they slid off the road and out of the rally with damaged suspension when seemingly destined for second place. It was a bitter blow after a storming drive. Ae claimed two more top 10 scalps on the second visit as Smith/Wakely ended a great run with a roll and Baz Jordan/Lee Carter also went out in their Escort Mk2 when looking good for a top 10. Their fresh Mark Solloway built car had been delivered new to scrutineering on Friday.

Guy Smith and Patrick Walsh

Bob Bean

Pascal Regnier

However, through all the drama, Evans continued to be the model of consistency and emerged from two runs of Newcastleton on Sunday evening with a whopping seven-minute lead over Stokes/Weaver. But there had been drama in the Evans camp when the gearbox failed in Twiglees and left him only fifth gear. The management service team changed the 'box in around 15 minutes and sent him off to Newcastleton. "The boys did a very good job," said Evans of the moment that could have ended his rally.

The second Ae had dealt Pearcey's bid to catch Stokes a blow when he caught a rear puncture five miles from the finish. "We were on an absolute mission," said Pearcey. He also now had to watch his mirrors for the flying Taylor, who had lost out on the first Twiglees with a puncture but flew the second run to end the day 43s adrift of Pearcey in the fight for third.

The amazing drive from Woodcock/Dance, one of the best of the entire rally, showed no sign of faltering as they stepped up to fifth, far ahead of Woodcock's pre-event ambition of a top 10 finish. Into sixth came Keith Robathan and Phil Clarke who got quicker and quicker as the Scot got used to the Rally Xtreme Escort Mk2, but he felt he was losing out on the night stages.

Packing out the lower reaches of the top 10 as the cars filed back into Carlisle came Phil and Mick Squires (Ford Escort Mk2), Guy Smith/Patrick Walsh (Escort Mk1), Christophe Jacob/Stephane Prevot (Escort Mk2) and Steve Perez/Paul Spooner (Lancia

Nick Woodman and Chris Parsons

Stratos). The Stratos was sounding better than ever and running superbly to the delight of thousands of fans in the forests.

Day four: Monday
The final day was intended to take in two runs through a mammoth 18-mile stage in Kershope, with some of it uncharted territory and tricky to read from the maps. But there was another twist in the story after around four inches of snow fell overnight. Rally manager Colin Heppenstall battled to get the stage running but cancelled the second run to get the rally back on schedule.

With over seven minutes in hand, Evans could afford to take a measured approach. "That was really tough," said Evans as he emerged from Kershope, with his lead intact. "There were tramlines in a few places; I was very cautious," he said.

However, the winning margin went out to nearly eight minutes as Stokes struggled on the wrong tyres. A smart call by Pearcey and his management vehicle, crewed by Darren Moon, put Pearcey's car on the Dunlop snow tyres that Moon ran in 2010 and he took nearly two minutes off a frustrated Stokes to grab second place. "We had an enormous moment half way through and I thought we were going off," said an elated Pearcey after a mighty result.

There was little change in the final top 10, but a jubilant Perez moved up to eighth as Smith slid off into a water-filled ditch. He took a maximum but salvaged a deserved tenth place.

The classes
The contest for victory in the Open Rally raged all the way to final stage as Martyn Hawkswell and Nick Welch (Ford Escort Mk2) had to cope with a relentless chase from the Toyota Corolla of Andy Madge and Pat Cooper. Despite consuming oil at a fair rate and going off on black ice on a road section, the Toyota was seldom little more than a minute down on the Vauxhall-powered Escort until dropping four minutes with an off in Kershope. Best of the F1000 pack after a great performance until they went off in Kershope were Mick Smith and Paul Osmond (Nissan Micra), so class victory fell to Mark Simpson and Richard Burdon.

2010 winners Stefaan Stouf and Joris Erard

Bob Bean and Malcolm Smithson were aiming for a top 15 overall finish in their Category 1 Lotus Cortina but slid off in Ae when the throttle stuck open and took a maximum. They had more than enough in hand over the three Saabs to still take the category as Nick Pinkett/Hugh Myers won Class B3 in their four-stroke 96 and Jim Valentine/Jonathan Lodge won Class B1 from Stephen Higgins/Caroline Lodge in a battle of the two-strokes.

In Class C1 Stuart and Linda Cariss drove a quietly impressive rally to win in their 1300cc Escort Mk1, while Class C2 was incredibly close among three Escort Mk1s. George and Jacqueline Bryson went into the final day just 1s up on Chris Blake/Tony Walker, with Dave Watkins/Paul Train only half a minute behind. Bryson emerged from Kershope still ahead. "That last stage was horrendous," said Bryson, who battled ahead after running third on the opening two legs.

Guy Smith/Patrick Walsh romped to Class C3 victory, with over five minutes in hand over the Saab 96 of Colin Hope and Nick Patrick, which set a cracking pace. In Class C4, Perez/Spooner scored a resounding victory over the Porsche 911 of Peter McDowell/Max Utting.

Woodcock/Dance won Class D3 by a huge margin after a fabulous performance, while in Class E for the FIA specification cars it was Robathan/Clarke from Jacob/Prevot.

Hemingway's way

Dave Hemingway is typical of the clubman competitors who make the Roger Albert Clark Rally such a special event. He'd been a loyal supporter of the rally from the very start back in 2004 and approached each event with determination, resourcefulness and good humour in equal parts.

The Yorkshireman and his co-driver Simon Ashton were attempting to win the Open Rally for the third time in four years, but the drama started even before the rally. On Thursday, a gearbox oil leak was found on their 2-litre Vauxhall powered Ford Escort Mk2. Out came the 'box for attention and then on Friday, the day of scrutineering and the rally start, a major electrical failure had the crew rushing around.

Worse was to come in Duncombe Park on Friday evening's third stage when a half shaft failed and

Personal view: the Stratos in Ae forest

Gwyndaf Evans

inflicted damage to the diff. They missed two stages while the car was towed back to service and the waiting crew. They had a spare shaft, but they had to scour the service area to find the parts needed to repair the diff. The volunteer crew then worked outside to rebuild the diff and finally finished at 2am.

Any chance of a good result was gone, but that didn't deter Hemmingway and he enjoyed a strong run through Saturday's stages in Yorkshire, playing his trademark ice cream van chimes through the forests. The drama continued on Sunday with propshaft and gearbox changes and an hour in a ditch in Ae. Ultimately, the final result was of little importance this time; the achievement of completing this special rally was reward enough.

Personal view: Paul Lawrence

I've always loved the noise that rally cars make. Standing in a damp forest on a winter day listening to the approach of a high-revving BDG just has to be one of the best things about this glorious sport.

But even the Escorts were upstaged on this year's Roger Albert Clark Rally by the Lancia Stratos of Steve Perez. As a loyal supporter of this fantastic event, Perez deserved a trouble-free run with the Italian super car, for it has severely tested his patience on previous editions.

This time around the Stratos sounded better than ever and I heard it approaching the downhill hairpin in Ae Forest from some distance. These were proper RAC conditions; it had just snowed, and the cloud was hanging low over the hills, threatening more snow.

Perez attacked the hairpin with gusto and then fired the Stratos into the fast, flowing section of stage that hugs the tumbling Water of Ae. The noise of the Stratos echoed off the valley sides for several minutes and it made the hairs on the back of my neck stand up. For a few moments, it was 1979 and I was 19 years old once more.

2011 ROGER ALBERT CLARK RALLY: ENTRY LIST

No	Driver	Co-driver	Car	Class
1	Stefaan Stouf	Joris Erard	Ford Escort Mk2	D5
2	Gwyndaf Evans	John Millington	Ford Escort RS	D5
4	Paul Griffiths	Sam Collis	Ford Escort RS1800	D5
5	Phil Collins	Nicky Grist	Opel Ascona 400	D5
6	Tim Pearcey	Neil Shanks	Ford Escort RS1800	D5
7	David Stokes	Guy Weaver	Ford Escort RS1600	C5
8	Tim Mason	Graham Wild	Porsche 911	C4
10	Nick Woodman	Chris Parsons	Ford Escort Mk2	D5
11	Phil Squires	Mick Squires	Ford Escort RS1800	D5
12	Steve Perez	Paul Spooner	Lancia Stratos	C4
14	Charlie Taylor	Steve Bielby	Ford Escort Mk2	D5
15	Leigh Armstrong	Chris Armstrong	Ford Escort Mk2	D5
16	Neville Jones	Chris Davies	Ford Escort Mk2 RS1800	D5
17	Barry Jordan	Lee Carter	Ford Escort Mk2	E5
18	Peter Smith	Paul Wakely	Ford Escort Mk1	C5
19	Matthew Robinson	Michael Gilby	Ford Escort Mk2	D5
20	Guy Woodcock	Graham Dance	Ford Escort RS2000	D3
21	Tim Freeman	Paul Barden	Ford Escort RS1800	D5
22	Christophe Jacob	Stephane Prevot	Ford Escort RS	E5
23	Terry Nowlan	Ben Giles	Ford Escort RS1600	C5
24	Marcus Dodd	Andrew Bargery	Ford Escort Mk2	D5
25	Robin Shuttleworth	Ron Roughead	Ford Escort Mk1 RS2000	C3
26	Pascal Regnier	Maryline Furnemont	Ford Escort Mk2	D5
27	Guy Smith	Patrick Walsh	Ford Escort Mk1	C3
28	David Watkins	Paul Train	Ford Escort Mk1 Twin Cam	C2
29	Gerald Braithwaite	Katy Mashiter	Talbot Sunbeam Lotus	D5
30	Peter McDowell	Matt Utting	Porsche 911RS	C4
31	Steve Graham	Tony Graham	Lancia Fulvia	C1
32	Andrew Borthwick	Dave Robson	Talbot Sunbeam Lotus	D5
33	Colin Hope	Nick Patrick	Saab 96 V4	C3
34	George Bryson	Jacqueline Bryson	Ford Escort Twin Cam	C2
35	Tony Ginns	Mark Ellis	Ford Escort Mexico	C2
36	David Lucking	Paul Lucking	Ford Escort Mk2	D3
37	Ian Hildreth	Stephen Stead	Ford Escort Mk2	D3
38	Mark Tugwell	Tim Tugwell	Hillman Avenger	C2
39	Chris Blake	Tony Walker	Ford Escort Mk1 Mexico	C2
40	Bob Bean	Malcolm Smithson	Ford Lotus Cortina Mk1	B4
41	Stuart Cariss	Linda Carris	Ford Escort Sport	C1
42	Jim Valentine	Jonathan Lodge	Saab 96 Sport	B1
43	Nick Pinkett	Hugh Myers	Saab 96 Sport	B3
44	Stephen Higgins	Caroline Lodge	Saab 96 Sport	B1
45	Lionel Hansen	Johan Jalet	Porsche 911SE	D5
46	Keith Robathan	Phil Clarke	Ford Escort Mk2	E5
51	Dave Hemingway	Simon Ashton	Ford Escort Mk2	G4
52	Martyn Hawkswell	Nick Welch	Ford Escort RS	G4
53	Richard Warne	Chris Deal	Ford Escort RS	G4
54	Malcolm Mawdsley	Kev Bardon	Subaru Impreza 2WD	G5
55	David Rawlings	Philip Weston	Porsche 911	G5
56	Magic McCombie	Craig Wallace	Saab 900	G4
57	Andy Madge	Pat Cooper	Toyota Corolla GT	G3
58	Nigel Barrett	Simon Law	Nissan Micra	G2
59	Kevin Jeffray	Joe Parsons	Nissan Micra	G1
60	Thomas Jordan	Nigel Hutchinson	Citroen C1	G1
61	Mick Smith	Paul Osmond	Nissan Micra	G1
62	Mark Simpson	Richard Burdon	Nissan Micra	G1

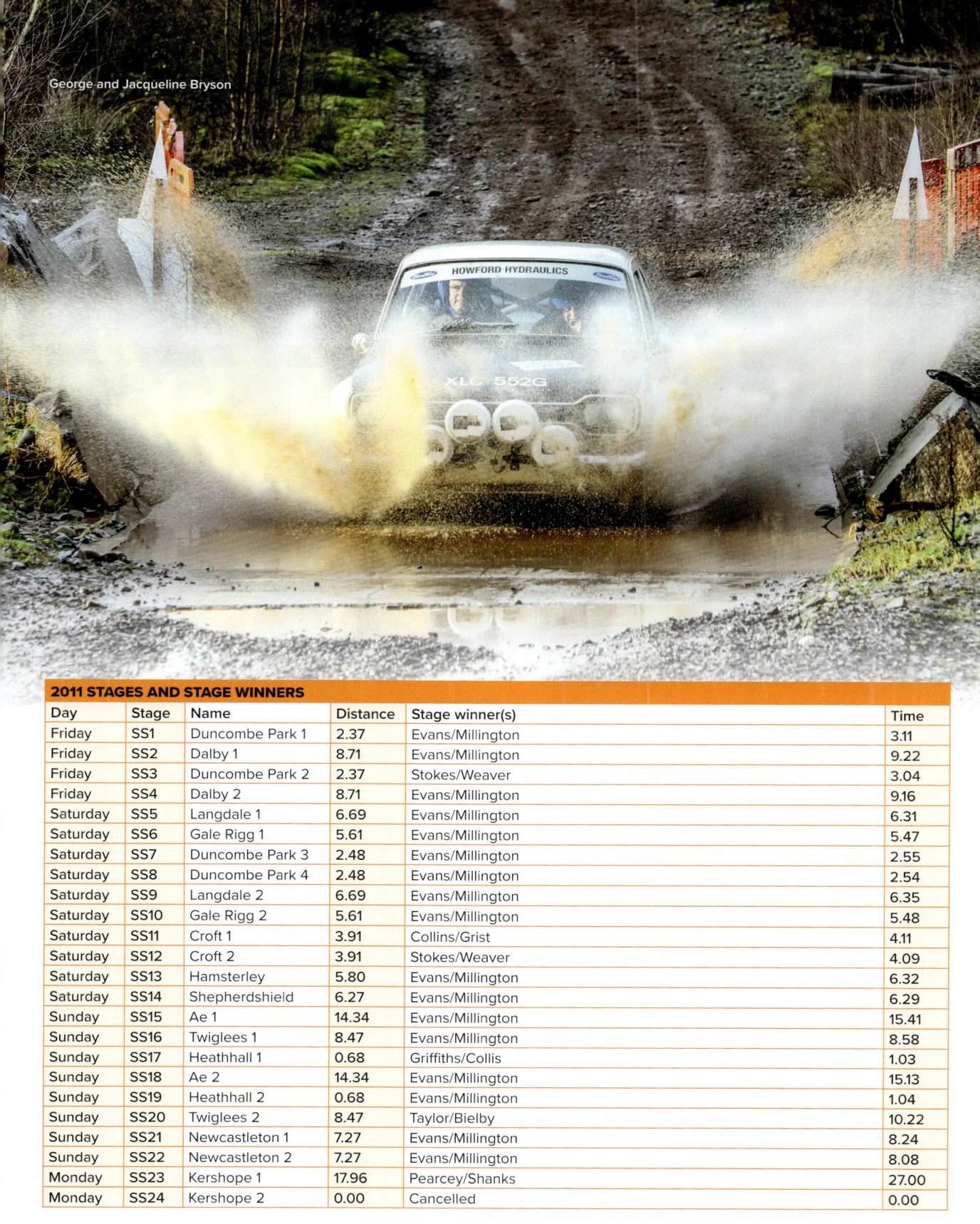

George and Jacqueline Bryson

2011 STAGES AND STAGE WINNERS

Day	Stage	Name	Distance	Stage winner(s)	Time
Friday	SS1	Duncombe Park 1	2.37	Evans/Millington	3.11
Friday	SS2	Dalby 1	8.71	Evans/Millington	9.22
Friday	SS3	Duncombe Park 2	2.37	Stokes/Weaver	3.04
Friday	SS4	Dalby 2	8.71	Evans/Millington	9.16
Saturday	SS5	Langdale 1	6.69	Evans/Millington	6.31
Saturday	SS6	Gale Rigg 1	5.61	Evans/Millington	5.47
Saturday	SS7	Duncombe Park 3	2.48	Evans/Millington	2.55
Saturday	SS8	Duncombe Park 4	2.48	Evans/Millington	2.54
Saturday	SS9	Langdale 2	6.69	Evans/Millington	6.35
Saturday	SS10	Gale Rigg 2	5.61	Evans/Millington	5.48
Saturday	SS11	Croft 1	3.91	Collins/Grist	4.11
Saturday	SS12	Croft 2	3.91	Stokes/Weaver	4.09
Saturday	SS13	Hamsterley	5.80	Evans/Millington	6.32
Saturday	SS14	Shepherdshield	6.27	Evans/Millington	6.29
Sunday	SS15	Ae 1	14.34	Evans/Millington	15.41
Sunday	SS16	Twiglees 1	8.47	Evans/Millington	8.58
Sunday	SS17	Heathhall 1	0.68	Griffiths/Collis	1.03
Sunday	SS18	Ae 2	14.34	Evans/Millington	15.13
Sunday	SS19	Heathhall 2	0.68	Evans/Millington	1.04
Sunday	SS20	Twiglees 2	8.47	Taylor/Bielby	10.22
Sunday	SS21	Newcastleton 1	7.27	Evans/Millington	8.24
Sunday	SS22	Newcastleton 2	7.27	Evans/Millington	8.08
Monday	SS23	Kershope 1	17.96	Pearcey/Shanks	27.00
Monday	SS24	Kershope 2	0.00	Cancelled	0.00

Roger Albert Clark Rally 2011: the eighth edition

Robin Shuttleworth

Steve Perez

2011 RESULTS

Overall	Class	No	Driver	Co-driver	Car	Class	Total
1	1	2	Gwyndaf Evans	John Millington	Ford Escort RS	D5	02:53:40
2	2	6	Tim Pearcey	Neil Shanks	Ford Escort RS1800	D5	03:01:32
3	1	7	David Stokes	Guy Weaver	Ford Escort RS1600	C5	03:02:06
4	3	14	Charlie Taylor	Steve Bielby	Ford Escort Mk2	D5	03:03:10
5	1	20	Guy Woodcock	Graham Dance	Ford Escort RS2000	D3	03:04:18
6	1	46	Keith Robathan	Phil Clarke	Ford Escort Mk2	E5	03:06:21
7	4	11	Phil Squires	Mick Squires	Ford Escort RS1800	D5	03:10:34
8	1	12	Steve Perez	Paul Spooner	Lancia Stratos	C4	03:11:21
9	2	22	Christophe Jacob	Stephane Prevot	Ford Escort RS	E5	03:12:02
10	1	27	Guy Smith	Patrick Walsh	Ford Escort Mk1	C3	03:17:24
11	5	45	Lionel Hansen	Johan Jalet	Porsche 911SE	D5	03:19:29
12	6	10	Nick Woodman	Chris Parsons	Ford Escort Mk2	D5	03:19:49
13	2	33	Colin Hope	Nick Patrick	Saab 96 V4	C3	03:23:03
14	2	30	Peter McDowell	Matt Utting	Porsche 911RS	C4	03:25:22
15	1	34	George Bryson	Jacqueline Bryson	Ford Escort Twin Cam	C2	03:30:47
16	2	39	Chris Blake	Tony Walker	Ford Escort Mk1 Mexico	C2	03:31:02
17	7	16	Neville Jones	Chris Davies	Ford Escort Mk2 RS1800	D5	03:31:24
18	3	28	David Watkins	Paul Train	Ford Escort Mk1 Twin Cam	C2	03:31:25
19	1	41	Stuart Cariss	Linda Carris	Ford Escort Sport	C1	03:34:19
20	1	40	Bob Bean	Malcolm Smithson	Ford Lotus Cortina Mk1	B4	03:34:49
21	8	32	Andrew Borthwick	Dave Robson	Talbot Sunbeam Lotus	D5	03:35:25
22	2	37	Ian Hildreth	Stephen Stead	Ford Escort Mk2	D3	03:39:24
23	4	35	Tony Ginns	Mark Ellis	Ford Escort Mexico	C2	03:56:29
24	1	43	Nick Pinkett	Hugh Myers	Saab 96 Sport	B3	04:00:54
25	1	42	Jim Valentine	Jonathan Lodge	Saab 96 Sport	B1	04:03:08
26	2	31	Steve Graham	Tony Graham	Lancia Fulvia	C1	04:24:40
27	2	44	Stephen Higgins	Caroline Lodge	Saab 96 Sport	B1	04:25:17
Ret		1	Stefaan Stouf	Joris Erard	Ford Escort Mk2	D5	Head gasket after SS10
Ret		4	Paul Griffiths	Sam Collis	Ford Escort RS1800	D5	Suspension damage SS18
Ret		5	Phil Collins	Nicky Grist	Opel Ascona 400	D5	Went off SS13
Ret		8	Tim Mason	Graham Wild	Porsche 911	C4	Gearbox and engine TC2B
Ret		15	Leigh Armstrong	Chris Armstrong	Ford Escort Mk2	D5	Accident SS15
Ret		17	Barry Jordan	Lee Carter	Ford Escort Mk2	E5	Stopped SS18
Ret		18	Peter Smith	Paul Wakely	Ford Escort Mk1	C5	Rolled SS18
Ret		19	Matthew Robinson	Michael Gilby	Ford Escort Mk2	D5	Engine SS9
Ret		21	Tim Freeman	Paul Barden	Ford Escort RS1800	D5	Engine failure after SS17
Ret		23	Terry Nowlan	Ben Giles	Ford Escort RS1600	C5	Engine MTC3
Ret		24	Marcus Dodd	Andrew Bargery	Ford Escort Mk2	D5	Accident damage SS4
Ret		25	Robin Shuttleworth	Ron Roughead	Ford Escort Mk1 RS2000	C3	Dropped valve MTC4
Ret		26	Pascal Regnier	Maryline Furnemont	Ford Escort Mk2	D5	Blown engine SS18
Ret		29	Gerald Braithwaite	Katy Mashiter	Talbot Sunbeam Lotus	D5	Broken propshaft SS10
Ret		36	David Lucking	Paul Lucking	Ford Escort Mk2	D3	Accident SS18
Ret		38	Mark Tugwell	Tim Tugwell	Hillman Avenger	C2	Dead engine

Gwyndaf Evans

Paul Griffiths and Sam Collis

2011 RESULTS: OPEN RALLY

Overall	Class	No	Driver	Co-driver	Car	Class	Total
1	1	52	Martyn Hawkswell	Nick Welch	Ford Escort RS	G4	03:13:30
2	1	57	Andy Madge	Pat Cooper	Toyota Corolla GT	G3	03:20:22
3	2	51	Dave Hemingway	Simon Ashton	Ford Escort Mk2	G4	03:38:02
4	1	62	Mark Simpson	Richard Burdon	Nissan Micra	G1	03:38:31
5	1	58	Nigel Barrett	Simon Law	Nissan Micra	G2	03:40:29
6	2	60	Thomas Jordan	Nigel Hutchinson	Citroen C1	G1	03:40:52
7	3	53	Richard Warne	Chris Deal	Ford Escort RS	G4	03:47:53
Ret		54	Malcolm Mawdsley	Kev Bardon	Subaru Impreza 2WD	G5	Alternator SS14
Ret		55	David Rawlings	Philip Weston	Porsche 911	G5	Misfire at service
Ret		56	Magic McCombie	Craig Wallace	Saab 900	G4	Detached flywheel
Ret		59	Kevin Jeffray	Joe Parsons	Nissan Micra	G1	Accident SS7
Ret		61	Mick Smith	Paul Osmond	Nissan Micra	G1	Went off SS23

Colin Hope

Dave Hemingway

Roger Albert Clark Rally 2011: the eighth edition

Leigh and Chris Armstrong

2011 RESULTS: KALL KWIK RALLY

Overall	Class	No	Driver	Co-driver	Car	Class	Total
1	1	121	Mathew Smith	Neil Colls	Ford KA	H2	00:46:25
2	1	141	Dave Brick	Rob Woodhouse	Ford Escort Mk2	H4	00:46:43
3	2	127	Rob Herrington	Charlotte Banner	Ford Escort Mk2	H4	00:50:23
4	1	135	Scott Smith	Jamie Couch	Ford Escort Mk2	H3	00:52:36
5	3	130	David May	David McLachan	BMW Compact	H4	00:53:01
6	2	137	Stewart Scott	Mark Casey	Ford Escort Mk1	H3	00:53:04
7	4	125	Robin Wilkinson	Ray Keith	Ford Focus RWD	H4	00:53:50
8	1	126	David Thirlwell	Dean Grabham	Ford Escort Mk1	H1	00:54:20
9	2	128	Nick Jarvis	Alan Carfrae	Suzuki Swift	H2	00:54:28
10	5	133	Bill Douglas	David Tearl	Volvo 244	H4	00:54:32
11	3	138	James Johns	Paul Watkins	Skoda Felicia	H2	00:56:14
12	4	140	Richard Sykes	Simon Taylor	Citroen C2 R2	H2	00:57:54
13	3	131	Brian Maguire	Ant Helliwell	Peugeot 205 GTi	H3	00:58:17
14	4	142	Charlie Blaney	Adrian Wilford	Ford Escort Mk2	H3	01:02:10
Ret		122	Philip Welch	Andrew Welborn	VW Golf Kit Car	H3	Mechanical SS9
Ret		123	Ian Coulson	Joe Jones	Talbot Sunbeam	H2	Retired
Ret		124	Mike Dowson	Dave Raw	Ford Escort Mk2	H3	Blown head gasket MTC2
Ret		129	Roger Priestnall	Jamie Forrest	Proton Satria	H2	Engine SS5
Ret		132	Ian Cartwright	Ian Jackson	Peugeot 205 GTi	H2	Rolled did not restart at MTC3
Ret		134	John O'Gorman	John Rutter	BMW E30	H4	Steering SS6
Ret		136	Mike Kent	Martin Knapp	Talbot Sunbeam Ti	H2	Brake failure after SS6

Andrew Borthwick

David Stokes

Paul Griffiths

2011 RESULTS: DE LACY RALLY

Overall	Class	No	Driver	Co-driver	Car	Class	Total
1	1	96	John Nicholson	Don Bramfoot	Ford Escort Sport	J3	00:37:27

2011 RESULTS: CLUBMANS RALLY

Overall	Class	No	Driver	Co-driver	Car	Class	Total
1	1	68	Iain Haining	Mairi Riddick	Vauxhall Nova	K2	01:00:30
2	1	66	Stephen Richards	Scott Smith	Ford Escort Mk2	K3	01:00:36
3	2	63	James Robertson	Claire Robertson	Citroen C2	K2	01:01:36
4	3	73	Dave Taylor	Katy Mashiter	Ford Escort	K2	01:02:28
5	4	71	Darren Martin	Martin Steele	Ford Puma	K2	01:07:47
Ret		64	Phil Jobson	Jerry Hettrick	Ford Escort Mk2	K2	Mechanical SS17
Ret		65	Mark Shaw	Ken Willan	Talbot Sunbeam Ti	K2	Went off SS15
Ret		67	Tam Brown	Mike Curry	Peugeot 205	K2	Rolled SS15
Ret		69	Greg McKnight	Chris McKnight	Vauxhall Nova	K2	Gearbox failure SS16
Ret		70	David Coleman	Josh Davison	Skoda Felicia	K1	Missed SS16
Ret		72	Roy Eide Johansen	Mark Simpson	Ford Escort Mk1	K3	Lost drive SS20

2011 RESULTS: KERSHOPE CHALLENGE

Overall	Class	No	Driver	Co-driver	Car	Class	Total
1	1	98	Alan Hughes	Ken Bills	Ford Escort RS2000	L3	00:59:15
2	1	99	Bill Lymburn	James Hastings	Ford Escort Mk2	L4	01:05:58

Peter Smith

Charlie Taylor

Roger Albert Clark Rally 2011: the eighth edition

Roger Albert Clark Rally 2012:
the ninth edition

Overall winners: Marty McCormack and Phil Clarke

McCormack the first

The 2012 rally

Friday 23 to Sunday 25 November
158 stage miles
24 special stages
Start: Pickering Showground
Overnight 1: Pickering Showground
Overnight 2: H&H Auctions, Carlisle
Finish: H&H Auctions, Carlisle
78 starters
51 finishers

Open Rally winners: Martyn Hawkswell and Nick Welch

Roger Albert Rally 2012: the ninth edition

Will Midgley and Jonathan Driver

Martin McCormack and Phil Clarke won the ninth Roger Albert Clark Rally after a sensational fight with Steve Bannister and Kevin Rae. As McCormack turned up the pressure on the final day, he edged ahead of Bannister to finally win by just 17s after 160 stage miles and nearly three hours of flat out driving.

The stop line of the final 17-miler in Kershope on Sunday afternoon was charged with atmosphere. Bannister, who led from Yorkshire on Friday evening, had lost the lead on the penultimate stage and started Kershope 2s down on McCormack. As ever, 'Banner' gave his all, but knew that a late spin had cost him dear as he sat on the stop line. He slumped forward in his seat, head in hands, knowing that the rally had slipped away from him.

Sure enough, 45s later, McCormack arrived to secure his win and his elation matched Bannister's dejection at the end of a rally that both men deserved to win. "It was so tricky in there and we didn't know if we'd done enough," said McCormack. "I love this event."

Their stunning battle had gripped thousands of fans who made this the biggest and best Roger Albert so far. While Will Onions and John Millington bagged third overall, 74-year old Bob Bean and Malcolm Smithson won Category 1 and Martyn Hawkswell and Nick Welch repeated their 2011 Open Rally win in their Ford Escort Mk2.

Day one: Friday
Twenty-five stage miles in the Dalby complex in the darkness of Friday evening was a tough start to the compact format for the 2012 rally and two themes

Julian Burch

Will Onions in Gale Rigg

Allan MacDowall

Lionel Hansen

were common among expert predictions for the opening leg. First, Bannister would set the pace in his own back yard and, second, there would be some notable casualties. Both proved correct.

Sadly, the big retirements were two crews expected to feature strongly as the rally unfolded and both went out within five miles of the start with engine dramas. Julian Reynolds and Patrick Walsh holed the sump of their Escort Mk2 against a tree stump and Matt Edwards/Sam Collis suffered a blown motor. Both crews were devastated to go out so early.

But life was not easy for those who did make it through. Heavy rain the previous day left the stages very slippery and many local experts reckoned that Dalby had seldom been more treacherous.

Even though he arrived back in Pickering with a 28s lead at the end of Friday's leg, Bannister had not escaped problems. A puncture late in the first stage cost him time, while a heavy landing into a hole could have cost him more on the third stage. "It pushed the radiator back," he reported. "They've got some work to do tonight," he added of his service crew.

McCormack led the chase but elected not to get drawn into an early fight. "Just steady away: it would have been very easy to go off in there," he said. One of the star performances came from Matthew Robinson and Mick Gilby, who ended the leg third in their Escort Mk2. On the first stage, they caught and passed the similar car of former WRC contender Gregoire de Mevius.

A spin on the first stage cost Onions/Millington around 20s, but there was a good vibe in the car as they rallied together for the first time. "It clicked in the last two," said Onions. "It's all coming together now and we'll have a push tomorrow."

Roger Albert Clark Rally 2012: the ninth edition

Stefaan Stouf and Joris Erard in Glen Dhu

Baz Jordan at Croft

Jean-Jacques Julien

Yorkshire crews Charlie Taylor/Steve Bielby and Darren Moon/Andrew Roughead packed out the top six, while seventh was a great result for Jeremy Easson and Alun Cook. On his first event since breaking his back in Belgium two years earlier, Easson was on it from the start. "We've still got it," he said with a grin after loving every minute of being back in a rally car following a lengthy recuperation.

Day two: Saturday
Across 50 stage miles, including the asphalt of Croft, the ice of Gale Rigg and the fog of Pundershaw, Bannister and McCormack matched each other to the second. By the time they arrived at the Carlisle overnight halt, the gap was unchanged at 28s.

However, it was a battle that ebbed and flowed, with Bannister taking profit in Gale Rigg and McCormack clawing it back with a supremely committed attack on the fog-bound Croft. The fog was back, in patches, in the concluding pair of stages in Pundershaw and McCormack managed to claw 8s back and leave Bannister's lead unchanged.

Robinson retained his excellent third, but the deficit to Bannister was out to three and a half minutes. "I had a moment in a Pundershaw ditch, but got away with it," said Robinson.

The next gaggle of crews was battling furiously, with eight cars covered by a minute after 15 of the event's 24 special stages. Tied in fourth place were Moon/Roughead and Paul Griffiths/Jon Madoc-Jones,

Darren Moon in Dalby

while Onions and Millington were just 11s back. "My co-driver knows those stages well," said Moon of the Hamsterley and Pundershaw tests. "He told me to keep it flat and I did: it was a good run." Conversely, Griffiths had not enjoyed the foggy patches, and was glad to simply get to Carlisle. Onions had lost time with a spin at Duncombe Park, where huge crowds showed just how popular the rally has become. "I've never seen crowds like it in Yorkshire," said Bannister.

In seventh and eighth overall were the crews fighting for Category 2 honours. Easson and Cook led Belgians Stefaan Stouf and Joris Erard by just 4s in the battle of the Escort Mk1s. "That was not a time for heroics: just a matter of getting through those two," said Easson of the double run through five and a half miles of Pundershaw.

As he headed north out of his native Yorkshire, Bannister was apprehensive about what was still to come. "I didn't expect to live with Martin," he said of the driver 34 years his junior. However, Bannister still had that 28s advantage as crews prepared for the long, tough Sunday.

Day three: Sunday
With 75 stage miles done, a whopping 85 competitive miles still lay ahead to make Sunday the big day of the rally. Crews headed out of a damp Carlisle to tackle the equivalent of two BTRDA rallies back-to-back, topped by a daunting 17-mile deciding stage in Kershope.

McCormack knew that the time had come to really attack and his mission was to build the pressure on his rival. Seven and a half miles in a wet and murky Glen Dhu delivered him a 9s profit to instantly slash the gap to 19s in what was a perfect opener for the Irishman. But Bannister responded in Newcastleton and they set exactly the same time over the nine miles, nearly half a minute quicker than anyone else.

McCormack stole one second in the short three-miler in Florida, but Bannister responded superbly in the flowing 13-miles of Riccarton. He went 8s faster to take his lead back to 26s as they arrived in Hawick for service. In 33 tough stage miles, McCormack's net gain had been just 2s and that was not enough.

John Everard's Alfa Romeo in Gale Rigg

Steve Bannister

Paul Griffiths

Two runs through nine miles of Craik, with service in between, was the focal point in this titanic struggle. "He took me in Craik," said Bannister. "That was the turning point. We thought we'd gone well," he said. To then find that McCormack had taken 8s and then 7s was a massive blow for the rally leader. The margin was just 11s as McCormack's crew did a precautionary gearbox change after he picked up a concern over third gear.

Next up was 13 miles in Wauchope, a reverse of the Riccarton stage. Having dropped time on the morning run, McCormack knew that he had to push to the max to press home his attack and stop Bannister rebuilding his lead. The result was a 6s advantage to bring the gap to just 5s. Bannister pushed as hard as he could and gave his all to try and fend off a relentless pursuit.

But McCormack flew the three miles of the reversed Florida stage and took 7s advantage in just over three miles. Suddenly, for the first time since the opening stage, McCormack was ahead but next came the big sting in the tail, 17.2 miles in Kershope and it was now dark.

Almost within sight of the finish, Bannister spun in what may well have been the defining moment of this monster battle between two brilliant drivers. McCormack stopped the clocks 15s to the good to win by 17s and Bannister was left to rue the Friday night puncture and the spin: the two moments that could have changed the result.

As he sat at the Kershope stop line waiting for the lights of his rival to pierce the darkness, Bannister was devastated as he had driven a mighty rally. "Martin just pushed that bit harder," said Bannister at the end

Andrew Haddon and Dale Furniss

of a battle that had been as sporting as it was fierce. "It's been unreal," said McCormack after the drive of his career to date.

Sunday gave the rest of the top 10 a big shake-up and first to go out was Robinson with a fuel problem. Moon lost time with wiper failure and Griffiths had to stop and change a puncture. With only second and third gears, Onions got through Kershope to take third, while Easson drove a blinder to hold off Stouf for Category 2 victory and fourth overall, with Moon and Seamus O'Connell/Andrew Sankey finishing between them. Charlie Taylor and Steve Bielby had yet another good RAC for eighth overall with Griffiths recovering for ninth ahead of the flying Guy Woodcock and Graham Dance in the only non-BDG Escort in the top 15.

Open Rally
For the second year running, Hawkswell and Welch won the Open Rally, a parallel event for any two-wheel drive car. Their Ford Escort Mk2 completed the rally with nearly two minutes in hand over the Vauxhall Astra of Nigel Barber and Stuart Popplewell.

"We've had a good run," said Hawkswell of a pretty clear rally. Barber, meanwhile, was fortunate to strike gearbox dramas on the road section to Croft on Saturday. With the 'box stuck in fifth, his crew changed it at Croft and no time was lost.

However, with three stages to run, the ever-spectacular Opel Kadett of Allan McDowall and Gavin Heseltine led the Open Rally by more than five minutes. It all ended badly with a substantial off in Wauchope.

Vauxhall Nova crew Nigel Barrett and Simon Law hit problems in the final stage, so the Nissan Micra of John Sutton/Paul Osmond topped the smallest class while Will Midgley and Jonathan Driver took Class G3 in their Toyota Corolla.

The classes
Despite a catalogue of dramas that included having the choke stuck open for two days, the Saab 96 of Jim Valentine again came home safely in Class B1, this time with Caroline Lodge on the maps. The car's four-stroke big brother also bagged Class B3 in the capable hands of Nick Pinkett and Richard Simpson.

McCormack in Craik on Sunday

Mark Schmidt

Ceiriog Hughes

The other Category 1 class, B4, fell to category winners Bean/Smithson who were sublime in their Lotus Cortina to win by 18 minutes. Truly elated to finish second to Bean were John Everard and James Sharpley, who pedalled their Alfa Romeo Sprint GT with gusto. "I've waited 40 years to do this," said a jubilant Everard as he reached the final control.

Class C1 fell to Stuart and Linda Cariss in their Ford Escort Mk1, despite missing two stages on Sunday after sliding into a ditch in the Florida stage. Victory in Class C2 for Robin Shuttleworth and Ronnie Roughead (Ford Escort Mk1) was a much better outcome than a blown engine 12 months earlier, though Shuttleworth scared himself with a moment a mile from the end of the rally. C3 was won by event newcomers Wayne Bonser and Richard Aston (Ford Escort Mk1), despite losing several minutes on Friday evening with a broken roll bar.

It took a lot of manpower to get the Porsche 911 of Tim Mason and 'Captain' Thompson back on track in Gale Rigg as brake problems dogged their progress. This early bid to collect a Christmas tree didn't stop them winning Class C4 as the same stage slowed the Datsun 240Z of Robert Close and Mike Reynolds with a broken driveshaft.

Grahame Standen and Bill Cook (Ford Escort Mk2) took Class D2, while Woodcock and Dance (Ford Escort Mk2) were as mighty as ever in winning D3 as well as bagging tenth overall with only Pinto power against the BDG hordes.

In D4, Julian Burch and Glyn Thomas (Sunbeam Lotus) had a pretty clear run apart from a fuel problem that halted the car for four minutes in Dalby. Finally, fresh back from New Zealand, Peter Smith and Ryland James (Ford Escort Mk1) won the class for FIA Appendix K cars.

The crowds in Gale Rigg

Winners Clarke (left) and McCormack with Colin Heppenstall

Winner's view: Martin McCormack

He was back on the event after a two-year gap
"This rally was unfinished business for me and I really wanted to win it a lot. I'd been here three times before and each time I'd been there or thereabouts. It was a rally I always wanted to come back and do and this proved to be the year. We did a lot of work and prep on the car before the rally and were on a fresh engine and gearbox. There was a bit of pressure being car number one but it was great having that position."

It was the best result of his career
"I've got to pay tribute to my co-driver Phil Clarke, who has been fantastic on the maps. We had a ding-dong battle for three days and to win it in the last stage was just magic. That's the only way I can describe it. Dalby was tricky because Steve Bannister had good knowledge of the stages. But it was all about getting to Sunday without doing anything silly."

It was an incredibly close finish
"At the finish of Kershope we didn't know if we'd done enough. But I said to Phil that whatever the result, we'd had one of best rallies we'd ever had and whoever won it would have deserved it. Luckily enough, it was us. I just couldn't believe that I'd finally won it. When we knew the result it just felt unreal. I'd always been quick, but I'd never had the consistency to keep it going."

Craik was the turning point
"It was nip and tuck and then we got to Craik, where I went off in 2008 chasing Malcolm Wilson. That's where I turned it around. The stage was very good to the map and it was a fast, flowing stage. I knew I had to turn it up and do something more. I knew that if I got a good run the first time through Craik, we could get him again on the second run."

He's keen to defend his win
"I'd love to come back and do it again next year. I love this rally: it's one of the best rallies I've ever done and the whole thing is fantastic."

The Perez Stratos in Craik

Nigel Barber

Bernard Munster

Personal view: Paul Lawrence

Does it really get any better? It was a clear moonlit Friday evening in Dalby Forest and I was standing with a group of good friends on the opening stage of the 2012 Roger Albert Clark Rally.

Barely a mile away, on another of the riggs that give Dalby its daunting high-speed character, the bark of a BDG revving hard as it hit 9000rpm in every gear signalled that battle had commenced. The banter and jokes fell away and everyone just listened: Marty McCormack was into the stage and the Irish ace clearly meant business.

However, so too did Steve Bannister who started a minute later and before long the air was alive with the glorious sound of BDG-powered Ford Escorts in the forest, in the dark. Down towards the Woodyard they went before looping back up Flax Dale, then turning south once more down Flainsey Rigg. After another brush with the Woodyard came the flat in fourth (or fifth) charge up White Cliff Rigg, the fastest of all the Riggs in Dalby, as they finally approached our spot, less than a mile from the end of the stage.

The atmosphere was electric as nine cars filled the stage before McCormack reached the finish line, nine and a half minutes later. Nine BDGs in full flight was a concerto that I will remember for a very long time: and the orchestra got even better a few minutes later when Steve Perez in the Lancia Stratos and Tim Mason in his Porsche 911 joined in. Both sounded gorgeous.

Bannister in flight in Dalby

If ever there was an overwhelming advert for the glory of historic rallying in general and the Roger Albert Clark Rally in particular, this was it. Our man on the stop watch was the first barometer of the way this epic rally was likely to unfold. Fighting a puncture as he stormed by, but barely easing his pace, 'Banner' dropped just 4s to McCormack. The rest were 20s down and more as the first battle lines were drawn.

This was all about two men at the top of their game. Bannister a complete legend and, at the top side of 60, still totally committed on stages he has rallied for over 35 years. And McCormack, the supremely gifted Irishman at less than half the age of the man they simply refer to as 'God' in these parts. It is easy to understand why, and their battle enthralled us all until the stop line of the final special stage.

For those of us simply watching, it was a dream evening. The pace was hot, the weather was sublime, the company was impeccable and the noise was out of this world. There was really only one downside to the whole experience: we have to wait 50 weeks before we can do it all over again.

Personal view 2: Paul Lawrence
My moment of the year came on the event of the year, the Roger Albert Clark Rally and it was at the stop line of the final stage that all the drama and emotion of this epic contest came to a conclusion.

For two and a half days we had marvelled as Steve Bannister and Kevin Rae battled against Marty McCormack and Phil Clarke, both in Ford Escort Mk2s.

Sunday was the big day and I knew the place to be was the stop line of the final stage, a daunting 17-miler in Kershope. It was dark and the atmosphere was electric as a select few awaited the leaders. The finish radio crew told us that McCormack had gone into the stage just 2s up.

But Bannister was first on the road and as he rolled to a stop, the look on his face told the story. He had spun near the finish and knew that McCormack was coming fast. Bannister craned his neck to look for the lights of his rival piercing the trees and, sure enough, McCormack arrived just 45s later to clinch victory.

The emotions of two great drivers were poles apart, but both were generous to their rival at the end of a magnificent contest. It was a truly memorable moment.

2012 ROGER ALBERT CLARK RALLY: ENTRY LIST

No	Driver	Co-driver	Car	Class
1	Martin McCormack	Phil Clarke	Ford Escort Mk2	D5
2	Steve Bannister	Kevin Rae	Ford Escort Mk2	D5
3	Julian Reynolds	Patrick Walsh	Ford Escort RS	D5
4	Paul Griffiths	Jon Madoc-Jones	Ford Escort RS1800	D5
5	Will Onions	John Millington	Ford Escort RS	D5
6	Tim Pearcey	Neil Shanks	Ford Escort RS1800	D5
7	Stefaan Stouf	Joris Erard	Ford Escort RS1600	C5
8	Seamus O'Connell	Andrew Sankey	Ford Escort RS1800 Mk2	D5
9	Steve Perez	Paul Spooner	Lancia Stratos	E4
10	Matt Edwards	Sam Collis	Ford Escort Mk2	D5
11	Gregoire de Mevius	Emmanuel Eggermont	Ford Escort RS	D5
12	Richard Lepley	Andy Richardson	Ford Escort RS1800	D5
14	Matthew Robinson	Mick Gilby	Ford Escort Mk2	D5
15	Andrew Haddon	Dale Furniss	Ford Escort Mk2	D5
16	Bernard Munster	Johan Gitsels	Porsche 911	D5
17	Charlie Taylor	Steve Bielby	Ford Escort Mk2	D5
18	Ernie Graham	Will Graham	Ford Escort RS1600	E5
19	Steve Magson	Geoff Atkinson	Vauxhall Chevette HSR	D4
20	Jeremy Easson	Alun Cook	Ford Escort Mk1	C5
21	Tim Mason	'Captain' Thompson	Porsche 911	C4
22	Guy Woodcock	Graham Dance	Ford Escort RS2000	D3
23	Nev Jones	Chris Davies	Ford Escort Mk2	E5
24	Peter Smith	Ryland James	Ford Escort	E5
25	Barry Jordan	James Gratton-Smith	Ford Escort Mk2	E5
26	Phil Squires	Mick Squires	Ford Escort RS1800	D5
27	Andrew Siddall	Iain Tullie	Ford Escort Mk1 RS1600	C5
28	Mark Bentley	Edward Bentley	Ford Escort Mk2	D5
29	Marcus Noble	Brian Hodgson	Ford Escort Mk2	D5
30	Dominique Depons	Jean Bourgoin	Ford Escort Mk2 RS1800	D5
31	Steve Graham	Tony Graham	Lancia Fulvia	C1
32	Geoff Bell	Paul Wakely	Ford Escort RS1800	E5
34	Guy Smith	Ian Oakey	Ford Escort	D5
36	Ashley Slights	Matthew Whattam	Ford Escort Mk1 RS2000	C3
37	Robert Close	Mike Reynolds	Datsun 240Z	C4
38	Wayne Bonser	Richard Aston	Ford Escort RS2000	C3
39	Julian Burch	Glyn Thomas	Talbot Sunbeam Lotus	D4
40	David Watkins	Paul Train	Ford Escort Mk1	C2
41	Robin Shuttleworth	Ronnie Roughead	Ford Escort Mk1 Mexico	C2
42	Bob Adamson	Dick Wardle	Ford Escort RS1800	E5
43	Magic McCrombie	Pete Gunson	Saab 900	G4
44	Colin Hope	Nick Patrick	Saab 96 V4	C3
45	Tom Hewick	Mick Johnson	Ford Escort Mk2	D5
46	James Stait	Marcus Cartwright	Talbot Sunbeam Lotus	D4
47	Lionel Hansen	Stephane Prevot	Porsche 911SC	D5
48	Guino Kenis	Filip Godde	BMW 2002	C3
49	Stewart Scott	Mark Casey	Ford Escort RS2000	C3
50	David Lucking	Paul Garside	Ford Escort Mk2	D3
51	Nick Jarvis	Alan Carfrae	Ford Escort Mk1	G4
52	Ian Hildreth	Stephen Stead	Ford Escort	D3
53	Grahame Standen	Bill Cook	Ford Escort Mk2	D2

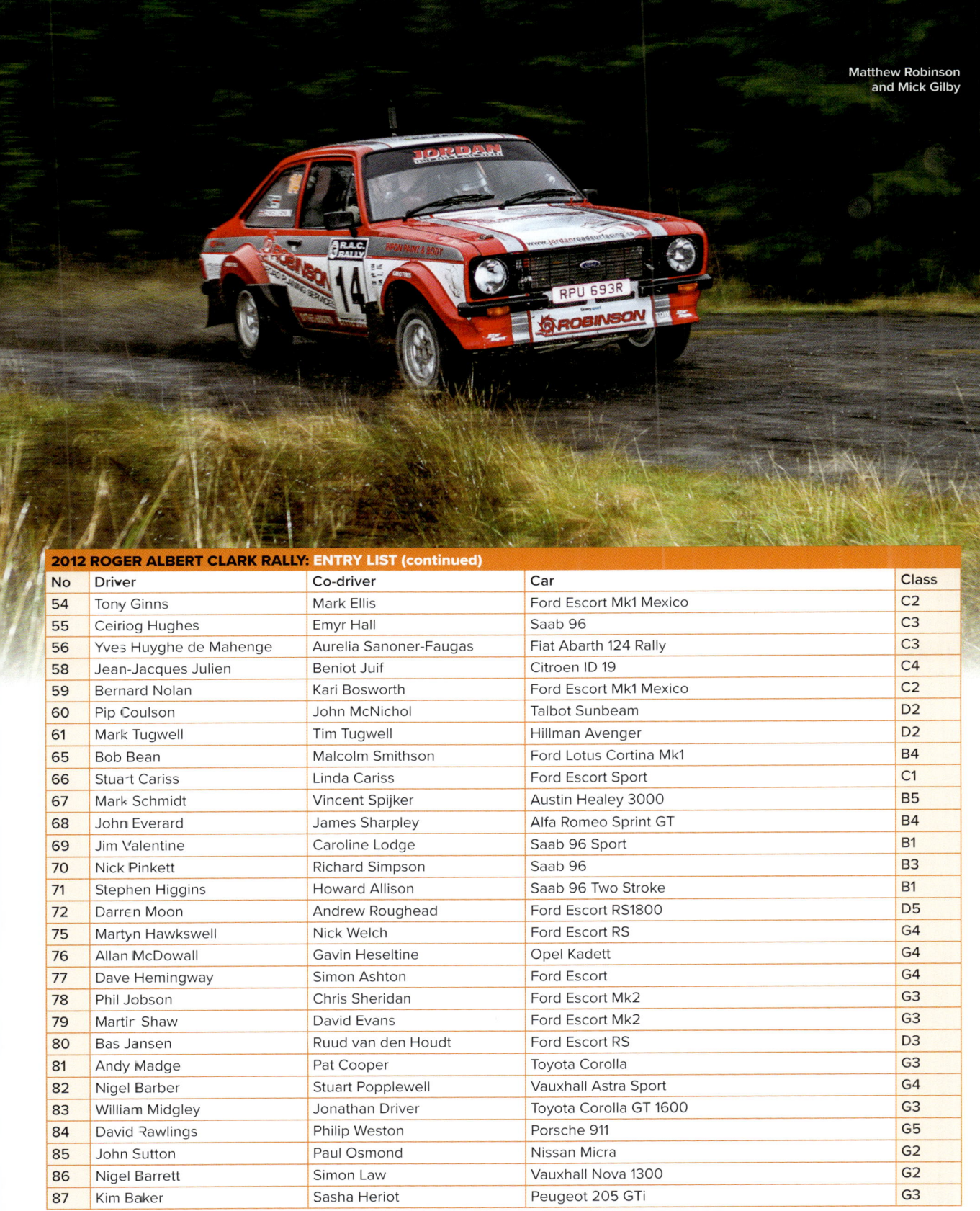

Matthew Robinson and Mick Gilby

2012 ROGER ALBERT CLARK RALLY: ENTRY LIST (continued)

No	Driver	Co-driver	Car	Class
54	Tony Ginns	Mark Ellis	Ford Escort Mk1 Mexico	C2
55	Ceiriog Hughes	Emyr Hall	Saab 96	C3
56	Yves Huyghe de Mahenge	Aurelia Sanoner-Faugas	Fiat Abarth 124 Rally	C3
58	Jean-Jacques Julien	Beniot Juif	Citroen ID 19	C4
59	Bernard Nolan	Kari Bosworth	Ford Escort Mk1 Mexico	C2
60	Pip Coulson	John McNichol	Talbot Sunbeam	D2
61	Mark Tugwell	Tim Tugwell	Hillman Avenger	D2
65	Bob Bean	Malcolm Smithson	Ford Lotus Cortina Mk1	B4
66	Stuart Cariss	Linda Cariss	Ford Escort Sport	C1
67	Mark Schmidt	Vincent Spijker	Austin Healey 3000	B5
68	John Everard	James Sharpley	Alfa Romeo Sprint GT	B4
69	Jim Valentine	Caroline Lodge	Saab 96 Sport	B1
70	Nick Pinkett	Richard Simpson	Saab 96	B3
71	Stephen Higgins	Howard Allison	Saab 96 Two Stroke	B1
72	Darren Moon	Andrew Roughead	Ford Escort RS1800	D5
75	Martyn Hawkswell	Nick Welch	Ford Escort RS	G4
76	Allan McDowall	Gavin Heseltine	Opel Kadett	G4
77	Dave Hemingway	Simon Ashton	Ford Escort	G4
78	Phil Jobson	Chris Sheridan	Ford Escort Mk2	G3
79	Martin Shaw	David Evans	Ford Escort Mk2	G3
80	Bas Jansen	Ruud van den Houdt	Ford Escort RS	D3
81	Andy Madge	Pat Cooper	Toyota Corolla	G3
82	Nigel Barber	Stuart Popplewell	Vauxhall Astra Sport	G4
83	William Midgley	Jonathan Driver	Toyota Corolla GT 1600	G3
84	David Rawlings	Philip Weston	Porsche 911	G5
85	John Sutton	Paul Osmond	Nissan Micra	G2
86	Nigel Barrett	Simon Law	Vauxhall Nova 1300	G2
87	Kim Baker	Sasha Heriot	Peugeot 205 GTi	G3

Roger Albert Clark Rally 2012: the ninth edition

2012 STAGES AND STAGE WINNERS

Day	Stage	Name	Distance	Stage winner(s)	Time
Friday	SS1	Dalby 1	8.71	McCormack/Clarke	9.31
Friday	SS2	Newclose Rigg 1	4.50	Bannister/Rae	4.08
Friday	SS3	Dalby 2	8.71	Bannister/Rae	9.10
Friday	SS4	Newclose Rigg 2	4.50	Bannister/Rae	4.11
Saturday	SS5	Gale Rigg 1	5.30	Bannister/Rae	5.21
Saturday	SS6	Duncombe Park 1	2.37	Griffiths/Madoc-Jones	3.18
Saturday	SS7	Duncombe Park 2	2.37	Stouf/Erard	3.09
Saturday	SS8	Gale Rigg 2	5.30	Bannister/Rae	5.15
Saturday	SS9	Duncombe Park 3	2.37	O'Connell/Sankey and McCormack/Clarke	3.01
Saturday	SS10	Duncombe Park 4	2.37	McCormack/Clarke	2.54
Saturday	SS11	Croft 1	3.91	McCormack/Clarke	5.55
Saturday	SS12	Croft 2	3.91	McCormack/Clarke	5.38
Saturday	SS13	Hamsterley	5.80	Bannister/Rae	6.12
Saturday	SS14	Pundershaw 1	6.10	Bannister/Rae	5.32
Saturday	SS15	Pundershaw 2	6.10	McCormack/Clarke	5.21
Sunday	SS16	Glen Dhu	7.43	McCormack/Clarke	7.49
Sunday	SS17	Newcastleton	8.99	McCormack/Clarke and Bannister/Rae	10.15
Sunday	SS18	Florida 1	3.32	McCormack/Clarke	3.54
Sunday	SS19	Riccarton	13.75	Bannister/Rae	13.22
Sunday	SS20	Craik 1	8.99	McCormack/Clarke	8.15
Sunday	SS21	Craik 2	8.99	McCormack/Clarke	8.10
Sunday	SS22	Wauchope	13.75	McCormack/Clarke	12.58
Sunday	SS23	Florida 2	3.32	McCormack/Clarke	3.46
Sunday	SS24	Kershope	17.00	McCormack/Clarke	19.51

2012 RESULTS

Overall	Class	No	Driver	Co-driver	Car	Class	Total
1	1	1	Martin McCormack	Phil Clarke	Ford Escort Mk2	D5	02:48:06
2	2	2	Steve Bannister	Kevin Rae	Ford Escort Mk2	D5	02:48:23
3	3	5	Will Onions	John Millington	Ford Escort RS	D5	02:58:21
4	1	20	Jeremy Easson	Alun Cook	Ford Escort Mk1	C5	02:58:36
5	4	72	Darren Moon	Andrew Roughead	Ford Escort RS1800	D5	02:59:09
6	5	8	Seamus O'Connell	Andrew Sankey	Ford Escort Mk2 RS1800	D5	02:59:11
7	2	7	Stefaan Stouf	Joris Erard	Ford Escort RS1600	C5	02:59:21
8	6	17	Charlie Taylor	Steve Bielby	Ford Escort Mk2	D5	03:00:26
9	7	4	Paul Griffiths	Jon Madoc-Jones	Ford Escort RS1800	D5	03:01:02
10	1	22	Guy Woodcock	Graham Dance	Ford Escort RS2000	D3	03:02:24
11	8	11	Gregoire de Mevius	Emmanuel Eggermont	Ford Escort RS	D5	03:03:04
12	9	12	Richard Lepley	Andy Richardson	Ford Escort RS1800	D5	03:03:54
13	10	26	Phil Squires	Mick Squires	Ford Escort RS1800	D5	03:08:17
14	1	24	Peter Smith	Ryland James	Ford Escort	E5	03:11:33
15	2	42	Bob Adamson	Dick Wardle	Ford Escort RS1800	E5	03:12:27
16	11	16	Bernard Munster	Johan Gitsels	Porsche 911	D5	03:12:40
17	1	21	Tim Mason	'Captain' Thompson	Porsche 911	C4	03:17:07
18	3	23	Nev Jones	Chris Davies	Ford Escort Mk2	E5	03:19:38
19	1	65	Bob Bean	Malcolm Smithson	Ford Lotus Cortina Mk1	B4	03:20:12
20	12	28	Mark Bentley	Edward Bentley	Ford Escort Mk2	D5	s 3:23:28
21	1	39	Julian Burch	Glyn Thomas	Talbot Sunbeam Lotus	D4	03:25:37
22	2	80	Bas Jansen	Ruud van den Houdt	Ford Escort RS	D3	03:26:00
23	13	29	Marcus Noble	Brian Hodgson	Ford Escort Mk2	D5	s 3:26:54
24	1	41	Robin Shuttleworth	Ronnie Roughead	Ford Escort Mk1 Mexico	C2	03:27:10
25	1	53	Grahame Standen	Bill Cook	Ford Escort Mk2	D2	s 3:28:01
26	3	50	David Lucking	Paul Garside	Ford Escort Mk2	D3	03:28:18

2012 RESULTS (continued)

Overall	Class	No	Driver	Co-driver	Car	Class	Total
27	4	52	Ian Hildreth	Stephen Stead	Ford Escort	D3	03:31:12
28	1	38	Wayne Bonser	Richard Aston	Ford Escort RS2000	C3	03:32:05
29	2	40	David Watkins	Paul Train	Ford Escort Mk1	C2	03:32:42
30	2	68	John Everard	James Sharpley	Alfa Romeo Sprint GT	B4	03:38:43
31	2	37	Robert Close	Mike Reynolds	Datsun 240Z	C4	s 3:41:19
32	1	66	Stuart Cariss	Linda Cariss	Ford Escort Sport	C1	s 3:46:43
33	2	60	Pip Coulson	John McNichol	Talbot Sunbeam	D2	03:51:52
34	2	49	Stewart Scott	Mark Casey	Ford Escort RS2000	C3	s 3:53:17
35	1	70	Nick Pinkett	Richard Simpson	Saab 96	B3	03:54:56
36	3	59	Bernard Nolan	Kari Bosworth	Ford Escort Mk1 Mexico	C2	s 3:57:53
37	3	61	Mark Tugwell	Tim Tugwell	Hillman Avenger	D2	s 4:02:30
38	3	56	Yves Huyghe de Mahenge	Aurelia Sanoner-Faugas	Fiat Abarth 124 Rally	C3	04:03:46
39	2	31	Steve Graham	Tony Graham	Lancia Fulvia	C1	04:08:45
40	2	46	James Stait	Marcus Cartwright	Talbot Sunbeam Lotus	D4	s 4:08:58
41	1	69	Jim Valentine	Caroline Lodge	Saab 96 Sport	B1	04:12:47
Ret		3	Julian Reynolds	Patrick Walsh	Ford Escort RS	D5	Holed sump SS1
Ret		6	Tim Pearcey	Neil Shanks	Ford Escort RS1800	D5	Stub axle SS16
Ret		9	Steve Perez	Paul Spooner	Lancia Stratos	E4	Mechanical SS22
Ret		10	Matt Edwards	Sam Collis	Ford Escort Mk2	D5	Blown engine SS1
Ret		14	Matthew Robinson	Mick Gilby	Ford Escort Mk2	D5	Mechanical SS17
Ret		15	Andrew Haddon	Dale Furniss	Ford Escort Mk2	D5	Stopped after SS22
Ret		18	Ernie Graham	Will Graham	Ford Escort RS1600	E5	Did not restart MTC3
Ret		19	Steve Magson	Geoff Atkinson	Vauxhall Chevette HSR	D4	Rolled SS24
Ret		25	Barry Jordan	James Gratton-Smith	Ford Escort Mk2	E5	Retired SS16
Ret		27	Andrew Siddall	Iain Tullie	Ford Escort Mk1 RS1600	C5	Stopped SS18
Ret		30	Dominique Depons	Jean Bourgoin	Ford Escort Mk2 RS1800	D5	Stopped SS24
Ret		32	Geoff Bell	Paul Wakely	Ford Escort RS1800	E5	Mechanical SF22
Ret		34	Guy Smith	Ian Oakey	Ford Escort	D5	Engine went bang SS11
Ret		36	Ashley Slights	Matthew Whattam	Ford Escort Mk1 RS2000	C3	Broken rocker TC7B
Ret		44	Colin Hope	Nick Patrick	Saab 96 V4	C3	In ditch SS24
Ret		45	Tom Hewick	Mick Johnson	Ford Escort Mk2	D5	Stopped SS17
Ret		47	Lionel Hansen	Stephane Prevot	Porsche 911SC	D5	Retired SS15
Ret		48	Guino Kenis	Filip Godde	BMW 2002	C3	Gearbox SS16
Ret		54	Tony Ginns	Mark Ellis	Ford Escort Mk1 Mexico	C2	Retired SS14
Ret		55	Ceiriog Hughes	Emyr Hall	Saab 96	C3	Stopped after SS22
Ret		58	Jean-Jacques Julien	Beniot Juif	Citroen ID 19	C4	Stopped SS22
Ret		67	Mark Schmidt	Vincent Spijker	Austin Healey 3000	B5	Gearbox MTC6
Ret		71	Stephen Higgins	Howard Allison	Saab 96 Two Stroke	B1	Stopped SS18

Marty McCormack

Yves Huyghe de Mahenge

Richard Lepley

2012 RESULTS: OPEN RALLY

Overall	Class	No	Driver	Co-driver	Car	Class	Total
1	1	75	Martyn Hawkswell	Nick Welch	Ford Escort RS	G4	03:09:12
2	2	82	Nigel Barber	Stuart Popplewell	Vauxhall Astra Sport	G4	03:11:03
3	3	77	Dave Hemingway	Simon Ashton	Ford Escort	G4	03:15:52
4	1	83	William Midgley	Jonathan Driver	Toyota Corolla GT 1600	G3	03:25:46
5	4	51	Nick Jarvis	Alan Carfrae	Ford Escort Mk2	G4	03:27:44
6	1	84	David Rawlings	Philip Weston	Porsche 911	G5	s 3:32:35
7	2	87	Kim Baker	Sasha Heriot	Peugeot 205 GTi	G3	03:39:35
8	1	85	John Sutton	Paul Osmond	Nissan Micra	G2	03:40:53
9	3	79	Martin Shaw	David Evans	Ford Escort Mk2	G3	s 3:58:31
10	4	78	Phil Jobson	Chris Sheridan	Ford Escort Mk2	G3	s 4:40:01
Ret		76	Allan McDowall	Gavin Heseltine	Opel Kadett	G4	Off road into river SS22
Ret		81	Andy Madge	Pat Cooper	Toyota Corolla	G3	OTL
Ret		86	Nigel Barrett	Simon Law	Vauxhall Nova 1300	G2	OTL
Ret		43	Magic McCrombie	Pete Gunson	Saab 900	G4	Retired SS3

2012 RESULTS: DE LACY RALLY

Overall	Class	No	Driver	Co-driver	Car	Class	Total
1	1	92	Mathew Smith	Giles Dykes	Ford Ka	J2	00:30:07
2	2	103	David Wood	Matt Edwards	Vauxhall Corsa	J2	00:32:48
3	3	91	Amanda Cornforth	Derek Cornforth	Ford Ka	J2	00:32:52
4	4	88	James Johns	John Thornton	Skoda Felicia	J2	00:36:17
5	5	93	Robert Pilcher	Roger Burkill	Ford Lotus Cortina Mk1	J2	00:36:37
6	6	89	John Nicholson	Don Bramfoot	Ford Escort Sport	J2	00:39:15
Ret		90	Clive Baty	Peter Scott	Renault 5 Alpine	J2	Stopped after SS1

2012 RESULTS: PEREGRINE PRINT RALLY

Overall	Class	No	Driver	Co-driver	Car	Class	Total
1	1	94	Michael Kent	Miles Cartwright	Talbot Sunbeam 1.6 Ti	H2	01:04:56

The scene in Gale Rigg

2012 RESULTS: CLUBMANS RALLY

Overall	Class	No	Driver	Co-driver	Car	Class	Total
1	1	96	Chris White	Chris Dewsnap	Ford Escort Mk2	K4	00:49:46
2	1	101	Alan Hughes	Ken Bills	Ford Escort Mk2	K3	00:50:00
3	2	99	Derek Belbin	John Stanger-Leathes	Ford Escort	K3	00:52:03
4	1	98	Mike Axford	Dave Thomason	Ford Fiesta RS	K2	00:53:12
5	3	97	Ian McAuley	Simon Buckles	Ford Escort Mk2	K3	00:56:01
6	1	105	David Coleman	Kyle Gass	Skoda Felicia	K1	01:07:09
Ret		100	Brian Middlemas	Kevin Crawford	Hilman Avenger	K2	Stopped SS19
Ret		102	Roy Eide-Johansen	Mark Simpson	Ford Escort Mk2	K3	Rolled SS19
Ret		104	Darren Martin	Martin Steele	Ford Escort Mk2	K4	Stopped SS16

2012 RESULTS: RETURN RALLY

Overall	Class	No	Driver	Co-driver	Car	Class	Total
1	1	101	Alan Hughes	Ken Bills	Ford Escort Mk2	L3	00:59:01
2	1	98	Mike Axford	Dave Thomason	Ford Fiesta RS	L2	01:00:50
3	2	97	Ian McAuley	Simon Buckles	Ford Escort Mk2	L3	01:06:01
Ret		99	Derek Belbin	John Stanger-Leathes	Ford Escort	L3	Mechanical SS24

Nick Pinkett

Tim Mason

Roger Albert Clark Rally 2012: the ninth edition

Roger Albert Clark Rally 2013:
the tenth edition

Overall winners: Steve Bannister and Kevin Rae

Bannister's second win

The 2013 rally

Friday 8 to Sunday 10 November
157 stage miles
23 special stages
Start: Pickering Showground
Overnight 1: Pickering Showground
Overnight 2: H&H Auctions, Carlisle
Finish: H&H Auctions, Carlisle
66 starters
37 finishers

Open Rally winners: Martyn Hawkswell and Nick Welch

Roger Albert Rally 2013: the tenth edition

Owen Murphy and James O'Brien

Steve Bannister joined Gwyndaf Evans as a double winner of the Roger Albert Clark Rally after he swept to a resounding victory on the tenth anniversary event.

Partnered by Kevin Rae, Bannister was the class of the field in his Ford Escort Mk2 and eventually built a winning margin of over four minutes after a typically tough rally in Yorkshire and the Scottish borders.

However, that does not tell the story of the first half of the rally when Matthew Robinson and Jason Pritchard both gave determined chase to Bannister. Ironically, the same brow in Punvershaw claimed the challengers on consecutive stages on Saturday afternoon.

With Robinson/Sam Collis and Pritchard/John Millington both rolling out over a deceptive crest, it was a mighty run by Paul Griffiths/Richard Wardle that netted second from Seamus O'Connell/Paul Wakely. Meanwhile, when they were sitting upside down in Duncombe Park on Saturday morning, fourth overall seemed an unlikely result for Tim Pearcey/Neil Shanks.

Bannister said that his victory went some way to making up for the disappointment of losing out in the famous 2012 battle with Marty McCormack and paid tribute to the challenge presented by Robinson and Pritchard. "It's been a brilliant rally," said Bannister. "The good thing for me, I suppose, is that they've gone off trying to beat me rather than break down. I was pleased with my pace for those two to have to push so hard."

Day one: Friday

There was no gentle run-in for the crews as the event plunged straight into Dalby in the darkness

Tim Pearcey

Steve and Tony Graham in the Lancia Fulvia

Mark Schmidt

David Goose

of Friday evening. Some dreams were dashed but Bannister took control to grab a lead he would never lose. However, Robinson signalled his intentions by returning to Pickering only 18s behind and Pritchard showed his class by taking third as he got used to new co-driver Millington and maps rather than route notes.

"I made a mess of the first stage with the wrong tyre choice," said Robinson who then matched or narrowly beat Bannister across the five remaining stages to underline his status as the key rival to his Rally Sport Developments stable mate.

"We had a good clean run," reported Bannister, but even he'd been off briefly on the slippery stages. The big losers were Rob Smith/Alun Cook who dropped six minutes with an off in Staindale and Matt Edwards/Will Rogers who dropped even more time with an engine bay fire after an electrical fault. Both crews then started superb recovery drives that would take them into the top ten at the finish, with Edwards eighth and Smith tenth.

Two Welsh crews, both new to the event, had strong opening runs to complete the early top five as Tomas Davies/Eurig Davies and Meirion Evans/Iwan Jones showed impressive pace on unfamiliar territory.

Day two: Saturday
Two runs through an extended Duncombe Park stage kicked off Saturday before the route headed north and west for stages at Croft, Hamsterley and Pundershaw. Duncombe Park claimed Evans/Jones with engine dramas, while Pearcey dropped nearly two minutes with a gentle roll. Darren Moon and Phil Clarke dropped over three minutes when the HT lead came off.

Roger Albert Clark Rally 2013: the tenth edition

Colin Wilkinson in a frosty Kershope

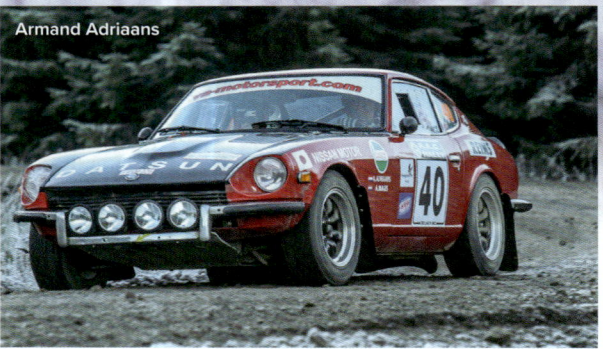

Armand Adriaans

Ceiriog Hughes

Meanwhile, the lead battle was brewing up nicely although Robinson dropped a little time on the asphalt at Croft. Pritchard, however, was flying and pulled back time to be within 45s of Bannister and all three then set exactly the same time in Hamsterley. But it was a double run through 12.5 miles of Pundershaw that changed the whole rally.

Pritchard was first to go, rolling heavily after a deceptive crest on the first run. On the second run, Robinson made a similar error at the same place and also rolled out as both drivers ended what had been impressive performances. At a stroke, Bannister's lead went out to four minutes, but he was genuinely gutted as he arrived at Carlisle to discover his rivals were gone. "That's a real shame," said the rally leader, who had relished another final day battle.

Griffiths had a great Saturday to move up to second but a delay for his management crew left him borrowing fuel to get through the second Pundershaw as Davies slotted into third from O'Connell and Owen Murphy/James O'Brien. Murphy found the lack of notes a real challenge in John Leahy's Sunbeam Lotus but upped his pace nicely on Saturday.

In Category 2, Belgians Stefaan Stouf and Joris Erard struggled all day with a broken exhaust manifold in their Ford Escort Mk1 but planned to get it welded up at Carlisle as they held a 55s margin over Peter Smith and Pat Walsh.

Day three: Sunday

This rally often delivers a sting in the tail and Sunday's leg of 70 stage miles in the Scottish borders opened after a sharp overnight frost. Icy patches lay in wait and duly claimed some casualties.

Bannister had a lead of just short of four minutes on Sunday morning. "I had it to lose rather than anyone else to win," said Bannister. "I pushed on in Craik and had two good times in there, because I get a bit

Seamus O'Connell in Craik

frustrated if you can't have a go. So, I had a go in Craik and really enjoyed it."

Sure enough, Bannister never put a wheel wrong and swept to victory by 4m12s after a glorious day of rallying over epic stages. Neither driver nor car had missed a beat in another stellar performance.

Griffiths, too, had turned in a fine rally to finish a best-yet second overall. "Brilliant: a really tough rally," he reported. Completing the overall podium was O'Connell who did well to deal with clutch and gearbox problems on Sunday to repeat his 2008 result.

"I loved the ice and the stages were fabulous," said Pearcey of a fine last day that took him to fourth as Murphy slipped back to fifth with two punctures. Moon charged back to sixth from the superbly consistent Charlie Taylor/Steve Bielby.

Stouf clinched Category 2 but it was close as the flying Chris Browne/Ali Cornwell-Browne stormed to within 38 seconds and pipped Smith in the closing stages. The elated Browne summed up his first and the tenth Roger Albert Clark Rally: "We loved everything about it! This is an incredible rally and we're coming back next year."

Open Rally

After an up and down rally, Martyn Hawkswell and Nick Welch finally emerged to win the concurrent Open Rally and complete a hat-trick of wins in their Ford Escort Mk2. Despite thinking his chance of victory was gone after a suspension breakage on the opening Duncombe Park stage on Saturday morning, Hawkswell battled back ahead and retook the lead when Nick Jarvis and Craig Thorley retired their Escort Mk1 on Sunday morning.

John Everard

Roger Albert Clark Rally 2013: the tenth edition

Matt Edwards in Duncombe Park

Ian Beveridge

Charlie Taylor

"I was fairly certain we were not going to win, but we set out Sunday morning to have a good go," said Hawkswell, who had taken a narrow lead on Friday evening. But limping through the second run of Duncombe Park lost him nearly a minute and a half.

Meanwhile, Jarvis was setting the pace and escaped from a high speed off at Croft with only minor panel damage to the back of the car. However, his rally ended with mechanical problems on Sunday and Hawkswell went back ahead having fended off the combined challenge from Barry Stevenson-Wheeler/John Pickavance and Dave Hemingway/Simon Ashton.

The classes
Class B1 among the Category 1 cars was an all-Saab 96 affair as the wonderful two-strokes of Stephen Higgins/Ronnie Roughead and Jim Valentine/Jonathan Lodge went head-to-head. Ultimately, Manxman Higgins had a great run to win by a handy margin with a typically attacking drive.

The event would not be complete without Bob Bean and Malcolm Smithson in their Lotus Cortina and they won Category 1 overall with another polished performance. However, over the opening leg, the Volvo PV544 of Ian Beveridge and Peter Joy made the running. Bean moved ahead on Saturday and the Volvo then suffered a snapped camshaft on Sunday.

Dutchmen Nykle Meijer and Fons Gosgens delighted the fans in their Austin Healey 3000 and overcame a catalogue of problems to win Class B5, while Steve and Tony Graham guided their Lancia Fulvia to Class C1 victory despite losing the brakes

Robinson and Collis in Dalby

in Staindale on Friday evening.

A clutch change on Friday night gave Darren Grimston and Tony Walker a late night with their Ford Escort Mexico but they bounced back to win Class C2. Dave Watkins and Paul Train should have been in the battle in their ex-Hannu Mikkola Escort Mk1, but alternator failure on Friday left them too far behind to challenge.

Kim Baker and Paul Heath (Ford Escort Mk1) bagged a fine victory in Class C3 as Baker had a ball in the XS Racing car for the first time. A heart-in-mouth moment in Pundershaw kept Kim on her toes but a top 20 overall finish was a great result. Sadly, things did not end well for class rivals Phil Jobson/Ali Proctor with a heavy off in Craik when caught out by a patch of ice.

Armand Adriaans and Anne-Marie Magis claimed Class C4 in their Datsun 240Z. The similar car of Jeremy Easson and Mike Reynolds was an early casualty when the propshaft failed on Friday evening, while Tim Mason and Graham Wild led until their Porsche 911 crashed on the ice of Sunday morning.

Chris Skill and Garry Middleton (Ford Escort Sport) had a ball on their way to Class D2 spoils in a car finished three days before the rally. The Montescorts car ran superbly and Middleton coped remarkably well on his first ever rally as they enjoyed running at the head of the field with the Category 1 cars.

Guy Woodcock and Graham Dance delivered yet another giant-killing performance in their Pinto-powered Ford Escort Mk2, which ran like a train. They were a mighty sixth overall at the end of Saturday but lost out to power on Sunday and slipped to ninth to record their third top 10 overall finish.

Tomas Davies

Edmund Peel and Dessie Nutt in the Clubman Rally

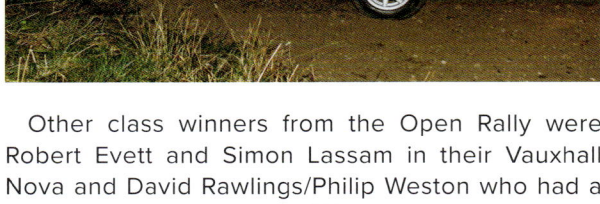

Falko Jansen

The Stratos in Duncombe Park

Other class winners from the Open Rally were Robert Evett and Simon Lassam in their Vauxhall Nova and David Rawlings/Philip Weston who had a good run in their Porsche 911.

Personal view: Paul Lawrence
It was around 7pm on the Saturday evening of the Roger Albert Clark Rally when Steve Bannister and Kevin Rae arrived at the 'service in' control in Carlisle. One of the service crew leant into the car and told 'Banner' that Matthew Robinson had rolled out in Pundershaw. We then confirmed to him what he had suspected: Jason Pritchard had done the same and was also out.

For a man who had just been handed a four-minute lead with one day to go, you might have expected Bannister to be elated at the prospect of an easy run to victory on Sunday. But you could not have been more wrong.

Bannister was genuinely gutted. Until the double run of Pundershaw, Robinson and Pritchard had pushed him hard and it was shaping up to be an epic three-way contest over 75 stage miles on Sunday. Earlier on Saturday, all three had set the same time in Hamsterley in a nip-and-tuck contest.

However, the same deceptive brow in Pundershaw had caught out both his rivals, and Bannister was dejected. He was particularly frustrated that his stable mate Robinson had crashed out despite a pre-stage warning. "Silly bugger," he said in typically direct Yorkshire style.

Winner's view: Steve Bannister
"After the fight with Marty McCormack last year and losing on the last stage, this has made up a little bit. But last year was such a fight, right to the death. This is the best event of the year for historic cars, so it is

Steve Bannister took his second overall win

great to win it again. As you get older there are all these young lads coming up and there are more and more of them coming in with Escorts. So it's nice to think I can stay on their pace. Next year? Well, maybe, we'll have to see!

"It's been a brilliant event. We've had no problems at all. To be fair, Kevin Theaker builds the car so well that we just do tyres and petrol and that's about it. I was very disappointed when Matthew Robinson went out. Both Matthew and Jason Pritchard were giving me a good fight: it was great when we all three set the same time in Hamsterley as that showed how close it was.

"The same crest caught them both out. We did that crest on the Pirelli Rally earlier this year. I kicked Matthew's ass for going off on the second run over the stage and told him he was a silly bugger. I said: 'what the hell were you doing?'

"I never had enough in hand to be comfortable. Sunday would have been very interesting with the ice if they had both stayed in the rally. Matthew was out watching and I said to him that probably none of us would have finished Sunday if we'd been battling.

We'd have all gone off on the ice.

"It was amazing really, especially with the ice on Sunday morning, and it was really tough. The ice in Kershope and Newcastleton was really bad. Craik was probably the least icy of them all, but even in the afternoon stages there were little patches of ice here and there to catch you out if you were not careful. You'd get a mile or two where it was really good and you were lulled into a false sense of security. Then you'd suddenly feel the car sliding.'

Robert Evett

2013 ROGER ALBERT CLARK RALLY: ENTRY LIST

No	Driver	Co-driver	Car	Class
1	Stefaan Stouf	Joris Erard	Ford Escort RS1600	C5
2	Matthew Robinson	Sam Collis	Ford Escort Mk2	D5
3	Matt Edwards	Will Rogers	Ford Escort Mk2	D5
4	Jason Pritchard	John Millington	Ford Escort RS1800	E5
5	Tomas Davies	Eurig Davies	Ford Escort Mk2	D5
6	Tim Pearcey	Neil Shanks	Ford Escort RS1800	D5
7	Rob Smith	Alun Cook	Ford Escort RS	E5
8	Owen Murphy	James O'Brien	Talbot Sunbeam Lotus	D4
9	Allan McDowall	Gavin Heseltine	Ford Escort RS1800	D5
10	Steve Perez	Paul Spooner	Lancia Stratos	E5
11	Jeremy Easson	Mike Reynolds	Datsun 240Z	C4
12	Paul Griffiths	Richard Wardle	Ford Escort RS1800	D5
14	Seamus O'Connell	Paul Wakely	Ford Escort Mk2	D5
15	Richard Lepley	Andy Richardson	Ford Escort RS1800	D5
16	Phil Squires	Mick Squires	Ford Escort RS1800	D5
17	Tim Mason	Graham Wild	Porsche 911RS	C4
18	Charlie Taylor	Steve Bielby	Ford Escort Mk2	D5
19	Meirion Evans	Iwan Jones	Ford Escort Mk2	D5
20	Guy Woodcock	Graham Dance	Ford Escort RS2000	D3
21	Darren Moon	Phil Clarke	Ford Escort RS1800	D5
22	Peter Smith	Patrick Walsh	Ford Escort Mk1	C5
24	Theo Bengry	Les Forsbrook	Ford Escort Mk2	E5
25	Chris Browne	Ali Cornwell-Browne	Ford Escort RS1600	C5
26	Barry Jordan	James Gratton-Smith	Ford Escort	C5
27	Phil Jobson	Ali Proctor	Ford Escort Mk1	C3
28	Nick Jarvis	Craig Thorley	Ford Escort	G4
29	Bas Jansen	Ruud van den Houdt	Ford Escort Mk2	D3
30	Rodger Mark Fowler	Chris Dewsnap	Ford Escort Mk2	D3
31	Steve Graham	Tony Graham	Lancia Fulvia	C1
32	Steve Bannister	Kevin Rae	Ford Escort Mk2	D5
33	Falko Jansen	Franz Gotz	Talbot Sunbeam	E3
34	John McIlwraith	Andy Irving	Ford Escort RS2000	D3
35	James Stait	Glyn Thomas	Talbot Sunbeam Lotus	D4
36	David Lucking	Paul Garside	Ford Escort Mk2	D3
37	Dave Forrest	Charlie Carter	Ford Escort Mk2	D3
38	Peter Egerton	Jamie Edwards	Ford Escort	E5
39	Jerry Bailey	Graham Lacey	Ford Escort RS	D5
40	Armand Adriaans	Anne Marie Magis	Datsun 240Z	C4
41	Andrew Haddon	Mark Crisp	Ford Escort Mk2	E3
42	Stewart Scott	Mark Casey	Ford Escort RS2000	C3
43	Ceiriog Hughes	Emyr Hall	Saab 96 V4	C3
44	Kim Baker	Paul Heath	Ford Escort Mk1	C3
45	Adrian Young	Gwynfor Jones	Ford Escort Mk2	D3
51	Bob Bean	Malcolm Smithson	Ford Lotus Cortina Mk1	B4
52	David Watkins	Paul Train	Ford Escort Mk1	C2
53	Darren Grimston	Tony Walker	Ford Escort Mexico	C2
54	Ian Beveridge	Peter Joy	Volvo PV544	B4
55	Paul Kendrick	Anton Bird	Ford Escort Mk1	C2
56	David John Goose	Robert H Oldershaw	Ford Escort Mk2	D2
57	Colin Wilkinson	John Stanger-Leathes	Hillman Avenger	C2

Jerry Bailey

2013 ROGER ALBERT CLARK RALLY: ENTRY LIST (continued)

No	Driver	Co-driver	Car	Class
58	John Everard	Mark Sharpley	Alfa Romeo 1600 Junior GT	B4
59	Mark Schmidt	Vincent Spijker	Austin Healey 3000	B5
60	Nykle Meijer	Fons Gosgens	Austin Healey 3000	B5
61	Chris Skill	Garry Middleton	Ford Escort 1600 Sport	D2
62	Jim Valentine	Jonathan Lodge	Saab 96 Sport Two Stroke	B1
63	Stephen Higgins	Ronnie Roughead	Saab 96 Two Stroke	B1
65	Martyn Hawkswell	Nick Welch	Ford Escort RS	G4
66	Dave Hemingway	Simon Ashton	Ford Escort Mk2	G4
67	Barry Stevenson-Wheeler	John Pickavance	Ford Escort RS	G4
68	Raj Jutley	Richard Hage	Ford Escort Mk1	G4
69	Andy Madge	Pat Cooper	Toyota Corolla GT Coupe	G3
70	Colin Hope	Nick Patrick	Ford Focus	G4
71	David Winstanley	Brynmor Pierce	BMW 320i	G5
72	David Rawlings	Philip Weston	Porsche 911	G5
74	Robert Evett	Simon Lassam	Vauxhall Nova SRi	G2
75	Mark Dickinson	Ken Sturdy	Rover 200	G2

Matthew Robinson

David Rawlings

Roger Albert Clark Rally 2013: the tenth edition

2013 STAGES AND STAGE WINNERS

Day	Stage	Name	Distance	Stage winner(s)	Time
Friday	SS1	Dalby 1	8.50	Bannister/Rae	8.52
Friday	SS2	Newclose Rigg 1	3.84	Bannister/Rae	4.11
Friday	SS3	Staindale 1	4.14	Griffiths/Wardle	5.14
Friday	SS4	Dalby 2	8.50	Pritchard/Millington	8.56
Friday	SS5	Newclose Rigg 2	3.84	Robinson/Collis	4.11
Friday	SS6	Staindale 2	4.14	Griffiths/Wardle	5.15
Saturday	SS7	Duncombe Park 1	4.33	Griffiths/Wardle	5.34
Saturday	SS8	Duncombe Park 2	4.33	Griffiths/Wardle	5.19
Saturday	SS9	Croft 1	5.42	Pritchard/Millington	5.04
Saturday	SS10	Croft 2	5.42	O'Connell/Wakely	4.53
Saturday	SS11	Hamsterley	5.76	Robinson/Collis, Pritchard/Millington and Bannister/Rae	5.54
Saturday	SS12	Pundershaw 1	12.53	Bannister/Rae	11.45
Saturday	SS13	Pundershaw 2	12.53	Bannister/Rae	11.57
Sunday	SS14	Kershope 1	6.41	Edwards/Rogers	7.19
Sunday	SS15	Newcastleton 1	4.71	Pearcey/Shanks	4.57
Sunday	SS16	Florida 1	3.28	Griffiths/Wardle	3.48
Sunday	SS17	Riccarton	13.61	Griffiths/Wardle	14.05
Sunday	SS18	Craik 1	9.01	Bannister/Rae	9.51
Sunday	SS19	Craik 2	9.01	Bannister/Rae	9.47
Sunday	SS20	Wauchope	12.77	Bannister/Rae	13.27
Sunday	SS21	Florida 2	3.22	Pearcey/Shanks and Griffiths/Wardle	3.53
Sunday	SS22	Newcastleton 2	4.52	Edwards/Rogers	4.54
Sunday	SS23	Kershope 2	6.81	Edwards/Rogers	8.09

2013 RESULTS

Overall	Class	No	Driver	Co-driver	Car	Class	Total
1	1	32	Steve Bannister	Kevin Rae	Ford Escort Mk2	D5	02:49:07
2	2	12	Paul Griffiths	Richard Wardle	Ford Escort RS1800	D5	02:53:19
3	3	14	Seamus O'Connell	Paul Wakely	Ford Escort Mk2	D5	02:55:55
4	4	6	Tim Pearcey	Neil Shanks	Ford Escort RS1800	D5	02:56:47
5	1	8	Owen Murphy	James O'Brien	Talbot Sunbeam Lotus	D4	02:57:04
6	5	21	Darren Moon	Phil Clarke	Ford Escort RS1800	D5	02:57:34
7	6	18	Charlie Taylor	Steve Bielby	Ford Escort Mk2	D5	02:58:10
8	7	3	Matt Edwards	Will Rogers	Ford Escort Mk2	D5	02:58:27
9	1	20	Guy Woodcock	Graham Dance	Ford Escort RS2000	D3	02:58:57
10	1	7	Rob Smith	Alun Cook	Ford Escort RS	E5	03:00:05
11	1	1	Stefaan Stouf	Joris Erard	Ford Escort RS1600	C5	03:01:32
12	2	24	Theo Bengry	Les Forsbrook	Ford Escort Mk2	E5	03:02:00
13	2	25	Chris Browne	Ali Cornwell-Browne	Ford Escort RS1600	C5	03:02:10
14	3	22	Peter Smith	Patrick Walsh	Ford Escort Mk1	C5	03:02:18
15	8	16	Phil Squires	Mick Squires	Ford Escort RS1800	D5	03:03:05
16	3	38	Peter Egerton	Jamie Edwards	Ford Escort	E5	03:14:05
17	1	61	Chris Skill	Garry Middleton	Ford Escort Mk2 1600 Sport	D2	03:15:07
18	1	51	Bob Bean	Malcolm Smithson	Ford Lotus Cortina Mk1	B4	03:17:14
19	1	53	Darren Grimston	Tony Walker	Ford Escort Mexico	C2	03:18:44
20	1	44	Kim Baker	Paul Heath	Ford Escort Mk1	C3	03:22:00
21	2	56	David John Goose	Robert H Oldershaw	Ford Escort Mk2	D2	03:24:13
22	2	36	David Lucking	Paul Garside	Ford Escort Mk2	D3	03:27:12
23	2	42	Stewart Scott	Mark Casey	Ford Escort RS2000	C3	03:30:19
24	1	40	Armand Adriaans	Anne Marie Magis	Datsun 240Z	C4	03:41:33
25	1	63	Stephen Higgins	Ronnie Roughead	Saab 96 Two Stroke	B1	03:41:42
26	2	62	Jim Valentine	Jonathan Lodge	Saab 96 Sport Two Stroke	B1	03:45:33

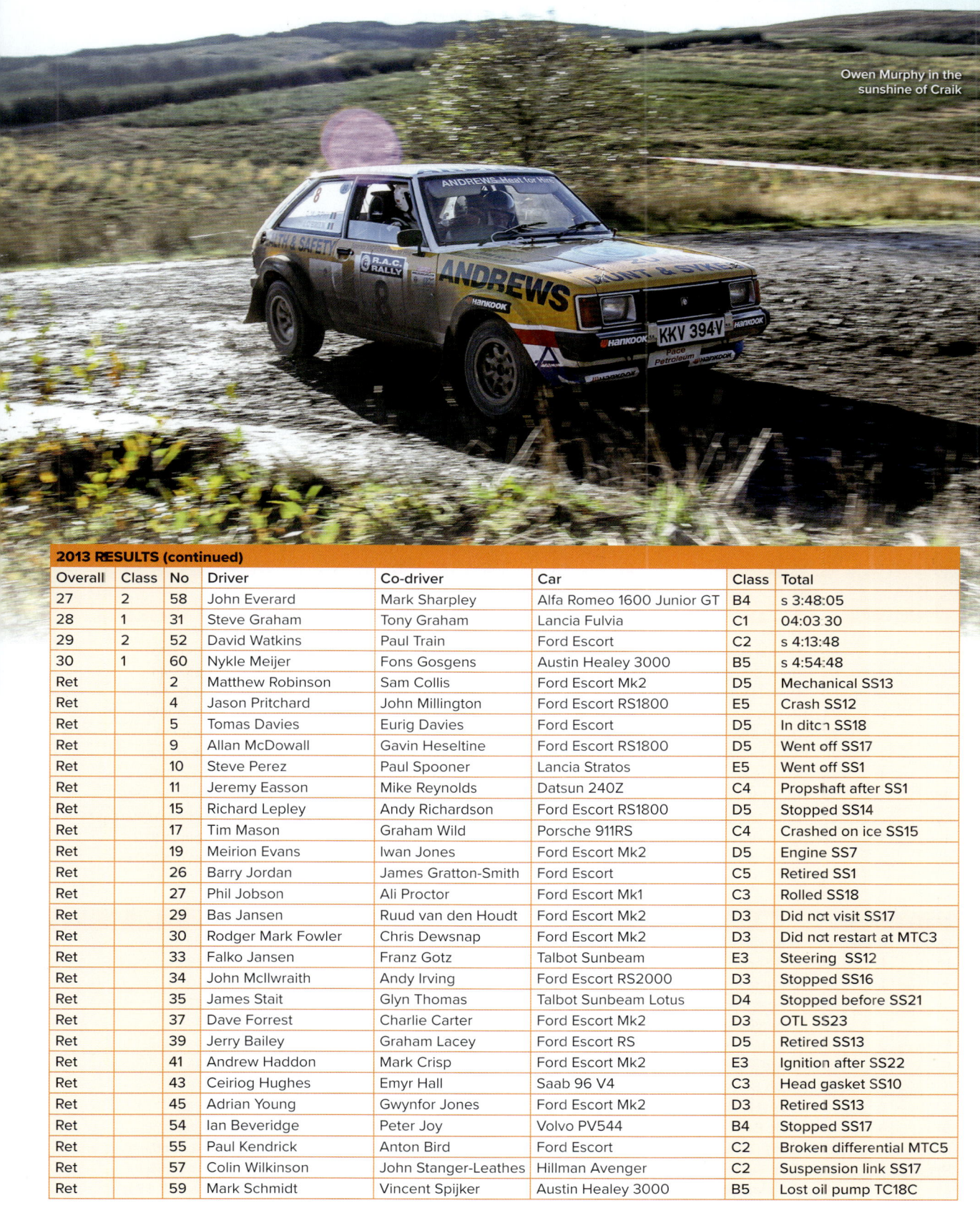

Owen Murphy in the sunshine of Craik

2013 RESULTS (continued)

Overall	Class	No	Driver	Co-driver	Car	Class	Total
27	2	58	John Everard	Mark Sharpley	Alfa Romeo 1600 Junior GT	B4	s 3:48:05
28	1	31	Steve Graham	Tony Graham	Lancia Fulvia	C1	04:03 30
29	2	52	David Watkins	Paul Train	Ford Escort	C2	s 4:13:48
30	1	60	Nykle Meijer	Fons Gosgens	Austin Healey 3000	B5	s 4:54:48
Ret		2	Matthew Robinson	Sam Collis	Ford Escort Mk2	D5	Mechanical SS13
Ret		4	Jason Pritchard	John Millington	Ford Escort RS1800	E5	Crash SS12
Ret		5	Tomas Davies	Eurig Davies	Ford Escort	D5	In ditch SS18
Ret		9	Allan McDowall	Gavin Heseltine	Ford Escort RS1800	D5	Went off SS17
Ret		10	Steve Perez	Paul Spooner	Lancia Stratos	E5	Went off SS1
Ret		11	Jeremy Easson	Mike Reynolds	Datsun 240Z	C4	Propshaft after SS1
Ret		15	Richard Lepley	Andy Richardson	Ford Escort RS1800	D5	Stopped SS14
Ret		17	Tim Mason	Graham Wild	Porsche 911RS	C4	Crashed on ice SS15
Ret		19	Meirion Evans	Iwan Jones	Ford Escort Mk2	D5	Engine SS7
Ret		26	Barry Jordan	James Gratton-Smith	Ford Escort	C5	Retired SS1
Ret		27	Phil Jobson	Ali Proctor	Ford Escort Mk1	C3	Rolled SS18
Ret		29	Bas Jansen	Ruud van den Houdt	Ford Escort Mk2	D3	Did not visit SS17
Ret		30	Rodger Mark Fowler	Chris Dewsnap	Ford Escort Mk2	D3	Did not restart at MTC3
Ret		33	Falko Jansen	Franz Gotz	Talbot Sunbeam	E3	Steering SS12
Ret		34	John McIlwraith	Andy Irving	Ford Escort RS2000	D3	Stopped SS16
Ret		35	James Stait	Glyn Thomas	Talbot Sunbeam Lotus	D4	Stopped before SS21
Ret		37	Dave Forrest	Charlie Carter	Ford Escort Mk2	D3	OTL SS23
Ret		39	Jerry Bailey	Graham Lacey	Ford Escort RS	D5	Retired SS13
Ret		41	Andrew Haddon	Mark Crisp	Ford Escort Mk2	E3	Ignition after SS22
Ret		43	Ceiriog Hughes	Emyr Hall	Saab 96 V4	C3	Head gasket SS10
Ret		45	Adrian Young	Gwynfor Jones	Ford Escort Mk2	D3	Retired SS13
Ret		54	Ian Beveridge	Peter Joy	Volvo PV544	B4	Stopped SS17
Ret		55	Paul Kendrick	Anton Bird	Ford Escort	C2	Broken differential MTC5
Ret		57	Colin Wilkinson	John Stanger-Leathes	Hillman Avenger	C2	Suspension link SS17
Ret		59	Mark Schmidt	Vincent Spijker	Austin Healey 3000	B5	Lost oil pump TC18C

Roger Albert Clark Rally 2013: the tenth edition

Allan McDowall

2013 RESULTS: OPEN RALLY

Overall	Class	No	Driver	Co-driver	Car	Class	Total
1	1	65	Martyn Hawkswell	Nick Welch	Ford Escort RS	G4	03:07:30
2	2	67	Barry Stevenson-Wheeler	John Pickavance	Ford Escort RS	G4	03:08:44
3	3	66	Dave Hemingway	Simon Ashton	Ford Escort Mk2	G4	03:09:26
4	1	74	Robert Evett	Simon Lassam	Vauxhall Nova SRi	G2	03:26:05
5	1	72	David Rawlings	Philip Weston	Porsche 911	G5	03:27:10
6	2	75	Mark Dickinson	Ken Sturdy	Rover 200	G2	03:29:53
7	4	68	Raj Jutley	Richard Hage	Ford Escort Mk1	G4	s 3:49:35
Ret		28	Nick Jarvis	Craig Thorley	Ford Escort	G4	Stopped SS16
Ret		69	Andy Madge	Pat Cooper	Toyota Corolla GT Coupe	G3	Did not restart at MTC3
Ret		70	Colin Hope	Nick Patrick	Ford Focus	G4	Retired SS7
Ret		71	David Winstanley	Brynmor Pierce	BMW 320i	G5	Retired SS12

2013 RESULTS: PEREGRINE NIGHT RALLY

Overall	Class	No	Driver	Co-driver	Car	Class	Total
1	1	102	Mat Smith	Giles Dykes	Ford Ka	H2	00:38:21
2	1	101	Steve Magson	Richard Boyes	Ford Escort Mk1 RS2000	H3	00:40:07
3	2	103	Marcus Tomlinson	Darren Smith	Ford Escort Mk2	H3	00:43:37
4	1	107	Simon Cole	Ian Jackson	BMW 325i	H4	00:44:21
5	2	114	David Wood	Matt Wood	Vauxhall Corsa	H2	00:45:05
6	3	109	David Mosey	Graham Hepworth	Hillman Avenger	H3	00:45:32
7	3	112	Peter Bennett	Alastair McNeil	Vauxhall Corsa	H2	00:48:52
8	2	104	Dean Hickling	Geoff Moss	Ford Sierra Sapphire	H4	00:52:41
9	4	113	Clive Baty	Richard Crozier	Renault 5 Alpine	H2	00:55:28
Ret		108	Harry Shephard	Stephen Shephard	Ford Escort Mk2 RS2000	H3	Brake problems after SS3
Ret		110	Pete Williams	Josh Pulleyn	Ford Escort Mk2	H2	Retired SS5
Ret		111	Amanda Cornforth	Derek Cornforth	Ford Ka	H2	Driveshaft SS4

Raj Jutley

Tim Mason

2013 RESULTS: CLUBMANS RALLY

Overall	Class	No	Driver	Co-driver	Car	Class	Total
1	1	82	James Potter	Bob Duck	Ford Escort RS	K3	00:41:13
2	1	83	Guy Anderson	Tony Phillips	Talbot Sunbeam Lotus	K4	00:41:27
3	2	81	Terry Brown	Tomos Whittle	Ford Escort RS1800	K3	00:41:55
4	2	90	Nigel Talton	Andrew Turner	Rover SD1	K4	00:47:54
5	1	89	Robert Rook	Bernard Nolan	Ford Escort Twin Cam	K2	00:48:16
6	2	93	David Wood	Matt Wood	Vauxhall Corsa	K2	00:49:32
7	3	84	Alan Mayhew	Bryan Newton	Ford Escort Mk2	K3	00:50:47
8	4	88	Edmund Peel	Dessie Nutt	Porsche 911	K3	00:50:55
9	5	87	Brian Maguire	David Curtis	Peugeot 205 GTI Mi16	K3	00:52:13
10	3	86	Thomas Heard	Amanda Burney	Volvo S70 T5	K4	01:02:03
Ret		85	Iain Heard	Alistair Maxwell	Ford Escort Mk2	K3	Stopped SS16
Ret		91	Darren Martin	Martin Steele	Peugeot 206	K3	Retired after SS16
Ret		92	Jeff Wincott	Martin Payne	Ford Escort Mk2	K3	Electrical did not start
Ret		94	Peter Roughan	Barry Sharpe	Ford Escort	K3	Did not visit SS14

2013 RESULTS: RETURN RALLY

Overall	Class	No	Driver	Co-driver	Car	Class	Total
1	1	82	James Potter	Bob Duck	Ford Escort RS	L3	00:42:35
2	1	83	Guy Anderson	Tony Phillips	Talbot Sunbeam Lotus	L4	00:44:03
3	2	81	Terry Brown	Tomos Whittle	Ford Escort RS1800	L3	00:45:10
4	2	90	Nigel Talton	Andrew Turner	Rover SD1	L4	00:49:49
5	3	87	Brian Maguire	Dave Curtis	Peugeot 205 GTi Mi16	L3	00:50:32
6	1	89	Robert Rook	Bernard Nolan	Ford Escort Mk1 Twin Cam	L2	00:50:52
7	4	91	Darren Martin	Martin Steele	Peugeot 206	L3	00:51:46
8	5	88	Edmund Peel	Dessie Nutt	Porsche 911	L3	00:54:51
Ret		92	Jeff Wincott	Martin Payne	Ford Escort Mk2	L3	Did not start
Ret		93	David Wood	Matt Wood	Vauxhall Corsa	L2	Stopped SS23

Darren Grimston

Bob Bean

Roger Albert Clark Rally 2013: the tenth edition

Roger Albert Clark Rally 2014:
the eleventh edition

Overall winners:
Matthew Robinson
and Sam Collis

Robinson takes over

The 2014 rally

Friday 28 to Sunday 30 November
152 stage miles
26 special stages
Start: Seaburn Centre, Sunderland
Overnight 1 & 2: Seaburn Centre, Sunderland
Finish: Seaburn Centre, Sunderland
61 starters
42 finishers

Open Rally winners:
Nigel Barber and Stuart Popplewell

Roger Albert Rally 2014: the eleventh edition

Thomas Schulz in Herrington Park

Action, drama and a final plot twist were all part of the 2014 Roger Albert Clark Rally with a first victory for Matthew Robinson and Sam Collis after initial victors Matt Edwards and Paul Morris were excluded from the results.

For two and a half days, the two Ford Escort Mk2 crews had wowed the fans in an intense contest that started in horrendous fog in Hamsterley. Edwards/Morris arrived in Sunderland on Sunday afternoon with a 34s margin but were later excluded from this map-based event. The exclusion was for having information on the stages that should not have been carried in the competing car.

It was a desperately sad end to another epic Roger Albert and what is certain is that both crews had driven superbly across a stunning array of stages in and around the Kielder complex. "We sent a lot of spectators home happy," said Robinson after a mature performance in tough conditions. "I'll have to come back next year and do it properly," he added.

Edwards was gutted to lose what had seemed like an emotional victory. He'd worked tirelessly to make it to the event and had set a searing pace, notably in the fog of Hamsterley. Then, a puncture led to a spin into a ditch in Kershope on Saturday evening and he had to set about overhauling Robinson again to rebuild his lead.

As ever with this demanding rally, the overall results were peppered with outstanding performances and heroic tales as crews, mechanics and sometimes spectators worked miracles to keep cars running.

Up into second overall went Nick Elliott and

Malcolm Davey

Nick Elliott and Dave Price in Redesdale

Kim Baker

Andrew Siddall

Dave Price, while a superb third was the Fiat 131 of Julian Reynolds and Patrick Walsh. That fine result completed a clean sweep of the podium for cars from Rallysport Developments.

This was an event that delivered variety, too, as Gregoire de Mevius/Andre Leyh (Porsche 911), Jeremy Easson/Mike Reynolds (Datsun 240Z) and Steve Perez/John Millington (Lancia Stratos) all joined the Fiat in the top 10. Another stand-out performance came from Open Rally victors Nigel Barber and Stuart Popplewell in their Vauxhall Astra. They set a fearsome pace only topped by the leading historics and took the first Open win for a front-wheel drive car. "I'm over the moon: it's been a fantastic event and it's a dream result," said Barber.

It all started in thick fog on Friday evening, with some crews groping their way along with dipped headlights and in second gear. However, upfront, the two runs through Hamsterley dramatically shaped the rally. Robinson caught the struggling Elliott and Edwards nearly caught them both as he took an overnight lead of nearly a minute over Robinson.

All through Saturday Robinson chased the leader and thought he'd got his opening when Edwards backed into a Kershope ditch trying to rejoin after a spin. However, willing spectators saved the day for Edwards and limited the damage to a minute and a half. Over the final three stages of the leg, Edwards attacked once more to lead by 44s as the weary survivors filed back into Sunderland.

Roger Albert Clark Rally 2014: the eleventh edition

Matt Edwards and Paul Morris

Mark Schmidt

Ceiriog Hughes

"Go large or go home," was Robinson's plan for Sunday's seven stages and he chipped away to end the rally just 34s down and rueing the time spent behind Elliott in Hamsterley. However, this rally had a final twist and victory became Robinson's. "When we come to this rally, we know we use a map and a poti and nothing else," he said.

Up to second went Elliott and Price after a measured performance, accepting that chasing the two pacesetters would require just too many risks. "After we dropped the time in the fog, we concentrated on being the best of the rest: the stages were very unfamiliar but excellent quality," said Elliott.

Third for Reynolds and Walsh in the still-new Fiat 131 was like a victory and the car ran remarkably strongly right from the start with only a modest crew looking after it. "The car has run so well and I'm just pleased for Kevin Theaker and the team," said Reynolds who also topped Category K after Paul Griffiths/Iwan Jones retired in Harwood with engine dramas.

Easily best of the growing European contingent was the Porsche of de Mevius and Leyh, who came back strongly after struggling badly in the fog. They topped Category 2 after overhauling the Datsun of Easson/Reynolds during the comeback drive. "It's been great," said the Belgian ace. "For sure we have enjoyed it and it was so much easier in the daylight!"

Easson was mighty in the fog, sensing the opportunity to lay the foundations of a great result for the Datsun. "I've thoroughly enjoyed it, but it was hard work," he said. However, splitting the two sports cars was another of the drives of the rally. Guy Woodcock and Graham Dance got their Pinto-powered Escort Mk2 into an amazing third place at the end of Friday after a blistering run in the fog. They slipped back a little as power told in the daylight, but

The Kershope sunset: David Goose

fifth overall and Class D3 victory was just reward.

Easson was nearly caught for sixth by Charlie Taylor and John Richardson as Taylor made it 10 top 10 finishes in a row. It nearly went wrong, however, as Taylor's Escort Mk2 spent three minutes in a Shepherdshield ditch before spectators could get it going again. Meanwhile, eighth overall was an excellent result for Steve Perez and John Millington in the Lancia Stratos, which ran stronger than ever.

Two more great runs rounded out the top 10. Ian Jones and Iestyn Williams took ninth and second in class D3 in their Escort Mk2, while Chris Browne and his wife Ali bounced back superbly after an early engine timing drama to take tenth and Class C5. "We did it, but it's been hard work," said Browne who spent all day Saturday overtaking cars after dropping well down the running order.

Finally, the tales of what might have been included Alan Walker and Jez Rogers (Escort Mk2) who were fourth after Friday but suffered a blown engine early on Saturday and Darren Moon/Phil Clarke (Escort Mk2) who retired after a second gearbox failure.

The classes

Aside from a scare with fuel right at the start of the rally, it was a mighty performance from Jim Valentine and Jonathan Lodge to claim Class B1 in the wonderful two-stroke Saab 96. The venerable car barely missed a beat all weekend to maintain a fine record on this rally. Sadly, class rivals Steve Higgins and Mark Casey retired their similar car early on with diff failure.

Thomas Kleinwachter

Roger Albert Clark Rally 2014: the eleventh edition

Jeremy Easson and Mike Reynolds took sixth place

Barry Stevenson-Wheeler

Tom Axelsson

Local crew Richard Holdsworth/John Stanger-Leathes (Ford Cortina GT) earned Cass B3 spoils the hard way after a challenging event. However, it all came together on the final day when the Cortina behaved impeccably on what was only the driver's sixth gravel rally.

Ian Beveridge and Peter Joy (Volvo PV 544) emerged from a tough rally to win Category 1 overall and, other than points failure at Croft, had a remarkably clean run. "The car has been great," said Beveridge, who finished the rally with a handsome margin. Bob Bean/Malcolm Smithson (Lotus Cortina) dropped out of contention with electrical dramas, while Paul Mankin/Peter Scott suffered two half shaft failures on their similar car.

Mark Schmidt and Midas Nellisen (Austin Healey 3000) bagged class B5 with their first finish after two previous attempts. "We enjoyed it tremendously but we were very nervous over the last three stages," said the Dutchman. Countrymen Nykle Meijer and Eef de Jong used Super Rally rules to get their Healey to the finish.

Steve and Tony Graham (Lancia Fulvia) scored a deserved Class C1 victory after the little Lancia behaved impeccably until the final loop of stages when a broken throttle linkage nearly signalled disaster. But it was sorted out in time and they claimed the class.

Class C3 went to Phil Jobson and Arwel Jenkins (Ford Escort Mk1) once the similar car of Steve Magson and Darren Smith was forced out when Smith felt unwell with a virus on Saturday afternoon. Jobson was on target for his aim of a top 20 overall finish when they lost a lot of time with a puncture on the final stage.

Graham Standen and Bill Cook (Ford Escort Mk1)

Julian Reynolds and Patrick Walsh

were top of a hard-fought Class D2 with only a minute in hand over the charging Kim Baker and John Connor. "The first night in the fog was not so good but the car has been absolutely perfect," said Standen after doing most of the rally on second-hand tyres.

In the Open Rally, Malcolm Davey and Paul Slingsby (Ford Escort Mk1) won Class G3 and recorded their thanks for the spectators who got them out of a ditch in Ogre Hill.

Clubmans Rally
Running over six stages on Sunday was the Clubmans Rally and it delivered a narrow victory for the Citroen C2R2 of Jim Robertson and Colin Maxwell. They arrived back at Kielder dam with just over half a minute in hand over the Ford Fiesta RS of Mike Axford and Dave Thomason.

Two laps of the Ogre Hill, Redesdale and Falstone stages made up the compact event, although the eight crews lost the opening run through Falstone while an earlier accident in the main event was dealt with.

Axford was straight out of the blocks in Ogre Hill to go 8s up on Robertson as Brian Middlemas and Kevin Mathers slotted their splendid Hillman Avenger into third. Axford then added another 7s in Redesdale but it was still only a 17s lead as they arrived back at Redesdale for the penultimate stage. In turn, Middlemas was just 2s down on the Citroen.

However, Robertson saved his best until last and went 9s better in Redesdale and a whopping 30s quicker in Falstone to seal victory.

Alan Walker

Roger Albert Clark Rally 2014: the eleventh edition

Robinson and Collis on Sunday afternoon

Philip Young

Petro Turchi's Fiat 125S

News in brief

The mighty performance by Vauxhall Astra crew Barber and Popplewell to win the Open Rally marked the first time in 11 years that anything other than a Ford Escort had taken a win on the event. Such was their pace that their total elapsed time was only bettered by the Ford Escort Mk2s of Matthew Robinson and Nick Elliott.

Among those to retire on Friday evening was the Audi Quattro of Swedish crew, Tom Axelsson and Krister Gull. Taking advantage of the later cut-off dates for cars running to FIA regulations, they tackled the event for the first time but rolled out in the fog of Hamsterley forest.

German crew Thomas Kleinwachter and Andreas Schwalie showed attacking pace in their Porsche 911 on their first attempt at the event. Unfortunately, they hit early trouble with electrical problems at Herrington Park on Friday evening and, after setting some good stage times, retired with more electrical issues on Saturday.

Colin Hope and Nick Patrick had a disastrous start to their rally when their Saab 96 suffered driveshaft problems as they tried to leave the start. They missed the first four stages while fixing the problem while later dramas included a trip into a ditch in Kershope.

Bob Bean and Malcolm Smithson ran some of the Friday night stages without any intercom. The problem was traced to Bob's helmet and eventually one of the service crew found the cause: Bob's flat cap was stuck inside his crash helmet. "I couldn't hear a thing," said the Yorkshire veteran.

The Italian Fiat 125S of Petro Turchi and Giorgio Pesavento won many fans for adding variety to the entry. They had to miss several stages on Saturday evening while sorting out starter motor problems but loved the whole experience and hoped to return in 2015 with more countrymen.

The mighty Ford Falcon of Swedes Per Goransson and Conny Abrahamsson proved very popular in the few stages that it managed on Friday night and

Personal View: the Kershope sky

Saturday morning. The 5-litre monster proved a handful in the tight confines of Herrington Park before retiring with engine maladies.

Andy Madge enlisted the services of a new co-driver for his annual assault on the rally in his Toyota Corolla. Up from the service crew after nine years working on the team's management vehicle, stepped Mike Smith for his debut as a co-driver. Unfortunately, a broken half shaft on Friday evening interrupted their progress and left them to finish under Super Rally rules.

Personal view: Paul Lawrence
There is something very special about historic rally cars in the dark and this year's Roger Albert Clark Rally gave us some more epic memories.

Best of all was the Kershope stage late on Saturday afternoon. The sky had cleared as we headed west from Hamsterley and the sun was setting as we walked in from the stage start to the first corner.

An incredible winter sky provided the backdrop for the Category 1 and 1600 field, but it was fully dark by the time the main field arrived.

We could hear the cars off the start line and up the 'box as the spotlights lit up the trees. With a Porsche 911, Datsun 240Z and Lancia Stratos in the top 10, the regular BDG orchestra had some fierce aural opposition.

Pride of place, of course, went to the Stratos of Steve Perez sounding and going better than ever with a fresh Ferrari engine. We listened in awe as Steve worked the Stratos down across the bridge at Blacklyne and round Skelton Pike, with the bark of the engine easily outgunning the local tawny owls.

It was a truly memorable experience.

Steve Perez in the Stratos

2014 ROGER ALBERT CLARK RALLY: ENTRY LIST

#	Driver	Co-driver	Car	Class
2	Nick Elliott	Dave Price	Ford Escort Mk2	D5
3	Matthew Robinson	Sam Collis	Ford Escort Mk2	D5
4	Matt Edwards	Paul Morris	Ford Escort RS	D5
5	Seamus O'Connell	Andy Richardson	Ford Escort Mk2	D5
6	Darren Moon	Phil Clarke	Ford Escort Mk2	F2
7	Julian Reynolds	Patrick Walsh	Fiat 131 Abarth	F2
8	Alan Walker	Jez Rogers	Ford Escort RS	D5
9	Paul Griffiths	Iwan Jones	Ford Escort RS1800	F2
10	Martin Hagman	Jan Hagman	Ford Escort RS1800	F2
11	Gregoire De Mevius	Andre Leyh	Porsche 911	C4
14	Guy Woodcock	Graham Dance	Ford Escort RS2000	D3
15	Leigh Armstrong	Chris Armstrong	Ford Escort Mk2	D5
16	Steve Perez	John Millington	Lancia Stratos	F2
17	Bernard Munster	Andrée Hansen	Porsche 911	C4
18	Thomas Kleinwachter	Andreas Schwalie	Porsche 911	C4
19	Charlie Taylor	John Richardson	Ford Escort Mk2	D5
20	Chris Browne	Ali Cornwell-Browne	Ford Escort RS1600	C5
21	Philip Young	Hans Sylvan	Triumph TR7 V8	D4
22	Martyn Hawkswell	Nick Welch	Ford Escort RS	G4
23	Arwel Lloyd Jones	J A 'Harold' Jones	Ford Escort Mk2	D5
24	Pascal Regnier	Maryline Furnemont	Ford Escort Mk2	D5
25	Rudi Lancaster	Brynmor Pierce	Ford Escort RS	D5
26	Andrew Siddall	Paul Wakely	Ford Escort RS1600	F2
27	Steve Magson	Darren Smith	Ford Escort Mk1	C3
28	Adrian Young	Gwynfor Jones	Ford Escort RS2000	D3
29	Tom Axelsson	Krister Gull	Audi Ur-quattro	F2
30	David Hemingway	Simon Ashton	Ford Escort Mk2	G4
31	Steve Graham	Tony Graham	Lancia Fulvia	C1
32	Barry Stevenson-Wheeler	John Pickavance	Ford Escort RS	G4
33	Ian Jones	Iestyn Williams	Ford Escort Mk2	D3
34	Mark Bentley	Ed Bentley	Ford Escort Mk2	D5
35	Tom Coughtrie	Jamie Edwards	Ford Escort RS1800	F2
36	Jeremy Easson	Mike Reynolds	Datsun 240Z	C4
37	Thomas Schulz	Martina Schulz	Ford Escort Mk2	D5
38	Phil Jobson	Arwel Jenkins	Ford Escort Mk1	C3
39	Mark Fowler	Christopher Dewsnap	Ford Escort Mk2	G4
40	Colin Hope	Nick Patrick	Saab 96 V4	C3
41	Bas Jansen	Bob van Tulder	Ford Escort RS1600	F2
42	Dave Lucking	Paul Garside	Ford Escort Mk2	D3
43	Nigel Barber	Stuart Popplewell	Vauxhall Astra Sport	G4
45	David Rawlings	Philip Weston	Porsche 911	G5
46	Magic McCrombie	Chris King	Saab 900	G4
47	Falko Jansen	Harald Gottlieb	Talbot Sunbeam	F2
51	Bob Bean	Malcolm Smithson	Ford Lotus Cortina Mk1	B4
52	Robin Shuttleworth	Ronnie Roughead	Ford Escort Mk1 Mexico	C2
53	David Goose	Richard Wardle	Ford Escort Mk2	D2
54	Martin Shaw	Ian Prout	Ford Escort RS1400	G2
55	Ceiriog Hughes	Emyr Hall	Toyota Corolla SR	D2
56	Paul Mankin	Peter Scott	Ford Lotus Cortina Mk1	B4
57	Ian Beveridge	Peter Joy	Volvo PV544	B4
58	Grahame Standen	Bill Cook	Ford Escort Mk2	D2
59	Andy Madge	Mike Smith	Toyota Corolla GT Coupe	G3
60	Per Goransson	Conny Abrahamsson	Ford Falcon	B5
61	Malcolm Davey	Paul Slingsby	Ford Escort Mk1	G3
62	Kim Baker	John Connor	Ford Escort Mk2	D2
63	Mark Han Schmidt	Midas Nelissen	Austin Healey 3000	B5
64	Richard Holdsworth	John Stanger-Leathes	Ford Cortina Mk1 GT	B3
65	Petro Turchi	Giorgio Pesavento	Fiat 125S	C3
66	Jim Valentine	Jonathan Lodge	Saab 96 Sport	B1
67	Stephen Higgins	Mark Casey	Saab 96 Sport	B1
68	Nykle Meijer	Eef de Jong	Austin Healey 3000	B5

Adrian Young and Gwynfor Jones

2014 STAGES AND STAGE WINNERS

Day	Stage	Name	Distance	Stage winner(s)	Time
Friday	SS1	Herrington Park 1	0.81	Robinson/Collis	1.36
Friday	SS2	Herrington Park 2	0.81	Woodcock/Dance and Elliott/Price	1.34
Friday	SS3	Pennington 1	6.16	Edwards/Morris	8.31
Friday	SS4	Pennington 2	6.16	Edwards/Morris	8.44
Friday	SS5	Herrington Park 3	0.81	Magson/Smith	1.30
Friday	SS6	Herrington Park 4	0.81	Robinson/Collis and Edwards/Morris	1.33
Saturday	SS7	Herrington Park 5	0.81	Robinson/Collis	1.15
Saturday	SS8	Herrington Park 6	0.81	Robinson/Collis	1.14
Saturday	SS9	Croft 1	5.42	Robinson/Collis	5.25
Saturday	SS10	Croft 2	5.42	O'Connell/Richardson	5.13
Saturday	SS11	Hamsterley 1	5.76	Edwards/Morris	5.02
Saturday	SS12	Hamsterley 2	5.76	Edwards/Morris	5.01
Saturday	SS13	Shepherdshield 1	6.27	Robinson/Collis	6.15
Saturday	SS14	Whitehill 1	11.64	Robinson/Collis and Edwards/Morris	10.45
Saturday	SS15	Kershope 1	8.83	Edwards/Morris	9.48
Saturday	SS16	Ash Park 1	4.59	Edwards/Morris	5.11
Saturday	SS17	Kershope 2	8.83	Robinson/Collis	10.17
Saturday	SS18	Ash Park 2	4.59	Edwards/Morris	5.05
Saturday	SS19	Whitehill 2	12.53	Edwards/Morris	13.12
Saturday	SS20	Shepherdshield 2	6.54	Edwards/Morris	7.05
Sunday	SS21	Harwood	11.77	Edwards/Morris	11.19
Sunday	SS22	Ogre Hill 1	7.28	Robinson/Collis	7.46
Sunday	SS23	Redesdale 1	5.07	Edwards/Morris	5.14
Sunday	SS24	Falstone 1	0.00	Cancelled	0.00
Sunday	SS25	Ogre Hill 2	7.28	Robinson/Collis	7.38
Sunday	SS26	Redesdale 2	5.07	Robinson/Collis	5.16
Sunday	SS27	Falstone 2	11.69	Robinson/Collis	12.03

Roger Albert Clark Rally 2014: the eleventh edition

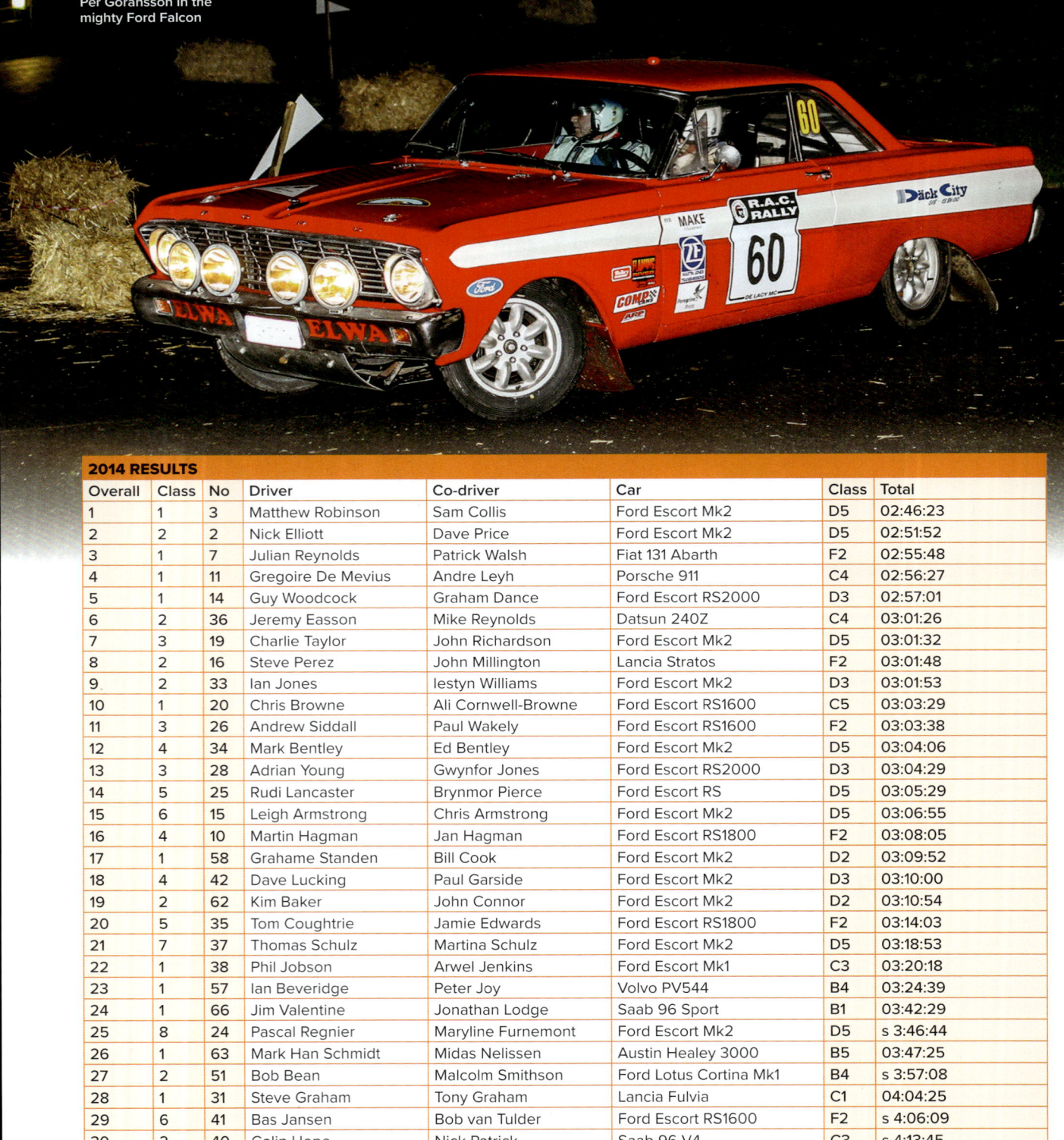

Per Goransson in the mighty Ford Falcon

2014 RESULTS

Overall	Class	No	Driver	Co-driver	Car	Class	Total
1	1	3	Matthew Robinson	Sam Collis	Ford Escort Mk2	D5	02:46:23
2	2	2	Nick Elliott	Dave Price	Ford Escort Mk2	D5	02:51:52
3	1	7	Julian Reynolds	Patrick Walsh	Fiat 131 Abarth	F2	02:55:48
4	1	11	Gregoire De Mevius	Andre Leyh	Porsche 911	C4	02:56:27
5	1	14	Guy Woodcock	Graham Dance	Ford Escort RS2000	D3	02:57:01
6	2	36	Jeremy Easson	Mike Reynolds	Datsun 240Z	C4	03:01:26
7	3	19	Charlie Taylor	John Richardson	Ford Escort Mk2	D5	03:01:32
8	2	16	Steve Perez	John Millington	Lancia Stratos	F2	03:01:48
9	2	33	Ian Jones	Iestyn Williams	Ford Escort Mk2	D3	03:01:53
10	1	20	Chris Browne	Ali Cornwell-Browne	Ford Escort RS1600	C5	03:03:29
11	3	26	Andrew Siddall	Paul Wakely	Ford Escort RS1600	F2	03:03:38
12	4	34	Mark Bentley	Ed Bentley	Ford Escort Mk2	D5	03:04:06
13	3	28	Adrian Young	Gwynfor Jones	Ford Escort RS2000	D3	03:04:29
14	5	25	Rudi Lancaster	Brynmor Pierce	Ford Escort RS	D5	03:05:29
15	6	15	Leigh Armstrong	Chris Armstrong	Ford Escort Mk2	D5	03:06:55
16	4	10	Martin Hagman	Jan Hagman	Ford Escort RS1800	F2	03:08:05
17	1	58	Grahame Standen	Bill Cook	Ford Escort Mk2	D2	03:09:52
18	4	42	Dave Lucking	Paul Garside	Ford Escort Mk2	D3	03:10:00
19	2	62	Kim Baker	John Connor	Ford Escort Mk2	D2	03:10:54
20	5	35	Tom Coughtrie	Jamie Edwards	Ford Escort RS1800	F2	03:14:03
21	7	37	Thomas Schulz	Martina Schulz	Ford Escort Mk2	D5	03:18:53
22	1	38	Phil Jobson	Arwel Jenkins	Ford Escort Mk1	C3	03:20:18
23	1	57	Ian Beveridge	Peter Joy	Volvo PV544	B4	03:24:39
24	1	66	Jim Valentine	Jonathan Lodge	Saab 96 Sport	B1	03:42:29
25	8	24	Pascal Regnier	Maryline Furnemont	Ford Escort Mk2	D5	s 3:46:44
26	1	63	Mark Han Schmidt	Midas Nelissen	Austin Healey 3000	B5	03:47:25
27	2	51	Bob Bean	Malcolm Smithson	Ford Lotus Cortina Mk1	B4	s 3:57:08
28	1	31	Steve Graham	Tony Graham	Lancia Fulvia	C1	04:04:25
29	6	41	Bas Jansen	Bob van Tulder	Ford Escort RS1600	F2	s 4:06:09
30	2	40	Colin Hope	Nick Patrick	Saab 96 V4	C3	s 4:13:45
31	9	23	Arwel Lloyd Jones	J A 'Harold' Jones	Ford Escort Mk2	D5	s 4:17:10
32	1	64	Richard Holdsworth	John Stanger-Leathes	Ford Cortina Mk1 GT	B3	s 4:23:16

Martin Hagman

2014 RESULTS (continued)

Overall	Class	No	Driver	Co-driver	Car	Class	Total
33	3	65	Petro Turchi	Giorgio Pesavento	Fiat 125S	C3	s 4:38:37
34	7	47	Falko Jansen	Harald Gottlieb	Talbot Sunbeam	F2	s 4:46:00
35	2	68	Nykle Meijer	Eef de Jong	Austin Healey 3000	B5	s 5:05:53
Ret		4	Matt Edwards	Paul Morris	Ford Escort RS	D5	Excluded
Ret		5	Seamus O'Connell	Andy Richardson	Ford Escort Mk2	D5	Retired after off SS15
Ret		6	Darren Moon	Phil Clarke	Ford Escort Mk2	F2	Second gearbox after SS10
Ret		8	Alan Walker	Jez Rogers	Ford Escort RS	D5	Blown engine SS8
Ret		9	Paul Griffiths	Iwan Jones	Ford Escort RS1800	F2	Engine SS21
Ret		17	Bernard Munster	Andrée Hansen	Porsche 911	C4	Engine SS13
Ret		18	Thomas Kleinwachter	Andreas Schwalie	Porsche 911	C4	Electrical after SS12
Ret		21	Philip Young	Hans Sylvan	Triumph TR7 V8	D4	Engine seized end of SS21
Ret		27	Steve Magson	Darren Smith	Ford Escort Mk1	C3	Co-driver unwell TC16C
Ret		29	Tom Axelsson	Krister Gull	Audi Ur-quattro	F2	Accident damage SS3
Ret		52	Robin Shuttleworth	Ronnie Roughead	Ford Escort Mk1 Mexico	C2	Crankshaft SS9
Ret		53	David Goose	Richard Wardle	Ford Escort Mk2	D2	Accident SS24
Ret		55	Ceiriog Hughes	Emyr Hall	Toyota Corolla SR	D2	Accident SS24
Ret		56	Paul Mankin	Peter Scott	Ford Lotus Cortina Mk1	B4	Broke both halfshafts SS17
Ret		60	Per Goransson	Conny Abrahamsson	Ford Falcon	B5	Engine after SS8
Ret		67	Stephen Higgins	Mark Casey	Saab Sport 96	B1	Differential SS3

Nigel Barber

Matt Edwards

Roger Albert Clark Rally 2014: the eleventh edition

Matthew Robinson in Hamsterley

2014 RESULTS: OPEN RALLY

Overall	Class	No	Driver	Co-driver	Car	Class	Total
1	1	43	Nigel Barber	Stuart Popplewell	Vauxhall Astra Sport	G4	02:55:41
2	2	32	Barry Stevenson-Wheeler	John Pickavance	Ford Escort RS	G4	03:01:36
3	3	22	Martyn Hawkswell	Nick Welch	Ford Escort RS	G4	03:04:51
4	1	61	Malcolm Davey	Paul Slingsby	Ford Escort Mk1	G3	03:18:23
5	2	59	Andy Madge	Mike Smith	Toyota Corolla GT Coupe	G3	s 3:28:25
6	4	39	Mark Fowler	Christopher Dewsnap	Ford Escort Mk2	G4	03:29:31
7	5	30	David Hemingway	Simon Ashton	Ford Escort Mk2	G4	s 3:53:20
Ret		45	David Rawlings	Philip Weston	Porsche 911	G5	Electrical problem SS25
Ret		46	Magic McCrombie	Chris King	Saab 900	G4	Blown engine SS12
Ret		54	Martin Shaw	Ian Prout	Ford Escort RS1400	G2	In ditch SS17

Iar Jones and Iestyn Williams

2014 RESULTS: CLUBMANS RALLY

Overall	Class	No	Driver	Co-driver	Car	Class	Total
1	1	83	Jim Robertson	Colin Maxwell	Citroen C2R2	L2	00:45:08
2	2	86	Mike Axford	Dave Thomason	Ford Fiesta RS	L2	00:45:44
3	3	85	Brian Middlemas	Kevin Mathers	Hillman Avenger	L2	00:46:09
4	1	82	Iain Heard	Alistair Maxwell	Ford Escort Mk2	L3	00:47:18
5	2	81	John Nicholson	Peter Littlefield	Ford Escort RS2000	L3	00:49:44
6	1	88	Darren Martin	Kyle Gass	Ford Ka	L1	00:57:49
7	2	87	Dave Coleman	Dan Hurst	Skoda Felicia	L1	01:01:47
Ret		84	Michael Farmer	Charlotte Sayer-Payne	Ford Focus	L2	Rear suspension SS26

Julian Reynolds

Martin Shaw

Roger Albert Clark Rally 2014: the eleventh edition

Roger Albert Clark Rally 2017:
the twelfth edition

Overall winners: Martin McCormack and Barney Mitchell

McCormack wins on the rally's return

The 2017 rally

Friday 10 to Monday 13 November
268 stage miles
30 special stages
Rally HQ: Brightwell's Auctions, Leominster
Start: Shelsley Walsh
Transport section from Leominster to Carlisle
Overnight 1, 2 & 3: H&H Auctions, Carlisle
Finish: Kielder Waterside
91 starters
64 finishers

Open Rally winners: David Hutchinson and Jeff Garnett

Roger Albert Rally 2017: the twelfth edition

Simon Webster and Jez Rogers in Gwibedog

After four days, 30 special stages and nearly 300 competitive miles, Marty McCormack and Barney Mitchell emerged victorious after the huge challenge presented by the 12th Roger Albert Clark Rally.

McCormack's second win on the event came after Jason Pritchard and Phil Clarke retired on Sunday afternoon with a failed half shaft. At the time Pritchard went out at the start of the first Twiglees stage, McCormack was chasing hard in a bid to claw back a 45s deficit. "It's been a long event and it has been absolutely brilliant," said McCormack.

It was a bitter disappointment for Pritchard who did not put a wheel wrong in nearly three days, but for most crews just finishing this epic rally was a huge achievement. Joining McCormack on the overall podium were Matthew Robinson/Sam Collis and early leaders Roger Chilman and Bryan Thomas.

While established drivers took the big prizes, a pack of younger drivers made their mark with some outstanding performances. Ultimately, Ben Friend and Adam Milner went unrewarded, but Josh Browne drove way beyond his experience to claim a top 10 finish.

Day one: Friday

Friday was the day the Roger Albert Clark Rally made its debut in Wales and the fans came out in good numbers, starting the other side of the border at Shelsley Walsh for a run up and down the famous hill.

However, that was just an aperitif before 14 miles in a wet and slippery Radnor and it was Chilman who

Dave Watkins

Robinson and Collis in Greskine 1

Steve Perez

Frank Cunningham

grabbed the rally by the throat to go a whopping 18s better than anyone else. But it so nearly went wrong on the finish line at Perez's Bend. Chilman got through the flying finish and then slid off. Luckily some spectators got him back on and the time put him into the lead over Pritchard.

Two stages on the Epynt gravel, with a couple of miles of asphalt added in, gave Pritchard the chance to claw it back and when the re-run of Radnor was cancelled due to marshalling issues, it was Pritchard who took a nine-second lead up the M6 to Carlisle.

Rudi Lancaster and Steve Bennett both had strong days in Wales to take third and fourth while McCormack and Robinson sat menacingly a few seconds back, content with their pace after running one and two on the road through the Radnor slime.

Far less happy was a tight-lipped Steve Bannister who was down in tenth after his first foray into Wales for a quarter of a century. A 1m30s gap to Pritchard left him plenty to do as he headed for more familiar ground.

Day two: Saturday
After relocating to Carlisle, Saturday was a long tough day with stages across Northumberland, concluding with double runs at Ogre Hill and Harwood in the dark.

Incredibly, as the leading crews arrived back in Carlisle at the end of the leg, the gap between Pritchard and McCormack was unchanged at 43s. However, behind the top two, much had changed and the gaps were starting to grow after more than 90 stage miles.

Alan Walker in Castle O'er

Chris White

Guy Anderson

Pritchard was wheel perfect through the day. "We're just keeping it neat and tidy and we're only half way there," he said at the end of the day. Up to third was Robinson, but he'd dropped some time in the second Harwood. "I'm a bit rubbish in the dark," he said with a grin.

Chilman, tackling these stages for the first time, turned in a good day to hold fourth. "Really happy with that: we found a pace we're happy with," he said. When Bennett rolled out of the rally on Whitehill 2, a slightly happier Bannister moved up to fifth. "Those lads at the front are going too quick for an old man," he said. Ben Friend, Alan Walker and Simon Webster all had good days to pack out the top 10, while Lancaster dropped to ninth after a tough day that included diff and gearbox changes.

Day three: Sunday
The action moved across the Scottish border for another long, tough day on Sunday with many crews reporting that the Twiglees stage was the best of the rally. Before that were double runs at a pair of stages in the Greskine and Ae region and it was here that Bannister had a quick roll. The car ended back on its wheels with minimum delay, but he dropped some time while regaining his composure.

McCormack set off in pursuit of Pritchard but made little in-road as the Welshman continued his superb performance. However, the start of the first Twiglees stage was as far as Pritchard would go. McCormack saw his rival parked up but took no pleasure. "I'm gutted for him. He's driven very well," said the Northern Irishman.

That left McCormack with a lead of over two minutes for the final day, but it was much closer for what became the contest for second. During Sunday Chilman took more than a minute out of Robinson to end the leg only 14s down. "We've had a good afternoon and we're keeping the pressure on," said Chilman after a day in stages that were new to him. Bent steering cost Robinson some time as the crews tackled icy patches on some of the higher ground.

Jason Pritchard and Phil Clarke

Walker was having the drive of his life and closed in on Bannister's fourth place for a while, but then had dramas of his own when a starter motor failed and melted some wiring. Northern Irishman Adrian Hetherington, running a historic specification car for the first time, had taken a while to find his pace but jumped ahead of the consistently quick Simon Webster for sixth place going into the final day.

On a day that shook-up the leader board, Friend lost his giant-killing top six place when he slid off an icy Greskine. The car was undamaged and later rejoined, but the prospect of an outstanding result for the Pinto-powered car was dashed. Meanwhile, Lancaster rolled out of the rally in Greskine 2 as Paul Griffiths/Iwan Jones and Stuart Egglestone/Brian Hodgson consolidated top 10 places. Another mighty performance came to an end in Twiglees 2 when Milner, battling head-gasket issues, slid his 1600cc Escort out the rally.

Day four: Monday

McCormack ran first on the road on Monday and faced some icy patches, but he barely put a wheel wrong.

"It was very tricky in the ice again this morning," said McCormack after winning the rally for a second time.

Robinson attacked the Kielder stages to make certain of second. "We're dead chuffed," he said after returning to his Escort following two seasons dedicated to the Fiat 131 project. Chilman was equally delighted with third place on his first attempt at the event and his first time over many of the northern stages. "It could not have gone any better for us," said Chilman.

Sadly, Bannister took a stage maximum in Newcastleton when he slid off, so Walker and John Conner moved up to a fantastic fourth overall in what he described as the best rally of his life. Webster and Jez Rogers stepped up to a fine fifth while Bannister dropped to sixth, just clear of Griffiths. Egglestone had a cracking run to a Class D3 winning eighth overall from Josh Browne, who was one of the stars of the event on only his seventh ever rally. Finally, despite losing seven minutes to a puncture, Barry Stevenson-Wheeler and John Pickavance rounded out the top 10 after Hetherington slid off in the final Falstone stage.

Roger Albert Clark Rally 2017: the twelfth edition

Guino Kenis in Gwibedog

Theo Bengry

Gavin Chisholm

Open Rally
David Hutchinson and Jeff Garnett tackled the event for the first time and came away with a resounding victory in the Open Rally for non-historic two-wheel drive cars.

Their Duratec-engined Ford Escort Mk2 was quick and consistent throughout, although Hutchinson admitted that the icy stages on Sunday had been a challenge. "Saturday was absolutely amazing and driving Harwood in the dark was an incredible experience," he said.

By Monday afternoon Hutchinson was three minutes clear of the Peugeot 205 GTi of James Nicholls and David Allman, which was the best front-wheel drive car on the event. A trip into a ditch on Sunday morning cost them little time but left the Peugeot looking rather battle scarred.

Remarkably, Dave Hemingway and Simon Ashton battled back to third in their Escort after a long time in a ditch on Saturday while Mick Plowman/Nigel Hutchinson chased the leader until they dropped a wheel into a ditch early on Sunday and broke a suspension joint. They later rejoined to take fourth.

Henri Grehan and Chris Ridge were often the fastest but a trip home for an engine rebuild and a roll on Saturday cost them any result. But they rejoined under super-rally rules to finish the event and set some impressive stage times.

News in brief
Three drivers set the standard in Class D3 and it was Ben Friend and Cliffy Simmons who set the pace until they slid off on the ice of Sunday morning. Instead, Stuart Egglestone and Brian Hodgson took over in

Chris Hellings in Shepherdshield

their Finto-powered Escort Mk2 to take an impressive win on Egglestone's first rally in a rear-wheel-drive car.

The Category K classes fell to the VW Golf GTi of Chris Hellings and Glyn Thomas and Griffiths/Jones. The Golf crew drove a great rally to win their class on their first attempt at an event of this scale. Griffiths took over in Class G2 when Pritchard went out of the lead of the rally.

Jimmy McRae and Pauline Gullick drove a rally befitting their combined experience to win Class C5 in the Chevrolet-powered Vauxhall Firenza. They had to fend off the Escort Mk1 of Chris Browne/Ali Cornwell-Browne on the way to yet another success for the British rallying legend. Another V8, this time the Triumph TR7 of David Kynaston/Val Thompson, won Class D4 after a great run punctuated by an off on Sunday's ice.

Dave Watkins and Graham Wride turned in an exemplary performance to win Class C2 in Watkins' ex-works Escort Mk1. The superbly presented car ran like a train across four tough days.

Victory in Class D2 was an absolute triumph in the face of adversity for Kim Gray and Tom Murphy in their Escort Mk2. It started with engine issues on Friday that dictated a return to Chesterfield for an overnight rebuild. Then, various gearbox and axle problems threatened to put them out but somehow Kim and her team got the car to the finish.

The two-stroke Saab 96 of Stephen Higgins and Sam Spencer won Class B2 after a wonderful performance in the low-power car. The Saab behaved impeccably over four days and even managed a stint in the outside lane of the M6 on the run back to service in Carlisle on Sunday evening.

Jimmy McRae

Ben Friend and Cliffy Simmons

Rikki Proffitt

Martin McCormack

A fine rally for veteran Bob Bean and co-driver Malcolm Smithson was well rewarded by victory in Class B4 among the Category 1 contenders. The freshly rebuilt Lotus Cortina of the 79-year-old Yorkshireman ran remarkably well and Bob drove as well as ever, more than half a century after his first attempt at the original RAC Rally.

Finally, Rikki Proffitt and Graham Wild (Porsche 911) won Class B5 despite a challenging event. They struggled to get to the start of the Roughside stage on Saturday and then hit gearbox problems on Sunday. After a change of box, they returned on Monday to clinch the class despite running under Super Rally rules.

Personal View 1: Paul Lawrence
Few rallies get the sort of reception from competitors, marshals and fans that the 2017 Roger Albert Clark Rally received.

After a gap of three years while the rally was reinvented, it came back with a bang in November and drew rave reviews. Under a general concept of 'go big or go home', rally manager Colin Heppenstall really went for it, with four days, 270 stage miles and three countries.

From Friday morning, when the car parks at Shelsley Walsh could barely cope, it was a runaway success and gave thousands of enthusiasts, whether competing or not, a truly epic experience in the forests of Wales, Northumberland and Scotland.

The competition was intense and the pace was more like a one-day sprint as Marty McCormack won the big prize. But rallying itself was the real winner for here was an event that created a unique buzz. The only problem is that there is a two-year wait until the next one.

Personal View 2: Paul Lawrence
The absolute memory of 2017 just has to be the

Roger Chilman in Capelstone Fell

Roger Albert Clark Rally.

After a gap of three years the event was back longer and tougher than ever before and the refreshed format really captured the hearts of everyone involved. On Monday morning, day four, we were in Caplestone Fell, a daunting 19-miler in the central block of Kielder.

This was everything that I had hoped for from the rally: a fourth straight day of rallying with good friends, classic Kielder locations and a remarkable tally of 65 cars still running and still committed.

Stage rallying has had some tough times recently, but here was an event that brought joy to thousands and showed what is possible with determination. There is no other UK rally that comes close for the atmosphere, buzz and sense of occasion.

Roger Albert reflections

We live in an ill-tempered world, full of argument, discord and threats. Yet for four days that was all forgotten by those lucky enough to be involved in the 2017 Roger Albert Clark Rally. Paul Lawrence reflects on what many people described as the rally of the year.

Two years earlier, rally manager Colin Heppenstall had just cancelled the 2015 event as a low entry made it financially unworkable. Many organisers would have given up and walked away, but Heppenstall is not a quitter. In equal measure determined, stubborn and full of energy, he worked away for 18 months to rebuild the event. It came back as a bigger, tougher and longer rally and it was a massive success.

For the first time it went to Wales and that was a canny decision. It bought entries and interest from a region that had never seen the rally before and Heppenstall broke new ground by running a transport section on Friday night as the whole rally relocated from Leominster to Carlisle. It worked well.

Although the final start list was down to 91, still close to a record for the rally, it was important that over 140 crews initially lodged deposits. It was clear that four days, three countries, 270 stage miles and 30 special stages had grabbed the attention of crews more used to under 45 miles in little more than half a day. This was nearly six BTRDA rallies in four days.

Seb Perez in Monday's Kielder Rally

However, this was not just a rally about the crews. Spectators, marshals and organisers were all part of an adventure that took you completely away from normal life for four days. Instead of unrelenting coverage of Trump, Isis and Brexit, it was a blur of forests, service areas, lights across the night sky, Escorts sideways, two-stroke Saabs ring-a-dinging, time controls, the noise of the Stratos, stunning scenery, wonderful humour and camaraderie, with the occasional visit to bed when time allowed. Everyone had a ball.

It is camaraderie that came up time and time again when talking to competitors. Everyone wanted to finish and see everyone else finish. Parts, tyres and fuel were all readily loaned out and service crews often worked on other people's cars as well as their own. When Kim Baker's crew were working overnight at Carlisle to rebuild her engine, the Den Motorsport team provided their awning, lights and fuel for the generator.

Ford Escort Mk1 driver Chris Browne says that camaraderie is a big factor for him. "The rally was amazing as always; the camaraderie is incredible. You don't get that anywhere else."

"Exactly like the RAC Rallies of old," said Roger Chilman Snr as he watched his son take a podium finish. "The cars, the sounds, the night stages and the fantastic camaraderie; glad I was there."

While BDG-powered Ford Escort Mk2s provided an incredible sound track to the rally, less expensive cars were still giving their crews the experience of a lifetime. James Nicholls and David Allman finished second in their Peugeot 205 GTi, which is probably a £10,000 car. "We'd never done an event of this scale before and it was a massive challenge," said Nicholls. "It was the best rally I've ever done, without a doubt. We had a warm reception for the 205, which started off as an accident-damaged project."

At the other end of the scale in experience terms was Jimmy McRae, who contested the former RAC Rally 17 times and was on his fifth Roger Albert Clark. "What an event! We'll be back in 2019," he said after hearing Heppenstall confirm that the 13th edition would be in two years' time.

For Escort Mk2 driver Alan Walker, it was his first rally as a driver since blowing the engine up

Reflection 1: James Nicholls

David Kynaston

Baz Jordan at Shelsley Walsh

comprehensively on the 2014 rally. With John Connor on the notes, he finished a superb fourth overall on what he said was the best rally he'd ever done. "They were fantastic stages and to do 20-mile stages was amazing. Stages like Twiglees and Castle O'er were brilliant." Hitting 9400rpm in top in Falstone added another chapter in Walker's rallying memories.

Paul Griffiths, an event regular, was seventh in his Escort Mk2. "What a great rally that was! The stages were so good and what a day Monday in Kielder was: one stage after the other and in top condition. I cannot wait till 2019."

This was an event that made memories that will last for years. Tony Graham was, as ever, co-driving for his brother Steve in their gorgeous Lancia Fulvia. "The organisers are responsible for enabling all competitors, marshals, officials and spectators to create and share those memories and hey, what is life about if we cannot leave a legacy of memories for those we share life with. Well done to everyone involved in the best Roger Albert Clark so far."

Spectators were more involved than on one-day sprints. For sure, they were more knowledgeable and responsible than on any other rally. John Pettit and a group of mates did all four days. "Fantastic event: what organisation that took! We watched eight stages starting in Wales on Friday and finishing in Kielder on Monday. Well done all the crews who entered; we were well and truly entertained."

Marshals turned out in good numbers to be part of the event and many did more than one day. "I had a great weekend and much respect to the very knowledgeable spectators out on this fabulous event," said Chris Mallows. "What a great weekend; it was a privilege to marshal on an event this good," said Brian Credland.

Reflections 2: Steve and Tony Graham

Phil Jobson

Mark Holmes

From the organising team, Peter Baker from RalliTrak summed up some common views. "Simply to be a part of the experience that is the Roger Albert Clark is without doubt unrivalled. This throwback is nothing short of magic. To work with a team who to a man, woman and child (under 18s) simply got on with anything and everything that was thrown at them was inspiring.

"To achieve something of this magnitude takes a very special person, in this case a very special couple, and the team who support them. I am proud to call myself one of them. I have a feeling the Roger Albert Clark will remain the gift to rallying that simply keeps on giving. I predict the next event will be bigger and better and create yet more memories."

The final word must go to the only man in British rallying who would even consider taking on such an event, Colin Heppenstall. "It was 18 months of hard work followed by four perfect days of rallying. The response proved that the decision to rest the event and run it every two years is right. My sincere thanks are due to all the people who helped to make it happen, including all the marshals."

Insight: Kim Gray (Ford Escort Mk2)
The first day didn't end well
"We snapped the camshaft on Friday but I didn't realise and it still drove. So I got it back to service in

Kim Gray battled to the finish

Leominster and they told me it was pretty terminal. So my husband Andy, our Welsh service guy Bryn and I drove home to Chesterfield, while the service crew took the car to Carlisle and started taking the engine out. However, the service van broke down on the M6."

They worked all night
"We got a new cam and took it to Carlisle and put it in. Most of us didn't go to bed at all on Friday night. We fired it up just after 7am on Saturday morning, ready to restart at 9.30am. Everything was okay in the morning but then the alternator started playing up just as it was getting dark. We did Ogre Hill and Harwood on just two spot lamps. It was nice to go to bed on Saturday night and, of course, Andy was driving as well in his Peugeot 205 GTi."

Then the gearbox failed
"On Sunday morning in Scotland I started struggling to get second gear. We thought it was the clutch as we'd had the engine out but by the time we got to the last three stages I couldn't get any gears other than third. We did the last stage and the run back to service in third. We then changed the gearbox."

More drama on Monday
"On Monday we flew through Newcastleton but I couldn't get the car moving at management service and thought the rear brakes were stuck on. But the crown wheel bolts had all come out. We managed to get that sorted and got to the long 20-mile Kielder stage just in time. In Falstone we caught and passed the Lancia Fulvia and managed to move up the running order for the second long stage, but we still caught three cars."

They finished!
"We finished and won the class and didn't quite make the top 20 overall, and I'd quite like to have done that for a third time. It was four days of rallying and just mental. Everyone comes together so much more than on a small event. Everyone wants everyone else to finish as it is such a big commitment. We had help from no end of people and it was great."

2017 ROGER ALBERT CLARK RALLY: ENTRY LIST

No	Driver	Co-driver	Car	Class
1	Matthew Robinson	Sam Collis	Ford Escort Mk2	D5
2	Martin McCormack	Barney Mitchell	Ford Escort Mk2	D5
3	Jason Pritchard	Phil Clarke	Ford Escort RS1800	G2
5	Steve Bannister	Callum Atkinson	Ford Escort Mk2	D5
6	Rudi Lancaster	Guy Weaver	Ford Escort RS1800	G2
8	Steve Bennett	Osian Owen	Ford Escort RS	D5
9	Simon Webster	Jez Rogers	Ford Escort RS1800	D5
10	Roger Chilman	Bryan Thomas	Ford Escort RS	D5
12	Paul Griffiths	Iwan Jones	Ford Escort RS1800	G2
14	Alan Walker	John Connor	Ford Escort Mk2	D5
15	Adrian Hetherington	Andrew Grennan	Ford Escort Mk2	D5
16	Henri Grehan	Christopher Ridge	Ford Escort Mk2	J5
17	Adam Milner	Roy Jarvis	Ford Escort Mexico Mk1	C2
18	Ben Friend	Cliffy Simmons	Ford Escort Mk2	D3
19	Chris Skill	Tom Jordan	Ford Escort RS1600	C5
20	Steve Perez	John Millington	Lancia Stratos	G2
21	Jimmy McRae	Pauline Gullick	Vauxhall Firenza Can-Am	C5
22	Callum Guy	Andrew Roughead	Ford Escort RS	G2
23	Mark Bentley	Ed Bentley	Ford Escort Mk2	D5
24	Seb Perez	Alex Lee	Ford Escort Mk2	D3
25	Christophe Jacob	Isabelle Regnier	Ford Escort Mk2	G2
26	Frank Cunningham	Ryland James	Ford Sierra Sapphire	F2
27	Josh Browne	Jane Edgington	Ford Escort Mk2	D3
28	Stuart Egglestone	Brian Hodgson	Ford Escort Mk2	D3
29	Barry Jordan	James Gratton-Smith	Hillman Avenger	C5
30	David Hutchinson	Jeff Garnett	Ford Escort Mk2	J5
31	Steve Graham	Tony Graham	Lancia Fulvia	C2
32	Theo Bengry	Les Forsbrook	Opel Ascona 400	D4
33	Barry Stevenson-Wheeler	John Pickavance	Ford Escort RS1800	D5
34	Chris Browne	Ali Cornwell-Browne	Ford Escort RS1600	C5
35	Leigh Armstrong	Chris Armstrong	Ford Escort RS	D5
37	Tom Coughtrie	Jamie Edwards	Mitsubishi Galant VR4	F2
38	Jerry Bailey	Sinclair Young	Ford Escort Mk1 Mexico	C2
39	Phil Jobson	Arwel Jenkins	Ford Escort Mk1	C5
40	Guy Anderson	Stephen Link	Talbot Sunbeam Lotus	D4
41	Phil Squires	Mick Squires	Ford Escort RS1800	D5
42	Duncan Williams	George Williams	Ford Escort Mk2	D3
43	Mark Holmes	Craig Simkiss	Ford Escort RS1600	C5
44	Adrian Young	Gwynfor Jones	Ford Escort RS2000	D3
45	Andrew Robinson	Kevin Wilson	Ford Escort Mk2	D5
46	Chris White	Chris Dewsnap	Ford Escort Mk2	G2
47	Alain Maria	Cedric Santini	Ford Escort Mk2	D3
48	Nick Carr	Richard Crozier	Ford Escort Mk2	D5
49	Wayne Bonser	Rich Aston	Ford Escort RS2000	C3
50	Dave Hemingway	Simon Ashton	Ford Escort Mk2	J4
52	Kim Gray	Tom Murphy	Ford Escort Mk2	D2
53	Bart-Jan Deenik	Egbert Kolvoort	Ford Escort RS1600	C5
54	Ceiriog Hughes	Emyr Hall	Saab 96 V4	C3
55	Colin Hope	Nick Patrick	Saab 96 V4	C3
56	Rikki Proffitt	Graham Wild	Porsche 911	B5
57	Paul Fry	Mike Steele	Ford Escort Mk2	D3
58	Dirk Deveux	Kris D'alleine	Ford Escort Mk2	J4
59	Jean Louis Thizy	Serge Mollar	Opel Manta 400	E2

2017 ROGER ALBERT CLARK RALLY: ENTRY LIST (continued)

No	Driver	Co-driver	Car	Class
60	Dominique Lesourd	Sebastien Chol	Ford Escort Mk1	C3
61	Dave Watkins	Graham Wride	Ford Escort Twin Cam	C2
62	David Kynaston	Val Thompson	Triumph TR7 V8	D4
63	Mark Fowler	Ashley Young	Ford Escort Mk2	D5
64	Tim Metcalfe	Sasha Heriot	Ford Escort RS1800	G2
65	Yves Huyghé de Mahenge	Anne-Marie Pomares	Ford Escort RS2000	D3
66	Jean Francois Berenguer	Aline Berenguer	Opel Manta 400	G2
67	Stuart Cariss	Linda Cariss	Ford Escort Sport	C2
68	David Gathercole	Martyn Donn	Ford Escort RS1800	C5
69	Robert Rook	Mark Sharpley	Ford Escort Mk1 Twin Cam	C2
70	Philip Rowland	Philip Woodcock	BMW 323	J5
71	Stewart Scott	Mark Casey	Ford Escort RS2000	C3
72	Andy Madge	Mike Smith	Toyota Corolla GT Coupe	J3
73	Francis Tuthill	Peter Lythell	Saab 96 V4	D3
74	Bob Bean	Malcolm Smithson	Ford Lotus Cortina Mk1	B4
75	Paul Mankin	Desmond Bell	Ford Lotus Cortina Mk1	B4
76	Mick Plowman	Nigel Hutchinson	Ford Escort Mk2	J4
77	David Pedley	Steven Warrington	Vauxhall Astra GTE	J4
78	Guino Kenis	Bjorn Vanoverschelde	BMW M3 E30	F2
79	Allan Clark	Iain Thorburn	Hillman Avenger	C3
80	Drexel Gillespie	Gill Cotton	Ford Escort Mk1	C3
81	Nigel Bancroft	John Buckley	Ford Escort Mk2	D5
82	Robert Evett	Michael Evett	Vauxhall Nova	J2
83	Jim Valentine	Jonathan Lodge	Saab 99	C3
84	Richard Phillipson	Stefan Arndt	Honda Civic EG6	J3
85	Andrew Gray	Emma Morrison	Peugeot 205 GTi	J3
86	Paul Rawson	Paul Wild	Ford Escort Mk1	C2
87	Pete Johnston	Charles Johnston	Datsun 240Z	H2
88	Richard Gemmell	Matt Beebe	MG ZR	J2
89	Gavin Chisholm	Shannon Turnbull	Saab 99	J4
90	Pete Gunson	Jonathan Haynes	Vauxhall Astra	J4
91	James Nicholls	David Allman	Peugeot 205 GTi	J4
93	Olaf Pothoven	Marvin Molenkamp	Volvo Amazon 122S	J4
94	Chris Hellings	Glyn Thomas	Volkswagen Golf GTi	G1
95	Magic McCombie	Kevin Mathers	Saab 900	J4
96	Mathew Evans	Daniel Evans	Peugeot 205	J2
97	Stephen Higgins	Sam Spencer	Saab 96 Two Stroke	B2
98	Keith Turner	Rob Brook	Ford Escort RS2000	D5

Christophe Jacob

Colin Hope

Roger Albert Clark Rally 2017: the twelfth edition

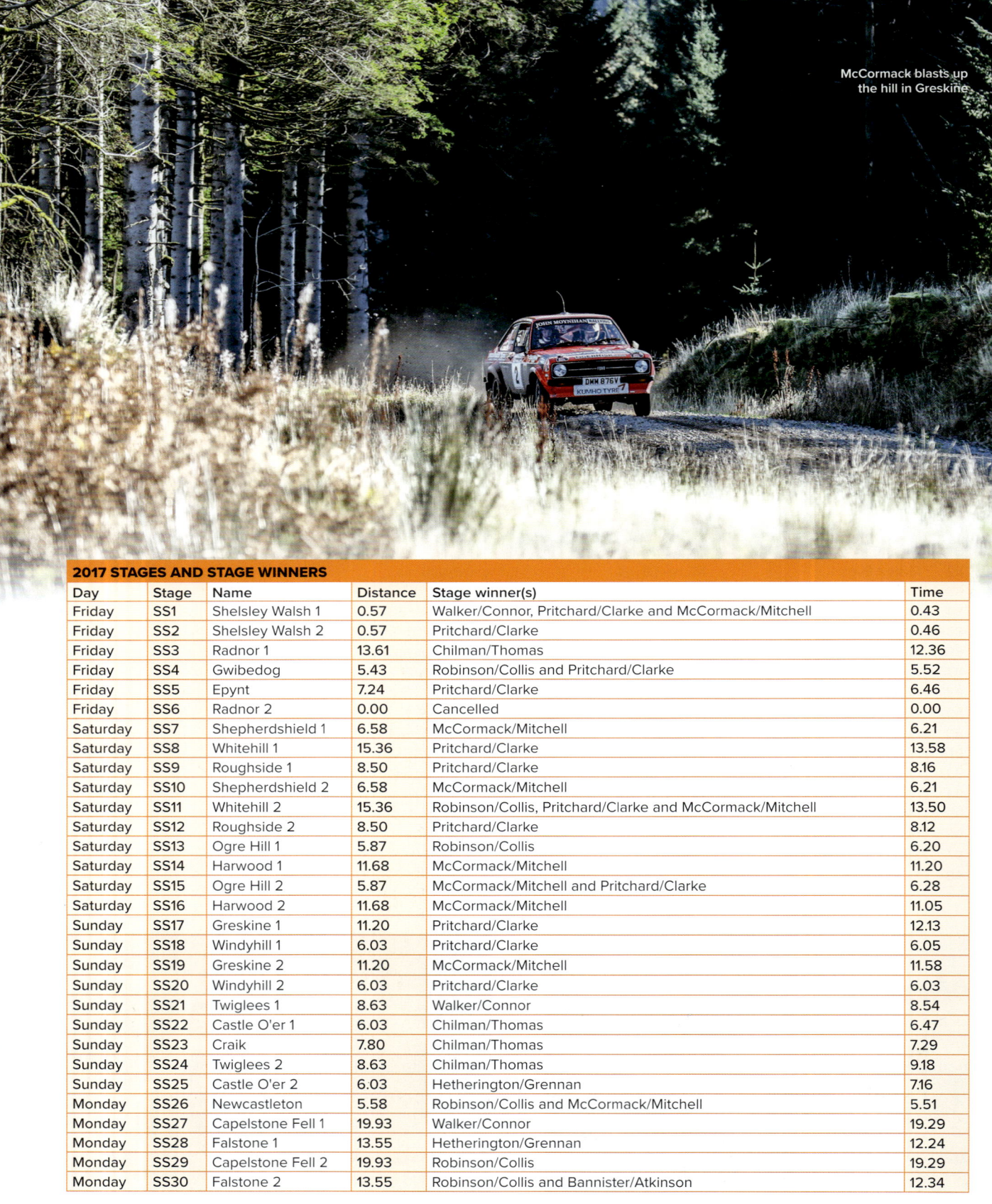

McCormack blasts up the hill in Greskine

2017 STAGES AND STAGE WINNERS

Day	Stage	Name	Distance	Stage winner(s)	Time
Friday	SS1	Shelsley Walsh 1	0.57	Walker/Connor, Pritchard/Clarke and McCormack/Mitchell	0.43
Friday	SS2	Shelsley Walsh 2	0.57	Pritchard/Clarke	0.46
Friday	SS3	Radnor 1	13.61	Chilman/Thomas	12.36
Friday	SS4	Gwibedog	5.43	Robinson/Collis and Pritchard/Clarke	5.52
Friday	SS5	Epynt	7.24	Pritchard/Clarke	6.46
Friday	SS6	Radnor 2	0.00	Cancelled	0.00
Saturday	SS7	Shepherdshield 1	6.58	McCormack/Mitchell	6.21
Saturday	SS8	Whitehill 1	15.36	Pritchard/Clarke	13.58
Saturday	SS9	Roughside 1	8.50	Pritchard/Clarke	8.16
Saturday	SS10	Shepherdshield 2	6.58	McCormack/Mitchell	6.21
Saturday	SS11	Whitehill 2	15.36	Robinson/Collis, Pritchard/Clarke and McCormack/Mitchell	13.50
Saturday	SS12	Roughside 2	8.50	Pritchard/Clarke	8.12
Saturday	SS13	Ogre Hill 1	5.87	Robinson/Collis	6.20
Saturday	SS14	Harwood 1	11.68	McCormack/Mitchell	11.20
Saturday	SS15	Ogre Hill 2	5.87	McCormack/Mitchell and Pritchard/Clarke	6.28
Saturday	SS16	Harwood 2	11.68	McCormack/Mitchell	11.05
Sunday	SS17	Greskine 1	11.20	Pritchard/Clarke	12.13
Sunday	SS18	Windyhill 1	6.03	Pritchard/Clarke	6.05
Sunday	SS19	Greskine 2	11.20	McCormack/Mitchell	11.58
Sunday	SS20	Windyhill 2	6.03	Pritchard/Clarke	6.03
Sunday	SS21	Twiglees 1	8.63	Walker/Connor	8.54
Sunday	SS22	Castle O'er 1	6.03	Chilman/Thomas	6.47
Sunday	SS23	Craik	7.80	Chilman/Thomas	7.29
Sunday	SS24	Twiglees 2	8.63	Chilman/Thomas	9.18
Sunday	SS25	Castle O'er 2	6.03	Hetherington/Grennan	7.16
Monday	SS26	Newcastleton	5.58	Robinson/Collis and McCormack/Mitchell	5.51
Monday	SS27	Capelstone Fell 1	19.93	Walker/Connor	19.29
Monday	SS28	Falstone 1	13.55	Hetherington/Grennan	12.24
Monday	SS29	Capelstone Fell 2	19.93	Robinson/Collis	19.29
Monday	SS30	Falstone 2	13.55	Robinson/Collis and Bannister/Atkinson	12.34

Chris Skill and Tom Jordan

2017 RESULTS

Overall	Class	No	Driver	Co-driver	Car	Class	Total
1	1	2	Martin McCormack	Barney Mitchell	Ford Escort Mk2	D5	04:28:27
2	2	1	Matthew Robinson	Sam Collis	Ford Escort Mk2	D5	04:30:11
3	3	10	Roger Chilman	Bryan Thomas	Ford Escort RS	D5	04:31:19
4	4	14	Alan Walker	John Connor	Ford Escort Mk2	D5	04:34:24
5	5	9	Simon Webster	Jez Rogers	Ford Escort RS1800	D5	04:35:51
6	6	5	Steve Bannister	Callum Atkinson	Ford Escort Mk2	D5	04:39:03
7	1	12	Paul Griffiths	Iwan Jones	Ford Escort RS1800	G2	04:40:28
8	1	28	Stuart Egglestone	Brian Hodgson	Ford Escort Mk2	D3	04:41:03
9	2	27	Josh Browne	Jane Edgington	Ford Escort Mk2	D3	04:43:32
10	7	33	Barry Stevenson-Wheeler	John Pickavance	Ford Escort RS1800	D5	04:50:05
11	8	15	Adrian Hetherington	Andrew Grennan	Ford Escort Mk2	D5	04:50:42
12	2	46	Chris White	Chris Dewsnap	Ford Escort Mk2	G2	04:50:49
13	1	21	Jimmy McRae	Pauline Gullick	Vauxhall Firenza Can-Am	C5	04:51:59
14	3	25	Christophe Jacob	Isabelle Regnier	Ford Escort Mk2	G2	04:53:38
15	2	34	Chris Browne	Ali Cornwell-Browne	Ford Escort RS1600	C5	04:54:33
16	9	35	Leigh Armstrong	Chris Armstrong	Ford Escort RS	D5	04:55:28
17	10	41	Phil Squires	Mick Squires	Ford Escort RS1800	D5	05:00:06
18	4	20	Steve Perez	John Millington	Lancia Stratos	G2	05:00:29
19	11	45	Andrew Robinson	Kevin Wilson	Ford Escort Mk2	D5	05:03:27
20	3	42	Duncan Williams	George Williams	Ford Escort Mk2	D3	05:03:45
21	4	44	Adrian Young	Gwynfor Jones	Ford Escort RS2000	D3	05:06:41
22	5	57	Paul Fry	Mike Steele	Ford Escort Mk2	D3	05:15:14
23	1	74	Bob Bean	Malcolm Smithson	Ford Lotus Cortina Mk1	B4	05:16:36
24	1	62	David Kynaston	Val Thompson	Triumph TR7 V8	D4	05:17:31
25	1	52	Kim Gray	Tom Murphy	Ford Escort Mk2	D2	05:17:42
26	1	49	Wayne Bonser	Rich Aston	Ford Escort RS2000	C3	s 5:23:54
27	5	64	Tim Metcalfe	Sasha Heriot	Ford Escort RS1800	G2	05:25:36
28	2	40	Guy Anderson	Stephen Link	Talbot Sunbeam Lotus	D4	s 5:26:44
29	1	61	Dave Watkins	Graham Wride	Ford Escort Twin Cam	C2	05:28:34

Roger Albert Clark Rally 2017: the twelfth edition

2017 RESULTS (continued)

Overall	Class	No	Driver	Co-driver	Car	Class	Total
30	12	63	Mark Fowler	Ashley Young	Ford Escort Mk2	D5	05:29:25
31	6	47	Alain Maria	Cedric Santini	Ford Escort Mk2	D3	05:33:54
32	2	67	Stuart Cariss	Linda Cariss	Ford Escort Sport	C2	s 5:37:09
33	1	94	Chris Hellings	Glyn Thomas	Volkswagen Golf GTi	G1	05:39:44
34	3	53	Bart-Jan Deenik	Egbert Kolvoort	Ford Escort RS1600	C5	05:40:50
35	2	55	Colin Hope	Nick Patrick	Saab 96 V4	C3	05:41:45
36	3	79	Allan Clark	Iain Thorburn	Hillman Avenger	C3	05:45:29
37	13	81	Nigel Bancroft	John Buckley	Ford Escort Mk2	D5	05:45:31
38	4	71	Stewart Scott	Mark Casey	Ford Escort RS2000	C3	05:50:54
39	2	75	Paul Mankin	Desmond Bell	Ford Lotus Cortina Mk1	B4	05:51:23
40	14	98	Keith Turner	Rob Brook	Ford Escort RS2000	D5	05:53:39
41	3	69	Robert Rook	Mark Sharpley	Ford Escort Mk1 Twin Cam	C2	05:58:23
42	4	68	David Gathercole	Martyn Donn	Ford Escort RS1800	C5	s 6:05:50
43	1	97	Stephen Higgins	Sam Spencer	Saab 96 Two Stroke	B2	06:06:07
44	4	86	Paul Rawson	Paul Wild	Ford Escort Mk1	C2	06:13:35
45	1	56	Rikki Proffitt	Graham Wild	Porsche 911	B5	s 6:27:40
46	5	83	Jim Valentine	Jonathan Lodge	Saab 99	C3	s 6:39:19
47	1	87	Pete Johnston	Charles Johnston	Datsun 240Z	H2	s 7:02:30
48	5	31	Steve Graham	Tony Graham	Lancia Fulvia	C2	07:20:16
Ret		19	Chris Skill	Tom Jordan	Ford Escort RS1600	C5	Retired SS24
Ret		22	Callum Guy	Andrew Roughead	Ford Escort RS	G2	Suspension TC18B
Ret		23	Mark Bentley	Ed Bentley	Ford Escort Mk2	D5	Went off SS21
Ret		24	Seb Perez	Alex Lee	Ford Escort Mk2	D3	Engine failure SS11
Ret		26	Frank Cunningham	Ryland James	Ford Sierra Sapphire	F2	Went off SS7
Ret		29	Barry Jordan	James Gratton-Smith	Hillman Avenger	C5	Smashed axle SS11
Ret		32	Theo Bengry	Les Forsbrook	Opel Ascona 400	D4	Gearbox MTC5
Ret		37	Tom Coughtrie	Jamie Edwards	Mitsubishi Galant VR4	F2	Gearbox SS11
Ret		38	Jerry Bailey	Sinclair Young	Ford Escort Mexico	C2	Engine SS10
Ret		39	Phil Jobson	Arwel Jenkins	Ford Escort Mk1	C5	Retired SS8
Ret		43	Mark Holmes	Craig Simkiss	Ford Escort RS1600	C5	Gearbox SS3
Ret		48	Nick Carr	Richard Crozier	Ford Escort Mk2	D5	Engine after SS17
Ret		54	Ceiriog Hughes	Emyr Hall	Saab 96 V4	C3	Gearbox before SS3
Ret		59	Jean Louis Thizy	Serge Mollar	Opel Manta 400	E2	Broken engine SS4
Ret		60	Dominique Lesourd	Sebastien Chol	Ford Escort Mk1	C3	Retired SS7
Ret		65	Yves Huyghé de Mahenge	Anne-Marie Pomares	Ford Escort RS2000	D3	Engine MTC5
Ret		66	Jean Francois Berenguer	Aline Berenguer	Opel Manta 400	G2	Personal reasons TC23
Ret		73	Francis Tuthill	Peter Lythell	Saab 96 V4	D3	Electrical after SS14
Ret		78	Guino Kenis	Bjorn Vanoverschelde	BMW M3 E30	F2	Gearbox TC18B
Ret		80	Drexel Gillespie	Gill Cotton	Ford Escort Mk1	C3	Stopped SS23

Pete Johnstone

Jason Pritchard

Jean-François Berenguer

2017 RESULTS: OPEN RALLY

Overall	Class	No	Driver	Co-driver	Car	Class	Total
1	1	30	David Hutchinson	Jeff Garnett	Ford Escort Mk2	J5	05:01:23
2	1	91	James Nicholls	David Allman	Peugeot 205 GTi	J4	05:04:2'
3	2	50	Dave Hemingway	Simon Ashton	Ford Escort Mk2	J4	05:12:49
4	3	76	Mick Plowman	Nigel Hutchinson	Ford Escort Mk2	J4	s 5:16:22
5	1	85	Andrew Gray	Emma Morrison	Peugeot 205 GTi	J3	05:25:08
6	1	84	Richard Phillipson	Stefan Arndt	Honda Civic EG6	J3	05:41:26
7	4	90	Pete Gunson	Jonathan Haynes	Vauxhall Astra	J4	05:49:44
8	1	96	Mathew Evans	Daniel Evans	Peugeot 205	J2	06:04:38
9	3	72	Andy Madge	Mike Smith	Toyota Corolla GT Coupe	J3	s 6:07:31
10	5	95	Magic McCombie	Kevin Mathers	Saab 900	J4	s 6:22:05
11	6	89	Gavin Chisholm	Shannon Turnbull	Saab 99	J4	06:23:02
12	7	58	Dirk Deveux	Kris D'alleine	Ford Escort Mk2	J4	s 6:23:57
13	2	70	Philip Rowland	Philip Woodcock	BMW 323	J5	s 6:48:42
14	2	82	Robert Evett	Michael Evett	Vauxhall Nova	J2	s 6:56:40
Ret		16	Henri Grehan	Christopher Ridge	Ford Escort Mk2	J5	OTL
Ret		77	David Pedley	Steven Warrington	Vauxhall Astra GTE	J4	Damaged floor after SS18
Ret		88	Richard Gemmell	Matt Beebe	MG ZR	J2	Body damage SS11
Ret		93	Olaf Pothoven	Marvin Molenkamp	Volvo Amazon 122S	J4	Stopped SS29

Mathew Evans

Philip Rowland

Roger Albert Clark Rally 2017: the twelfth edition

Roger Albert Clark Rally 2019:
the thirteenth edition

Overall winners: Martin McCormack and Barney Mitchell

McCormack does it again
The 2019 rally

Thursday 21 to Monday 25 November
286 stage miles
31 special stages
Start: Brightwell's Auctions, Leominster
Overnight 1: Brightwell's Auctions, Leominster
Transport section from Leominster to Carlisle
Overnight 2, 3 & 4: H&H Auctions, Carlisle
Finish: Kielder Waterside
126 starters
93 finishers

Open Rally winners: Baz Jordan and Arwel Jenkins

Roger Albert Rally 2019: the thirteenth edition

Marty McCormack and Barney Mitchell were the heroes of the day when they won the Roger Albert Clark Rally for a second time running as the mammoth event finished on Monday afternoon.

Ultimately, this biennial event became a two-way contest as McCormack went head to head with the similar Ford Escort Mk2 of Jason Pritchard and Phil Clarke. The gap ebbed and flowed and they were seldom more than a few seconds apart on each stage. However, when Pritchard dropped 50s with a puncture in Greskine on Sunday morning, McCormack extended his lead to an uncatchable margin.

McCormack said: "Absolutely fantastic! We've had a brilliant rally and fought hard from the start. Jason and Phil are great lads to race against and it's been a tough battle all weekend. Monday was the toughest day: trying to manage the lead is so difficult."

The 13th edition of the event was longer and tougher than those that went before with 286 stages miles across 32 special stages and four and a half days. From Thursday night in Wales to Saturday evening it was fog that was the biggest challenge and for many of the 130 starters, just getting to the finish in Carlisle was a huge victory.

Days one and two: Thursday and Friday
It turned out to be just six and a half miles for only the front-runners, but the visit to Radnor set the tone for the weekend. The Welsh hills were at their most malevolent as thick fog hung over the higher parts of the stage. The route was trimmed to one run

Tomas Ebegard

The Toyota Corolla of Emmanuel Eggermont

Wayne Sisson

Steve Graham

only and the action was further curtailed when Alan Walker's Escort caught fire.

But before then, McCormack and Pritchard established themselves at the head of the rally. Pritchard caught and passed Matthew Robinson in the truly demanding conditions and went 4s up on McCormack with Roger Chilman a further 4s back. Robinson dropped over a minute and others suffered more before notional times kicked in after the stoppage.

Paul Barrett had struggled in the fog but that was the least of his problems come Friday morning in Wales when he went out on the opening Crychan stage with terminal engine problems. He was quickly joined by fellow Northern Irishman Adrian Hetherington with similar issues.

However, McCormack was more than holding up Northern Irish honours in Pritchard's back yard and won six of the eight stages. But it was still close and only 13s split them as they loaded up on Epynt for the trek north to Carlisle. "We've had a fantastic day and I'm really pleased to be on the pace in Wales," said McCormack. "I maybe tried a bit too hard this morning and was a bit ragged," said Pritchard.

Roger Albert Clark Rally 2019: the thirteenth edition

Ben Friend in Kershope 1

Andy Pidden

Andrew Siddall

Half a minute back, Chilman was doing his own thing but fourth-placed Robinson was left to rue the Radnor fog. "If we'd not dropped that time last night, we'd have been with them," he said after a strong day in Wales. Simon Webster and Rudi Lancaster rounded out the top six before younger guns Henri Grehan and Ben Friend. "That feels like a win," said Friend after a generally disastrous season, although he did need a quick gearbox change at service.

The fierce pace at the head of the Pinto pack put Josh Browne and Stuart Egglestone into the top 10 but out went the glorious Toyota Celica of Gregoire de Mevius with engine woes.

Day three: Saturday
Saturday was one of those days that will go down in Roger Albert Clark folklore as a massive challenge with over 100 stage miles, persistent rain and, later on, fog to rival Radnor. "Thicker than Devon clotted cream," said Lancaster of his home county.

There was no gentle lead-in after the haul north: nearly 17 miles in Kershope was the starter for a day of long stages across Kielder and back. Robinson knew he had to attack and was just 1s down on McCormack in the first Kershope, went quickest in Ash Park and then parked up in the second Kershope with a gearbox problem. It was

McCormack in Crychan 1 on Friday

a sad end to the start of his charge and he'd been pushing hard. "Nobody likes a short-shifter," he had joked at the start.

Pritchard took just a second back from McCormack in Clintburn and McCormack grabbed six back in Chirdonhead. The rally then left the main block of Kielder for 12 miles in the now fog-bound Harwood and Pritchard drove an epic stage to slash the lead margin from 37s down to just 4s. "It was very difficult in there and I was probably a bit slow," said McCormack before learning of Pritchard's time. "We got through it, thanks to Phil on the notes. But there's a long way to go yet," said Pritchard.

Suitably stung, McCormack immediately bounced back in Pundershaw to grab half a minute back and end the day 33s up. With Robinson gone, Chilman settled back into third but was now over five minutes down and running his own rally.

Josh Browne had been absolutely flying in his Pinto-engined Escort and was third quickest through Clintburn, but then rolled out of the rally in Chirdonhead. The same stage claimed Webster when he went off and before the end of the leg Friend was out with alternator failure.

Through it all came Egglestone into fifth from Wayne Sisson who had his Mitsubishi Galant running much better after a troubled time in Wales. Lancaster slotted into sixth from the increasingly impressive US-based Irishman Barry McKenna.

Stefaan Stouf

Jeremy Easson and Mike Reynolds in Castle O'er

Day four: Sunday

Sunday was another big day with 70 stage miles in southern Scotland, starting with 11 miles in Greskine where low cloud hung broodingly over the higher parts of the stage.

Nothing much changed at the head of the rally as Pritchard edged McCormack by a single second after 12 minutes of flat-out motoring. After losing 10 minutes in a Kershope ditch on Saturday, Grehan was back with a bang to go third fastest from the quietly consistent Chilman.

However, it was the second run of Greskine that played a pivotal role in the lead contest. Around halfway through the stage, Pritchard picked up a front puncture. He carried on but had dropped 50s by the finish and that put McCormack's lead out to 1m26s.

Over the balance of Sunday's stages, McCormack was peerless and took a string of fastest times to extend his lead to 1m49s by the time the weary survivors arrived back in Carlisle.

"We kept our noses clean and had a good day, but there was a bit of patchy fog," said McCormack, who was now firmly on course to become the first driver to win the event for a third time. Once again, the Scottish leg had dealt Pritchard a killer punch.

In the wake of the big two, Chilman ran another strong day but accepted that a gap of seven minutes meant that third would be his lot unless either of the top two went out. Egglestone had a good day to edge ahead of Sisson for fourth while McKenna moved up to fifth at the expense of Lancaster who dropped a lot of time.

A misfire stopped brothers Leigh and Chris Armstrong in Twiglees and dropped them out of the top 10, while Grehan tigered his way back up to ninth to split Christophe Jacob and Stefaan Stouf. Their fight was for the honour of Belgium and Jacob took just 14s lead into the final stage.

Day five: Monday

Monday was no walk in the park as another 60 stage miles awaited in the central block of Kielder to deliver a proper sting in the tail, climaxing with a second run through the daunting 17-miler in Bewshaugh.

Keith McIvor in Falstone

Andy Madge

Chris Melling

For McCormack and Pritchard, the day started as one of stalemate. "We're not going to catch Marty on pace alone," said the chaser, knowing that his Greskine puncture had cost him too much. McCormack, meanwhile, was not about to throttle back. "We'll just keep doing what we're doing," said the leader.

However, McCormack did rather misjudge the pace on the opener in Whitrope and dropped 20s. That was his alarm call and over the next three stages he dropped only a handful more to take a margin of 1m22s into the final stage.

There was a poignant moment for the leading duo when McCormack suffered his only puncture of the rally when a rear tyre deflated in the regroup control after Falstone 2. Crucially, it had not impacted his pace through the stage. "The luck of the Irish," said Pritchard with a wry grin as he looked at the flat tyre.

And so it all came down to the final 17 miles in Bewshaugh as the rain settled in to make sure the stage was a fittingly tough climax to a truly challenging rally. Pritchard did all he could and clawed back 30s to bring the margin back to less than a minute, but McCormack was the victor.

Chilman remained third as Sisson pipped Egglestone for fourth by a second. McKenna was a last stage casualty, so Grehan took sixth from Geoff Bell. Further down the top 10 there was disaster for Jacob when he slid off right at the end of the first Falstone stage and dropped around 10 minutes. Lancaster, too, was in trouble and lost a lot of time with ongoing fuel problems that dropped him to eighth as Paul Street and Dave Bennett took mighty top 10 finishes.

McCormack and Mitchell in Kershope on Saturday morning

Kevin Jeffray

Bob Beales

The classes

For the Category 1 (pre '68) historics, this is a very tough rally and every finisher had climbed a mountain to keep their car running. Sadly, Class B1 went unclaimed when the two-stroke Saab 96 of Stephen Higgins/Sam Spencer cried enough. Somehow, father and son Andy and Thomas Pidden dragged their ailing Ford Cortina Mk1 home for B3 victory.

A Class B2 finish for sole starters Bob Seager and Geraldine McBride (MG Midget) was a massive achievement after they were badly hobbled by a batch of dirty fuel on Saturday night. They worked until 0400hrs to drain and clean the system. Clutch issues finally prevented them restarting on Monday but they had done enough to be classified. The legend that is Bob Bean dominated Class B4 with a fabulous run in his Ford Lotus Cortina with the redoubtable Captain Thompson alongside. A last day off in Bewshaugh 1 failed to dampen Bean's enthusiasm.

From the FIA classes, another class winner was the amazing VW Beetle of Bob Beales/Mike Leflay. They had all sorts of excitement and nearly ended

Drew Struthers and Fiona Muir

their rally in a Kershope culvert while passing the MG Midget. Later, they went off after the flying finish of Falstone, but the Beetle just kept on going.

Class C1 was the domain of Steve and Tony Graham in their magnificent Lancia Fulvia while a consummate victory in Class C2 fell to Dave Bennett/Alistair McNeil (Ford Escort Mk1). Dominating the class was one thing but pushing the little Escort into the top 10 overall was the real measure of one of the drives of the rally.

Despite having to rejoin under Super Rally rules, Josh Carr/Richard Wardle (Ford Escort Mk1) still won Class C3 and in C4 the irrepressible Jeremy Easson and Mike Reynolds came out on top in Mike's Datsun 240Z.

On their return to the UK forests, 2010 overall winners Stefaan Stouf and Joris Erard (Ford Escort Mk1) triumphed in Class C5 after spending some time dialling themselves back into the challenge of gravel rallying.

Class D2, for the 1600cc Category 3 cars, went to John Mennell and Adrian Wilford (Ford Escort Mk2) after an excellent run in the ex-Kim Gray car while Egglestone/Brian Hodgson were runaway winners in Class D3. Despite a visit to a Greskine ditch, David Kynaston and Val Thompson did a fine job to win Class D4 in their Triumph TR7 V8.

The F2 Class, for the latest generation of historics from up to 1990, was always the domain of Wayne Sisson and Neil Shanks in their 4x4 Mitsubishi Galant. They got quicker and quicker after some time-consuming issues in Wales and delivered by far and away the best result on the rally for a four-wheel-drive historic car.

Open Rally
The concurrent Open Rally ran for any two-wheel-drive cars and after several different leaders there was a well-deserved win for Baz Jordan and Arwel Jenkins.

By the end of the Welsh leg, Yorkshiremen Nick Cook and Dave Raw had a slender lead over the hard-charging Peugeot 205 GTi of James Nicholls/David Allman and the Toyota GT86 of 2017 Open winners David Hutchinson and Jeff Garnett.

Pritchard and Clarke
in Greskine

Paul Mankin

David Gathercole

The Kershope stage was not kind to the leading contenders and both Nicholls and Hutchinson suffered punctures and limped out, with Hutchinson dropping a massive six minutes. Nicholls was unlucky enough to puncture his front left tyre on both runs through the stage.

By the end of the long Saturday, Cook's lead was out to 2m40s as Dale Glover moved into second with an awesome drive in his Vauxhall Nova, while Jordan was up to third in his Vauxhall-engined Hillman Avenger. Then, a failed CV joint cost Glover a lot of time.

Cook continued to control the division through Sunday until fuel pressure dramas struck over the last five stages and he dropped a lot of time. That put Jordan into a useful three-minute lead over Nicholls going into the final day, which he retained with a nicely measured drive.

Personal view: Paul Lawrence
After more than four days of rallying, the finish of the final stage of the Roger Albert Clark Rally can be a place of tension and drama. But in persistent drizzle by Kielder Water, Marty McCormack and Barney Mitchell confirmed a mighty victory on the stop line of Bewshaugh 2.

Bob Seager and Geraldine McBride

For 31 special stages and 300 stage miles, they had fought tooth and nail with the similar Ford Escort Mk2 of Jason Pritchard and Phil Clarke as they dropped the rest of the field.

Pritchard punctured in Greskine 2 on Sunday and dropped 40s and McCormack took 1m22s into the final 17 miles in Bewshaugh. Pritchard clawed back half a minute but the McCormack reception party, headed by his family and team, was not to be disappointed.

It was starting to go dark on a wintery afternoon, but McCormack's faultless drive to a record-breaking third Roger Albert victory shone through the gloom.

Insight: Marty McCormack (Ford Escort Mk2)
The Roger Albert is a challenge
"It's a very tough event. When you're in the middle of the event and its long hours and fast driving, it's hard on the body and the arms and shoulders. It's long hours in the car and you have to dig deep and get a bit of resolve now and again and keep going."

He had strong pace
"It's a very rewarding rally and you know it's the big one and the special one and that's what it is all about. I'm really happy to have won it for the third time and we were really pleased with our pace all weekend. We kept the pace on and kept our heads down. Maybe I was always known for my pace but maybe not consistency and two years ago we struggled with Jason Pritchard on the Friday in Wales. We dropped a lot of time."

McCormack's only puncture of the rally

Roger Albert Clark Rally 2019: the thirteenth edition

David Greer and
Brian Crawford

He led after the Welsh leg
"I was aware not to let that happen this year and the Pirelli tyres were very good. Coming out of Wales with an advantage was a big positive for me. That was very important because I knew our pace would be okay when we got up north."

Fog was a big issue
"Then we got the fog thrown in and we all know that Jason's co-driver Phil Clarke is very experienced in the fog. They took 30 seconds out of us in 12 miles in Harwood. Barney Mitchell and I went down the road after that and said we had to do something about it. Barney got his head down and away we went. This rally is all about the variables and never more than this year. Barney really dug deep and came up a level on Saturday night. He hasn't done a lot in fog and he really stepped up."

Monday was a difficult day
"The last day on Monday was so tough because you're watching for punctures and trying to keep yourself right and just keep driving the stages to the notes. Don't cut too much and risk a puncture."

He won for the third time
"It takes a while for it all to sink in and it's a brilliant feeling. I must say a special thanks to the organisers and all the marshals: it's a fantastic event and Colin Heppenstall is always thinking on his feet and really on point. It was a really top class rally. It's an absolutely fantastic experience."

Martin McCormack

2019 ROGER ALBERT CLARK RALLY: ENTRY LIST

No	Driver	Co-driver	Car	Class
1	Martin McCormack	Barney Mitchell	Ford Escort Mk2	D5
2	Matthew Robinson	Sam Collis	Ford Escort Mk2	D5
3	Jason Pritchard	Phil Clarke	Ford Escort RS1800	G2
5	Roger Chilman	Patrick Walsh	Ford Escort Mk2	D5
6	Paul Barrett	Gordon Noble	Ford Escort Mk2	G2
7	Simon Webster	Jez Rogers	Ford Escort RS1800	D5
8	Wayne Sisson	Neil Shanks	Mitsubishi Galant VR4	F2
9	Adrian Hetherington	Andrew Grennan	Ford Escort RS1800	D5
10	Alan Walker	John Connor	Ford Escort RS1800	D5
12	Ghislain de Mevius	Johan Jalet	Nissan 240RS	E2
14	Stefaan Stouf	Joris Erard	Ford Escort RS1600	C5
15	Rudi Lancaster	Dave Price	Ford Escort RS1800	G2
16	Grégoire de Mévius	Andre Leyh	Toyota Celica	G2
17	Phil Collins	Den Golding	Opel Ascona 400	D4
18	Ben Friend	Cliffy Simmons	Ford Escort Mk2	D5
19	Stuart Egglestone	Brian Hodgson	Ford Escort Mk2	D3
20	Guy Woodcock	Will Rutherford	Ford Escort RS2000	D3
21	Henri Grehan	Jack Bowen	Ford Escort Mk2	D5
22	Keith McIvor	David Burns	Ford Escort Mk2	G2
23	Nick Carr	Joe Sturdy	Ford Escort Mk2	D5
24	Barry Stevenson-Wheeler	John Pickavance	Ford Escort RS1800	D5
25	Josh Browne	Jane Edgington	Ford Escort Mk2	D3
26	Christophe Jacob	Isabelle Regnier	Ford Escort RS	G2
28	Geoff Bell	Tim Challen	Ford Escort Mk2	D5
29	Jerry Bailey	Sinclair Young	Ford Escort RS	D5
30	David Hutchinson	Jeff Garnett	Toyota GT86	J4
31	Steve Graham	Tony Graham	Lancia Fulvia	C1
32	Leigh Armstrong	Christopher Armstrong	Ford Escort RS	D5
33	Philippe Tollemer	Christelle Tollemer	Ford Escort Mk2	D5
34	Barry McKenna	Arthur Kierans	Ford Escort Mk2	D5
35	Chris White	Chris Dewsnap	Ford Escort Mk2	G2
36	Lee Ashberry	Terry Mallin	Ford Escort RS1800	D5
37	David Greer	Brian Crawford	Opel Manta 400	G2
38	Pete Littler	Andy Marchbank	Ford Escort Mk2	D5
39	Arne Bäckström	Björn Wessel	Volvo 240	G2
40	Paul Street	Ian Jones	Ford Escort Mk2	D5
41	Andrew Siddall	Alex Lee	Fiat 131 Abarth Rally	G2
43	Baz Jordan	Arwel Jenkins	Hillman Avenger	J4
44	Chris Browne	Ali Cornwell-Browne	Ford Escort RS1600	C5
45	Phil Squires	Mick Squires	Ford Escort Mk2	D5
46	Jeremy Easson	Mike Reynolds	Datsun 240Z	C4
47	David Kynaston	Val Thompson	Triumph TR7 V8	D4
48	Alexandre Felsenhart	Adelin Philippe	Ford Escort Mk1	J4
49	Grant Inglis	Robert Gray	Ford Escort Mk2	D5
50	Nick Cook	Dave Raw	Ford Escort Mk1	J4
51	Roger Matthews	Tom Marrott	Ford Escort Mk1	C5
52	Raymond Barnes	Clive Jones	Talbot Lotus Sunbeam	D4
53	Mike Tomkinson	Shaun Whitehurst	Ford Escort RS1800	D5
54	Josh Carr	Richard Wardle	Ford Escort Mk1	C3
55	Tony Shields	Graham Whitaker	Ford Escort Mk1	C3
56	Wayne Bonser	Rich Aston	Ford Escort RS2000	C3
57	Martin Freestone	James Luton	Ford Escort RS1600	C5
58	Seamus Burke	Martin Brady	Ford Escort Mk2	G2

2019 ROGER ALBERT CLARK RALLY: ENTRY LIST (continued)

No	Driver	Co-driver	Car	Class
59	Harold de Hemptinne	Antoine del Marmol	Ford Escort Mk2	D3
60	Steve Magson	Kevin Bardon	Mercedes 2.3 16V	J5
63	Pascal Regnier	Maryline Furnémont	Ford Escort RS1800	G2
64	David Gathercole	Martyn Donn	Ford Escort RS1600	C5
65	David Tomlin	Keith Ashley	Ford Escort Mk2	G2
66	Pascal Delporte	Geoffrey Brion	Ford Escort Mk2	D3
67	Franco Tundo	Adrian Cavenagh	Ford Escort Mk2 RS1800	D5
69	David Jones	Glyn Price	BMW E30	J5
70	Dave Hemingway	Simon Ashton	Ford Escort Mk2	J4
71	Paul Fry	Mike Steele	Ford Escort Mk2	D5
72	Dave Forrest	Charlie Carter	Ford Escort Mk2	D3
73	Mike Reed	John Millington	Ford Escort Mk2	D3
74	Paul Kynaston	Rupert Barker	Opel Ascona 400	D4
75	Steve Ward	Alan Jones	Ford Escort Mk2	D5
77	Derek Belbin	James Burns	Ford Escort Mk2	D5
78	Owain Lloyd	Peter Scott	Ford Escort RS2000	D3
79	Mick Plowman	Paul Hudson	Ford Escort Mk2	J4
80	Andy Madge	Mike Smith	Toyota Corolla GT Coupe	J3
82	Donald Brooker	Tony Booth	Subaru Legacy Turbo	F2
83	Keith Turner	Rob Brook	Ford Escort Mk2 RS	D5
84	Ernie Lee	Steven Brown	BMW E30 325i	E2
85	Steve Hopewell	Mike Smith	Ford Escort Mk2	D5
86	Tomas Ebegård	Hamish Campbell	Porsche 911RS	G2
88	Jim Robertson	Paul Gribben	Ford Escort Mk2	D3
89	Bart Jan Deenik	Egbert Kolvoort	Ford Escort Mk1 RS1600	C5
90	Tim Metcalfe	Caron Tomlinson	Ford Escort RS1800	G2
91	James Nicholls	David Allman	Peugeot 205 GTi	J4
92	Kevin Jeffray	Iain Macleod	Vauxhall Astra GSi	J4
93	Rodger Mark Fowler	Ashley Young	Ford Escort Mk2	D5
94	Graham Samuel	Guy Desmet	Ford Escort Mk2	D3
95	Kris Hopkins	Martin Melsome-Smith	Triumph TR7 V8	D4
96	Colin Hope	Nick Patrick	Saab 96 V4	C3
97	Paul Kendrick	Luke Green	Ford Escort RS1600	C5
98	Richard Spink	Nigel Hutchinson	Ford Escort	J4
99	Dominique Lesourd	Sebastien Chol	Ford Escort Mk2	D3
100	Timothy Cains	Richard May	Peugeot 309	J4
101	John Leckie	Jon Madoc-Jones	Proton Satria GTi	J4
102	Graham Palmer	Mike Webb	Ford Escort	J4
103	Magic McCombie	Jonathan Haynes	Saab 900	J4
104	Chris Melling	Nick West	Peugeot 205 GTi	J3
105	Ian Newton	Ian Jones	Ford Escort Mk2	J4
106	Robert Williams	Iestyn Williams	Ford Escort Mk1 RS2000	C3
107	Michael Sawyer	Matthew Hewlett	Datsun 1600	C4
108	David Pedley	Steve Warrington	Vauxhall Astra	J4
109	Richard Phillipson	Stefan Arndt	Honda Civic EG6	J3
110	Simon Malins	Mark Casey	Vauxhall Firenza	C4
111	Gavin Chisholm	Shannon Turnbull	Saab 99	J5
112	Lorraine Gathercole	Chris Skill	Ford Escort RS	C5
113	Trevor Godwin	Ian Harrop	MG Maestro	F2
120	David Bennett	Alistair McNeil	Ford Escort Mk2	C2
121	John Mennell	Adrian Wilford	Ford Escort Mk2	D2
122	David Goose	Will Atkins	Ford Escort Sport	D2
123	Stuart Cariss	Linda Cariss	Ford Escort Sport	C2
125	Drew Struthers	Fiona Moir	Hillman Avenger GT	C2

2019 ROGER ALBERT CLARK RALLY: ENTRY LIST (continued)

No	Driver	Co-driver	Car	Class
126	Bob Bean	'Captain' Thompson	Ford Lotus Cortina Mk1	B4
128	Emmanuel Eggermont	Edouard de Braekeleer	Toyota Corolla GT AE 86	J3
129	Iain Freestone	Nick Kennedy	Rover 200 BRM	J3
130	Malcolm Rich	Ryland James	Ford Anglia 105E	B3
131	Robert Evett	Michael Evett	Vauxhall Nova	J2
132	Drexel Gillespie	Gill Cotton	Volvo 122S	B4
133	Paul Rawson	Graham Wild	Ford Escort Mk1	C2
134	Paul Mankin	Pete Phennah	Porsche 911	B5
135	Malcolm Mounsey	Ronald Mounsey	Talbot Sunbeam Ti	D2
136	Allan Clark	Iain Thorburn	Hillman Avenger	C2
137	Pete Johnston	Charles Johnston	Peugeot 205 GTi	J3
138	Charles Campbell	Kenny Owen	Davrian Mk8	D2
139	Alex Waterman	Glyn Thomas	Skoda 130L	F1
140	Dale Glover	Sean Ward	Vauxhall Nova SRi	J2
141	Mathew Evans	Daniel Evans	Peugeot 205	J2
142	Bob Seager	Geraldine McBride	MG Midget	B2
143	Andy Pidden	Thomas Pidden	Ford Cortina Mk1 GT	B3
144	Stephen Higgins	Sam Spencer	Saab 96 Sport	B1
145	Robert Beales	Mike Leflay	VW Beetle	G1

2019 STAGES AND STAGE WINNERS

Day	Stage	Name	Distance	Stage winner(s)	Time
Thursday	SS1	Radnor 1	6.64	Pritchard/Clarke	8.14
Thursday	SS2	Radnor 2	0.00	Cancelled	0.00
Friday	SS3	Crychan 1	6.34	McCormack/Mitchell	6.47
Friday	SS4	Gwibedog 1	5.43	McCormack/Mitchell	5.48
Friday	SS5	Epynt 1	4.05	Robinson/Collis	4.23
Friday	SS6	Halfway 1	4.20	McCormack/Mitchell	4.39
Friday	SS7	Crychan 2	6.34	McCormack/Mitchell	6.48
Friday	SS8	Gwibedog 2	5.43	McCormack/Mitchell and Pritchard/Clarke	5.53
Friday	SS9	Epynt 2	4.05	Chilman/Walsh	4.27
Friday	SS10	Halfway 2	4.20	McCormack/Mitchell	4.41
Saturday	SS11	Kershope 1	16.69	McCormack/Mitchell	18.28
Saturday	SS12	Ash Park	5.33	Robinson/Collis	5.35
Saturday	SS13	Kershope 2	16.69	McCormack/Mitchell	17.55
Saturday	SS14	Clintburn 1	13.52	Pritchard/Clarke	12.20
Saturday	SS15	Chirdonhead	14.71	McCormack/Mitchell	14.52
Saturday	SS16	Harwood	11.83	Mckenna/Kierans	14.04
Saturday	SS17	Pundershaw	9.35	McCormack/Mitchell	9.05
Saturday	SS18	Paddaburn	15.03	McCormack/Mitchell and Pritchard/Clarke	16.36
Sunday	SS19	Greskine 1	11.07	Pritchard/Clarke	11.59
Sunday	SS20	Ae 1	8.93	McCormack/Mitchell	8.46
Sunday	SS21	Greskine 2	11.07	McCormack/Mitchell	11.48
Sunday	SS22	Ae 2	8.93	McCormack/Mitchell	8.43
Sunday	SS23	Twiglees 1	5.55	McCormack/Mitchell	6.02
Sunday	SS24	Castle O'er 1	6.04	Chilman/Walsh and McCormack/Mitchell	7.08
Sunday	SS25	Craik	7.75	McCormack/Mitchell	7.58
Sunday	SS26	Twiglees 2	5.55	McCormack/Mitchell	6.05
Sunday	SS27	Castle O'er 2	6.04	McCormack/Mitchell	6.53
Monday	SS28	Whitrope	6.11	Pritchard/Clarke	5.58
Monday	SS29	Falstone 1	11.98	Pritchard/Clarke	12.01
Monday	SS30	Bewshaugh 1	17.67	Pritchard/Clarke	17.32
Monday	SS31	Falstone 2	11.98	McCormack/Mitchell	11.58
Monday	SS32	Bewshaugh 2	17.67	Pritchard/Clarke	17.41

2019 RESULTS

Overall	Class	No	Driver	Co-driver	Car	Class	Total
1	1	1	Martin McCormack	Barney Mitchell	Ford Escort Mk2	D5	05:03:12
2	1	3	Jason Pritchard	Phil Clarke	Ford Escort RS1800	G2	05:04:04
3	2	5	Roger Chilman	Patrick Walsh	Ford Escort Mk2	D5	05:14:23
4	1	8	Wayne Sisson	Neil Shanks	Mitsubishi Galant VR4	F2	05:18:30
5	1	19	Stuart Egglestone	Brian Hodgson	Ford Escort Mk2	D3	05:18:31
6	3	34	Barry McKenna	Arthur Kierans	Ford Escort Mk2	D5	S 5:32:10
7	4	21	Henri Grehan	Jack Bowen	Ford Escort Mk2	D5	05:37:59
8	5	28	Geoff Bell	Tim Challen	Ford Escort Mk2	D5	05:40:32
9	2	15	Rudi Lancaster	Dave Price	Ford Escort RS1800	G2	05:41:39
10	1	120	David Bennett	Alistair McNeil	Ford Escort Mk1	C2	05:43:16
11	6	40	Paul Street	Ian Jones	Ford Escort Mk2	D5	05:43:51
12	1	14	Stefaan Stouf	Joris Erard	Ford Escort RS1600	C5	05:44:12
13	2	59	Harold de Hemptinne	Antoine del Marmol	Ford Escort Mk2	D3	s 5:44:26
14	7	24	Barry Stevenson-Wheeler	John Pickavance	Ford Escort RS1800	D5	s 5:44:48
15	3	20	Guy Woodcock	Will Rutherford	Ford Escort RS2000	D3	05:47:35
16	1	46	Jeremy Easson	Mike Reynolds	Datsun 240Z	C4	05:49:42
17	3	58	Seamus Burke	Martin Brady	Ford Escort Mk2	G2	05:49:48
18	4	41	Andrew Siddall	Alex Lee	Fiat 131 Abarth Rally	G2	05:51:49
19	8	36	Lee Ashberry	Terry Mallin	Ford Escort RS1800	D5	s 5:56:05
20	5	63	Pascal Regnier	Maryline Furnémont	Ford Escort RS1800	G2	05:57:52
21	9	45	Phil Squires	Mick Squires	Ford Escort Mk2	D5	05:59:40
22	10	53	Mike Tomkinson	Shaun Whitehurst	Ford Escort RS1800	D5	06:00:17
23	2	123	Stuart Cariss	Linda Cariss	Ford Escort Sport	C2	S 6:02:11
24	4	72	Dave Forrest	Charlie Carter	Ford Escort Mk2	D3	06:02:21
25	1	121	John Mennell	Adrian Wilford	Ford Escort Mk2	D2	06:03:18
26	11	38	Pete Littler	Andy Marchbank	Ford Escort Mk2	D5	S 6:03:50
27	1	54	Josh Carr	Richard Wardle	Ford Escort Mk1	C3	s 6:04:36
28	6	37	David Greer	Brian Crawford	Opel Manta 400	G2	06:05:21
29	5	88	Jim Robertson	Paul Gribben	Ford Escort Mk2	D3	06:09:14
30	12	75	Steve Ward	Alan Jones	Ford Escort Mk2	D5	06:09:17
31	7	22	Keith McIvor	David Burns	Ford Escort Mk2	G2	s 6:09:46
32	6	99	Dominique Lesourd	Sebastien Chol	Ford Escort Mk2	D3	06:15:53
33	2	57	Martin Freestone	James Luton	Ford Escort RS1600	C5	06:16:10
34	8	90	Tim Metcalfe	Caron Tomlinson	Ford Escort RS1800	G2	06:16:35
35	2	107	Michael Sawyer	Matthew Hewlett	Datsun 1600	C4	s 6:17:14
36	2	56	Wayne Bonser	Rich Aston	Ford Escort RS2000	C3	s 6:17:37
37	3	64	David Gathercole	Martyn Donn	Ford Escort RS1600	C5	s 6:18:10
38	13	29	Jerry Bailey	Sinclair Young	Ford Escort RS	D5	s 6:19:23
39	1	47	David Kynaston	Val Thompson	Triumph TR7 V8	D4	s 6:24:43
40	1	126	Bob Bean	'Captain' Thompson	Ford Lotus Cortina Mk1	B4	s 6:29:23
41	14	67	Franco Tundo	Adrian Cavenagh	Ford Escort Mk2 RS1800	D5	s 6:30:47
42	2	74	Paul Geoffery Kynaston	Rupert Barker	Opel Ascona 400	D4	06:32:00
43	2	82	Donald Brooker	Tony Booth	Subaru Legacy Turbo	F2	06:38:01
44	9	65	David Tomlin	Keith Ashley	Ford Escort Mk2	G2	06:40:52
45	15	83	Keith Turner	Rob Brook	Ford Escort Mk2 RS	D5	06:41:11
46	16	93	Rodger Mark Fowler	Ashley Young	Ford Escort Mk2	D5	06:41:48
47	17	49	Grant Inglis	Robert Gray	Ford Escort Mk2	D5	S 6:43:54
48	3	133	Paul Rawson	Graham Wild	Ford Escort Mk1	C2	s 6:44:43
49	4	89	Bart Jan Deenik	Egbert Kolvoort	Ford Escort Mk1 RS1600	C5	06:49:04
50	1	84	Ernie Lee	Steven Brown	BMW E30 325i	E2	06:51:48
51	18	71	Paul Fry	Mike Steele	Ford Escort Mk2	D5	S 6:56:54
52	4	125	Drew Struthers	Fiona Moir	Hillman Avenger GT	C2	06:56:55
53	7	66	Pascal Delporte	Geoffrey Brion	Ford Escort Mk2	D3	S 7:14:03
54	1	139	Alex Waterman	Glyn Thomas	Skoda 130L	F1	s 7:15:20

2019 RESULTS (continued)

Overall	Class	No	Driver	Co-driver	Car	Class	Total
55	3	52	Raymond Barnes	Clive Jones	Talbot Lotus Sunbeam	D4	s 7:20:38
56	8	94	Graham Samuel	Guy Desmet	Ford Escort Mk2	D3	07:28:21
57	3	106	Robert Williams	Iestyn Williams	Ford Escort Mk1 RS2000	C3	07 30:51
58	1	143	Andy Pidden	Thomas Pidden	Ford Cortina Mk1 GT	B3	s 7:32:08
59	1	134	Paul Mankin	Pete Phennah	Porsche 911	B5	S 7:37:41
60	5	112	Lorraine Gathercole	Chris Skill	Ford Escort RS	C5	s 7 40:02
61	2	132	Drexel Gillespie	Gill Cotton	Volvo 122S	B4	s 7:44:09
62	6	97	Paul Kendrick	Luke Green	Ford Escort RS1600	C5	s 7:45:16
63	3	113	Trevor Godwin	Ian Harrop	MG Maestro	F2	S 7:57:53
64	3	110	Simon Malins	Mark Casey	Vauxhall Firenza	C4	08:06:36
65	1	31	Steve Graham	Tony Graham	Lancia Fulvia	C1	08:36:00
66	1	142	Bob Seager	Geraldine McBride	MG Midget	B2	S 8:47:25
67	4	95	Kris Hopkins	Martin Melsome-Smith	Triumph TR7 V8	D4	08:47:41
68	1	145	Robert Beales	Mike Leflay	VW Beetle	G1	S 8:54:09
Ret		16	Grégoire de Mevius	Andre Leyh	Toyota Celica	G2	Stopped after SS4
Ret		17	Phil Collins	Den Golding	Opel Ascona 400	D4	Clutch arm SS12
Ret		18	Ben Friend	Cliffy Simmons	Ford Escort Mk2	D5	Alternator failure SS18
Ret		23	Nick Carr	Joe Sturdy	Ford Escort Mk2	D5	Rolled SS13
Ret		25	Josh Browne	Jane Edgington	Ford Escort Mk2	D3	Went off SS15
Ret		26	Christophe Jacob	Isabelle Regnier	Ford Escort RS	G2	Retired in service before SS31
Ret		32	Leigh Armstrong	Christopher Armstrong	Ford Escort RS	D5	Electrical SS24
Ret		33	Philippe Tollemer	Christelle Tollemer	Ford Escort Mk2	D5	Retired after TC30B
Ret		35	Chris White	Chris Dewsnap	Ford Escort Mk2	G2	Engine SS22
Ret		39	Arne Bäckström	Björn Wessel	Volvo 240	G2	In ditch, heavy damage SS29
Ret		44	Chris Browne	Ali Cornwell-Browne	Ford Escort RS1600	C5	Broken propshaft SS19
Ret		51	Roger Matthews	Tom Marrott	Ford Escort Mk1	C5	Clutch before SS21
Ret		55	Tony Shields	Graham Whitaker	Ford Escort Mk1	C3	Stopped SS17
Ret		73	Mike Reed	John Millington	Ford Escort Mk2	D3	Low oil pressure SS14
Ret		77	Derek Belbin	James Burns	Ford Escort Mk2	D5	Engine SS27
Ret		78	Owain Lloyd	Peter Scott	Ford Escort RS2000	D3	Rolled SS13
Ret		85	Steve Hopewell	Mike Smith	Ford Escort Mk2	D5	Went off SS29
Ret		86	Tomas Ebegård	Hamish Campbell	Porsche 911RS	G2	Gearbox SS28
Ret		96	Colin Hope	Nick Patrick	Saab 96 V4	C3	Car broken after SS12
Ret		122	David Goose	Will Atkins	Ford Escort Sport	D2	Kielder ditch SS15
Ret		130	Malcolm Rich	Ryland James	Ford Anglia 105E	B3	Engine SS3
Ret		135	Malcolm Mounsey	Ronald Mounsey	Talbot Sunbeam Ti	D2	Rolled SS15
Ret		136	Allan Clark	Iain Thorburn	Hillman Avenger	C2	Seized axle SS7
Ret		138	Charles Campbell	Kenny Owen	Davrian Mk8	D2	Gearbox broken SS1
Ret		144	Stephen Higgins	Sam Spencer	Saab 96 Sport	B1	Incurable misfire SS23

Steve Magson

David Hutchinson

Josh Browne and Jane Edgington

2019 RESULTS: OPEN RALLY

Overall	Class	No	Driver	Co-driver	Car	Class	Total
1	1	43	Baz Jordan	Arwel Jenkins	Hillman Avenger	J4	05:51:11
2	2	91	James Nicholls	David Allman	Peugeot 205 GTi	J4	05:53:47
3	3	50	Nick Cook	Dave Raw	Ford Escort Mk1	J4	05:54:16
4	4	105	Ian Newton	Ian Jones	Ford Escort Mk2	J4	06:02:20
5	5	30	David Hutchinson	Jeff Garnett	Toyota GT86	J4	S 6:04:32
6	6	98	Richard Spink	Nigel Hutchinson	Ford Escort	J4	06:06:29
7	7	48	Alexandre Felsenhart	Adelin Philippe	Ford Escort Mk1	J4	06:12:48
8	8	100	Timothy Cains	Richard May	Peugeot 309	J4	06:16:03
9	1	80	Andy Madge	Mike Smith	Toyota Corolla GT Coupe	J3	s 6:20:22
10	9	70	Dave Hemingway	Simon Ashton	Ford Escort	J4	s 6:23:47
11	10	92	Kevin Jeffray	Iain Macleod	Vauxhall Astra GSi	J4	06:35:31
12	1	131	Robert Evett	Michael Evett	Vauxhall Nova	J2	06:37:03
13	2	104	Chris Melling	Nick West	Peugeot 205 GTi	J3	S 6:38:09
14	11	101	John Leckie	Jon Madoc-Jones	Proton Satria GTi	J4	06:40:56
15	2	140	Dale Glover	Sean Ward	Vauxhall Nova SRi	J2	s 6:43:00
16	12	102	Graham Palmer	Mike Webb	Ford Escort	J4	s 6:49:53
17	3	128	Emmanuel Eggermont	Edouard de Braekeleer	Toyota Corolla GT AE 86	J3	S 6:50:31
18	4	129	Iain Freestone	Nick Kennedy	Rover 200 BRM	J3	s 6:52:08
19	3	141	Mathew Evans	Daniel Evans	Peugeot 205	J2	s 7:05:46
20	5	137	Pete Johnston	Charles Johnston	Peugeot 205 GTi	J3	s 7:10:00
21	13	108	David Pedley	Steve Warrington	Vauxhall Astra	J4	07:12:53
22	1	60	Steve Magson	Kevin Bardon	Mercedes 2.3 16V	J5	S 7:30:06
23	2	111	Gavin Chisholm	Shannon Turnbull	Saab 99	J5	s 8:17:52
Ret		69	David Jones	Glyn Price	BMW E30	J5	Ripped axle off mounting SS12
Ret		79	Mick Plowman	Paul Hudson	Ford Escort Mk2	J4	Gearbox broken SS30
Ret		103	Magic McCombie	Jonathan Haynes	Saab 900	J4	Broken axle SS29
Ret		109	Richard Phillipson	Stefan Arndt	Honda Civic EG6	J3	Beached on big rocks SS4

Alex Waterman and Glyn Thomas

2019 RESULTS: CLUBMANS RALLY

Overall	Class	No	Driver	Co-driver	Car	Class	Total
1	1	150	Mark McCulloch	Michael Hendry	Ford Escort Mk2	J	00:59:20
2	2	163	Bryan Jardine	Darragh Sheridan	Ford Escort	J	01:01:33
3	1	152	Phil Jobson	Chris Sheridan	Ford Escort Mk1	C	01:02:53
4	1	157	Noel Lappin	David Fitzsimons	Ford Escort Mk2 1400	I	01:06:25
5	2	158	Donald Peacock	Albert Connelly	Peugeot 205 GTi	I	01:06:26
6	3	159	Anthony Harrison	Simon Barnes	Ford Escort Mk2	J	01:08:56
7	4	165	Darren Martin	Dan Hurst	Ford Escort Mk2	J	01:10:36
8	1	167	Steve Forster	Terry Martin	Ford Escort	D	01:10:40
9	3	151	Mike Axford	Dave Thomason	Ford Fiesta RS	I	01:11:47
10	5	162	Colin Smith	Adrian Lloyd	Vauxhall Astra	J	01:18:56
11	2	164	Alan McMorran	Scott Gourlay	Chrysler Avenger	D	01:21:05
12	3	160	Martin Oglesby	John Parker	Opel Kadett GT/E	D	01:22:26
Ret		153	David Dobson	Graeme Wood	Opel Manta	J	Electrical SS21
Ret		154	Andy Turner	Steve Harris	Subaru Impreza RWD	K	Stopped after SS20
Ret		155	Ian Forgan	Chris Lees	Ford Ka	J	Stopped SS19
Ret		156	Alistair Brearley	Paul Barbet	Ford Escort RS	J	Off in ditch SS20

Roger Matthews

Ghislain de Mevius

Roger Albert Clark Rally 2019: the thirteenth edition

Roger Albert Clark Rally 2021:
the fourteenth edition

Overall winners:
Ryan Champion and
Craig Thorley

Champion the wonder Porsche

The 2021 rally

Thursday 25 to Monday 29 November
227 stage miles
21 special stages
Start: H&H Auctions, Carlisle
Overnight 1 & 2: H&H Auctions, Carlisle
Transport section from Carlisle to Welshpool
Overnight 3: Welshpool
Overnight 4: Walter's Arena
Finish: Town centre, Carmarthen
139 starters
100 finishers

Open Rally winners:
Neil Weaver and Jack Morton

Roger Albert Rally 2021: the fourteenth edition

Seb Perez in Dyfnant 2

After one of the most challenging rallies for decades, Ryan Champion and Craig Thorley won the 2021 Roger Albert Clark Rally after a superbly measured performance in their Porsche 911.

The 14th edition of the rally was every bit as tough as the snow-hit 2010 event as Storm Arwen wreaked havoc across the north of England and Scotland and threatened to derail the event completely. But, after being forced to cancel Saturday's leg in Southern Scotland, the rally regrouped for two days in Wales and the action was relentless.

The Ford Escort Mk2s of Jason Pritchard/Phil Clarke, Paul Barrett/Gordon Noble and Osian Pryce/Noel O'Sullivan could all have won but went out in Wales. Instead, Champion became the event's first overall winner in anything but a Ford Escort.

"I can't quite believe it honestly," said Champion at the finish in Carmarthen on Monday afternoon. "We just did what we've been doing for the last couple of days and just played our own game. I'm a little bit shell shocked. Actually, I still can't quite believe it's happened!"

Day one: Thursday
The rally started with a bang, literally in some cases, with four stages on Thursday evening in Newcastleton and Kershope on a clear, cold, frosty night. The pace was fierce from the start, but incredibly, the first corner of the rally claimed three

Adrian Hetherington

Osian Pryce and Noel O'Sullivan in Bewshaugh 1

Andrew Pidden

leading contenders as Roger Chilman, Josh Browne, and Harry Hunt all went off the road at the first real corner of the rally.

Chilman in particular rolled several times, and his rally was over. Meanwhile, Pritchard settled into the groove despite a misfire in the first pair of stages to take an early advantage over Pryce, who admitted that he was unsure about just where to set his pace. He ended the evening 56s down on Pritchard as Barrett slotted into second place.

Others to struggle through the evening included Matthew Robinson, who admitted he didn't get on well in the dark, while Jerry Bailey's rally ended with an engine fire on the second Kershope stage.

Pritchard said: "We're being very cautious and there's a long way to go." Pryce commented: "It was a job to judge the pace. But we'll find a balance by tomorrow." Barrett was in striking form, setting times to rival Pritchard and Pryce. "There was a bit of fog at the top of Kershope," said Barrett. "But we're definitely going better than we did in 2019. We've done nothing radical."

Jason Pritchard and Phil Clarke in SS1

Rory McCann

Malcolm Rich

Day two: Friday

This was the big day with more than 100 stage miles across eight stages in the central block of Kielder, always an unforgiving place to go rallying. By the end of the day, blizzard conditions in gale force winds made it even more of a challenge and the final stage was curtailed in the interest of competitor and marshal safety.

Barrett set a searing pace on Friday morning to keep the pressure on Pritchard and after the first run through the mighty 17-mile Bewshaugh stage, the lead gap was down from 46s overnight to 36s.

However, as conditions worsened, Pritchard took a massive profit in Falstone by beating Barrett by 52s, having come close to catching the Northern Irishman in the falling snow. Now only the second run through Bewshaugh was left and it was incredibly tough as crews faced a raging blizzard and lying snow. Pritchard was back to running first on the road in the main field but as he crossed the flying finish another set of lights was right behind him. Barrett had all but caught his rival and so the day ended with them 37s apart, marking a 9s gain for Barrett in 105 stage miles.

Star drive: Adam Milner and Roy Jarvis

"Absolutely horrendous in there," said Pritchard on the stop line, visibly relieved to have simply got through. "Just push, push, push," said Barrett of his remarkable performance.

Pryce was one of many to drop time in Bewshaugh and ended the day nearly four minutes down but still third ahead of Champion's Porsche 911 as Seb Perez and Adrian Hetherington rounded out the top six overall. In the Open Rally, Neil Weaver and Jack Bowen set a ferocious pace in their Super 1600 Vauxhall Corsa to lead by a huge margin.

Day three: Saturday

The situation in the forests on Friday deteriorated rapidly as the evening developed and the rally was halted before trees started coming down. However, trees down across the road sections made life increasingly difficult and around 30 crews were stranded in Langholm as fallen trees even blocked the main A7. It was 1000hrs on Saturday before some of them made it back to Carlisle.

With the Scottish stages and access roads blocked by fallen trees, rally manager Colin Heppenstall took the responsible decision to cancel Saturday's leg, putting the safety of everyone involved ahead of all other considerations.

The service area was full of tales of a challenging night and many crews were grateful to the Crown Inn at Langholm, which opened its doors to everyone and ensured those stranded were safe, warm and fed.

Drexel Gillespie

Roger Albert Clark Rally 2021: the fourteenth edition

Richard Jordan in Walter's Arena

Day four: Sunday

After the transport section south, crews regrouped in Welshpool for two runs through three classic mid-Wales stages. However, the storm had left the Gartheiniog stage littered with trees and so only Dyfnant and Dyfi lay in wait. Even on Sunday afternoon, the higher sections harboured snow and ice and that only got worse for the second runs on Sunday evening.

Dyfi changed the complexion of the rally as Pritchard rolled out of the lead as the mighty battle with Barrett finally reached its conclusion. But Barrett had no time to savour his new-found lead as Pryce was on the attack and pulled back 1m34s in just three stages. The front-runners were red flagged on the first Dyfi stage after Pritchard's roll and that denied Pryce the chance to take back more time in his own backyard.

"It's not easy," said Barrett. "That last stage was sheet ice, but we'll just keep at it," he said of his plan for Monday. Champion moved into a secure third, but fourth-placed Perez had a single second in hand over the charging Hetherington. Despite stopping in Dyfnant 2 with sheared wheel studs, Weaver's lead in the Open Rally was such that even with two stage maximums, he still led by nearly five minutes.

David Hutchinson

Day five: Monday

The final day's action opened with seven miles in Walters Arena and soon after 0900hrs came an

Paul Rawson and Paul Wild in Dyfnant 1

Andy Johnson

Ricky Evans

incredible five-minute period that stood the rally on its head. Barrett, running first on the road in the main field, rolled over a deceptive brow near the finish and, though damage was light, a broken track control arm signalled that his rally was over.

In a cruel twist of irony for Barrett, moments earlier his major rival had gone out when Pryce suffered a front stub axle failure mid-stage and his rally was also over. Moments later, Hetherington went off early in the icy stage and dropped around 1m50s. Champion, running third on the road, struggled to keep concentration as he saw first Pryce and then Barrett out of the rally. "I just didn't expect it to be as icy as it was and we lost 20s with a spin," said Champion, who instantly took a lead of over four minutes.

Knowing that Pryce would continue hunting him down on Monday, Barrett had started the day with no choice but to push. "I didn't known Osian had stopped and I was just trying to keep him honest," said Barrett. "It was a crest with a sudden six right and we just slid wide and that was it." It was a poor reward for one of the drives of his life.

The rally winner at the start of SS4

Tim Metcalfe

Ben Friend

Pryce took his bitter rallying blow with good grace. "I didn't enjoy the snow, to be honest. But in the back of my mind, I knew if I just got through, I could get to Wales and then do the work there. We started doing the work yesterday. But obviously, we didn't quite finish the job. I think we could have done it."

As the full impact of those few moments in Walters Arena became clear, Champion led the rally to Crychan with a commanding margin and knew that he could ease his pace over the final four stages and duly reached the finish with his four minute lead intact. "We didn't know if we would be fast enough and we couldn't live with the fastest guys," said Champion." So we just settled in our pace and kept somewhere near and amazingly it's come to us. It's a fantastic rally to win."

Behind the Porsche, Perez was quietly impressive as he worked his way up to second. Clobbering a deer in Kielder was his major concern as it took out his spotlights, but Seb drove with his head to underline his outstanding all-rounder credentials. "A clean, consistent run," reported Perez. "We were a

Rhys Yates and Max Freeman on Monday morning

bit off the pace in the ice on Sunday night. On Friday I think it was lucky that the deer hit the lamp pod because it would have done the radiator otherwise. So you need a bit of luck on this event."

Despite his off on the first stage of Monday, Hetherington bounced back to take the final podium place but it was very close as a mighty late charge from Ben Friend and Cliffy Simmons narrowed the gap to just 6s. On a mission, Friend was 22s faster than everyone through the final Crychan stage and slashed Hetherington's advantage from 32s to just six. A cautious approach at the start of the rally ultimately denied Friend a podium place. Hetherington said: "That was some rally we've done. We had to push on Monday to hold him off."

Rhys Yates/Max Freeman and Robert Gough/Jack Bowen delivered fine debut Roger Albert performances to round out the top six, with Yates being impressed by the camaraderie among the leading contenders. Meanwhile, Simon Webster and Jez Rogers were consistently strong on the way to seventh ahead of the remarkable Adam Milner/Roy Jarvis. Paul Street/Ian Jones turned in another great Roger Albert Clark drive for ninth while Sacha Kakad/James Aldridge rounded the overall top 10.

The Open Rally
Running alongside the historic event was the Open Rally for all two-wheel drive cars and after a see-saw rally it was the Super 1600 Opel Corsa of Weaver and Jack Morton that took victory.

David Goose

Roger Albert Clark Rally 2021: the fourteenth edition

Champion and Thorley on Sunday evening

Tony Jardine

Ian Beveridge

Weaver set a scorching pace from the start and took a 26s lead into the second day as Andy Davison and Tim Murphy chased in their Talbot Sunbeam VXR. However, twice on Friday Davison dropped big chunks of time and then was one of the crews stranded overnight in Langholm. Weaver, running in the first group of cars, had no such problems and led the Open Rally by 17 minutes by Welshpool. Up into second had come the Escort Mk2 of Steve Hopewell and Mike Smith.

In Dyfnant, it nearly all went wrong for Weaver as he was forced to stop with sheared wheel studs and he took two stage maximums as a result. That wasn't the end of Weaver's drama as he took another maximum in Walter's Arena with a broken driveshaft. However, he then set a stunning pace over the final four stages to reclaim control and win by nearly two minutes as Davison clawed his way back to second from Hopewell.

The classes
The clear star of Category 1 for the pre '68 cars was the Ford Anglia of Malcolm Rich and Ryland James which needed a gearbox change on its way to a remarkable 26th overall. They went back to base in Brecon on Sunday night and worked until 0400hrs

Robinson and Collis in Bewshaugh

Terry Cree

changing the gearbox. Aside from the winning Porsche 911, the Anglia was the only other non-Escort in the top 28 cars. Rich marked his birthday on Monday with a truly memorable result.

The wonderful two-stroke Saab 96 of Steve Higgins/Sam Spencer and the Volvo PV544 of Swedes Martin Linden and Rickard Forsell joined the Porsche 911 of Rikki Proffitt and Graham Wild as other class winners in Category 1.

Milner/Jarvis blitzed the BDA-powered Escorts in Category 2 (up to 1974) and won Class C2 by more than half an hour over the Toyota Corolla of Ian Beveridge and Paul Price. The lovely Lancia Fulvia

Stephen Higgins

of Steve and Tony Graham successfully completed every stage on its way to Class C1 victory, while Tony Shields and Mark Mason topped Class C3 in their Escort Mk1 Pinto.

Roger Albert Clark Rally 2021: the fourteenth edition

Adrian Drury and Cat Lund in Dyfnant 2

The strong Class C5, for the BDA-powered Escort Mk1s, was commandingly taken by 2010 overall winners Stefaan Stouf and Joris Erard from Belgium as they finished just outside the overall top 10.

In Category 3, for the pre '81 cars, one of the closest class finishes came among the 1600cc cars in Class D2 where the VW Golf of Chris and Tim Hellings beat the Sunbeam Talbot of Dave Hopkins/Richard Wise by just half a minute. Hopkins and Wise only met at scrutineering after a last-minute deal when Hopkins' planned co-driver Tony Vart was side-lined by a family bereavement. Hopkins and Wise had run in the top 30 overall until clutch problems slowed them on the final day. In D1, the Vauxhall Nova of Keir and Paul Beaton survived a roll on its way to winning the class.

When Mike Reed was unwell in the week before the rally, he offered his planned management car driver Ken Sturdy his Escort Mk2 for the event, complete with the talents of John Millington in the co-driver's seat. Sturdy repaid his friend's generous offer by bringing the Pinto-engined car home unmarked and winner of Class D3.

Other class winners included father and son Ricky and Dan Evans (Peugeot 205 GTi), Keith McIvor/David Burns (Escort Mk2) and Richard Phillipson/Stefan Arndt in the magnificent Safari-style Peugeot 504.

Star drive: Adam Milner (Ford Escort Mk1)
Typically, for such a long and challenging event, there were lots of impressive performances. In overall terms, Seb Perez was a stand-out in a new build Escort Mk2 from Dansport and the Ford Anglia of Malcolm Rich/Ryland James, just about the oldest car on the rally, thrilled the fans as it claimed the scalps of many newer and more powerful cars.

However, the absolute star of the rally was young Adam Milner, co-driven by the not quite so young Roy Jarvis. In the 1600cc crossflow-engined Ford Escort Mk1 they had spent the last three years rebuilding, Milner was stunningly fast and spectacular, showing off a prodigious natural talent.

"I've not driven it since we crashed on the Pirelli

Simon Webster and Jez Rogers

Mike Tomkinson

Paul Barrett

Rally in 2018," said Milner. "We've had a big push to finish it over the last few months. This is a baptism of fire," he said before Thursday's opening leg.

The pace was strong from the start and they were 9s outside the overall top 10 as they headed into Wales. The slippery Welsh stages didn't faze Milner one bit and his uncanny balance, honed on trials bikes, served him well on the icy sections. "We've not backed off yet and the car's going well," he said in Machynlleth at the end of Sunday.

Through the final day, Milner still didn't back off and continued to thrill the spectators with his sublime lock-to-lock car control, which finally took them to an incredible eighth overall, only beaten by the winning Porsche 911 and six BDG-engined Escorts. Thirteen BD-powered Escorts followed them home.

"There's not a mark on it; I'm amazed," said Milner at the finish. "It's been mint," added one of Britain's most under-rated rallying talents.

2021 ROGER ALBERT CLARK RALLY: ENTRY LIST

No	Driver	Co-driver	Car	Class
2	Jason Pritchard	Phil Clarke	Ford Escort RS1800	G2
3	Osian Pryce	Noel O'Sullivan	Ford Escort Mk2	G2
4	Matthew Robinson	Sam Collis	Ford Escort Mk2 RS	D5
5	Roger Chilman	Patrick Walsh	Ford Escort Mk2	D5
6	Paul Barrett	Gordon Noble	Ford Escort Mk2	G2
7	Rhys Yates	Max Freeman	Ford Escort Mk2	D5
8	Seb Perez	Gary McElhinney	Ford Escort Mk2	D5
9	Ben Friend	Cliff Simmons	Ford Escort Mk2	D5
10	Steve Bannister	Callum Atkinson	Ford Escort Mk2	D5
11	Simon Webster	Jez Rogers	Ford Escort RS1800	D5
12	Alan Walker	John Connor	Ford Escort RS1800	D5
14	Steve Bennett	Osian Owen	Ford Escort Mk2	D5
15	Josh Browne	Jane Edgington	Ford Escort Mk2	D5
16	Harry Hunt	Steven McPhee	Ford Escort RS1800	D5
17	Robert Gough	Jack Bowen	Ford Escort RS1800	D5
18	Ryan Champion	Craig Thorley	Porsche 911	D4
20	Adrian Hetherington	Ronan O'Neill	Ford Escort RS1800	D5
21	David Condell	Paul Kelly	Ford Escort Mk2	J5
22	David Brown	Steve Bielby	Ford Escort RS1800	D4
23	Barry Stevenson-Wheeler	John Pickavance	Ford Escort RS1800	D5
24	Rudi Lancaster	Guy Weaver	Ford Escort RS1800	G2
25	John Lowe	James Whitaker	Ford Escort Mk2	D5
26	Jeremy Bailey	Sinclair Young	Ford Escort RS1800	D5
27	Chris Skill	Simon Jones	Ford Escort RS1600	C5
28	David Hutchinson	Jeff Garnett	Ford Escort Mk2	J5
29	Rob Dennis	Andy Boswell	Ford Escort Mk2	D5
30	Leigh Armstrong	Chris Armstrong	Ford Escort RS	D5
31	Steve Graham	Tony Graham	Lancia Fulvia	C1
32	Christophe Jacob	Isabelle Regnier	Ford Escort Mk2	G2
33	Stefaan Stouf	Joris Erard	Ford Escort RS1600	C5
34	Sacha Kakad	James Aldridge	Ford Escort Mk2	D5
35	Paul Street	Ian Jones	Ford Escort Mk2	D5
36	Keith McIvor	David Burns	Ford Escort Mk2	G2
37	Frank Tundo	Natasha Tundo	Triumph TR7 V8	G2
38	Chris Browne	Ali Cornwell-Browne	Ford Escort RS1600	C5
39	Adrian Young	Gwynfor Jones	Ford Escort RS2000	D3
40	Grant Inglis	Michael Cruickshank	Ford Escort Mk2	D5
41	Andrew Siddall	Alex Lee	Ford Escort RS1800	D5
42	Jeremy Easson	Alun Cook	Datsun 240Z	C4
43	Mike Stuart	Neil Shanks	Ford Escort Mk1	C5
44	Theo Bengry	Les Forsbrook	Opel Ascona 400	D4
46	David Tomlin	Keith Ashley	Ford Escort Mk2	G2
47	Lee Ashberry	Terry Mallin	Ford Escort Mk2	D5
48	Alun Horn	Ian Beamond	Ford Escort	J4
49	Nick Cook	Dave Raw	Ford Escort Mk1	J4
50	Richard Jordan	James Gratton-Smith	Ford Escort Mk2	D5
51	Fintan McGrady	Cormac McGrady	Ford Escort Mk2	D5
52	Pete Littler	Andy Marchbank	Ford Escort RS1800	D5
53	Seamus Burke	Martin Brady	Ford Escort Mk2	G2
54	Ken Sturdy	John Millington	Ford Escort RS2000	D3
55	James Nicholls	David Allman	Peugeot 205 GTi	J4
56	Mike Tomkinson	Shaun Whitehurst	Ford Escort Mk2	D5
57	Philip Squires	Mick Squires	Ford Escort Mk2	D5
58	Jim Robertson	Paul Gribben	Ford Escort Mk2	D5
59	David Pedley	Paul Stringer	Ford Mk2 RS1800	D4
60	Phil Jobson	Ali Proctor	Ford Escort Mk1	C5
61	Gary Smith	Clive Jones	Ford Escort Mk1	C5
62	Chris Harris	Brynmor Pierce	Ford Escort Mk2	J5

2021 ROGER ALBERT CLARK RALLY: ENTRY LIST (continued)

No	Driver	Co-driver	Car	Class
63	Andy Davison	Tom Murphy	Talbot Sunbeam VXR	J5
64	Andy Johnson	Jim Mc Sherry	Vauxhall Chevette HSR	D4
65	Andrew Stokes	Jonny 'Tad' Evans	Ford Escort Mk1	C5
66	David Kirby	Martin Corbett	Ford Escort Mk1	C5
67	Richard Warne	Chris Deal	Ford Escort Mk2	J4
69	Terry Cree	Richard Shores	BMW 2002 Ti	C3
70	Tony Shields	Mark Mason	Ford Escort Mk1	C3
71	Mick Plowman	Paul Hudson	Ford Escort Mk2	J4
72	Mike Roberts	Ken Bowman	Ford Escort RS2000	D3
73	Richard Spink	Nigel Hutchinson	Ford Escort RS1800	D5
74	Dave Forrest	Jamie Forrest	Ford Escort Mk2	D3
75	David Kynaston	Val Thompson	Triumph TR7 V8	D5
76	Alexandre Felsenhart	Andre Leyh	Ford Escort Mk1	J4
77	Dave Hemingway	Simon Ashton	Ford Escort Mk2	J4
78	Paul Fry	Mike Steele	Ford Escort RS1800	D5
79	Darren Martin	Peter Johnson	Ford Escort RS2000	J4
80	George Bryson	Jacqueline Bryson	Ford Escort RS1600	C5
81	David Goose	Will Atkins	Ford Escort Sport	D2
82	David Jones	Glyn Price	BMW E30	F2
83	Steve Hopewell	Mike Smith	Ford Escort	J4
84	Miguel Henry de Frahan	Stéphane Prevot	Ford Escort Mk2 RS1800	D5
85	Tim Metcalfe	Mark Casey	Ford Escort RS1800	G2
86	Dominique Lesourd	Sebastien Chol	Ford Escort Mk2	D3
87	Bart Jan Deenik	Egbert Kolvoort	Ford Escort RS1600 Mk1	C5
88	Paul Kynaston	Andy Conibear	Opel Ascona	D4
89	Christian Becker	Frederic Hebert	Ford Escort Mk2	D3
90	Paul Thompson	Josh Davison	Ford Escort	J4
91	Graham Palmer	Mike Webb	Ford Escort Mk1	C3
92	Rodger Mark Fowler	Ashley Young	Ford Escort Mk2	D5
93	Donald Brooker	Tony Booth	Subaru Legacy RS	F2
94	Steve Benton	John Henderson	Ford Mk2 Escort	D5
96	Conrad Bos	Geoff Crabtree	Ford Escort RS2000	D3
97	John McIlwraith	Jonathan Fowler	Ford Escort Mk2	D3
98	Keith Turner	Brian Hodgson	Ford Escort Mk2	D5
99	Ricky Evans	Daniel Evans	Peugeot 205	F2
100	Derek Belbin	James Burns	Ford Escort Mk2	D5
101	Colin Hope	Nick Patrick	Saab 96 V4	C3
102	Ben Jemison	Dean Kellett	Vauxhall Chevette	D4
103	Stuart McLaren	Simon Hunter	Opel Kadett GT/E	D3
105	Drexel Gillespie	Gill Cotton	Ford Escort Mk1	C3
106	Jean Louis Meynart	Yves Huyghe de Mahenge	Ford Escort Mk2	G2
107	Ron Morgan	Marc Clatworthy	Ford Escort Mk2	D3
108	Adrian Drury	Cat Lund	Talbot Sunbeam	D2
109	Phillip Harris	Richard Suter	Ford Escort	J4
110	Colin Smith	John Pinder	Vauxhall Astra Mk3	J4
112	Eddie Gale	Andy Hollingham	Ford Escort Mk2	J5
113	Richard Phillipson	Stefan Arndt	Peugeot 504	H2
114	Gavin Chisholm	Jonathan Lodge	Saab 99	J4
115	Keith Shepherd	Rowan Corney	Ford Escort	J4
121	Neil Weaver	Jack Morton	Vauxhall Corsa S1600	J3
122	Adam Milner	Roy Jarvis	Ford Escort Mexico Mk1	C2
123	Rory McCann	Paul McCann	Hillman Avenger	C2
124	Rikki Proffitt	Graham Wild	Porsche 911S	B5
125	Stuart Cariss	Linda Cariss	Ford Escort Sport	C2
126	John Mennell	Tom Spencer	Ford Escort Mk2	J3
127	Alan Jardine	Chris McSherry	Ford Escort Mk2	D2
128	Alex Waterman	Glyn Thomas	Datsun 1600 SSS	C2
129	Matthew Fowle	Andy Pullan	Ford Escort Mk1	C2

Roger Albert Clark Rally 2021: the fourteenth edition

2021 ROGER ALBERT CLARK RALLY: ENTRY LIST (continued)

No	Driver	Co-driver	Car	Class
130	Chris Hellings	Tim Hellings	VW Golf Mk1 GTi	D2
131	Tony Jardine	Allan Harryman	Hillman Avenger	C2
132	Andy Madge	Matt Cooper	Toyota Corolla GT Coupe	J3
133	Ian Beveridge	Paul Price	Toyota Corolla TE27	C2
134	Bob Bean	'Captain' Thompson	Ford Lotus Cortina Mk1	B4
135	David Hopkins	Richard Wise	Talbot Sunbeam	D2
136	Dave Watkins	Graham Wride	Ford Escort Mk1 Twin Cam	C2
137	Mark Tugwell	Nigel Graham	Ford Escort Mk1	C2
138	Keir Beaton	Paul Beaton	Vauxhall Nova	D1
139	Malcolm Rich	Ryland James	Ford Anglia	B3
141	Iain Freestone	Nick Kennedy	Rover 200 BRM	J3
142	Paul Mankin	Pete Phennah	Porsche 911	B5
143	Dale Glover	Sean Ward	Vauxhall Nova SRi	J2
144	Chris Melling	Nick West	Peugeot 205 GTi	J3
145	Paul Rawson	Paul Wild	Ford Escort Mk1	C2
146	Allan Clark	Iain Thorburn	Hillman Avenger	C2
147	Martin Lindén	Rickard Forsell	Volvo PV 544 Sport	B4
148	Julian Birley	Emyr Hall	Talbot Sunbeam Ti	D2
149	Robert Evett	Michael Evett	Vauxhall Nova	J2
150	Andrew Pidden	Thomas Pidden	Ford Cortina GT Mk1	B3
151	Rob Aslett	Ashley Aslett	Peugeot 205 GTi	J3
152	Anthony Harrison	Andrew Darbyshire	Ford Escort Mk1 Mexico	C2
153	Steve Higgins	Sam Spencer	Saab 96 Sport	B1

2021 STAGES AND STAGE WINNERS

Day	Stage	Name	Distance	Stage winner(s)	Time
Thursday	SS1	Newcastleton 1	3.58	Pritchard/Clarke and Barrett/Noble	3.35
Thursday	SS2	Kershope 1	12.90	Pritchard/Clarke	14.42
Thursday	SS3	Newcastleton 2	4.95	Pritchard/Clarke and Barrett/Noble	5.17
Thursday	SS4	Kershope 2	12.90	Walker/Connor	14.08
Friday	SS5	Clintburn	13.18	Barrett/Noble	11.58
Friday	SS6	Chirdonhead 1	14.41	Pritchard/Clarke	13.26
Friday	SS7	Falstone 1	10.15	Pritchard/Clarke	9.39
Friday	SS8	Bewshaugh 1	17.20	Barrett/Noble	17.18
Friday	SS9	Pundershaw	9.01	Barrett/Noble	8.12
Friday	SS10	Chirdonhead 2	14.41	Pryce/O'Sullivan	13.41
Friday	SS11	Falstone 2	10.15	Pritchard/Clarke	10.43
Friday	SS12	Bewshaugh 2	17.20	Barrett/Noble	20.04
Saturday	SS13	Greskine 1	0.00	Cancelled	0.00
Saturday	SS14	Ae 1	0.00	Cancelled	0.00
Saturday	SS15	Greskine 2	0.00	Cancelled	0.00
Saturday	SS16	Ae 2	0.00	Cancelled	0.00
Saturday	SS17	Twiglees 1	0.00	Cancelled	0.00
Saturday	SS18	Craik 1	0.00	Cancelled	0.00
Saturday	SS19	Twiglees 2	0.00	Cancelled	0.00
Saturday	SS20	Craik 2	0.00	Cancelled	0.00
Sunday	SS21	Dyfnant 1	11.02	Pryce/O'Sullivan	12.14
Sunday	SS22	Gartheiniog 1	0.00	Cancelled	0.00
Sunday	SS23	Dyfi 1	13.29	Pryce, Barrett, Perez, Friend, Champion and Hetherington	15.32
Sunday	SS24	Dyfnant 2	11.02	Pryce/O'Sullivan	12.33
Sunday	SS25	Gartheiniog 2	0.00	Cancelled	0.00
Sunday	SS26	Dyfi 2	13.29	Pryce/O'Sullivan	15.36
Monday	SS27	Walters 1	7.12	Davison/Murphy	8.32
Monday	SS28	Glasfynydd	3.09	Friend/Simmons	4.01
Monday	SS29	Crychan 1	10.47	Friend/Simmons	11.58
Monday	SS30	Walters 2	7.12	Hetherington/O'Neill	7.46
Monday	SS31	Crychan 2	10.47	Friend/Simmons	11.50

2021 RESULTS

Overall	Class	No	Driver	Co-driver	Car	Class	Total
1	1	18	Ryan Champion	Craig Thorley	Porsche 911	D4	04:13:10
2	1	8	Seb Perez	Gary McElhinney	Ford Escort Mk2	D5	04:17:14
3	2	20	Adrian Hetherington	Ronan O'Neill	Ford Escort RS1800	D5	04:18:30
4	3	9	Ben Friend	Cliff Simmons	Ford Escort Mk2	D5	04:18:36
5	4	7	Rhys Yates	Max Freeman	Ford Escort Mk2	D5	04:20:49
6	5	17	Robert Gough	Jack Bowen	Ford Escort RS1800	D5	04:22:38
7	6	11	Simon Webster	Jez Rogers	Ford Escort RS1800	D5	04:25:26
8	1	122	Adam Milner	Roy Jarvis	Ford Escort Mexico Mk1	C2	04:27:12
9	7	35	Paul Street	Ian Jones	Ford Escort Mk2	D5	04:27:23
10	8	34	Sacha Kakad	James Aldridge	Ford Escort Mk2	D5	04:30:24
11	1	33	Stefaan Stouf	Joris Erard	Ford Escort RS1600	C5	04:31:26
12	9	30	Leigh Armstrong	Chris Armstrong	Ford Escort RS	D5	04:32:14
13	1	36	Keith McIvor	David Burns	Ford Escort Mk2	G2	04:33:48
14	10	12	Alan Walker	John Connor	Ford Escort RS1800	D5	04:35:11
15	11	23	Barry Stevenson-Wheeler	John Pickavance	Ford Escort RS1800	D5	04:35:35
16	2	24	Rudi Lancaster	Guy Weaver	Ford Escort RS1800	G2	04:39:16
17	12	50	Richard Jordan	James Gratton-Smith	Ford Escort Mk2	D5	04:39:53
18	2	38	Chris Browne	Ali Cornwell-Browne	Ford Escort RS1600	C5	04:42:17
19	13	73	Richard Spink	Nigel Hutchinson	Ford Escort RS1800	D5	04:45:55
20	3	32	Christophe Jacob	Isabelle Regnier	Ford Escort Mk2	G2	04:48:14
21	4	53	Seamus Burke	Martin Brady	Ford Escort Mk2	G2	04:51:32
22	1	54	Ken Sturdy	John Millington	Ford Escort RS2000	D3	04:53:46
23	3	27	Chris Skill	Simon Jones	Ford Escort RS1600	C5	04:55:47
24	1	70	Tony Shields	Mark Mason	Ford Escort Mk1	C3	04:57:18
25	1	97	John McIlwraith	Jonathan Fowler	Ford Escort Mk2	D3	04:59:54
26	1	139	Malcolm Rich	Ryland James	Ford Anglia	B3	05:00:22
27	14	52	Pete Littler	Andy Marchbank	Ford Escort RS1800	D5	05:00:25
28	2	72	Mike Roberts	Ken Bowman	Ford Escort RS2000	D3	05:00:57
29	1	130	Chris Hellings	Tim Hellings	VW Golf Mk1 GTi	D2	05:01:07
30	2	135	David Hopkins	Richard Wise	Talbot Sunbeam	D2	05:01:37
31	15	51	Fintan McGrady	Cormac McGrady	Ford Escort Mk2	D5	05:02:19
32	2	133	Ian Beveridge	Paul Price	Toyota Corolla TE27	C2	05:04:01
33	1	124	Rikki Proffitt	Graham Wild	Porsche 911S	B5	05:05:00
34	16	10	Steve Bannister	Callum Atkinson	Ford Escort Mk2	D5	s 5:05:57
35	3	81	David Goose	Will Atkins	Ford Escort Sport	D2	05:06:25
36	17	40	Grant Duncan Inglis	Michael Cruickshank	Ford Escort Mk2	D5	s 5:06:35
37	3	136	Dave Watkins	Graham Wride	Ford Escort Mk1 Twin Cam	C2	05:06:43
38	18	57	Philip Squires	Mick Squires	Ford Escort Mk2	D5	s 5:06:52
39	19	100	Derek Belbin	James Burns	Ford Escort Mk2	D5	05:07:47
40	1	138	Keir Beaton	Paul Beaton	Vauxhall Nova	D1	s 5:08:10
41	4	65	Andrew Stokes	Jonny 'Tad' Evans	Ford Escort Mk1	C5	s 5:09:16
42	1	147	Martin Lindén	Rickard Forsell	Volvo PV 544 Sport	B4	05:10:39
43	20	94	Steve Benton	John Henderson	Ford Escort Mk2	D5	05:13:07
44	2	22	David Brown	Steve Bielby	Ford Escort RS1800	D4	s 5:15:01
45	3	102	Ben Jemison	Dean Kellett	Vauxhall Chevette	D4	05:16:12
46	21	29	Rob Dennis	Andy Boswell	Ford Escort Mk2	D5	s 5:16:35
47	22	41	Andrew Siddall	Alex Lee	Ford Escort RS1800	D5	s 5:17:31
48	1	99	Ricky Evans	Daniel Evans	Peugeot 205	F2	05:17:33
49	23	84	Miguel Henry de Frahan	Stéphane Prevot	Ford Escort Mk2 RS1800	D5	05:18:07
50	5	61	Gary Smith	Clive Jones	Ford Escort Mk1	C5	05:19:22
51	4	127	Alan Jardine	Chris McSherry	Ford Escort Mk2	D2	05:20:30
52	4	64	Andy Johnson	Jim McSherry	Vauxhall Chevette HSR	D4	05:21:05
53	24	56	Mike Tomkinson	Shaun Whitehurst	Ford Escort Mk2	D5	s 5:21:48
54	5	46	David Tomlin	Keith Ashley	Ford Escort Mk2	G2	s 5:22:11
55	2	93	Donald Brooker	Tony Booth	Subaru Legacy RS	F2	05:23:09
56	6	60	Phil Jobson	Ali Proctor	Ford Escort Mk1	C5	s 5:23:25
57	6	37	Frank Tundo	Natasha Tundo	Triumph TR7 V8	G2	05:23:25
58	5	148	Julian Birley	Emyr Hall	Talbot Sunbeam Ti	D2	05:25:26

Roger Albert Clark Rally 2021: the fourteenth edition

2021 RESULTS (continued)

Overall	Class	No	Driver	Co-driver	Car	Class	Total
59	25	92	Rodger Mark Fowler	Ashley Young	Ford Escort Mk2	D5	05:25:28
60	3	89	Christian Becker	Frederic Hebert	Ford Escort Mk2	D3	s 5:28:34
61	3	82	David Jones	Glyn Price	BMW E30	F2	05:28:46
62	5	59	David Pedley	Paul Stringer	Ford Escort Mk2 RS1800	D4	s 5:31:05
63	2	69	Terry Cree	Richard Shores	BMW 2002 Ti	C3	05:31:42
64	26	98	Keith Turner	Brian Hodgson	Ford Escort Mk2	D5	05:33:15
65	4	107	Ron Morgan	Marc Clatworthy	Ford Escort Mk2	D3	s 5:33:38
66	3	91	Graham Palmer	Mike Webb	Ford Escort Mk1	C3	05:34:48
67	7	80	George Bryson	Jacqueline Bryson	Ford Escort RS1600	C5	05:40:11
68	4	145	Paul Rawson	Paul Wild	Ford Escort Mk1	C2	s 5:40:54
69	8	87	Bart Jan Deenik	Egbert Kolvoort	Ford Escort RS1600 Mk1	C5	s 5:46:54
70	2	150	Andrew Pidden	Thomas Pidden	Ford Cortina Mk1 GT	B3	s 5:47:53
71	1	153	Steve Higgins	Sam Spencer	Saab 96 Sport	B1	05:48:28
72	6	108	Adrian Drury	Cat Lund	Talbot Sunbeam	D2	05:51:05
73	2	142	Paul Mankin	Pete Phennah	Porsche 911	B5	s 6:10:01
74	1	113	Richard Phillipson	Stefan Arndt	Peugeot 504	H2	06:10:39
75	5	131	Tony Jardine	Allan Harryman	Hillman Avenger	C2	s 6:20:23
76	5	103	Stuart McLaren	Simon Hunter	Opel Kadett GT/E	D3	s 6:25:17
77	6	88	Paul Kynaston	Andy Conibear	Opel Ascona	D4	s 6:32:42
78	1	31	Steve Graham	Tony Graham	Lancia Fulvia	C1	06:53:46
Ret		2	Jason Pritchard	Phil Clarke	Ford Escort RS1800	G2	Rolled SS23
Ret		3	Osian Pryce	Noel O'Sullivan	Ford Escort Mk2	G2	Front wheel missing SS27
Ret		4	Matthew Robinson	Sam Collis	Ford Escort MK2 RS	D5	Went off SS11
Ret		5	Roger Chilman	Patrick Walsh	Ford Escort Mk2	D5	Went off SS1
Ret		6	Paul Barrett	Gordon Noble	Ford Escort Mk2	G2	Went off SS27
Ret		14	Steve Bennett	Osian Owen	Ford Escort Mk2	D5	Gearbox TC23B
Ret		15	Josh Browne	Jane Edgington	Ford Escort Mk2	D5	Stopped SS29
Ret		16	Harry Hunt	Steven McPhee	Ford Escort RS1800	D5	Stopped SS1
Ret		25	John Lowe	James Whitaker	Ford Escort Mk2	D5	Did not restart at MTC9
Ret		26	Jeremy Bailey	Sinclair Young	Ford Escort RS1800	D5	Fire SS4
Ret		39	Adrian Young	Gwynfor Jones	Ford Escort RS2000	D3	Stopped SS30
Ret		42	Jeremy Easson	Alun Cook	Datsun 240Z	C4	Did not restart at MTC9
Ret		43	Mike Stuart	Neil Shanks	Ford Escort Mk1 Mexico	C5	Stopped SS6
Ret		44	Theo Bengry	Les Forsbrook	Opel Ascona 400	D4	Stopped in service TC29C
Ret		47	Lee Ashberry	Terry Mallin	Ford Escort Mk2	D5	Stopped SS9
Ret		58	Jim Robertson	Paul Gribben	Ford Escort Mk2	D5	Stopped SS3
Ret		66	David Kirby	Martin Corbett	Ford Escort Mk1 Mexico	C5	Stopped SS8
Ret		74	Dave Forrest	Jamie Forrest	Ford Escort Mk2	D3	Stopped SS2
Ret		75	David Kynaston	Val Thompson	Triumph TR7 V8	D5	Axle expired SS29
Ret		78	Paul Fry	Mike Steele	Ford Escort RS1800	D5	Blown diff SS7
Ret		85	Tim Metcalfe	Mark Casey	Ford Escort RS1800	G2	Driver personal reasons TC10C
Ret		86	Dominique Lesourd	Sebastien Chol	Ford Escort Mk2	D3	No electrics SS4
Ret		96	Conrad Bos	Geoff Crabtree	Ford Escort RS2000	D3	Stopped in Service TC29C
Ret		101	Colin Hope	Nick Patrick	Saab 96 V4	C3	Stopped SS11
Ret		105	Drexel Gillespie	Gill Cotton	Ford Escort Mk1 Mexico	C3	Oil pressure after SS12
Ret		106	Jean Louis Meynart	Yves Huyghe de Mahenge	Ford Escort Mk2	G2	Stopped SS12
Ret		123	Rory McCann	Paul McCann	Hillman Avenger	C2	Rolled SS6
Ret		125	Stuart Cariss	Linda Cariss	Ford Escort Sport	C2	Went off SS6
Ret		128	Alex Waterman	Glyn Thomas	Datsun 1600 SSS	C2	Stopped SS30
Ret		129	Matthew Fowle	Andy Pullan	Ford Escort Mk1 Mexico	C2	Did not restart MTC3
Ret		134	Bob Bean	'Captain' Thompson	Ford Lotus Cortina Mk1	B4	Mechanical MTC4
Ret		137	Mark Tugwell	Nigel Graham	Ford Escort Mk1 Mexico	C2	Mechanical after SS29
Ret		146	Allan Clark	Iain Thorburn	Hillman Avenger	C2	Did not restart at MTC9
Ret		152	Anthony Harrison	Andrew Darbyshire	Ford Escort Mk1 Mexico	C2	Stopped SS6

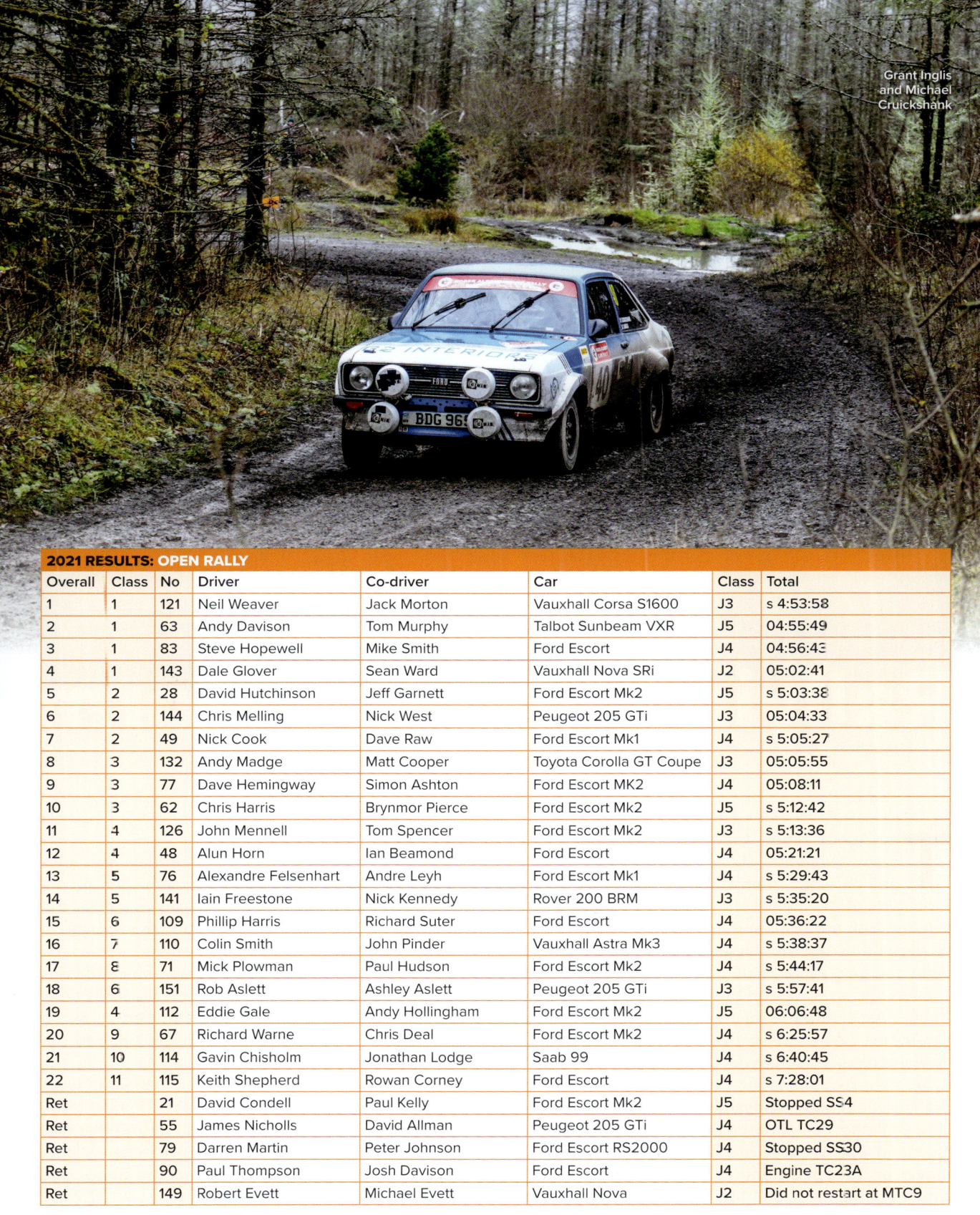

Grant Inglis and Michael Cruickshank

2021 RESULTS: OPEN RALLY

Overall	Class	No	Driver	Co-driver	Car	Class	Total
1	1	121	Neil Weaver	Jack Morton	Vauxhall Corsa S1600	J3	s 4:53:58
2	1	63	Andy Davison	Tom Murphy	Talbot Sunbeam VXR	J5	04:55:49
3	1	83	Steve Hopewell	Mike Smith	Ford Escort	J4	04:56:43
4	1	143	Dale Glover	Sean Ward	Vauxhall Nova SRi	J2	05:02:41
5	2	28	David Hutchinson	Jeff Garnett	Ford Escort Mk2	J5	s 5:03:38
6	2	144	Chris Melling	Nick West	Peugeot 205 GTi	J3	05:04:33
7	2	49	Nick Cook	Dave Raw	Ford Escort Mk1	J4	s 5:05:27
8	3	132	Andy Madge	Matt Cooper	Toyota Corolla GT Coupe	J3	05:05:55
9	3	77	Dave Hemingway	Simon Ashton	Ford Escort MK2	J4	05:08:11
10	3	62	Chris Harris	Brynmor Pierce	Ford Escort Mk2	J5	s 5:12:42
11	4	126	John Mennell	Tom Spencer	Ford Escort Mk2	J3	s 5:13:36
12	4	48	Alun Horn	Ian Beamond	Ford Escort	J4	05:21:21
13	5	76	Alexandre Felsenhart	Andre Leyh	Ford Escort Mk1	J4	s 5:29:43
14	5	141	Iain Freestone	Nick Kennedy	Rover 200 BRM	J3	s 5:35:20
15	6	109	Phillip Harris	Richard Suter	Ford Escort	J4	05:36:22
16	7	110	Colin Smith	John Pinder	Vauxhall Astra Mk3	J4	s 5:38:37
17	8	71	Mick Plowman	Paul Hudson	Ford Escort Mk2	J4	s 5:44:17
18	6	151	Rob Aslett	Ashley Aslett	Peugeot 205 GTi	J3	s 5:57:41
19	4	112	Eddie Gale	Andy Hollingham	Ford Escort Mk2	J5	06:06:48
20	9	67	Richard Warne	Chris Deal	Ford Escort Mk2	J4	s 6:25:57
21	10	114	Gavin Chisholm	Jonathan Lodge	Saab 99	J4	s 6:40:45
22	11	115	Keith Shepherd	Rowan Corney	Ford Escort	J4	s 7:28:01
Ret		21	David Condell	Paul Kelly	Ford Escort Mk2	J5	Stopped SS4
Ret		55	James Nicholls	David Allman	Peugeot 205 GTi	J4	OTL TC29
Ret		79	Darren Martin	Peter Johnson	Ford Escort RS2000	J4	Stopped SS30
Ret		90	Paul Thompson	Josh Davison	Ford Escort	J4	Engine TC23A
Ret		149	Robert Evett	Michael Evett	Vauxhall Nova	J2	Did not restart at MTC9

Roger Albert Clark Rally 2021: the fourteenth edition

The snow started to fall on Friday afternoon

Rallying and the storm
2021: Storm Arwen

The Roger Albert Clark Rally is designed to be a challenge. Long days, tough stages and a unique atmosphere make it one of the highlights of UK special stage rallying. But the 2021 edition took the challenge to a new level as Storm Arwen did its best to wreak havoc. Paul Lawrence reflected on a remarkable rally.

Everyone who was on the 2010 Roger Albert will have clear memories of the incredible event that ran in the year of the snow. The 2021 rally will go down in history as the year of the blow.

As ever, rally manager Colin Heppenstall pulled off the seemingly impossible by organising a five-day, 31-stage, 320-stage mile epic across England, Scotland and Wales. Only the ongoing impact of Covid on European entries reduced the capacity entry of 150 cars, but 139 cars took the start in Carlisle on Thursday afternoon.

Everything went well through Friday as crews tackled a daunting 105 competitive miles in the central block of Kielder Forest. However, as the light faded and the snow began, the arrival of Storm Arwen was to have a dramatic impact on the event. Having monitored worsening conditions Heppenstall called a halt to the rally on Friday evening but later running crews and officials faced a rapidly increasing challenge to get back to the Carlisle base.

By around 9pm, all roads out of Kielder were blocked by fallen trees and the planned rally route back to Carlisle was blocked by a big tree that was down across the road just north of Kielder village, close to the start of the Bewshaugh stage. The snow, which had fallen heavily as the wind got up,

Conrad Bos demonstrated other talents

didn't really get much worse but fallen trees were a huge problem and that was not limited to the smaller roads. The main A7 trunk road from Carlisle to Edinburgh was blocked either side of the border town of Langholm and it was in Langholm that as many as 30 crews and some officials realised that they were going no further on Friday night. Though not on rally route, Langholm was where they ended up as they exhausted attempts to find a way out.

To the enormous credit of the management and staff, the Crown Inn in Langholm opened its doors and offered food, drink and shelter to at least 50 rally people. Bar trade was brisk before sleep was attempted. However, in many ways they were the lucky ones, as a few crews and officials spent an uneasy night in the car. By 9am on Saturday, the key routes were open again, but it was the middle of the day before the final officials escaped the forest.

Among those with a big tale to tell were rallying veterans Bob Bean (83) and 'Captain' Thompson (70). They had punctured in Bewshaugh and slid their Lotus Cortina off into a big ditch, which they only escaped three hours later thanks to the hard work of the recovery crew. By now, roads out of Kielder were blocked and they were short of fuel having missed the planned meet with their management vehicle. The fuel ran out in the early hours, and it was 7.30am before a farmer came by and offered a jerry can of fuel. "We didn't panic, but it was a cold night," said Thompson. "The main road through Kielder was like a scene from a Spielberg blockbuster with the amount of debris. It was exciting... afterwards!"

It was sunny and calm on Friday morning

Among the crews stuck in Langholm was Top Gear presenter Chris Harris and co-driver Bryn Pierce, tackling the Open Rally in a non-historic Ford Escort Mk2. "Friday evening felt like a Top Gear challenge that went catastrophically wrong, but the rally spirit has been incredible, and people helped us so much," said Harris, who impressed many with his approach to the event and speed on the stages. "The stages on Friday when the sun was shining were as good as I've experienced in terms of driving of any sort. It was an utter privilege and I just feel so lucky to have been on this event. It was the most fantastic experience."

Another driver new to the event was Lotus Elan racer Conrad Bos, a veteran of just two gravel rallies in his Pinto-engined Ford Escort Mk2 before the start of the Roger Albert Clark. With fellow racers Adam Cunnington and John Moon in his support crew, this was way outside any established comfort zone, but Bos showed his versatility by helping behind the bar at the Crown Inn. They regrouped on Saturday morning and rejoined in Wales, only to retire at final service on Monday when the Escort resolutely refused to fire. They loved the whole adventure and 10 laps at Snetterton will not be such a big deal anymore.

Dave Hemingway and Simon Ashton are members of a very small club, having started and finished all 14 Roger Alberts in their Open category Escort Mk2. Fumes from the newly painted car once it got hot made Ashton feel groggy, but they had bigger issues on Friday night with an epic tale of getting back to Carlisle, possibly as the final car to do so.

"We adopted the same pedestrian pace of the

The Crown Hotel in Langholm

Bob Bean and 'Captain' Thompson

Chris Harris rose to a different type of challenge

previous night and decided that a night in the hotel would be much more productive than a night in a Falstone ditch," said Hemingway of Friday's penultimate stage. "Bewshaugh 2 was even worse. The driving snow which made it difficult to see was almost non-existent in the trees, so you could push on only to be met by a wall of snow as you exited the trees. To make it worse, we had to crash over two fallen trees which were completely blocking the stage. We exited safely but may possibly be the last crew to finish the stage as the two trees we jumped were quickly being joined by many others."

The road through Newcastleton was blocked so they headed north into Scotland. "We descended to the deserted A7 which looked ominous, but we continued through Langholm and out the other side where we were met by an artic lorry reversing up the road. A tree with a 2ft thick trunk was laying across the road at shoulder height, supported by two collapsed walls. We headed west for the M74, but the route was blocked so a south-westerly route was plotted. An upturned sheep shed in the road was lifted out of the way and plonked over the wall by a farmer driving a telehandler. On arrival in Carlisle, we were told that we were the first car into the control for over an hour and I'm not sure that any made it back after us either. We abandoned the car in service and beat a retreat to the hotel!"

By around 10am on Saturday, everyone was either back at Carlisle or accounted for and Heppenstall confirmed that Saturday's leg was cancelled. Privately, he had been concerned that the whole rally would have to be called off, but better news soon arrived from Wales.

During Saturday, local volunteers had concentrated on clearing the Dyfi stage and the adjoining Gartheiniog stage was cancelled to consolidate resources. Dyfnant, meanwhile, was clear of trees but, even in the daylight of Sunday afternoon, harboured patches of snow and ice on the higher stretches just to keep up the challenge. Crews later reported that the second run through Dyfi on Sunday evening was treacherously icy.

All of that made Monday's leg of five stages pretty straightforward with only some ice on the opening Walter's Arena stage to keep everyone on their toes. Remarkably, 100 of the 139 starters made the finish in Carmarthen after a rally that no-one will forget. Just as he had in 2010, Heppenstall had pulled a rabbit out of a hat to keep the event running. The night that Storm Arwen hit Kielder will go down in rallying folklore.

The view from the top
Rally manager Colin Heppenstall faced some tough decisions when Storm Arwen hit. "This is his view of a truly challenging 24 hours.

"On Friday at 3pm the skies were blue and clear and there was no wind. But by early evening the weather conditions were coming in and getting worse. Snow started to fall, it was getting colder, and the wind was reasonable as we went into the final stage of the day. Then we could hear that the wind was getting up to the level where there was a possibility of trees coming down.

"In consultation with Forestry England, who were with me all the time, I made the decision to stop the event because we could tell the wind was now at a dangerous level. We stopped the final Bewshaugh stage with about 10 cars left to go into the stage.

"What happened next happened very quickly. Within

The A7 at Langholm on Saturday morning

two or three minutes the stage was blocked in multiple locations with trees that had fallen. We then launched red flags to stop all the cars and opened all the forest gates just to get everybody, the crews, the marshals and the spectators, out of the forests as quickly as possible and back onto the public highway.

"Eventually every road out of Kielder was blocked with trees. Even we were blocked in Kielder, and we had to cut our way out. The Crown Inn in Langholm did a wonderful job looking after some of our competitors and I really thank them for that. But then Saturday morning was calm, and the weather was gorgeous. There was no wind, and nobody would believe we'd had the night before that we'd had.

"We couldn't get into any of the Saturday stages in Scotland as far too many trees were down across all four stages and the access roads. The only option we had was to follow our major incident plan, which we had also done the night before, and we followed it through on Saturday morning as the health and safety of everybody was paramount: not only the competitors, but the marshals and the spectators as well.

"Most of the time, we know where the competitors are and we know where the marshals are, but we haven't a clue where the spectators are. And we found out on Saturday morning that some spectators had gone into the Greskine on Friday night and had got blocked in there. So, they had to be cut out on Saturday morning. We ask people not to go into the forest the night before and it's for these reasons, we don't do it lightly.

"So, we had to cancel the Saturday stages and we then started looking at what we were going to do in Wales. By 11am on Saturday we had a call from the stage commander to say the Dyfnant stage was all open and clear. At least we had a start for the rest of the event."

Roger Albert Clark Rally 2023:
the fifteenth edition

Overall winners: Martin McCormack and Barney Mitchell

McCormack the fourth as Solberg stars

The 2023 rally

Thursday 23 to Monday 27 November
334 stage miles
31 special stages
Start: Carmarthen Showground
Overnight 1: Walter's Arena
Transport section from Sweet Lamb to Carlisle
Overnight 2, 3 and 4: Carlisle
Finish: H&H Auctions, Carlisle
155 starters
103 finishers

Open Rally winners: Neil Weaver and Jack Morton

Roger Albert Rally 2023: the fifteenth edition

Robert Woodside in his Tuthill Porsche 911

Osian Pryce and Rhodri Evans

Martin McCormack and Barney Mitchell emerged from the dramatic closing stages of the 2023 Roger Albert Clark Rally to scoop victory as the star names fell by the wayside. This was the biggest and toughest edition of the rally so far and the presence of stars like Kris Meeke, Oliver Solberg, Chris Ingram and Osian Pryce helped boost spectator numbers to record levels. An unrivalled media package ensured that all the drama and action was available on-line for a global audience.

Day one: Thursday

Thursday was supposed to be the easy day, a gentle lead into what lay ahead with just under 40 miles in some classic Welsh stages. However, the drama started right from the off and continued all day as all sorts of people hit all sorts of problems.

First in grief was newly crowned BHRC champion Roger Chilman, who hit terminal engine problems on the opening stage in Crychan. That was a crushing blow given that his 2021 rally had ended a mile into the opening stage with an off.

Across the road in Cefn, Matthew Robinson and Sam Collis came to a sudden and expensive halt, with a major flywheel drama. They rejoined on Saturday, but their challenge for overall glory was over.

After Walters Arena, a second lap of Crychan and Cefn continued the carnage and immediately in trouble were Meeke and Noel O'Sullivan, who

The Roger Albert Clark Rally: The first 20 years

Seb Perez was a star in the Lancia Stratos

The Stimson/Butler Ford Anglia won Category 1

punctured in Crychan 2 and had to stop and change a wheel. However, worse was to come in the middle of Cefn when their Escort ground to a halt with an electrical issue and refused to run on more than two cylinders. The car was eventually manhandled out of the stage, but their rally was over. Stefaan Stouf and Dai Roberts were also in trouble when, two corners earlier, their Escort Mk1 shed a wheel.

Through it all, Pryce and Rhodri Evans drove a storming day to finish the leg with just a single second advantage over Solberg and Elliot Edmondson. "I'm happy with how it's gone," said Pryce. "Stage one was my test and we can improve on things for tomorrow," promised the overnight leader.

Solberg, too, had a strong day in unfamiliar surroundings and was very happy with his situation. "It's been a great day, super tough, but amazing to keep up with the other guys," said Oliver who was surrounded by fans every time he got out of the car.

McCormack and Mitchell had a scare at the start of Cefn 2 with smoke coming from their Escort after an electrical short, but they resolved the problem and carried on in some style.

Meanwhile, Seb Perez and Gary McElhinney had the Lancia Stratos going remarkably well, despite spending some of the morning loop on less than six cylinders after a distributor problem.

Ingram and Hannah McKillop battled a gearbox issue on the TR7 V8 but that was resolved at service and they pressed on, starting to show the new car's potential.

Roger Albert Clark Rally 2023: the fifteenth edition

Tony Jardine in Glengap forest

Jim Robertson in Cefn

Class D two winners David Hopkins and Richard Wise

Day two: Friday

Friday was the first big day with 75 stage miles in mid Wales centred on the classics of Myherin and Hafren and it was here that Solberg started to assert his authority on the rally in front of a bumper crowd. In fact, so popular was the event that the organisers had to close the Sweet Lamb car park before the first cars arrived.

The day opened with another stage in the Crychan complex and Solberg pinched a second off Pryce and made it all square going into Myherin. Up across the fast and flowing stage past the wind farm, Solberg took a seven second lead. But it was in the 15 miles of Hafren that he really pushed home his advantage. On the first run, he added nine over Pryce.

But on the second run of Hafren in the dark of Friday early evening, Solberg added another 17 to take his advantage out to 44s as the crews headed north out of Wales.

Pryce remained the biggest challenger to the flying Swede while McCormack slipped away a little, ending the day over two minutes down on the leader

Daniel Mennell was one of the stars of the rally

after a monster moment in Hafren persuaded him to reign it back a little. Pritchard ended the leg fourth after a strong day on home ground, while Perez was one of the stars of Friday by wailing the glorious Lancia Stratos into fifth place overall.

Cathan McCourt, Ben Friend and James Ford were next up but the big losers for the day included Ingram, who retired the TR7 V8 with transmission issues and Paul Barrett, who dropped nearly five minutes in the second run of Hafren South.

US-based Irishman Barry McKenna had been well up into the top 10 but broke the steering and a damper in Myherin and quickly stopped and removed the entire front corner towards the end of the stage so that he could drive out on one wheel and the sump guard. Somehow his crew got him going, and he flew again but he was now 15 minutes down on the leaders.

Day three: Saturday

On Saturday, after the haul north, it was into new territory for the event for a tough leg of stages, centred on the forests of Dumfries and Galloway. A gloriously bright and sunny morning heralded a heavy frost and icy stretches that never really cleared all day, and later returned with a vengeance as the temperature dropped towards the end of the afternoon.

Jason Pritchard and Phil Clarke took third overall

Roger Albert Clark Rally 2023: the fifteenth edition

Solberg set the pace until Sunday evening

But that made little difference to Solberg who continued his relentless pace at the head of the field. While Solberg stormed through stage after stage, around him the opposition was starting to come unstitched and first to go was Pryce who parked the Escort up on the first run of Glengap when oil concerns signalled the end of his rally.

Solberg had no such worries. "That was an incredible day, fantastic! Really difficult stages and very icy as well," said Solberg, who ended the day with a lead of more than four minutes. In his wake, McCormack and Pritchard both dropped time with moments but were able to continue and McCormack overcame a bent steering rack to end the day 1m46s up on Pritchard as Perez and the increasingly impressive McCourt and Friend rounded out the top six.

Out went Paul Barrett, another to fall victim to engine dramas as the Wales Motorsport squad lost its third top 10 runner in three days. Several others also didn't fare well. The second run through Glengap took Ford's Porsche 911 out of the rally with broken suspension and Richard Tuthill failed to finish the day in his 911.

Once again, it had been a tough day and even the loss of the two runs through Arroch Hill due to route authorisation issues didn't diminish the challenge of a full day in Scotland.

Richard Holdsworth in his Ford Cortina Mk1

The Roger Albert Clark Rally: The first 20 years

Craig Jones and Ian Taylor.

Aaron Rix and Abi Haycock in the Open category

Mike Stuart won Category two

Day four: Sunday

Anyone who thought that Friday and Saturday were tough days was in for a wake-up call on Sunday when six long stages in the central block of Kielder delivered 88 stage miles in a 13-hour day.

Many had predicted that Sunday would shape the leader board but much of that work had been concluded in the preceding three days and now it was a case of maintaining his lead and keeping out of trouble for rally leader Solberg. He did that remarkably well and took his lead out to more than five and a half minutes before disaster struck on the final stage of the day. A broken halfshaft in the second run of Harwood was a cruel blow and the resulting stage maximum dropped him to fourth, over five minutes adrift of McCormack.

The Alfa Romeo of Dutch crew Maarten and Jeanette Buitenhuis

Dyfrig James was one of the stars with fourth overall

Baz Jordan and Arwel Jenkins

"Big commiserations to Oliver," said McCormack. "But we've still got a long way to go," he added of the final day of 80 stage miles in Kielder. Incredibly, Perez was now up to second and battling with McCourt despite a scare with a water pipe on the Lancia. By the end of the day, McCourt was just 15s behind while Pritchard and Friend rounded out the top six though Prichard had suffered two punctures.

Day five: Monday
With the halfshaft that stopped them on Sunday evening replaced, Solberg and Edmondson restarted on Monday morning knowing that a clear run should take them back ahead of Perez/McElhinney and McCourt/Liam Moynihan into second place. McCormack's lead was too great to be clawed back in the 80 stage miles available unless the Northern Irish driver had a problem and with the epic 39-mile closing stage still to come, nothing was certain.

However, close to the end of the opening stage of the day in Shepherdshield, Solberg slid off the road and nosed the undamaged Escort into a ditch. His rally was over, but the young Swede had gained

Andrew Haddon returned to the event in a Ford Escort Mk1

so much experience and so many new fans that it was still a big success.

"We were going to try to push this morning to try to get up to second," said Solberg as he waited for the car to be recovered. "Pushing it a bit too hard, maybe, and just slid into the ditch. So very annoying. The guys were up all night trying to fix the car and they did an amazing job. This was very frustrating.

"It's been an amazing race to be honest. At least I did four days. Four amazing days, I really enjoyed myself and there were so many people out there. It's been amazing, you know, so we have to take the positives. It's been a great, great rally. But you know, just that slight mistake and the ditches are so close in Kielder."

There were no such dramas for McCormack and Mitchell, who set out on Monday at a controlled pace and with a little less exuberance than normal. They actually extended their lead through the day and emerged safely from the end of the Big One, the concluding 39-mile stage in Kielder, to a rapturous reception from friends, family and supporters.

"To do this for the fourth time is unbelievable," said McCormack. "We're just a team of part timers. The world has been watching this event this weekend, and it's a real privilege to compete in it." While McCormack and his crew celebrated, there was a devastating final stage retirement for Perez. He had

Conrad Bos and Geoff Crabtree

Roger Albert Clark Rally 2023: the fifteenth edition

McCormack scored his fourth win

Aaron McClure in his Peugeot 205 GTi

Anthony Harrison and Marcus Pomfret

driven a sublime rally in the Stratos and had matched all but Solberg to show just how far the car has come. Sadly, in the final stage water pump failure signalled the end and Seb had to pull over and park the Lancia. But he had proved so much and won the hearts of so many fans. The loss of Perez elevated McCourt and Moynihan into a superb second overall, a result that no one, crew included, could have predicted when the rally started.

Third place was a great result for Jason Pritchard and Phil Clarke, but it could have been more. They had a tough event and the crushing blow came on Sunday morning when they punctured on each of the Kershope stages. They had to stop and change twice and the eight minutes they lost doing so probably cost them overall victory. Being pushed out of a Crychan ditch, and running very close to time limit after an alternator failure were more challenges from an event that could have delivered even more. Co-driver Clarke was the only Englishman in the overall top six.

Fourth overall was an amazing result for Dyfrig James and Emyr Jones, who had started down at 46 in their Escort Mk2. The road rally ace drove a great rally, kept out of trouble and picked up an

Barry McKenna overcame various challenges to get a finish

Chris Ingram in the Appleby Engineering Triumph TR7 V8

Mike Roberts and Ken Bowman

outstanding result, finishing just nine seconds ahead of Mike Stuart and Sinclair Young in their Category 2 winning Ford Escort Mk1. "It's been a blur, but the car has been superb," said Stuart. Two gearbox changes and a spare rushed down from Perth kept the crew on their toes but it was a great result for the Scots.

Vivian Hamill and Andrew Grennan rounded out the top six to give Ireland three of the top six finishers while another great performance came from Daniel Mennell and Steven Brown who were seventh in their Escort. They spent 10 minutes in a Kershope ditch and were grateful to the spectators who got them back on. That moment potentially cost them fourth place and they were just 10 seconds down on Hamill at the finish.

Another Yorkshire crew, Paul Thompson and Josh Davison were close behind in a fine eighth position and ninth place was a quietly impressive result for Robert Woodside and Dean Beckett in their Tuthill Porsche 911 as the Irish tarmac ace tackled the event for the first time. Rounding out the top 10 for a class winning run in their Pinto-engined Ford Escort Mk1 were son and father Ben and Steven Smith, with another of the great performances from this amazing rally.

The top six (L-R): Clarke, Pritchard, McCormack, Mitchell, Moynihan and McCourt

The Open Rally

Neil Weaver and Jack Morton dominated the Open Rally for the non-historic two-wheel drive cars. Repeating their 2021 victory, Weaver and Morton finished an incredible 23 minutes ahead of the rest of the Open field with a faultless performance and times that took them well inside the overall top 10 rankings. With a busy schedule of preparing cars for other drivers across the season Weaver, nicknamed the 'Ludlow Loeb', condenses most of his rallying into this five-day marathon and drove as well as ever.

Second in the Open went to Northern Irish crew Bryan Jardine and Declan Campbell with a great performance in their Escort Mk1 to finish well clear of former winners Dave Hemingway and Simon Ashton in their Escort Mk2.

A class winning fourth went to event debutant Aaron Rix with Abi Haycock co-driving in his Vauxhall-engined Ford Escort Mk2 with a strong performance from car and crew. Up into fifth came Italians Simone Calzia and Fabrizio Filicicchia in their Peugeot 208. They had an absolute ball and loved the event, while demonstrating that a modern front wheel drive car has a place in the rally.

The classes

As ever with the Roger Albert Clark Rally, there were tales of heroic efforts to keep cars running right down the field and every one of the 103 finishers and their support teams deserves enormous credit.

In Category 1, for the pre '68 cars, victory went to the Ford Anglia of Pete Stimson and Mark Butler, who drove a canny event to keep the little Anglia out of trouble. They moved ahead when Swedes Martin Linden and Rickard Forsell slid their Volvo PV544 off the road in Mount Common on Sunday. The Swedish crew got back on to win their class with second in the category, narrowly heading Richard Holdsworth and Harry Walshaw in their Ford Cortina GT.

Stuart and Young dominated Category 2 for the pre '74 cars finishing 13 minutes up on Ben and

Berry Stevenson-Wheeler and John Pickavance in Glengap

Craig Jones and his crew celebrate reaching the finish

Steven Smith. The Smiths easily won Class C3 while C2 was a great victory for Alex Waterman and Chris Davies in their Datsun 1600 from the hard charging Escort Mk1 Mexico of Antony Harrison and Marcus Pomfret.

In Category 3 for the pre '81 cars, the overall event winners took the glory but there was a tremendous performance from David Hopkins and Richard Wise who battled their 1600cc Talbot Sunbeam Ti to class D2 victory and a fantastic 19th overall in the historic event. Adrian Young and Gwynfor Jones headed Class D3 for the Pinto Mk2s, but only just from Eddie O'Donnell and Cameron Fair.

In the classes for the later historics, Mark and Andrew Constantine took class glory in their Vauxhall Nova Sport along with Ian Tunney/Chris Sanderson (Mitsubishi Starion) and Aaron McLure/Simon Taylor (Peugeot 205 GTi).

Roger Albert Clark Rally 2023: the fifteenth edition

Cathan McCourt finished a fine second overall

2023 ROGER ALBERT CLARK RALLY: ENTRY LIST

No	Driver	Co-driver	Car	Class
1	Martin McCormack	Barney Mitchell	Ford Escort Mk2	D5
2	Kris Meeke	Noel O'Sullivan	Ford Escort Mk2	D5
3	Oliver Solberg	Elliot Edmondson	Ford Escort Mk2	G2
4	Osian Pryce	Rhodri Evans	Ford Escort Mk2	G2
5	Jason Pritchard	Phil Clarke	Ford Escort Mk2 RS1800	G2
6	Richard Tuthill	Stephane Prevot	Porsche 911	D4
7	Roger Chilman	Patrick Walsh	Ford Escort Mk2	D5
8	Chris Ingram	Hannah McKillop	Triumph TR7 V8	G2
9	Paul Barrett	Gordon Noble	Ford Escort Mk2	G2
10	Matthew Robinson	Sam Collis	Ford Escort Mk2	D5
11	Ghislain de Mevius	Johan Jalet	Ford Escort Mk2	G2
12	Adrian Hetherington	Ronan O'Neill	Ford Escort RS1800	D5
14	Ben Friend	Cliff Simmons	Ford Escort Mk2	D5
15	Seb Perez	Gary McElhinney	Lancia Stratos HF	G2
16	James Ford	Neil Shanks	Porsche 911 Carrera RS	D4
17	Cathan McCourt	Liam Moynihan	Ford Escort Mk2	D5
18	Daniel Alonso Villaron	Alejandro Lopez Fernandez	Ford Escort Mk2	J5
19	Richard Jordan	James Gratton Smith	Ford Escort Mk2	G2
20	Steve Bannister	Callum Atkinson	Ford Escort Mk2	D5
21	Simon Webster	Jez Rogers	Ford Escort RS1800	D5
22	Grégoire de Mevius	Andre Leyh	Toyota Celica	G2
23	Stefaan Stouf	Dai Roberts	Ford Escort RS1600	C5
24	Gareth James	Daniel Petrie	Ford Escort RS1800	D5
25	Daniel Mennell	Steven Brown	Ford Escort Mk2	D5
26	Rudi Lancaster	Guy Weaver	Ford Escort RS1800	G2
27	Mike Stuart	Sinclair Young	Ford Escort Mk1	C5

The Vauxhall Chevette of Ben Jemison

Rally veteran Andy Madge

2023 ROGER ALBERT CLARK RALLY: ENTRY LIST (continued)

No	Driver	Co-driver	Car	Class
28	Paul Thompson	Josh Davison	Ford Escort	D5
29	Kevin Procter	Jamie Edwards	Ford Sapphire Cosworth 4X4	F2
30	Sacha Kakad	James Aldridge	Ford Escort Mk2	D5
31	Steve Graham	Tony Graham	Lancia Fulvia	C1
32	Craig Jones	Ian Taylor	Ford Escort RS2000	C5
33	Ken Sturdy	Alex Lee	Ford Escort RS1800	G2
34	David Hutchinson	Jeff Garnett	Ford Escort Mk2	D5
36	Barry McKenna	James Fulton	Ford Escort Mk2	D5
37	Barry Stevenson-Wheeler	John Pickavance	Ford Escort RS1800	D5
38	Baz Jordan	Arwel Jenkins	Ford Escort Mk2	D5
40	Theo Bengry	Les Forsbrook	Opel Ascona 400	D4
41	Andrew Haddon	Mark Crisp	Ford Escort Mk1	C5
42	Robert Woodside	Dean Beckett	Porsche 911	C4
43	Robert Barrett	Andy Coupland	Ford Escort Mk2	J4
44	Ben Jemison	Dean Kellett	Vauxhall Chevette	D4
46	Dyfrig James	Emyr Jones	Ford Escort Mk2	G2
47	Ieuan Evans	Dafydd Evans	Ford Escort RS1800	D5
48	Ben Smith	Steven Smith	Ford Escort Mk1	C3
49	Andrew Stokes	Jonny Tad Evans	Ford Escort Mk1	C5
51	Phil Squires	Mick Squires	Ford Escort Mk2	D5
52	Eddie O'Donnell Jnr	Cameron Fair	Ford Escort Mk2	D3
53	Vivian Hammill	Andrew Grennan	Ford Escort Mk2	D5
54	Tony Thompson	Matthew Thompson	Ford Escort RS1800	D5
55	Rob Dennis	Andy Boswell	Ford Escort Mk2	D5
56	Mark Holmes	John Connor	Ford Escort Mk1	C5
57	Dave Forrest	Jamie Forrest	Ford Escort Mk2	D3
58	Mike Reed	John Millington	Ford Escort RS2000	D3
59	Neal James	Kevin Jones	Ford Escort Mk2	D3
60	Keith McIvor	David Burns	Ford Escort Mk2	G2
61	Mike Simpson	Dale Gibbons	Ford Escort Mk2 RS1800	D5
62	Darren Martin	Peter Johnson	Subaru Legacy	F2
63	Chris Harris	Brynmor Pierce	Porsche 911	D4
64	Barry Renwick	Paul Hughes	Ford Escort RS1800	D5
65	David Pedley	Paul Stringer	Ford Escort RS1800	G2
66	Alun Horn	Ryan Griffiths	Ford Escort Mk2	J4
67	Steven Ormond-Smith	John Tear	Ford Escort RS1600	C5
68	Aaron McClure	Simon Taylor	Peugeot 205 GTi	F2
69	Andy Wolfe	James Crook	Ford Escort Mk1	C5

French crew Gregory Perrard and Cesar Delbecque

Ken Sturdy in the Mount Common stage

2023 ROGER ALBERT CLARK RALLY: ENTRY LIST (continued)

No	Driver	Co-driver	Car	Class
70	Gavin Edwards	Caron Tomlinson	Ford Escort Mk2	D5
71	Christopher Ingram	Paul Turner	Ford Escort Mk2	G2
72	Grant Inglis	Gavin Chisholm	Ford Escort Mk2	D5
73	David Tomlin	Keith Ashley	Ford Escort Mk2	G2
74	Dave Hemingway	Simon Ashton	Ford Escort Mk2	J4
75	Fintan McGrady	Cormac McGrady	Ford Escort RS1800	D5
76	Stuart Ranby	Ian Bass	Ford Escort Mk2	D5
77	Conrad Bos	Geoff Crabtree	Ford Escort RS2000	D3
78	Remy Thomissen	Christopher Davies	Ford Escort Mk1	C3
80	Phil Morton	Chris Dodds	Mitsubishi Starion	J4
81	Paul Fry	Mike Steele	Ford Escort RS1800	D5
82	Adrian Young	Gwynfor Jones	Ford Escort RS2000	D3
83	Maxime Vilmot	Marie-Noelle Ratier	Ford Escort Mk2	G2
84	Geraint Davies	Eurig Davies	Ford Escort Mk2	D5
85	Jim Robertson	Paul Gribben	Ford Escort Mk2	D5
87	Donald Peacock	Craig Wallace	Ford Escort Mk2	D5
88	Mike Roberts	Ken Bowman	Ford Escort RS2000	D3
89	Alexandre Felsenhart	Jean-Louis Hottelet	Ford Escort Mk1	J4
91	Gianni Anassarette	Ismaele Barra	Peugeot 208	J3
92	Colin Richard Hope	Billy Dalgleish	SAAB 96 V4	C3
93	Federico Polese	Nicola Arena	Porsche 911SC	H2
94	Tim Metcalfe	Stephen McAuley	Ford Escort RS1800	G2
95	Miguel Henry de Frahan	Emmanuel Eggermont	Ford Escort Mk2 RS1800	D5
96	Alan Carfrae	Liam Carfrae	Ford Escort RS1600	C5
97	John Brazier	Damian Bird	Ford Escort RS1800	G2
98	Bart-Jan Deenik	Egbert Kolvoort	Ford Escort RS1600 Mk1	C5
99	James Brady	Jack Brady	Porsche 911	F2
100	Keith Turner	Tracy Wood	Ford Escort Mk2	D5
101	Maarten Buitenhuis	Jeanette Buitenhuis	Alfa Romeo Guilietta	D3
102	Chris Cleghorn	Ryland James	Ford Escort RS1800	G2
103	Robin Hamilton	Philip Sandham	Talbot Sunbeam	D4
104	Paul Holmes	Elizabeth Beesley	Ford Escort Mk2 RS2000	D3
105	Nick Mason	Pete Smith	Datsun 240Z	H2
106	Frank Tundo	Alan Jones	Triumph TR7 V8	H2
107	Alec Cooper	Mark l'Anson	Ford Escort RS1600	C5
108	Ray Barnes	Ula Budzynska	Lotus Sunbeam	D4
109	Ian Tunney	Chris Sanderson	Mitsubishi Starion Turbo	E2
110	David Calvert	Colin Blunt	Ford Escort Mk2	J4

Ian Beveridge and Paul Price

2023 ROGER ALBERT CLARK RALLY: ENTRY LIST (continued)

No	Driver	Co-driver	Car	Class
111	Rodger Mark Fowler	Malcolm Johnson	Ford Escort Mk2	D5
112	Stu McLaren	Mark Ammonds	Opel Kadett GT/E	D3
113	Douglas Menzies	Graeme Menzies	Ford Escort Mk2	D3
114	Lyn Davies	Aled Richards	Ford Escort Mk2	D5
115	Howard Allan	John Buckley	Ford Escort Mk2	D3
117	Gordon McCombie	Russell Smith	Saab 900	J4
118	Colin Smith	John Pinder	Vauxhall Astra Mk3	J4
119	Robin Hernaman	Ray Crowther	BMW 318ti Compact	J4
120	Martin Oglesby	John Parker	Opel Kadett	D3
121	Chris Lonnon	Mark Courtier	MG ZR 160	J4
122	A an Young	Ashley Young	Ford Escort Mk2	D3
131	Adam Milner	Roy Jarvis	Ford Escort Mexico Mk1	C2
132	Neil Weaver	Jack Morton	Opel Corsa S1600	J3
133	Rory McCann	Paul McCann	Hillman Avenger	C2
134	Bryan Jardine	Declan Campbell	Ford Escort Mk1 RS1600	J3
135	Aaron Rix	Abi Haycock	Ford Escort Mk2	J2
136	David Hopkins	Richard Wise	Talbot Sunbeam Ti	D2
137	Alex Waterman	Chris Davies	Datsun 1600 SSS	C2
138	Simone Calzia	Fabrizio Filicicchia	Peugeot 208	J3
139	Chris Hellings	Glyn Thomas	VW Mk1 Golf GTI	D2
140	Stuart Cariss	Linda Cariss	Ford Escort Mk1	C2
141	Philip Clarke	Richard Bonner	Ford Escort Mk2	J3
142	Dave Watkins	Dave Shepherd	Ford Escort Mk1	C2
143	Noel Lappin	Charlie Mason	Ford Escort Mk2	J2
144	Lyndon Barton	Simon Hunter	Ford Escort Mk2	J3
145	Anthony Harrison	Marcus Pomfret	Ford Escort Mk1 Mexico	C2
146	Tony Jardine	Allan Harryman	Chrysler Avenger	C2

Ben Friend and Cliff Simmons

2023 ROGER ALBERT CLARK RALLY: ENTRY LIST (continued)

No	Driver	Co-driver	Car	Class
147	Greg Mills	Andrew Sankey	Ford Escort Mk2	J3
148	Wyn Hughes	David Davies	Ford Escort Mk2	D2
149	Mark Constantine	Andrew Constantine	Vauxhall Nova Sport	E1
151	Paul Rawson	Mike Curry	Ford Escort Mk1	C2
152	Mark Tugwell	Debora Tugwell	Ford Escort Mk1	C2
153	Andy Madge	Matt Cooper	Toyota Corolla GT Coupe	J3
154	Pete Johnston	Charles Johnston	Peugeot 205GTi	J3
155	Pete Stimson	Mark Butler	Ford Anglia	B3
156	Paul Mankin	Graham Wild	Ford Lotus Cortina	B4
157	Alan Kitson	John Roberts	Ford Escort Mk1	C2
158	William Jones	Martin Davies	Hillman Avenger	C2
159	Domenico Ramoino	Fabiana Ramoino	Renault Clio Rally5	J5
160	Charles Knifton	Stephen Gozzard	Peugeot 205 GTi	E1
161	Grégory Perrard	César Delbecque	Renault Clio Rally	J5
162	Richard Holdsworth	Harry Walshaw	Ford Cortina Mk1 GT	B3
163	Andrew Pidden	Thomas Pidden	Ford Cortina k1	B3
164	Martin Lindén	Rickard Forsell	Volvo PV 544 Sport	B4
165	Ian Beveridge	Paul Price	Toyota Corolla TE27	C2
167	Patrick Messer	Natalie Messer	Peugeot 205 XS	J2
168	Robert Evett	Michael Evett	Morris Marina	C1
169	James Rudd	Oliver Foster	Nissan Micra	J2
170	John Cotton	Gill Cotton	MG ZR	J2
171	Roger Mustoe	Andrew Hebron	VW Polo 16V	J2
172	Rob Aslett	Rob Aslett	Peugeot 205 GTi	J3
173	Owen Turner	Ryan Pickering	Mitsubishi Lancer	C2
174	Stephen Higgins	Corey Powell-Jones	SAAB 96	B3

2023 STAGES AND STAGE WINNERS

Day	Stage	Name	Distance	Stage winner(s)	Time
Thursday	SS1	Crychan 1	10.47	Pryce/Evans	11.34
Thursday	SS2	Cefn 1	2.87	Meeke, Solberg and Pryce	3.23
Thursday	SS3	Walters Arena 1	4.38	Solberg/Edmondson	4.30
Thursday	SS4	Glasfynydd	3.03	Meeke/O'Sullivan and Solberg/Edmondson	3.49
Thursday	SS5	Crychan 2	10.47	Pryce/Evans	11.40
Thursday	SS6	Cefn 2	2.87	Pryce/Evans and Solberg/Edmondson	3.27
Thursday	SS7	Walters Arena 2	4.38	Solberg/Edmondson	4.36
Friday	SS8	Esgair Berfedd	5.86	Solberg/Edmondson	5.51
Friday	SS9	Myherin 1	11.12	Solberg/Edmondson	11.18
Friday	SS10	Sweet Lamb/Hafren 1	15.08	Solberg/Edmondson	16.29
Friday	SS11	Hafren South 1	8.24	Pryce/Evans	8.41
Friday	SS12	Myherin 2	11.12	Solberg/Edmondson	11.32
Friday	SS13	Sweet Lamb/Hafren 2	15.08	Solberg/Edmondson	17.00
Friday	SS14	Hafren South 2	8.24	Solberg/Edmondson	9.13
Saturday	SS15	Ae	8.79	Solberg/Edmondson	8.39
Saturday	SS16	Dalbeattie	4.69	Pryce/Evans and McKenna/Fulton	5.54
Saturday	SS17	Glengap 1	9.77	Solberg/Edmondson	10.13
Saturday	SS18	Glencaird Hill 1	10.66	Solberg/Edmondson	9.34
Saturday	SS19	Arroch Hill 1	0.00	Cancelled	
Saturday	SS20	Glengap 2	9.77	Solberg/Edmondson	10.34
Saturday	SS21	Glencaird Hill 2	10.66	Solberg/Edmondson	10.01
Saturday	SS22	Arroch Hill 2	0.00	Cancelled	
Sunday	SS23	Kershope 1	16.77	Solberg/Edmondson	17.56
Sunday	SS24	Kershope 2	16.77	Solberg/Edmondson	17.19
Sunday	SS25	Mount Common 1	16.43	Solberg/Edmondson	17.16
Sunday	SS26	Harwood 1	10.81	Solberg/Edmondson	10.27
Sunday	SS27	Mount Common 2	16.43	Solberg/Edmondson	17.25
Sunday	SS28	Harwood 2	10.81	Pritchard/Clarke	10.45
Monday	SS29	Shepherdshield	6.69	Pritchard/Clarke	6.18
Monday	SS30	Pundershaw	13.26	Pritchard/Clarke	12.04
Monday	SS31	Roughside	9.98	Pritchard/Clarke	9.35
Monday	SS32	Hopehouse	8.01	Pritchard/Clarke and McCormack/Mitchell	7.15
Monday	SS33	The Big One	38.92	Pritchard/Clarke	36.12

Stuart McLaren in Kielder on Sunday

The modified escort of Villaron and Lopez

Roger Albert Clark Rally 2023: the fifteenth edition

Neil Weaver and Jack Morton in their Opel Corsa

2023 RESULTS

Overall	No	Driver	Co-driver	Car	Class	Total
1	1	Martin McCormack	Barney Mitchell	Ford Escort Mk2	D5	05:48:26
2	17	Cathan McCourt	Liam Moynihan	Ford Escort Mk2	D5	05:53:56
3	5	Jason Pritchard	Phil Clarke	Ford Escort Mk2 RS1800	G2	05:55:22
4	46	Dyfrig James	Emyr Jones	Ford Escort Mk2	G2	06:05:02
5	27	Mike Stuart	Sinclair Young	Ford Escort Mk1	C5	06:05:11
6	53	Vivian Hammill	Andrew Grennan	Ford Escort Mk2	D5	06:11:35
7	25	Daniel Keith Mennell	Steven Brown	Ford Escort Mk2	D5	06:11:45
8	28	Paul Thompson	Josh Davison	Ford Escort Mk2	D5	06:12:06
9	42	Robert Woodside	Dean Beckett	Porsche 911	C4	06:15:32
10	48	Ben Smith	Steven Smith	Ford Escort Mk1 RS2000	C3	06:18:03
11	70	Gavin Edwards	Caron Tomlinson	Ford Escort Mk2	D5	06:19:28
12	38	Baz Jordan	Arwel Jenkins	Ford Escort Mk2	D5	06:19:59
13	20	Steve Bannister	Callum Atkinson	Ford Escort Mk2	D5	06:23:30
14	84	Geraint Davies	Eurig Davies	Ford Escort Mk2	D5	06:25:26
15	60	Keith McIvor	David Burns	Ford Escort Mk2	G2	06:25:34
16	41	Andrew Haddon	Mark Crisp	Ford Escort Mk1	C5	06:27:45
17	87	Donald Peacock	Craig Wallace	Ford Escort Mk2	D5	06:29:14
18	26	Rudi Lancaster	Guy Weaver	Ford Escort RS1800	G2	06:32:05
19	136	David Hopkins	Richard Wise	Talbot Sunbeam Ti	D2	06:37:06
20	37	Barry Stevenson-Wheeler	John Pickavance	Ford Escort RS1800	D5	s 6:40:11
21	44	Ben Jemison	Dean Kellett	Vauxhall Chevette	D4	06:42:37
22	85	Jim Robertson	Paul Gribben	Ford Escort Mk2	D5	06:46:07
23	82	Adrian Young	Gwynfor Jones	Ford Escort RS2000	D3	06:46:10
24	51	Phil Squires	Mick Squires	Ford Escort Mk2	D5	06:46:50
25	36	Barry McKenna	James Fulton	Ford Escort Mk2	D5	s 6:47:01
26	49	Andrew Stokes	Jonny Tad Evans	Ford Escort Mk1	C5	06:47:13
27	52	Eddie O'Donnell Jnr	Cameron Fair	Ford Escort Mk2	D3	06:47:55

2023 RESULTS (continued)

Overall	No	Driver	Co-driver	Car	Class	Total
28	32	Craig Jones	Ian Taylor	Ford Escort RS2000	C5	06:48:02
29	72	Grant Inglis	Gavin Chisholm	Ford Escort Mk2	D5	06:49:24
30	98	Bart-Jan Deenik	Egbert Kolvoort	Ford Escort RS1600 Mk1	C5	06:50:52
31	137	Alex Waterman	Chris Davies	Datsun 1600 SSS	C2	06:51:42
32	19	Richard Jordan	James Gratton Smith	Ford Escort Mk2	G2	06:51:46
33	65	David Pedley	Paul Stringer	Ford Escort RS1800	G2	06:52:14
34	69	Andy Wolfe	James Crook	Ford Escort Mk1	C5	s 6:53:47
35	57	Dave Forrest	Jamie Forrest	Ford Escort Mk2	D3	06:54:57
36	145	Anthony Harrison	Marcus Pomfret	Ford Escort Mk1	C2	06:58:53
37	75	Fintan McGrady	Cormac McGrady	Ford Escort RS1800	D5	07:00:46
38	140	Stuart Cariss	Linda Cariss	Ford Escort Sport	C2	07:01:50
39	148	Wyn Hughes	David Davies	Ford Escort Mk2	D2	07:04:40
40	61	Mike Simpson	Dale Gibbons	Ford Escort Mk2	D5	s 7:06:01
41	93	Federico Polese	Nicola Arena	Porsche 911 SC	H2	07:08:17
42	81	Paul Fry	Mike Steele	Ford Escort RS1800	D5	07:08:19
43	71	Christopher Ingram	Paul Turner	Ford Escort Mk2	G2	s 7:11:53
44	149	Mark Constantine	Andrew Constantine	Vauxhall Nova Sport	E1	07:12:57
45	68	Aaron McClure	Simon Taylor	Peugeot 205 GTi	F2	s 7:14:39
46	78	Remy Thomissen	Christopher Davies	Ford Escort Mk1	C3	s 7:15:21
47	40	Theo Bengry	Les Forsbrook	Opel Ascona 400	D4	S 7:16:37
48	88	Mike Roberts	Ken Bowman	Ford Escort RS2000	D3	s 7:17:49
49	158	William Jones	Martin Davies	Hillman Avenger	C2	s 7:21:06
50	96	Alan Carfrae	Liam Carfrae	Ford Escort RS1600	C5	s 7:22:16
51	92	Colin Richard Hope	Billy Dalgleish	SAAB 96 V4	C3	07:28:31
52	111	Rodger Mark Fowler	Malcolm Johnson	Ford Escort Mk2	D5	07:28:40
53	106	Frank Tundo	Alan Jones	Triumph TR7 V8	H2	07:31:14
54	103	Robin Hamilton	Philip Sandham	Talbot Sunbeam	D4	07:31:40
55	97	John Brazier	Damian Bird	Ford Escort RS1800	G2	s 7:32:57
56	77	Conrad Bos	Geoff Crabtree	Ford Escort Mk2	D3	s 7:35:48
57	142	Dave Watkins	Dave Shepherd	Ford Escort Mk1	C2	07:37:36
58	95	Miguel Henry de Frahan	Emmanuel Eggermont	Ford Escort Mk2 RS1800	D5	07:40:57
59	113	Douglas Menzies	Graeme Menzies	Ford Escort Mk2	D3	s 7:45:35
60	173	Owen Turner	Ryan Pickering	Mitsubishi Lancer	C2	s 7:54:50
61	114	Lyn Davies	Aled Richards	Ford Escort Mk2	D5	07:56:36
62	102	Chris Cleghorn	Ryland James	Ford Escort RS1800	G2	s 7:57:17
63	165	Ian Beveridge	Paul Price	Toyota Corolla TE27	C2	S 7:59:47
64	155	Pete Stimson	Mark Butler	Ford Anglia	B3	08:00:21
65	58	Mike Reed	John Millington	Ford Escort RS2000	D3	s 8:00:58
66	146	Tony Jardine	Allan Harryman	Chrysler Avenger	C2	s 8:05:04
67	115	Howard Allan	John Buckley	Ford Escort Mk2	D3	08:06:31
68	104	Paul Holmes	Elizabeth Beesley	Ford Escort Mk2 RS2000	D3	s 8:09:36
69	164	Martin Lindén	Rickard Forsell	Volvo PV 544 Sport	B4	s 8:11:37
70	162	Richard Holdsworth	Harry Walshaw	Ford Cortina GT	B3	s 8:12:58
71	109	Ian Tunney	Chris Sanderson	Mitsubishi Starion Turbo	E2	s 8:30:20
72	56	Mark Holmes	John Connor	Ford Escort Mk1	C5	s 8:30:55
73	101	Maarten Buitenhuis	Jeanette Buitenhuis	Alfa Romeo Guilietta	D3	s 8:36:36
74	105	Nick Mason	Pete Smith	Datsun 240Z	H2	s 8:42:14
75	112	Stu Mclaren	Mark Ammonds	Opel Kadett GT/E	D3	S 8:42:54
76	122	Alan Young	Ashley Young	Ford Escort Mk2	D3	08:45:33
77	64	Barry Renwick	Paul Hughes	Ford Escort RS1800	D5	s 9:36:11
78	163	Andrew Pidden	Thomas Pidden	Ford Cortina Mk1	B3	s 9:36:46
79	31	Steve Graham	Tony Graham	Lancia Fulvia	C1	09:41:18

2023 RESULTS (continued)

Overall	No	Driver	Co-driver	Car	Class	Total
Ret	2	Kris Meeke	Noel O'Sullivan	Ford Escort Mk2	D5	Mechanical issue after SS6
Ret	3	Oliver Solberg	Elliot Edmondson	Ford Escort Mk2	G2	Slid off road - SS29
Ret	4	Osian Pryce	Rhodri Evans	Ford Escort Mk2	G2	Stopped - SS17
Ret	6	Richard Tuthill	Stephane Prevot	Porsche 911	D4	Did not restart from MTC7
Ret	7	Roger Chilman	Patrick Walsh	Ford Escort Mk2	D5	Mechanical - SS1
Ret	8	Chris Ingram	Hannah McKillop	Triumph TR7 V8	G2	Mechanical - SS10
Ret	9	Paul Barrett	Gordon Noble	Ford Escort Mk2	G2	Engine after SS15
Ret	10	Matthew Robinson	Sam Collis	Ford Escort Mk2	D5	Stopped - SS33
Ret	11	Ghislain de Mevius	Johan Jalet	Ford Escort RS Mk2	G2	Stopped - SS17
Ret	12	Adrian Hetherington	Ronan O'Neill	Ford Escort RS1800	D5	Stopped after SS23
Ret	14	Ben Friend	Cliff Simmons	Ford Escort Mk2	D5	Stopped - SS30
Ret	15	Seb Perez	Gary McElhinney	Lancia Stratos HF	G2	Stopped - SS33
Ret	16	James Ford	Neil Shanks	Porsche 911 Carrera	D4	Stopped - SS20
Ret	21	Simon Webster	Jez Rogers	Ford Escort RS1800	D5	Mechanical - after SS23
Ret	22	Grégoire de Mevius	Andre Leyh	Toyota Celica	G2	Stopped - SS10
Ret	23	Stefaan Stouf	Dai Roberts	Ford Escort RS1600	C5	Stopped - SS10
Ret	24	Gareth James	Daniel Petrie	Ford Escort RS1800	D5	Engine failure after SS10
Ret	29	Kevin Procter	Jamie Edwards	Ford Sapphire Cosworth 4X4	F2	Went off into ditch SS24
Ret	30	Sacha Kakad	James Aldridge	Ford Escort Mk2	D5	Stopped - SS27
Ret	33	Ken Sturdy	Alex Lee	Ford Escort RS1800	G2	Stopped - SS33
Ret	34	David Hutchinson	Jeff Garnett	Ford Escort Mk2	D5	Went off - SS15
Ret	47	Ieuan Evans	Dafydd Evans	Ford Escort RS1800	D5	Stopped - SS31
Ret	54	Tony Thompson	Matthew Thompson	Ford Escort RS1800	D5	Stopped - SS33
Ret	55	Rob Dennis	Andy Boswell	Ford Escort Mk2	D5	Stopped at end of SS11
Ret	59	Neal James	Kevin Jones	Ford Escort Mk2	D3	Blown engine - SS24
Ret	62	Darren Martin	Peter Johnson	Subaru Legacy	F2	Stopped - SS32
Ret	63	Chris Harris	Brynmor Pierce	Porsche 911	D4	Stopped - SS13
Ret	67	Steven Ormond-Smith	John Tear	Ford Escort RS1600	C5	Stopped - SS30
Ret	73	David Tomlin	Keith Ashley	Ford Escort Mk2	G2	Engine fire - SS1
Ret	76	Stuart Ranby	Ian Bass	Ford Escort Mk2	D5	Stopped in SS10
Ret	83	Maxime Vilmot	Marie-Noelle Ratier	Ford Escort Mk2	G2	Mechanical - SS12
Ret	94	Tim Metcalfe	Stephen McAuley	Ford Escort RS1800	G2	Retired after SS23
Ret	99	James Brady	Jack Brady	Porsche 911	F2	Retired after MTC6
Ret	100	Keith Turner	Tracy Wood	Ford Escort Mk2	D5	Stopped - SS29
Ret	107	Alec Cooper	Mark I`Anson	Ford Escort RS1600	C5	Stopped - SS29
Ret	108	Ray Barnes	Ula Budzynska	Lotus Sunbeam	D4	Stopped SS16
Ret	120	Martin Oglesby	John Parker	Opel Kadett	D3	Stopped - SS26
Ret	131	Adam Milner	Roy Jarvis	Ford Escort Mexico Mk1	C2	Stopped - SS23
Ret	133	Rory McCann	Paul McCann	Hillman Avenger	C2	Stopped - SS18
Ret	139	Chris Hellings	Glyn Thomas	VW Mk1 Golf GTI	D2	Stopped after SS8
Ret	151	Paul Rawson	Mike Curry	Ford Escort Mk1	C2	Stopped - SS15
Ret	152	Mark Tugwell	Debora Tugwell	Ford Escort Mk1	C2	Stopped after SS15
Ret	156	Paul Mankin	Graham Wild	Ford Lotus Cortina	B4	Stopped - SS9
Ret	157	Alan Kitson	John Roberts	Ford Escort Mk1	C2	Stopped after SS29
Ret	160	Charles Knifton	Stephen Gozzard	Peugeot 205 GTi	E1	Engine - SS12
Ret	168	Robert Evett	Michael Evett	Morris Marina	C1	Stopped - after SS18
Ret	174	Stephen Higgins	Corey Powell-Jones	SAAB 96	B3	Stopped - SS15

Bryan Jardine was second in the Open Rally

2023 RESULTS: OPEN RALLY

Overall	No	Driver	Co-driver	Car	Class	Total
1	132	Neil Weaver	Jack Morton	Opel Corsa S1600	J3	06:06:23
2	134	Bryan Jardine	Declan Campbell	Ford Escort Mk1 RS1600	J3	06:29:24
3	74	Dave Hemingway	Simon Ashton	Ford Escort Mk2	J4	06:47:19
4	135	Aaron Rix	Abi Haycock	Ford Escort Mk2	J2	06:53:10
5	138	Simone Calzia	Fabrizio Filicicchia	Peugeot 208	J3	s 6:56:10
6	143	Noel Lappin	Charlie Mason	Ford Escort Mk2	J2	06:58:08
7	153	Andy Madge	Matt Cooper	Toyota Corolla GT Coupe	J3	06:59:06
8	43	Robert Barrett	Andy Coupland	Ford Escort Mk2	J4	s 7:06:52
9	141	Philip Clarke	Richard Bonner	Ford Escort Mk2	J3	07:07:26
10	144	Lyndon Barton	Simon Hunter	Ford Escort Mk2	J3	07:14:16
11	167	Patrick Messer	Natalie Messer	Peugeot 205 XS	J2	07:18:38
12	161	Gregory Perrard	Cesar Delbecque	Renault Clio Rally	J5	07:26:54
13	171	Roger Mustoe	Andrew Hebron	VW Polo 16V	J2	s 7:32:56
14	18	Daniel Alonso Villaron	Alejandro Lopez Fernandez	Ford Escort Mk2	J5	s 7:34:23
15	121	Chris Lonnon	Mark Courtier	MG ZR 160	J4	07:45:15
16	172	Rob Aslett	Rob Aslett	Peugeot 205 GTi	J3	07:49:50
17	118	Colin Smith	John Pinder	Vauxhall Astra Mk3	J4	S 7:53:30
18	170	John Cotton	Gill Cotton	MG ZR	J2	08:09:01
19	119	Robin Hernaman	Ray Crowther	BMW 318ti Compact	J4	08:27:43
20	159	Domenico Ramoino	Fabiana Ramoino	Renault Clio Rally5	J5	s 8:33:11
21	169	James Rudd	Oliver Foster	Nissan Micra	J2	s 8:50:57
22	89	Alexandre Felsenhart	Jean-Louis Hottelet	Ford Escort Mk1	J4	s 8:50:57
23	80	Phil Morton	Chris Dodds	Mitsubishi Starion	J4	s 9:11:51
24	110	David Calvert	Colin Blunt	Ford Escort	J4	s 9:28:31
Ret	66	Alun Horn	Ryan Griffiths	Ford Escort Mk2	J4	Stopped - SS33
Ret	91	Gianni Anassarette	Ismaele Barra	Peugeot 208	J3	Stopped - SS33
Ret	117	Gordon McCombie	Russell Smith	Saab 900	J4	Stopped - SS23
Ret	147	Greg Mills	Andrew Sankey	Ford Escort Mk2	J3	Stopped - SS18
Ret	154	Pete Johnston	Charles Johnston	Peugeot 205GTi	J3	Did not restart at MTC7

One of the rescue units

The unsung heroes

No rally can run without the support and dedication of many, many people. An event on the scale of the Roger Albert Clark Rally involves hundreds of volunteers who give up their time and experience on a largely voluntary basis to make the event what it is.

As we celebrate 20 years of this remarkable rally, we wish to record heartfelt gratitude to every single person who has played a role, no matter how small, in helping run this incredible rally.

Whilst we do not plan to name too many individuals, there are several people we simply must acknowledge and they include Brian Avery, who was central to getting the event off the ground in the first place. He helped take the idea originally put forward by the late Paul Adams, to run what they call a proper rally, to being a reality.

Victoria, Colin, Nicola and Thomas Heppenstall

The Heppenstall family, of course, have been absolutely central to everything that has happened since 2003. Colin and Nicola and their children, Robert, Victoria and Thomas have all lived and

Flying finish marshals in Kielder

breathed this rally for two decades. But in the earlier years so did their parents, Brian and Margaret Heppenstall and Graham James.

Always at Colin's right hand has been Bob Lodge who has played a remarkable role, often behind the scenes, in simply ensuring that things happen and the rally runs as planned.

The Heppenstalls have their rallying heritage in De Lacy Motor Club and the club was central to the early years of the event, notably through the use of its Schedule 4 permission to run an event of this scale.

Out on the special stages has been an army of marshals who have worked tirelessly in all weathers and conditions, in daylight and in darkness to keep the rally running safely.

They are the stage marshals, the radio crews, the start and finish crews, the passage control teams and, importantly, the stage commanders who pull the stages together and ensure they are set up to the required standard.

On each stage, there is a team of rescue and recovery crews, some who have done every event,

Marshals in Falstone, 2019

and the medical staff who are on hand should anything serious happen. Back at rally base, there is a dedicated team of scrutineers, stewards, service area teams, secretarial and results teams who all play an absolutely vital role in such an event.

Every one of them is important to the running of the Roger Albert Clark Rally!

The unsung heroes

Phil Clarke (left) with Colin Heppenstall and Marty McCormack in 2012

What the rally means to me

My Roger Albert Clark Rally

This incredible rally has brought challenge, adventure, excitement, success and failure to many people in varying amounts. We asked 10 people involved in the event, from a range of perspectives, to explain what the rally means to them.

Phil Clarke: co-driver (winner in 2012)

I've done 13 editions so I've missed two. I think I missed the very first one in 2004 and I missed the third one in 2006. I've done every one since.

I think in the early days what made it special was the fact that it was on maps. Obviously we can't run maps now, it's just not feasible.

It's become an iconic event, and it seems to be the one to do. Colin and the rest of the Heppenstall family and the Roger Albert Clark Rally Motor Club just created this amazing event which captures the spirit of the old rallies with the mileage, the atmosphere and the camaraderie between crews and the volunteers.

On an event of this size it's the person with the least issues and the least problems. If you can get through without a puncture, or anything else, then you stand a better chance of winning.

Marty McCormack and I went off in Greystoke in 2007 and I got on the back of the rope. There must

have been 20 or 30 people pulling on this rope. I got on the back of it and the rope broke and I ended up with them all on top of me!

With Jason Pritchard, a halfshaft broke in 2017. We got about 200 yards into Twiglees and we were leading by 46s at the time. In 2019 we had a puncture in Greskine. Marty was leading and we were just keeping him honest. In 2021 we had a 42s lead in Dyfi when we hit the mud and that took the front end and over we went. we were the first of the very quick guys to go through. Quite possibly

John Cooper (far right) at scrutineering in Carlisle

it would have caught any of the top five given the pace we were on.

John Cooper: Chief Scrutineer
It's hard work, but it's worth it. I've been involved since the very beginning with Paul Adams. Paul asked me to be chief scrutineer when he first started the idea. Then I worked on an event in Europe with Colin Heppenstall and he was having a cup of coffee on the ferry crossing home. I sat down and he told me about his plans for the event. I said I was chief for Paul and he said: 'Well, you're my chief now!' And I've regretted it ever since.

It takes some organising but I have a great team around me. I've got one scrutineer who has done every event with me, which is Chris Williams. I have a great team. Every two years now it's stressful at scrutineering but after that it's great.

I remember the first year in Gisburn forest. It was like the old RAC Rallies because the roads were just jam packed with spectators and it's great fun. Once you get into Heppenstall family, you can't get out! There is no escape.

The Fulvia in Pundershaw

Steve Graham: driver (contested all 15 editions)
We've started all of them and only failed to finish twice in the first 14. We didn't finish the first one when our Peugeot 205 broke a half shaft and we had another non-finish when the rear suspension failed on the Lancia Fulvia. Getting a free entry for 2023 was a very generous act from Colin and the organisers and we really appreciated it.

From my perspective it was what started me rallying, watching the old RAC Rally in the 1970s and 1980s. In 2004, my co-driver and brother Tony persuaded me to start competing and the whole point of me starting rallying was to do the Roger Albert Clark rally in 2004. Our Fulvia was a four year project to turn a road car into a rally car.

It gets harder and harder each time. Our shakedown was the Goodwood Festival of Speed in July. We are one of the crews that still does the rally on maps, rather than on route notes.

Dave Hemingway: driver (contested all 15 editions)
It was very kind of Colin to give us a free entry for 2023: it was a nice gesture. The Roger Albert Clark is very special. I wanted to get involved in organising it in 2004 and I was one of the first ones to volunteer, and I said I'd do whatever job they wanted me to do. But Brian Avery said: 'Dave, you've got a car so you're doing it. We need the entries.'

So I had to find the money and every year since, until it went to every two years. It's a love hate thing! It's a lot of pressure getting ready for it and a lot of pressure getting around and when you finish there is this sense of euphoria that you've actually done it and completed it.

I used to try hard and in 2004 I was swapping stage times with some really famous people and I learnt that I wasn't that good. We found ourselves in a ditch in Kielder and lost a load of time and we finished the event. We did all stages, but we were OTL at one of the time controls. Apart from that we've finished every

Hemingway in 2017 in the Gwibedog stage

time. I paid £1800 for the car and I re-shelled it for £200 so it doesn't stand me a lot.

It is a highlight of everybody's calendar really. Everybody that you see on rallies, the marshals and other competitors are either doing it or want to do it.

Nicola Heppenstall: Clerk of the Course

Here we are with two grown up children. The kids were just babies when we started it. And if it hadn't been for the fact that there were babies I don't think it would have run. Colin had the time off work because I'd had major surgery and that's the only reason that the event ran. He had six weeks at home doing the paperwork and getting the road books ready.

It is a big part of our life but we enjoy it or we wouldn't do it. We enjoy seeing how much enjoyment it brings to the everyone.

It's just become a way of life and as far as we're concerned, there's no plan to stop and Colin has retired from his main job to concentrate more time on it. He's also on two different committees within Motorsport UK.

It wouldn't work if I was anti-rallying. Most wives say you can't go rallying but with me you can't go rallying if you're not taking me with you! It was the same with Colin's dad Brian. I hope Brian and my dad Graham are looking down on us and hopefully they are proud.

Bob Lodge: Deputy Clerk of the Course

It is truly an honour to be a part of this event. I've been out on all but one and have been proud to be able to work alongside Colin, Nicola and more lately, Victoria and Thomas along with the rest of the growing team. Seeing how the event unfolds from the first ideas through to its conclusion is truly a remarkable experience.

The most memorable year must be 2010 and the snow. Colin's notes on that particular year go a long way to explaining what we went through but don't quite tell the whole story. It was an experience and adventure to match anything I can imagine.

Long hard days and even harder and longer nights are the norm for the five days of the rally, with always a sting waiting round the corner to test our nerves and adaptability.

The friendliness, support and camaraderie between the competitors, service crews, the organising team, the marshals and spectators is what makes the event extra special. The unwavering trust they put in us to provide them with their own special rally experience is aways encouraging.

Nicola Heppenstall

Bob Lodge (far right) ensuring it all works

My Roger Albert Clark Rally

Martin McCormack

Martin McCormack: driver
(winner in 2012, 2017 and 2019)

Back in 2007 when I first started to come across from Northern Ireland everybody always talked about the Roger Albert Clark Rally. We wanted to do it that year to actually give us a goal and as usual it was quite tight with funding, but we wanted to give it a go.

What an epic event! I guess motor sport was always a journey and I never really expected to go as far as I did. I never really expected to go on a journey. It was the pleasure I got from being behind the wheel and the characters you met. Like David Winstanley and the people that are out there. Everybody was coming out covered in oil like me, trying to fix old cars and keep them going.

I love the atmosphere with the whole thing. And, in fact, to be competitive at that stage. The fact that you were starting 20 miles in Kielder and it was pouring with rain and you came in to a square right and there's no brakes in the car!

I met Phil Clarke for the first time at the start of the rally one year. Then hitting a park bench on the first corner of the 2008 rally. I had bruised ribs and the driver's door wouldn't open in the car for three days.

The fact that we've been so successful there and don't get me wrong, a lot of it is down to preparation.

John Millington: co-driver
(winner in 2008, 2009 and 2011)

When I first did it, which was 2008, with Malcolm Wilson we were using maps. That threw back to the days of road rallies, which I really loved. I loved working with maps and to actually be able to read the forests from a map gave me a real kick. I really enjoyed it.

The challenge then was being able to read the road from a map and help your driver as much as possible. So that's what the initial attraction of it was.

I have to say that when it went to route notes, I was one that thought, well, could you still do it on maps? But I do realise now, for safety as much as anything else, with the increase in speeds that notes was the way to go.

In all honesty, I think I was very, very fortunate because I went with some very good drivers. I attribute a lot of the victories down to the driver, because at the end of the day, there's only so much information you can get off a map, I don't care how good you are.

With the spread of the event, you would have had people in certain areas that were very, very good because they knew the roads very well. But then you'd move out of that area, so it balanced out.

The really special event was 2010 in the snow. So many memories from that year out shine the snapshot memories of all the other years. I think it typifies the spirit of the event and the willingness of competitors and Colin to work together and to rescue the rally. We'll never see that again, that was a one off. Nowadays, as we saw on the 2023 Malcolm Wilson, if it snows they stop.

Hats off to Colin, and it was so nice at the end when he was awarded spirit of the rally. That was the icing on the cake for me and I thought that was brilliant.

John Millington, head down as usual, with Malcolm Wilson

Jason Pritchard

Guy Weaver with David Stokes in Langdale

Jason Pritchard: leading driver

I grew up watching video clips and hearing all about Roger Clark as he was my dad's idol and dad obviously owns Roger Clark's Escort POO 505R. That is the car he won his first World Championship Rally in on the old RAC Rally in 1976. So it's very special in that sense.

Dad actually competed on the first ever running of the Roger Albert Clark and I was in the management vehicle using tulip diagrams. Don't tell my teachers as I was probably off sick!

I watched it many years after and what got me in was when Marty McCormack and Phil Clarke won it in 2012. Me and dad and a few boys went to watch it and it was hearing the cars coming for miles and miles through the forest and the buzz that was around on the event. On the way home, we were looking at the programme and in the back was the schedule for the RAC Championship.

A lot of the events were local to home, so that next week a few phone calls were made, a test was organised in the Mk2 and the rest is history.

We've always been there battling at the front, but it's not been the luckiest rally for me though. It's a whole championship in one week.

The 2021 accident still hurts me now. But if I approach that corner, or that straight, I wouldn't do anything any different now. It's just one of those things as we were first on the road in the quicker cars.

Guy Weaver: co-driver (second in 2008)

The first time I did it was 2007 with David Stokes. It was always with David and then with Rudi Lancaster. We came second in 2008 against Malcolm Wilson and then we came third 2011 behind Gwyndaf Evans and Tim Pearcey.

It's a unique event and provides a massive challenge with lots of preparation. The amount of hard work that Colin and the family puts into it is just unbelievable and how they get things to work. It's got a unique place in the British calendar and it's the most prestigious event in the country.

Sometimes you have to understand that it will work on the event and don't particularly worry about it, because it will work itself out. I've been in places like Newcastleton in the snow and there have been French crews trying to get their time and I'm telling them not to worry about climbing up the hill, because it will sort itself out. Because I know how it will work.

Preparing for 2021, for three consecutive weekends I was down at Rudi's in Devon. One weekend to do one day and then another weekend to do another day and another weekend to finish it off. It is hard sometimes to find the time to prepare for it properly. You just have to try and find the time from somewhere but work and family and all these other things get in the way of rallying!

Jason Pritchard and Phil Clarke

The former winners

Historic Rally
2004 Stig Blomqvist/Ana Goni (Ford Escort Mk2)
2005 Mark Higgins/Peter Martin (Ford Escort Mk1)
2006 Jimmy McRae/Andy Richardson (Ford Escort Mk2)
2007 Steve Bannister/Kevin Rae (Ford Escort Mk2)
2008 Malcolm Wilson/John Millington (Ford Escort Mk2)
2009 Gwyndaf Evans/John Millington (Ford Escort Mk2)
2010 Stefaan Stouf/Joris Erard (Ford Escort Mk1)
2011 Gwyndaf Evans/John Millington (Ford Escort Mk2)
2012 Marty McCormack/Phil Clarke (Ford Escort Mk2)
2013 Steve Bannister/Kevin Rae (Ford Escort Mk2)
2014 Matthew Robinson/Sam Collis (Ford Escort Mk2)
2017 Marty McCormack/Barney Mitchell (Ford Escort Mk2)
2019 Marty McCormack/Barney Mitchell (Ford Escort Mk2)
2021 Ryan Champion/Craig Thorley (Porsche 911)
2023 Marty McCormack/Barney Mitchell (Ford Escort Mk2)

Open Rally
2004 Steve Bannister/Kevin Rae (Ford Escort Mk2)
2005 Steve Bannister/Kevin Rae (Ford Escort Mk2)
2006 Steve Bannister/Kevin Rae (Ford Escort Mk2)
2007 Richard Hill/Patrick Cooper (Ford Escort Mk2)
2008 Dave Hemingway/Simon Ashton (Ford Escort Mk2)
2009 Marcus Noble/Brian Hodgson (Ford Escort Mk2)
2010 Dave Hemingway/Simon Ashton (Ford Escort Mk2)
2011 Martyn Hawkswell/Nick Welch (Ford Escort Mk2)
2012 Martyn Hawkswell/Nick Welch (Ford Escort Mk2)
2013 Martyn Hawkswell/Nick Welch (Ford Escort Mk2)
2014 Nigel Barber/Stuart Popplewell (Vauxhall Astra Sport)
2017 David Hutchinson/Jeff Garnett (Ford Escort Mk2)
2019 Baz Jordan/Arwel Jenkins (Hillman Avenger)
2021 Neil Weaver/Jack Morton (Vauxhall Corsa S1600)
2023 Neil Weaver/Jack Morton (Vauxhall Corsa S1600)

The numbers

15 rallies covering 55 days
400 special stages with 2933 competitive miles
1183 entries
32 support rallies
Competed on all 15 events: Dave Hemingway and Tony Graham

MOST STAGE WINS: HISTORIC RALLY	
Martin McCormack	72
Gwyndaf Evans	38
Jason Pritchard	36
Steve Bannister	34
Malcolm Wilson	22
Matthew Robinson	22
Jimmy McRae	21
Mark Higgins	21
Paul Griffiths	21
Oliver Solberg	20
Matt Edwards	16
David Stokes	13
Stig Blomqvist	12
Jeremy Easson	10
Osian Pryce	10
Stefan Stouf	9
Gareth Lloyd	6
Roger Chilman	6
Paul Barrett	6
Andrew Haddon	5
Hannu Mikkola	5
Alan Walker	4
Charlie Taylor	4
Ray Bellm	4
Seamus O'Connell	4
Adrian Hetherington	3
Ben Friend	3
Nick Elliott	3
Tim Pearcey	3
Darren Moon	2
Richard Lepley	2
Richard Tuthill	2
Rob Smith	2
Steve Smith	2
Kris Meeke	2
Barry Mckenna	2
Seb Perez	1
Grant Shand	1
Guy Woodcock	1
Leigh Armstrong	1
Mark Bennett	1
Phil Collins	1
Reg Britton	1
Steve Magson	1
Tim Mason	1
Warren Philliskirk	1
Will Onions	1

MOST STAGE WINS: OPEN RALLY	
Steve Bannister	65
Neil Weaver	40
Dave Hemmingway	30
'Mad' Mick Jones	27
Martyn Hawkswell	26
Nigel Barber	26
Richard Hill	26
Henri Grehan	20
Marcos Noble	17
Barry Stevenson-Wheeler	16
Allan McDowell	15
Phil Burton	11
David Hutchinson	10
Nick Cook	10
Andy Madge	9
James Nicholls	9
Andy Davison	8
Matthew Robinson	8
Baz Jordan	6
Malcolm Mawdsley	4
Nick Jarvis	4
Alan Gardiner	3
Dave Rawlings	3
Robert Dick	3
Dale Glover	2
David Condell	2
Jason Lepley	2
Will Onions	2
Dirk Deveux	1
Matt Barker	1
Mick Plowman	1
Paul Thompson	1
Stephen French	1
Stuart Newby	1
Robert Barrett	1
Daniel Villaron	1

Neil Weaver and Jack Morton

Roger Albert Clark Rally: the former winners and statistics

In memory

Over the 20 year story of the Roger Albert Clark we have sadly lost some of the people who played key roles in the rally, as organisers and competitors. Though not exhaustive, here are some of the people we remember.
Paul Adams, Brian Heppenstall, Steve Higgins, Graham James, Hannu Mikkola, Bob Milloy, Ian Rix, Mike Sones, David Stokes and David Winstanley.

Four time winner Marty McCormack